THE
READER'S DIGEST ILLUSTRATED
BOOK
OF
CATS

Reader's Digest

Published by The Reader's Digest Association Limited

LONDON ● NEW YORK ● SYDNEY ● CAPE TOWN ● MONTREAL

The Reader's Digest Illustrated Book of Cats

Consultants:

Dr. P. K. Basrur, professor of veterinary medical genetics, University of Guelph, Guelph, Ont. • **Leslie Bowers,** executive secretary, The International Cat Association • **R. G. Brown,** Ph.D., University of Massachusetts, Amherst, Mass., nutritional consultant to the Canadian Veterinary Medical Association • **John Burch,** all-breeds judge • **Dr. Charlotte Cushman,** Chaton Santé Clinique vétérinaire, Montreal, Que. • **Dr. Deborah Edwards,** All Cats Hospital, Largo, Fla. • **Dr. Michael Fox,** veterinarian, animal behaviourist and author of *The Healing Touch* and *Love Is a Happy Cat* • **Richard Gebhardt,** author of *The Complete Cat Book* • **Julia May,** veterinarian and member of Supreme Show Committee of the Governing Council of the Cat Fancy • **Yvonne Patrick,** all-breeds judge • **Dr. James Richards,** Cornell Feline Health Center, Cornell University, Ithaca, N.Y. • **Gloria Stephens,** feline geneticist, all-breeds judge and author of *The Legacy of the Cat*

ISBN 0 276 42212 0

The credits and acknowledgements that appear on page 256 are hereby made a part of this copyright page.

Based on the book first published in France as Guide des chats
Copyright © 1992, Sélection du Reader's Digest, S.A.

Copyright © 1992 The Reader's Digest Association (Canada) Ltd.
Copyright © 1992 The Reader's Digest Association Inc.
Copyright © 1992 The Reader's Digest Association Limited, London
Copyright © 1992 The Reader's Digest (Australia) Pty. Limited
Copyright © 1992 The Reader's Digest (New Zealand) Limited
Copyright © 1992 The Reader's Digest Association Far East Ltd.
Philippines Copyright © 1992 The Reader's Digest Association Far East Ltd.
Copyright © 1992 The Reader's Digest South Africa (Pty.) Limited

Copyright in this revised edition © 1995 The Reader's Digest Association Limited,
Berkeley Square House, Berkeley Square, London W1X 6AB

Designed and edited for Reader's Digest by NB Design/Cathy Meeus
Typeset by SX Composing, Rayleigh, Essex

® Reader's Digest, The Digest and the Pegasus logo are registered trademarks of
The Reader's Digest Association, Inc. of Pleasantville, New York, USA.

Printed in the United States of America

Introduction

The cat is the only animal that leads a solitary existence in the wild to have become domesticated. It is now the most popular household pet in many countries, and its numbers worldwide have increased to many millions.

Perhaps it chose to become domesticated, just as it chooses to do as it pleases today. This strength of personality is one of the reasons for its popularity. The others are immediately evident. Its small size, impeccable cleanliness and fierce independence make it the perfect household pet. A cat is also beautiful to look at – its movements are neat and fluid and its posture is elegant. Its companionship is tactile as well as audible, often in the most charming way. The sensuous rubbing of its fur against you, the sinuous winding of its tail around your legs, and its rumbling purr of pleasure when you stroke it can be irresistible. And most of us cannot fail to be touched by the warm affection of the gaze of a cat, with its eyes half-closed. It is not surprising that cats have gained recent status as therapists – their presence has been found to lower blood pressure in the sick and improve the well-being of the old, the feeble, and the emotionally disturbed.

In our appreciation of cats we have created many new breeds, mostly for showing. Today, most cat registry associations recognise between 40 and 50 breeds as eligible for championship contests. This book describes 51 breeds of cat. They were selected from cat registries in Australia, Britain, Canada, New Zealand, South Africa and the United States, and from the various associations that link cat fanciers around the world. But cat associations also recognise the beauty of non-pedigree cats and encourage their owners to show them in classes such as Household Pet or Other Variety.

Apart from telling you how to show your cat, this book covers all aspects of living with it – feeding, care, health, breeding and behaviour. Here is something for every cat-lover, whether you are a breeder of fancy cats or the devoted owner of a humble moggy.

—The Editors

Table of Contents

YOUR CAT'S PHYSIOLOGY

THE CAT AND ITS OWNER

UNDERSTANDING CATS

THE CAT THROUGH HISTORY

Feline ancestry

Fossilised remains of Miacis, one of the forest-dwelling Miacids, early ancestors of the carnivorous animals.

The polecat, an important member of the mustelid family, distant relatives of the cat.

The common genet, a viverrid native to the forests of central and southern Africa.

Despite what cat lovers might like to believe, the cat has not always been around. In fact, over millions of years, it was preceded by scores of species. For close to one million of those years, the dinosaurs ruled the world by dint of their sheer size. They became extinct some 65 million years ago, when some as yet unexplained cataclysm wiped them out. Mammals, of which the cat is one, had to wait for their disappearance to thrive.

The disaster that killed the dinosaurs also claimed other families. Between 65 and 60 million years ago, all marine and flying reptiles disappeared, as did most land animals of any size – say 10 kg (22 pounds) or more. The only ones to survive this upheaval were small creatures, mostly primitive long-nosed insect-eating mammals. During the Palaeocene epoch, which marked the dawn of the Cainozoic era (from some 65 million years ago to recent times: see chart, pages 12-13), these insectivores developed rapidly in many directions. The primates, a distinctive forest group, appeared quite early, giving rise to lemurs, monkeys, apes and, eventually, man. The ungulates or hoofed animals evolved, and these in turn led to horses, cattle, elephants, rhinoceroses, raccoons, and aardvarks. Rabbits, hares and rodents appeared, as did seals, bats, whales and sabre-toothed cats.

Forerunner to today's cat

To find the forerunner to today's cat we must return to the species explosion that occurred following the dinosaurs' disappearance. In this 'era of new life', as the Cainozoic era is known, mammals split into plant-eaters and flesh-eaters. Among the latter were the claw-footed, short-legged (and short-lived) fish-eating Creodonts, once mistakenly thought to be feline ancestors.

About the time the Creodonts began dying off (some 60 million years ago), the insect-eating Miacids were emerging. These short-legged, long-bodied, weasel- to wolf-size forest dwellers are generally regarded as ancestors of the felids (cats, lynxes, and cheetahs), as well as of other carnivorous land mammals: canids (wolves, foxes and dogs), hyaenids (hyenas), mustelids (weasels, minks, badgers and skunks), procyonids (raccoons), ursinids (bears) and viverrids (civets and mongooses), all of which feed chiefly on the flesh and blood of other vertebrates.

That the Miacids were better hunters than the Creodonts may have been a factor in the extinction of the latter. The Miacids may have been more intelligent – they had larger brains than the Creodonts – but sharper teeth might also have played a role. Although the Miacids had only 40 teeth compared to the Creodonts' 44, four of these were carnassial, ideal for holding and shearing flesh.

One identifying characteristic of all carnivores is their carnassial or shearing teeth – large sharp molars or premolars in the upper and lower jaws that cut food with a scissoring action. Through the study of early carnivores' teeth, and sometimes through the evidence of traces of tooth enamel, it has been possible to retrace some of these animals' history. (Tooth enamel survives for aeons in the ground, where soft tissue and sometimes even bones decompose.)

From the mid-Eocene to the early Oligocene epochs (50 to 40 million years ago: see chart, pages 12-13), carnivores developed and diversified rapidly, perhaps responding to changes in climate, plant life and prey. The diversification followed two distinct paths, producing the Carnivora superfamilies *Aeluroidea* (or *Feloidea*), which evolved into felids, hyaenids and viverrids, and the *Arctoidea* (or *Canoidea*), which contains the other carnivorous families.

Eusmilus *was a primitive felid of the late Oligocene epoch. We do not know whether it was a hunter or, like the modern hyena, subsisted on carrion.*

Fossils from that time include a lynx-sized animal known as *Dinictis*, which is generally regarded as an important evolution in feline development. It had longer legs and tail than the Creodonts or Miacids, and cat-like teeth for stabbing prey. Around the time it appeared, feline evolution took off in two directions. One branch produced the now extinct *Nimravidae* or paleofelids, large sabre-toothed cats that flourished in the Oligocene epoch (some 34 to 23 million years ago). Smaller teeth characterised the second group, which diverged into several subspecies in the late Miocene epoch (some 15 million years ago) and continued developing through to the Pliocene epoch (1 million years ago), evolving into *Felidae* (the neofelids), today's family of cats.

The *Nimravidae* existed for some 30 million years. One striking example of *Nimravidae* was *Eusmilus*, a sabre-toothed tiger, somewhere between a lynx and a puma in size, but with claws that were not completely retractable. Its upper jaw had two remarkable canine teeth: slightly flattened like sabre blades, they were edged like saws. This creature's claws were not as efficient as those of today's felines. Because it walked on its pads, rather than on its toes as today's cats do, it could not run very fast.

Was *Eusmilus,* then, simply a clumsy carrion-eater, and its sabre teeth just butcher's meat hooks for scavenging dead flesh, as some have suggested? Or, as others are equally convinced, was *Eusmilus* a predator? Whatever their survival techniques, these sabre-toothed tigers spread out across Africa, Asia, Europe and North America. Their huge size, limited intelligence, and cumbersome teeth are believed to have led to their extinction 5 million years after they first appeared.

Another paleofelid, *Nimravus*, developed about the same time as *Eusmilus*, but it flourished for 10 million years. As big as a jaguar and sometimes the size of

THE FOSSA

To get an idea of what the ancestors of cats looked like, consider the incredible fossa *Cryptoprocta ferox* of Madagascar. Originally thought to belong to the cat family, zoologists eventually classed it as a primitive viverrid, a member of the same family as genets, civet cats, and mongooses. The fossa looks like a small puma with a long tail, walks partly on its pads, and has completely retractable claws. Like a cat, its eyes have vertical pupils. It weighs about 10 kg (22 pounds), making it Madagascar's largest native carnivore, and it hunts lemurs and birds in the trees by night.

The remains of a similar creature have been found in rocks that were formed an estimated 10 to 20 million years ago. These fossils are thought to be one of the cat's early ancestors.

Most likely the fossa survived in Madagascar, protected by the ocean from competition with more highly evolved carnivores. But how did it get there in the first place? According to one theory, when a large African river, which disappeared some 5 million years ago, overflowed into the straits of Madagascar, it carried with it rafts of whole trees pulled up from its banks, virtual Noah's Arks supporting a lot of animals. It is possible that several of these rafts and the animals aboard reached the shores of Madagascar. This could explain why all the island's mammals belong to species that live in trees and represent versions of species long extinct everywhere else. Millions of years later, other mammals were introduced to the island by man.

a lion, *Nimravus* roamed Europe and North America. It had unusually long canine teeth and long slender legs, with four-toed back paws similar to a cat's that would have enabled it to run and hunt efficiently.

While the larger paleofelids, the *Nimravidae*, dominated the scene during the Oligocene epoch (see chart, pages 12-13), some of the smaller neofelids developed a similar form and structure. The neofelid *Proailurus*, for example, not only preceded *Nimravus* but survived it by centuries.

The cat's true ancestor

Another small neofelid, *Pseudoailurus*, appeared in Europe and North America during the Miocene epoch (about 23 million years ago). This direct ancestor of today's cats had a flattish skull, acute hearing through two chambers in the middle ear, and walked almost flat-footed. It and the earlier *Proailurus* were very similar to the present-day fossa, a 'living fossil', native to Madagascar (see box at left).

An odd sort of regression appeared in the first descendants of *Pseudoailurus*: they were sabre-toothed felines much like the ancient paleofelids, which had already died out. This phenomenon, called convergence, happens when groups of animals more or less distant from each other on the zoological scale are exposed to the same food sources and environmental conditions. The dolphin and the shark, for example, both gradually acquired a very similar streamlined shape, an adaptation dictated by their everyday problems of living in and moving through an aquatic environment and by their quest for similar food.

These sabre-toothed neofelids appeared 12 million years ago in the Miocene epoch (see chart, pages 12-13). By the Pliocene epoch (3 million years ago), this family had evolved into two slightly built species, *Homotherium* and *Machairodus*, and the heavier *Megantereon* and *Smilodon*. *Smilodon* (see facing page) would survive until 2 million years ago, dying out in the Holocene, or Recent epoch, relatively close to our own time.

The lighter of the neofelid sabre-tooths had serrated blade-like teeth while their heavier cousins had longer, curving, conical fangs that were obviously suited for piercing, not cutting. The lighter cats probably cut the throats or disembowelled the soft underbellies of their victims, while the heavier cats like *Smilodon* stabbed.

These larger cats, though formidable, had problems: their deadly teeth were fragile because they were long and exposed. They were useless for tearing apart prey and were so long – up to 13 cm (6 inches) that when the mouth was wide open to deliver a fatal blow, the animal could dislocate its neck.

Fossil links on the feline trail

Of all the sabre-toothed beasts, the neofelid *Smilodon* is the one we know most about. The remains of many of them have been found reasonably well preserved in the La Brea tar pits in West Hollywood, California. The tar pits are pools of viscous asphalt formed by seepage from petroleum deposits. They were natural death traps for animals – camels, condors, coyotes, mammoths and mastodons – that came to drink from pools of water atop the asphalt, but became bogged in the tar. The *Smilodons*, coming to feed off what appeared to be sitting prey, then became trapped in the tar themselves.

Their remains suggest that *Smilodon,* with its stocky legs, short tail and sharp claws, was more suited to ambushing game than to chasing it. About the size of a tiger, it had very few teeth: just two premolars and one molar on either side of each jaw – ideal for crushing bones. The lower jaw, which could drop open vertically, did not have the same bony projection on the chin that had supported the tips of *Eusmilus's* canines when its mouth was closed.

As with *Eusmilus* (see page 9), there are several theories about *Smilodon's* eating habits. Some scientists think that *Smilodon* stabbed its victims and then sucked their blood. Others believe that it ate only rotting meat, which seems likely because even modern-day predators find it hard to tear open the tough skin of an elephant or rhino carcass. The sharp canines might have been useful in this respect, but this conjecture is based on the small number of other teeth *Smilodon* had. This would seem to indicate that the animal would only be able to chew meat that was already decomposing.

It seems certain that *Smilodon's* muscular neck gave it extraordinary strength for lowering its head and embedding its canine teeth. Those who believe *Smilodon* to have been a predator, however, claim to have found corroborating evidence to bolster their case: one of its canine teeth embedded in the skull of a kind of jackal.

Primitive man did not appear on the evolutionary scale until the Pleistocene epoch some 1 to 2 million years ago, and modern man did not arrive until the Holocene, or Recent, epoch 10,000 years ago. By then many of the massive prehistoric animals had disappeared. The coming of the Ice Age was partly responsible for this extinction of the giant relatives of many animals alive today, but another important factor in the disappearance was the hunting activities of the original big game hunter, early man. By the time that man was using fire, the paleofelid sabre-toothed cats had died out, yielding place to the final version of the neofelid *Felidae.*

For the most part, these *Felidae* were cats of the kind we know today: panthers, lynxes, leopards, and so on. These animals had a number of recognisable physical characteristics: powerfully muscled jaws, teeth designed for cutting rather than grinding, bones and muscles adapted to running and, in most cases, retractable claws.

The domesticated cat appeared first in the Middle East more than 3,500 years ago, though there is some evidence – a jawbone discovered on Cyprus in 1983 – that such cats existed in 6000 B.C.

At first, man and cat must have competed as predators. Then, after domesticating horses for transportation, cattle and pigs for food, and dogs and leopards for hunting, man began a cautious relationship with the equally cautious, but always independent, somewhat solitary, and ever-delightful domestic cat.

Smilodon: *the last example of sabre-toothed tigers. Early man may well have encountered one. Above: artist's reconstruction and skull.*

The cat's

*PALAEOCENE	*EOCENE	*OLIGOCENE
From 65 million years ago	From 53 million years ago	From 34 million years ago

The Miacids appeared early in the Cainozoic era, the age of advanced mammals, birds, and molluscs, which followed the extinction of the dinosaurs and other ruling reptiles. Insect-eating, forest-dwelling creatures, they are ancestors to felids (cheetahs and small and roaring cats) and other carnivorous land mammals such as canids (wolves, foxes, and dogs), hyaenids (hyenas), mustelids (weasels, minks, badgers, and skunks), procyonids (raccoons), ursinids (bears), and viverrids (civets and mongooses). Only the evolution of the felid families is shown here.

Proailurus

FELIDAE
'NEOFELIDS'

MIACIDS

Dinictis

NIMRAVIDAE
'PALEOFELIDS'

Eusmilus

Nimravus

*Epochs of the Cainozoic era, which began some 65 million years ago

12

family tree

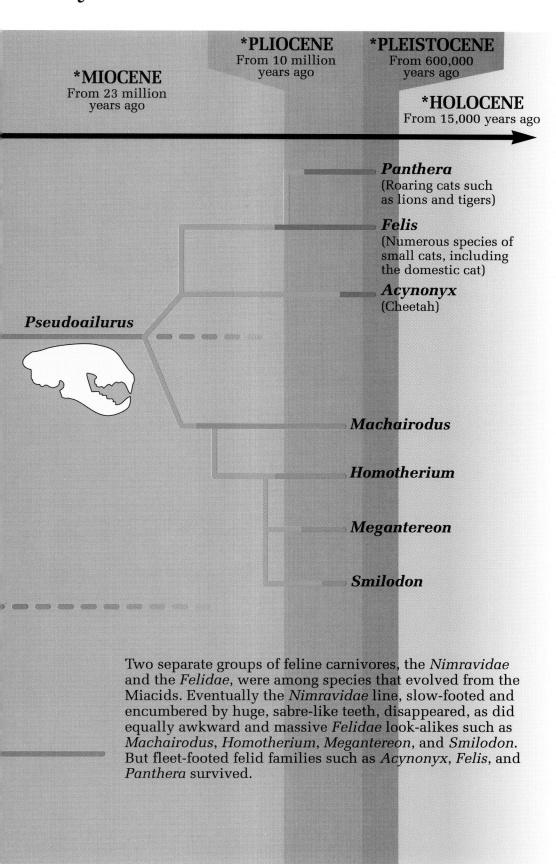

*MIOCENE
From 23 million
years ago

*PLIOCENE
From 10 million
years ago

*PLEISTOCENE
From 600,000
years ago

*HOLOCENE
From 15,000 years ago

Panthera
(Roaring cats such
as lions and tigers)

Felis
(Numerous species of
small cats, including
the domestic cat)

Acynonyx
(Cheetah)

Pseudoailurus

Machairodus

Homotherium

Megantereon

Smilodon

Two separate groups of feline carnivores, the *Nimravidae*
and the *Felidae*, were among species that evolved from the
Miacids. Eventually the *Nimravidae* line, slow-footed and
encumbered by huge, sabre-like teeth, disappeared, as did
equally awkward and massive *Felidae* look-alikes such as
Machairodus, *Homotherium*, *Megantereon*, and *Smilodon*.
But fleet-footed felid families such as *Acynonyx*, *Felis*, and
Panthera survived.

The cat's kith and kin

Cats, a very uniform animal group, are sometimes classified into big and small species, distinguished by a surprising but fundamental difference: the big cats' roar. This awe-inspiring sound is actually due to the absence of a section of hyoid bone on each side of the big cat's throat. Normally this bone is made up of two symmetrical chains of bones attaching the base of the tongue to the skull. The joints linking these little bones control movements connected with swallowing and the production of vocal sounds.

In the big cats (lions, tigers, leopards, panthers and jaguars), one of these bones is replaced on each side by a pliable sheath of cartilage that allows greater movement of the larynx, and thus enables the animal to emit a roar. Cats with ordinary hyoid bones can only mew or caterwaul.

Taxonomists, specialists in scientific classification of animals, classify the cat family in different ways. Three genera are used here: *Panthera* for the Big Cats, *Acynonyx* for the cheetah, and *Felis* for all other feline species. Naturalists have had a hard time classifying some species because many avoid man. This is one reason why classifications vary.

THE BIG CATS

- *Panthera leo*, the lion
- *Panthera tigris*, the tiger
- *Panthera onca*, the jaguar
- *Panthera pardus*, the leopard
- *Panthera uncia*, the snow leopard
- *Panthera nebulosa*, the clouded leopard

The Big Cats

The Panthera, although less closely related to our domestic cats than the members of genus *Felis*, display many characteristics that we can recognise in our own cats.

Lion

Lions live in Africa and India, and their tawny coats blend into the open grassland. Unlike most cats, male and female show marked physical differences (dimorphism), only the male having a mane of long hair. Adult lions are almost uniform in colour, but the cubs have spotted markings that fade as they mature.

Tiger

The tiger and lion, both roaring cats, are the largest of the big cats.

The tiger is found in Asia, from India and southeast Asia to Siberia. Markings vary considerably between different species. In addition to the usual tawny-gold and black colour, 'white tigers' occur, with slightly paler stripes against an off-white background.

Jaguar

The third largest of the big cats, the jaguar is found only in the New World. Its golden coat is patterned with clusters of dark spots forming rosettes, but a black form is also found.

Leopard

With a wide range of habitat from Africa through Asia to the Far East, the leopard has similar markings to the jaguar and is also found in a dark form – the black panther. The leopard is, however, smaller and more graceful than the jaguar.

Snow Leopard

The snow leopard is a slightly smaller cat than the leopard, with a greyish thick coat and dark blurred rosettes; it is found only in central Asia.

Clouded Leopard

The smallest of the big cats, the clouded leopard has distinctive blotchy markings on a pale background. It is found throughout southern and southeast Asia.

The leopard (or panther), a magnificent and dangerous big cat, is widespread in the equatorial regions of Africa and Asia.

Cheetah: swift and gentle

A streamlined shape, unretractable claws, small head and two black markings running like tears from the inside corners of the eyes to the outer corners of the mouth distinguish the cheetah from every other big cat. It used to be common across the Middle East and India, and throughout the less densely forested areas of Africa. Today not only has its African habitat shrunk considerably (the main populations are now in Namibia and Zimbabwe in southern Africa), but also it has

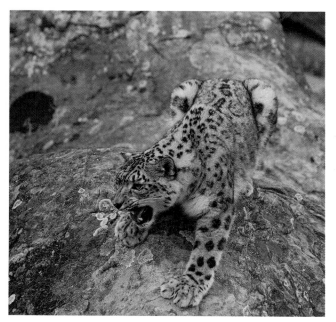

The snow leopard, with its mottled grey coat is well camouflaged as it stalks its prey in the mountains of central Asia. Its diet is varied, including deer, gazelle and even the occasional wild boar.

Cheetahs of Italy's merchant princes. The cheetah, a phenomenal short-distance runner, was first tamed and used for coursing hares in Ancient Egypt. The great lords of the Italian Renaissance were among scores of rulers who owned hunting cheetahs. Here, a nobleman has a cheetah riding pillion on a saddle cloth, while another rider has dismounted and is preparing to loose his cheetah.

become rare in the Middle East, and has disappeared entirely from India.

A diurnal rather than nocturnal cat that hunts hares, gazelles, and low-flying birds, the cheetah is the fastest runner of all land-based animals. It has been known to reach speeds of more than 100 km/h (65 miles an hour) in 500-m (550-yard) sprints. A gentle creature, the cheetah has always been easily tamed. Egyptian Pharaohs were the first to do this, and from 1500 B.C. onwards cheetahs and dogs were their hunting animals. The Greek geographer and historian Strabo, who died in A.D. 23, described how the people of India captured cheetahs found in great numbers in the bamboo forests along the Ganges, trained them to hunt, and tamed them so well that they wandered freely through palaces and gardens.

When the native Indian species died out, maharajas imported cheetahs from Africa, mostly Kenya, and continued to use them for hunting until the early 20th century. Cheetah hunting was somewhat like falconry or coursing hares with greyhounds. The cheetah was taken by cart to the hunting area, blindfolded, and restrained by a body harness. Once the quarry was in sight, the blindfold was removed and the cheetah freed. On a good day, the cheetah could run down its prey in less than a minute. It would then wait for its master to arrive and complete the kill. If the chase was too long, the cheetah collapsed, exhausted from its efforts.

During the Middle Ages this form of hunting was all the rage throughout eastern Europe and Asia, but was practised only intermittently in the Western World. Cheetahs were trained to ride on the horse's crupper behind the rider, as can be seen in the reproduction below of a detail from *The Journey of the Magi,* a mural by Benozzo Gozzoli, who died in the late 15th century. The fresco was commissioned by Piero de Medici of the Italian family of bankers and merchants. The Medicis ruled Florence, and later Tuscany, for all but 21 years between 1434 and 1737. The cheetah was a Medici family symbol.

Russian princes, British royals and numerous French kings have hunted with cheetahs. The Austrian Emperor Leopold I used cheetahs on deer hunts in the Vienna woods. Indeed many blame the huge cheetah stables of various royal houses for the eventual decline of this superb cat.

Felis

All species of *Felis* are solitary, generally nocturnal, and frequently arboreal. They are predominantly meat-eaters, although the Asian flat-headed cat relies heavily on fruit and the fishing cat, also found in the Far East, is so partial to fish that it catches them in its claws (see page 20). All cats have well-developed sight and very sharp hearing, which allow them to make successful hunting forays at dawn and dusk. They have a strong sense of smell, which is used more for detecting and communicating with other animals than for hunting.

A single cat usually has several lairs in its territory, one of which is used by the female to give birth. The male and female will live together only during the mating season, and few males actually take any part in rearing the young. The litter may number from one to six cubs depending on the species. All feline offspring are born blind but covered in fur.

Small cats of the Americas

Various ecological niches produce different kinds of creatures. Neither Antarctica nor even Australia with its particularly rich fauna has native cat species. Yet native species of small cats are abundant in South America. Descriptions of some of these cats, a few of them also found in North America, follow. (See also Lynxes, page 22.)

Puma

This cat, which ranges from Canada to southern South America, is known by many names: cougar, mountain lion, painter, panther, catamountain. Spanish colonists in Argentina called it the American lion, and the Portuguese in Brazil knew it as the red jaguar. The biggest of the genus *Felis*, it is comparable in size to the lion or leopard. It can weigh up to 100 kg (220 pounds) and flourishes in habitats as diverse as conifer forests and swamps. Because pumas prey on domestic animals, they have been hunted mercilessly since Europeans settled in the Americas. It is now the most endangered of the cats. The puma has a yellow-brown coat, lighter on the underbody. Like the jaguar, the large American feline, it plays a major role in the mythology of most pre-Columbian civilisations, which have left highly stylised images of these animals.

Colocolo or pampas cat

This cat is also called *gato pajero* (straw cat), because of its straw-coloured fur. The colocolo is the size of a domestic cat and has a long-haired striped coat that

---

THE CATS OF LATIN AMERICA

They are divided into five sub-groups:

- *Felis concolor*: the puma
- *Felis colocolo*: the colocolo or pampas cat
- *Felis leopardus*, with five species:
  - *Felis pardalis*: the ocelot
  - *Felis wiedi*: the margay
  - *Felis tigrinus*: the tiger cat
  - *Felis geoffroyi*: Geoffroy's cat
  - *Felis guigna*: the kodkod
- *Felis jacobita*: the mountain cat
- *Felis yagouaroundi*: the jaguar-undi

The colocolo hunts guinea pigs.

varies from yellowish white to a greyish brown. It lives mostly on the pampas, but has been found in the rain forests and even in mountainous regions. The coloco-lo lives mostly on the ground and preys on ground-nesting birds, small mammals, especially guinea pigs, and sometimes domestic fowl. When excited, the hairs on its back become erect, giving it a most formidable appearance. Found from Ecuador south to northern Chile and Argentina, it is said to be aggressive, and difficult to tame.

Felis leopardus (ocelot, margay, tiger cat, Geoffroy's cat and kodkod)

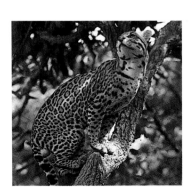

The ocelot, an arboreal cat of the Americas, has paid dearly for having a coat that became very fashionable.

The ocelot, once the most widely distributed feline in Central and South America, has been hunted almost to extinction for its handsome tawny coat, marked with jaguar-like, black-ringed brown spots. Its present range is from the southern United States to northern Argentina. An accomplished climber, it not only hunts in trees, but naps among the branches in the daytime. Rarely more than 45 cm (18 inches) high at the withers, the ocelot weighs 11 to 15 kg (24-33 pounds). Ocelots mark their territory with droppings, appear to live in couples, but hunt separately.

The margay, also known as the long-tailed spotted cat, looks like a miniature ocelot, has huge eyes, and excellent night vision. A tree-dweller, it moves easily among the branches, spiralling upwards and hanging by its back legs. Its acrobatic prowess is largely due to the specialised structure of its rear paws, which have wide toes that can grip a surface readily. An endangered species, it is now extinct in most of what was its range – Panama to Paraguay.

The tiger cat, also known as the oncilla or little Spotted cat, is sometimes mistaken for the margay. It too is a tree-dweller, but a less skilled climber. This endangered species is now rare in its range – Costa Rica south to Argentina.

Geoffroy's cat comes in various colours, but is often a spotted grey. It climbs well and, like all members of the subgenus *Leopardus*, is a fine swimmer. It ranges from Bolivia and Brazil south through Argentina.

The kodkod is a very small grey-brown spotted tree-dweller weighing from 2 to 3 kg (4½-6½ pounds). Found in parts of Argentina but mostly in central Chile, it is reputed to raid henhouses.

The jaguar, largest of the American cats, played a major role in Aztec mythology.

Mountain cat

This animal is also called the Andean highland cat. In Chile and Argentina, it inhabits arid zones of the Andes Mountains up to 5,000 m (16,000 feet) above sea level. It can tolerate the bitter night cold of such high altitudes thanks to its very thick silver-grey fur, which is spotted and striped in brown or orange. Now very rare, it has been a protected species since 1978.

Jaguarundi

This cat looks somewhat like an otter or a weasel: in fact its German name is *Weisel Katze* (weasel cat). Found from Texas southwards through Central America to Paraguay and northern Argentina, the jaguarundi's favourite habitat is the rain forest or dense undergrowth. Despite being an agile climber, it prefers to live on the ground. Since its fur is not valuable, hunters leave it alone. A short-legged animal with a long supple body, its smooth coat varies in colour from one cat to the next. Kittens from a single litter may be grey, almost black, or reddish-brown. The Indians say this cat had been tamed and used for rodent control long before the Spanish reached South America. Present-day jaguarundis still eat rodents as well as rabbits, birds, frogs, fish and poultry. They are most active in the morning and the evening.

The Andean or mountain cat, an extremely rare feline.

The jaguarundi.

Small Cats of the far East

All cats must be able to blend in with their surroundings, to escape the hunter and to track their prey. In jungles, stripes hide the tiger well; in deserts, the lion's sandy colouring is good camouflage when the pride sets out on a hunt; in light-dappled forests, the spotted coats of the cheetah and the leopard are all but invisible, as is the black leopard hunting by night. The cats of the Far East have especially distinctive coats.

Felis pardofelis (marbled cat, bay cat of Borneo)

The marbled cat used to inhabit the eastern Himalayas, Burma, Indo-China and Malaysia. It weighs between 2

Like many wild species, the marbled cat has suffered from encroachment on its habitat.

and 5 kg (4½-11 pounds), and has a yellowish coat with irregular spots ringed in black and a similarly marked long bushy tail. It generally lives on forested slopes but is found in low country in Borneo. This rare cat is now protected in India and Thailand.

The bay cat, also called the Bornean red cat, has a bright chestnut-brown coat, and is limited to a few areas of Borneo. Some cats with bluish fur have also been seen there. They too are found in rocky forested areas, but only a few have been spotted in recent years.

Felis prinailurus (leopard cat, Iriomote cat, rusty-spotted cat, fishing cat, flat-headed cat)

The leopard cat, a protected species, has an extremely broad range. It extends from Manchuria to India and includes all southeast Asia together with Borneo, Java and Sumatra. In areas as far apart as these, the leopard cat varies considerably in size and colouring. In tropical regions it weighs about 5 kg (11 pounds) and is brown with black markings, while further north in Manchuria it can reach 15 kg (3 pounds) and be a silvery grey with pale ring-like markings. Because it needs a lot of water, this cat is not found in dry or desert regions. An accomplished swimmer and climber, it lives in scrubland and forests.

The Iriomote cat was discovered by scientists in 1967 on a Japanese-owned island (Iriomote) off Taiwan. Naturalists initially classified it as a separate subgenus of the leopard cat, but now believe it to be an insular form of that animal. By night, it hunts small rodents, small water animals such as crabs, and water birds, each cat keeping to a territory of 2.5 square km (1 sq mile). As the island's agricultural development has encroached on the forests that are this cat's normal habitat, only a few dozen specimens are left.

The rusty-spotted cat, found in southern Sri Lanka and southern India, is also believed to be a variation of the leopard cat. It is smaller and more vividly coloured than the leopard cat.

The fishing cat or tarai is found in Sri Lanka, India, China, and as far south as Myanmar (formerly Burma). It is semiaquatic and seen in mangrove swamps and fishing from rocks on riverbeds, scooping up fish with its front paws. Some people have seen it dive into water and grab fish in its jaws. It also eats shellfish, snakes and small mammals. Quite a big cat, it can

The leopard cat was formerly widespread in southeast Asia, but is now so rare that it is a protected species.

The fishing cat is the only feline that lives almost exclusively on fish and other freshwater creatures.

weigh up to 14 kg (30 pounds). Its long body, grey with dark regular markings, resembles that of the civet cat.

The flat-headed cat, also known as the marten cat, is found in India, from Sri Lanka to southern China, and in Sumatra, Java and Bali. Its most striking feature is its long, flat head. Its longish soft fur is a dark reddish brown tipped with white, which gives it a silvery shimmer.

Other cats of Europe, Africa and Asia

Most big cats are solitary animals, a trait found also in today's domestic cat. Lions, which live in family prides ruled by one leader, are an exception. Other male and female big cats cohabit only for mating. The tiger is not only a loner, but can be a dangerous one at that. It was nicknamed 'man-eater' many years ago for good reason. Records from the mid-1800s show that at that time tigers ate 400 human victims a year in the Singapore area alone.

The following cats are neither as large as lions nor probably as fierce as tigers, except perhaps when cornered, but they do live in a wide range of habitats in Europe, Africa and Asia.

Golden cats

As their names indicate, the African and Asian golden cats are usually a dark auburn colour but sometimes their fur is slate grey. A darker band of colour runs along the golden cat's back from head to tail. The underbelly is lighter, with round dark markings, and the tail is ringed and sometimes white at the tip. Medium-sized animals, they can weigh from 6 to 16 kg (13-35 pounds).

The African golden cat lives in equatorial jungles of Senegal, Kenya and northern Angola. Although it can climb quite well, it tends to live on the ground, making its lairs under rocks or in holes dug by other animals. In some of its habitats, local tribes credit the cat with magical powers and trap it to use its whiskers in poisonous potions, and its fur in ceremonial robes. Other tribes believe possession of a golden's tail will guarantee success in the elephant hunt.

The Asian golden cat, often called Temminck's golden cat in honour of the Dutch naturalist who described

---

OTHER SUBGENERA OF EUROPE, AFRICA AND ASIA

- *Profelis*, the golden cats
  - *Felis temmincki*, Temminck's golden cat
  - *Felis aurata*, the African golden cat
- *Otocolobus*
  - *Felis manul*, the manul cat or Pallas's cat
- *Lynx*, with three subgenera
  - *Felis lynx*, the Northern lynx
  - *Felis pardina*, the parded lynx or Spanish lynx
  - *Felis rufus*, the bobcat, bay lynx, red cat, or American wildcat
- *Caracal*
  - *Felis caracal*, the caracal
- *Leptailurus*
  - *Felis serval*, the serval

The golden cat.

Many bizarre beliefs surround the lynx.

the African golden cat, makes its home from Nepal to south China and Sumatra.

Temminck's cats often hunt in pairs, and the male plays a part in rearing the offspring, which is unusual for the genus *Felis*. It roams the forested Himalayan foothills hunting birds, lizards and small deer. Like its African relative, it has a fondness for rocky terrain. It is now a protected species.

Lynxes

The northern lynx, distinguished by its pricked-up, tufted ears, small head, rear paws higher than the forepaws, and short tail ranges from Europe to Siberia, is widespread in Canada and the northern United States, but is not found in Africa. Lynxes ordinarily dwell in coniferous forests, but they have been seen on rocky outcrops in Mongolia's Altai Mountains and above the tree line in Tibet. They sleep by day, often in caves or hollow trees, but are very active at night, often travelling long distances in search of prey. Expert stalkers, they can creep close to their prey, then bound for the kill. But they also hunt by lying in ambush, waiting quietly for hours on a limb over a trail.

Seldom seen, the lynx's wariness gave rise to strange beliefs in the Middle Ages. It was said the lynx could see through the thickest walls, that its urine crystallised into precious stones, and that it was a gigantic cat. In reality, it is rather a small animal, weighing about 30 kg (65 pounds). Hunters say a wounded lynx is particularly dangerous animal.

Slightly smaller than the northern lynx, the Spanish lynx is the only wild cat restricted entirely to Europe, being found in remote parts of Spain and Portugal.

The manul or Pallas's cat. Because of its thick fur, it was once wrongly thought to be an ancestor of the Persian cat.

Pallas's cat

Also called the manul cat (from its scientific name *Felis manul*), Pallas's cat lives in the rocky deserts and steppes stretching across central Asia from the Caspian Sea to western China. This small, short-legged animal weighs between 4 and 5 kg (9-11 pounds). It is remarkable mainly for its fur, a uniform light brown colour with black markings on the head and some stripes running across the hindquarters and tail. The fur is very long on the lower part of the body, an aid to survival in the snow and bitter winter cold of its native habitat. Because of the long fur, this cat was once incorrectly considered to be a branch of the Angoras.

Pallas's cat has small round ears set back on the sides of the skull, and wide bushy whiskers that make its head look broad and flat. It eats mainly rodents and other small animals.

The caracal.

Caracal

This cat, a lynx that has adapted to the heat and humidity of the tropics, has a short-haired, fawn-coloured coat with rust-coloured spots, and weighs between 8 to 18 kg (17½-40 pounds). It is found everywhere in Africa except in dense jungles, in the Middle East, and in western India on territory once native to the cheetah. Like the cheetah, it has been domesticated by Indian hunters and has been used for running down

The serval.

hares. However, it is not so gentle a creature as the cheetah; while some caracals have been tamed, others remain incorrigibly ferocious.

Serval

The serval is found throughout Africa, except for the great rain forests, and it ranges from South Africa up to the northern coastal hills of the Sahel. It looks and moves like a long-legged cat, stands about 50 cm (20 inches) high at the withers, and weighs about 14 kg (30 pounds). It is a pale fawn with black spots and stripes, and a tail ringed in black. Like the leopard, it often has a darker coat in wet regions; some servals are almost black. Servals have a high-pitched cry, but they can also purr. Though a wily and solitary animal, and a henhouse thief, the serval is easily tamed. It can jump 3 m (10 feet) to bring down a bird.

Other feline family members

Jungle cat

The jungle cat is misnamed, although nobody seems to be quite sure why. Its habitats are many – dense woods, open country, reedy areas near rivers and lakes – but it cannot be found in tropical jungles. Commonly found in the deltas of the Nile and Volga rivers, and in low-lying swampy regions in the Near East, in Turkestan, India, China and Indo-China, it is sometimes more aptly named the reed cat, swamp cat or marsh cat.

A large cat that can weigh up to 16 kg (35 pounds), the jungle cat has a short tail reaching only to the hocks. It has tufts on its ears, though they are not as noticeable as those of the lynx. This greyish-brown cat – depending on the habitat, it may be coloured differently – has ring markings on its tail. Mainly active at twilight, it feeds on frogs, reptiles and small mammals such as hares. It lives in the abandoned lairs of badgers and porcupines, sometimes even in old buildings. Although they are excellent climbers, jumpers, runners and swimmers, most of the time jungle cats tend to move slowly and cautiously.

Sand cat or Márgueritte's cat

The size of a domestic cat, the sand cat, also known as Márgueritte's cat (*Felis margarita*), is short-legged and sandy-coloured, with a head that seems bigger

> **THE SUBGENUS FELIS**
> - *Felis chaus*, the jungle cat
> - *Felis margarita*, the sand cat or Márgueritte's cat
> - *Felis nigripes*, the black-footed cat
> - *Felis silvestris*, wildcat
>   - *Felis silvestris*, the European wildcat
>   - *Felis lybica*, the Caffre cat or African wildcat
>   - *Felis ornata*, the Indian desert cat
> - *Felis bieti*, the Chinese desert cat
> - *Felis catus*, the domestic cat

than it is because of large ears set on the sides. The placement of the ears and their oversized resonating chambers, or tympanic bullae, are an adaptation for desert life: in vast empty spaces with little wildlife, acute hearing is a great advantage to animals that hunt by night. The sand cat has adapted to desert life in other ways too. It can apparently go without drinking at all, finding enough liquid in its prey – jerboas and other rodents, reptiles, birds and locusts.

Its pads are covered with thick fur, and it was once believed that this thick fur was to protect the cat's paws from burning desert sands. It is now known, however, that the sand cat spends much of the hot day prudently underground, rarely emerging before nightfall. The hairy pads are now thought more likely to be the desert version of snowshoes: they enable the cat to walk on soft sand without sinking.

Found only in the Sahara and Arabian deserts, the sand cat is a rare species whose survival has been threatened as traffickers sought it for its fur, for study, and for sale as a household pet. As always, capturing wild animals for pets not only leaves them open to inappropriate care, but endangers the species as a whole. The sand cat has been an endangered species since the late 1970s.

The sand cat is perfectly adapted to its existence as a desert predator.

Black-footed cat

This smallest of the wild felines is even smaller than the domestic cat. It weighs at the most 2.5 kg (5½ pounds). Well adapted to desert life, it has furry pads for easy movement on sand and huge tympanic bullae that give it excellent hearing. For its size, it has an extraordinarily strong voice: this tiny cat can roar as loudly as any tiger – although with the pitch an octave higher, the effect is less awesome. The roar is a signal enabling male and female of this exceptionally solitary species to find each other during the mating season. It has to be loud enough to attract a mate which, by its solitary nature, lives some distance away. And there is little time to spare. The female's heat is said to last 5 to 10 hours.

Immediately after copulation, male and female go their separate ways, a way of life that persists in captivity where the black-footed cat demonstrates strong antisocial tendencies. This is most likely its survival mechanism at work. The paucity of desert fauna in its natural habitat limits how many predators can survive in one spot.

The black-footed cat is found in the Namib, the Kalahari and the Great Karroo deserts of Namibia, Botswana and South Africa respectively.

Wildcat

The wildcat lives on birds, mice, and other small mammals, seeking out insects such as grasshoppers as needed. (Contrary to folklore, wildcats are incapable of attacking a hare, much less a deer.) It leads a solitary life on a territory of some 50 ha (25 acres). In spring, the female produces a single litter of two or three kittens.

No one disputes the close kinship between the wildcat and the domestic cat. What is uncertain is which of the various subspecies of wildcat is the ancestor of the domestic species.

The wildcat must not be confused with 'wild' or feral domestic cats although it has been known to interbreed with them. A major difference between the two is their inherited capacity for domesticity: feral kittens removed at birth and reared with domestic cats will grow up to be domestic cats – wildcat kittens will always retain the wildness of their forebears.

Like all widely distributed species, wildcats vary greatly in appearance and habits; they are so different that they have never been classified, even though more than 20 subspecies have been identified. However, these subspecies can be placed in three groups:
• the wildcat of Asia Minor, the Caucasus and Europe, including the Mediterranean islands;
• the African wildcat or gloved cat;
• the Indian desert cat, the Asian link between the first two species.

The European wildcat is a third bigger than the domestic cat, and weighs up to 8 kg (17½ pounds). But a large percentage of this is muscle weight, as opposed to the fat weight of the less active domestic cat. The European wildcat's coat is a yellowish grey, with markings more pronounced on the feet and on the ringed tail than on the rest of the body. The throat is almost white. This wildcat has long thick fur, and a bushy tail that looks the same thickness along its whole length, unlike the more usual tapering tail of the domestic cat.

The European wildcat dislikes snow, which hinders its progress and deprives it of mice. It lives in

Felis silvestris,
the European wildcat.

OTHER BRITISH WILDCATS

Sightings of various large cats are reported quite frequently and give rise to stories about 'Beast of Exmoor', and 'Surrey Puma' or the 'Fen Tiger'. Many of these are undoubtedly due to over-active imaginations, but several wild cats, including a puma, a jungle cat and some leopards have died or been killed in different parts of the country and their identities have been verified after their death.

It is extremely likely that there are wildcats, which have either escaped from zoos or been released by owners who had no licences to keep them, living loose in the British Isles. Although these cats cannot be considered natives, they have every chance of surviving on the prey available to them.

The wildcat of the European forests is not the ancestor of our domestic cat, although it is a close relative. It is larger in size, and its solitary nature makes it impossible to domesticate. Even kittens taken from the wild when very young cannot be tamed.

forests or rocky terrain, sometimes even open country, and hunts at dusk or during the night. In daytime it rests in thick bush, often seeking shelter in the hollow of a dead tree or under a rock, though it also likes to sun itself.

Systematically hunted and almost wiped out in 19th-century Europe for preying on game and domestic animals, the European wildcat had some respite during the two world wars. When the hunt ceased, populations in Scotland, Germany, eastern France and the Pyrenees recovered. Meantime, the wildcats have clearly on occasion mated with domestic cats. Cat experts say that present-day specimens are noticeably different from the original stock.

The Scottish wildcat differs only slightly from its relatives in continental Europe, from whom it has been

The Scottish wildcat is shy of humans and is seen only rarely.

separated since Britain became an island. The wild-cat was originally found over most of the country but probably died out in southern England 400 years ago and then, due to killing by gamekeepers, became less and less widespread and is now restricted to northern Scotland, where it does its best to hide from man.

The African wildcat, also known as the gloved cat or Caffre cat, is smaller and more elegant than the European wildcat. It has a narrow head, big ears, a long tapering tail, and lives on African savannahs, not in jungles or deserts.

The Indian desert cat, found throughout Asia as far east as China and central India, keeps to dry regions and avoids snow and cold. Its thick soft fur, resembling that of the domestic cat, is a pale yellow or sand colour with spots. The Indian desert cat has a long tapering tail.

Biet's cat, or the Chinese desert cat, is very similar to the Indian desert cat. This cat is found only in southern Mongolia and central China.

The Origins of the Domestic Cat

Many naturalists consider the domestic cat to be a variation of the African wildcat (the gloved or Caffre cat), changed by domestication. The domestic cat has undergone minor genetic changes since it was more or less isolated from its wild relatives and subjected to breeding programmes by man. This directed breeding has brought out many previously unknown fur colourings and textures.

As shipboard companion to those sailing the high seas, the domestic cat spread all over the world with the explorers and colonisers. A female Siamese that spent 16 years aboard a British cargo ship is credited with being the most travelled cat on record. In many areas, especially on the American continents, the wildcat (*Felis silvestris*) was previously unknown. The domestic cat might easily have reverted to its wild state once it was set free to explore its comparatively wild surroundings of the New World. But this did not happen. The cat remained domesticated, serving a useful role in homes and on farms, and relying on human protection in the New World as it had in the Old.

Sadly that protection has not always been given. At times, the cat has been persecuted and ritually tortured. Even in relatively good times, it often had to fend for itself. Man tended to care for horses, goats and cattle, but to leave cats to hunt down their own rodent nourishment.

Whenever wars and accidents separated cats from their caretakers, the cats did what their primitive ancestors did and what homeless cats do today. They gather together in a kind of loose co-operative on rooftop or fenced-off area, forget their domesticated manners, and revert to the wild. Secluded in groups, they sit peacefully, each night, grooming each other, making vocal exchanges, and moving from group to group much like people at a cocktail party. Before dawn, the gathering breaks up and they all drift away to their daytime hideouts. The behaviour of these feral cats seems very close to that of their wildcat cousins, even if their habitat is a gutted urban building rather than the bush or jungle.

INGRAINED INSTINCT

'We really didn't need a domestic cat until the Egyptians invented the silo and began storing their crops,' writes Roger A. Caras in *A Cat Is Watching.* 'When the mice found out, they put out the word and engaged in one long picnic. The better mousetrap had to be adapted from wild stock. That was barely two thousand years before the dawn of Christianity. When we speak of wild species and their behavioural evolution, we speak of hundreds of thousands of years and sometimes millions. Dogs and bears, for instance, had a common ancestor in Miacids 60 million years ago.

'It just doesn't seem likely that we have been the cause of much in the way of instinctive changes or additions in the short time there has been anything like domestic cats. They probably had all the instincts they needed from the outset to handle us. There is another factor: the matter of training. Dogs for instance have been with us for almost six times as long as cats, and have been trained as cats never have been trained. Cats in general have always had as their chief assignment our aesthetic satisfaction. The cat's one economic value has been the result of an instinct, hunting small animals like mice and rats.

'But I believe cats have an instinctive knowledge of man taken directly from their instinctive knowledge of all other life forms. They are, however, conditioned by us from birth. And they do have another strong influence— a parent. All the mammals identified as Carnivora spend long periods with one parent, as do primates and whales.

'Guinea pigs, on the other hand, are off almost immediately after birth. But then, what can a guinea pig teach anyone?'

Ancient Egypt: the cat's first home

A wall painting from the tomb of Nakht, in the Valley of the Kings near Luxor, shows a cat waiting to retrieve waterfowl from the riverside marshes of the Nile. The ancient Egyptian hunters used throwing-sticks to kill the birds. The tomb dates from the period of the New Kingdom (1560-1080 B.C.).

The domestication of the cat is a relatively recent event. Some evidence suggests that small wild feline species may have been tamed in different parts of the world only about 8,000 years ago. By comparison, the dog was domesticated as early as 50,000 years ago.

The remains of a cat excavated at Jericho (now Eriha, Jordan) date from 6700 B.C. At Harappa (Pakistan), once the centre of the Indus Valley civilisation, archaeologists have discovered other cat remains roughly 4,000 years old. The remains probably belong to the Asiatic desert cat (*Felis sylvestris ornata*), also known as the Asiatic steppe wildcat, which still exists in Afghanistan, Iran and Pakistan. There is no evidence to suggest the cats were domesticated. However, some scientists believe the Asiatic wildcat may be an ancestor of today's cat. They point out that the skulls of the wildcat and the modern domestic cat are about the same size.

Gods and tombs

The overwhelming body of evidence points to ancient Egypt as the place where the cat was first domesticated. The ancestor of the ancient Egyptian cat is known to be the African wildcat (*Felis sylvestris lybica*), also called the 'gloved' or Caffre cat. It probably entered early farming villages along the Nile to hunt river rats infesting granaries. Farmers, recognising a useful ally, took the first step towards domestication by trying to keep the cat near their homes. But the process was to take thousands of years.

The cat first found a niche in the ancient Egyptian imagination. As early as 3500 B.C., the Book of the Dead refers to the 'great cat at the pool of the Persea in Heliopolis'. In this religious work, the cat seems to be a symbol for the sun god Osiris or Re (also known as Ra) who overcomes a serpent – Set or Apophis – who is the ruler of darkness. The image of the cat slicing off the head of snake-like Apophis – representing the victory of good in the battle with evil – recurs in other Egyptian works of art, including two papyrus manuscripts, now in the British Museum in London.

Evidence of the cat as a part of daily Egyptian life appears in wallpaintings in tombs built during the

A satirical illustration of cats and mice, from a papyrus manuscript prepared by Egyptian scribes about 100 B.C.

A wall painting from the tomb of Nebamun, built about 1400 B.C., depicts a cat holding two fallen birds by its paws and another in its mouth. The painting is now in the British Museum.

New Kingdom (1560-1080 B.C.). The paintings show an animal resembling today's domestic cat in size and appearance. For example, an image of a cat crouched under a table eating a fish appears in the tomb of the scribe Nakht, found in the Valley of the Kings near present-day Luxor, Egypt. Another painting from the time of the New Kingdom, now in the collection of the British Museum, shows a man, known as Nebamun, hunting waterfowl and using a cat apparently trained as a retriever.

Birth of the cat goddess

Traditionally, the Egyptians revered certain animals – the bull, lion, baboon, ibis and dog – for admired or feared qualities. Eventually they began to think of the sacred animals as deities with human traits. One such deity was named Bastet, originally depicted as a lion-headed woman.

According to legend, Bastet was the daughter or the wife-sister of Re, the sun god of Lower Egypt. She fled in anger from Re to Upper Egypt, where she disguised herself as a lion. The sun god sent for her to fight his enemies. At the beginning of her journey down the Nile, Bastet drowned her rage by bathing at Philae, where she assumed the shape of a cat. As Bastet sailed down the Nile, she was acclaimed by people on the banks, before making a triumphant entry into a city in the Nile delta known as Bubastis (now Tell Basta, near the modern city of Zagazig).

Statue of a cat, Late Period, 26th dynasty (664-525 B.C.).

A sanctuary for sacred cats

A great stone temple in Bastet's honour was built at Bubastis between 2050 and 1800 B.C. According to Herodotus, the Greek 'father of history', who visited Bubastis in the 5th century B.C., the city was situated on a high mound of earth dredged up during the creation of the canal system in the Nile delta. However, the walled temple was situated – at ground level – in a small valley at the centre of the city. It was almost surrounded by a moat, except for a causeway linking the city market to the temple. The sanctuary that contained the image of the goddess was at the heart of the temple complex. Within the temple, the priests watched over the sacred cats. They searched for signs of Bastet's wishes and warnings, and interpreted the vagaries of feline behaviour for the devout who came to worship the goddess.

Lion into cat

At first, Bastet was depicted as a lion-headed goddess, who symbolised light, heat and solar energy. But when she assumed the role of a cat, she became a symbol of the night and of the moon. Egyptians believed she controlled fertility, cured illness and guarded the dead. She was considered a gentle, benevolent guardian of home, family and love, but she – like many other ancient deities – was sometimes cruel and wrathful.

Bastet was also revered as the Corn Spirit that protected crops and ensured rich harvest. She acquired this role when she bathed at Philae during her journey down the Nile to Bubastis. Philae was the site of the main temple to Isis, who symbolised the fertile land of Egypt. The image of Bastet as the Corn Spirit appears on an ancient Egyptian wall painting (see page 32), now at the Louvre Museum in Paris. According to the ancient Egyptians, a farmer who dreamt of a large cat was sure to enjoy a rich harvest.

The priests in charge of the cult of Bastet may have transformed the goddess – symbolically – from a lion to a cat. (They probably found the lion too ferocious and cumbersome to handle, preferring the cat that was easy to manage.) After the transformation, Bastet was shown as a cat-headed woman. Her right hand held a sistrum – a metal rattle for beating out rhythm – and the left hand a semicircular pendant on which was inscribed a lion's head. She also carried an aegis, or ceremonial basket, in the crook of her left arm.

Bastet had other names: Ubastes and Pasht, which may be the source of the endearment 'puss'. Bubastis meant 'the house of Bast' – yet another one of her names. Further up the Nile, near Beni Hassan, she was worshipped by another cult whose members referred to her as Pekhet.

Mummy of a cat. The face was covered with a painted mask, and the embalmed body swathed in colourful wrappings.

Flutes and sistrums

Initially, Bastet was merely a local deity. About 950 B.C., when Bubastis became the capital of Egypt, the cat goddess assumed greater significance. For the next six centuries, she was revered as one of the greatest deities of the land. When the Greek historian Herodotus came in Egypt in the 5th century B.C., her cult was nearing its zenith. Bastet's festival at Bubastis was one of the most popular religious events of the year.

In the second book of his *Histories,* Herodotus says 700,000 pilgrims (excluding children) thronged to the celebration at Bubastis from every part of Egypt. Following Bastet's legendary journey, men and women sailed in barges down the Nile. Many of the men played flutes, while some of the women beat out wild rhythms with sistrums. Everyone else sang and clapped in time. Along the way, the barges stopped near riverside communities. Some pilgrims started to dance, while others bantered with the local people on the bank. The barges followed the canals to the temple at Bubastis. At the ensuing celebration, there were sacrifices, feasting, drinking, revelry, promiscuity and licentiousness. Herodotus viewed the spectacle with a certain amount of distaste.

Tattoos, blood and ashes

Rituals enlisting the protection of the cat pervaded Egyptian life. Parents dedicated their newborn babies to Bastet, hanging a pendant inscribed with her image around their necks. In adolescence, the cat's silhouette was tattooed on the arms to attract the goddess's gifts. At special ceremonies, a few drops of blood from a sacred cat might be injected to ward off sickness and evil spirits.

When a child fell seriously ill, the family shaved their heads and sold the hair for gold or silver, which was used to buy fish offerings for sacred cats. The family gathered at the temple to study the cat for signs of their child's recovery.

For Egyptians, Herodotus reports, there was no loss more painful than the death of a cat. At fires, people showed more concern for saving cats than putting out the blaze. (Herodotus also mentions that Egyptian cats had a strange propensity for running into fires.) If a cat died in a house fire, its inhabitants covered themselves with ashes and ran about the streets, beating their breasts and tearing their clothes to shreds.

Bastet, the cat goddess, holds a sistrum (a metal rattle) in her right hand, and a pendant showing the head of a lion, in her left hand. The aegis, or ceremonial basket, is in the crook of her left arm.

MUMMIFIED CATS

In 1890, archaeologists discovered more than 300,000 cat mummies buried in an underground sanctuary at Ben Hassan. The site had once been a temple dedicated to the cat goddess Bastet. Built about 1400 B.C. the temple was situated at the top of a cliff; and the sanctuary, at its base. The mummified cats had been placed in small cases. Beside the cases were mummified mice – food for the cat's long journey to the afterworld. Sadly, the significance of the discovery escaped the archaeologists. As a result, all the mummies – weighing 24 tons – were sent to Britain, where they were ground up and used as fertiliser.

In recent years, researchers at the British Museum in London X-rayed unopened cat mummies. They discovered that the necks of many of the cats had been broken. This suggested that the cats may have been strangled to death. In some cases, the creatures died before they were 4 months old. Researchers speculate that these cats may have been bred as sacrificial offerings. The mummies date from the Ptolomaic period (330 to 30 B.C.). The practice of animal sacrifice was completely abhorrent to the Egyptians before this time.

Researchers have also unwrapped the bandages and shrouds covering the cats and discovered the vestiges of striped and spotted fur on the desiccated bodies. The colour of the fur is light ginger or reddish yellow. In some cases, researchers have found cat mummies containing only parts of the animal – paws, hindquarters, and bodies without legs. They believe embalmers may have divided cats to meet the demand of the devotees of Bastet for mummies.

The responsibility and care of the domestic cat passed from father to son. At a cat's death, every member of the family shaved off their eyebrows in mourning. (However, they shaved the whole of their heads and bodies when a dog died.) The dead cat was embalmed and swathed in rich-coloured wrappings before it was packed in straw and placed in a wooden case. The face was covered with a mask, on which the nose, the eyes, ears and whiskers were painted. Embalmed mice were included for the voyage to the hereafter and were tucked into the sarcophagus beside the cat. The wealthier the family, the more lavish the arrangements for the cat's funeral, though even the most humble household went into mourning.

An Egyptian wall painting, now in the Louvre in Paris, shows the cat goddess Bastet in her symbolic role as the Corn Spirit, helping harvesters.

A shield of cats

The killing of cats (and other sacred animals) was an unthinkable offence, punishable by death. Because cows and fish were also considered sacred, the ancient Egyptians remained resolutely vegetarian throughout most of their history.

According to legend, the prohibition against killing cats led to a major military defeat. In 522 B.C., Cambyses II, the king of Persia (present-day Iran), invaded Egypt, attacking the strategically important city of Pelusium in the Nile delta. To overcome Egyptian resistance, Cambyses' soldiers marched into battle with cats affixed to their shields. The Egyptians, appalled at the possibility of killing or even wounding the animals, threw down their arms, leaving Pelusium to the Persians.

Cat, falcon and baboon inscribed on an Egyptian pottery fragment known as an ostracon.

Five centuries later, a cat complicated Egypt's uneasy relations with Rome. According to the Greek historian Diodorus Siculus, a Roman visiting Egypt killed a cat and, even though the incident was said to be accidental, the outraged public demanded his execution. Although the Egyptian king – Ptolemy XII, father of Cleopatra – was unwilling to antagonise the Romans, he could not stay the offender's execution.

Egypt eventually fell to Rome in 30 B.C., when Cleopatra – the last monarch of Egypt's Ptolemaic dynasty – committed suicide. Despite Roman domination, the ancient Egyptian religious cults lingered on for more than 400 years. At the end of the 4th century A.D., Emperor Theodosius the Great, who ruled from A.D. 379 to 395, abolished pagan practices, and established Christianity throughout the Roman Empire. But the heyday of the Egyptian cat – and its cult – had already ended.

The cat in Greece and Rome

Ancient Egyptians guarded their cats closely, prohibited their export from Egypt, and bought back many that had been illegally exported or smuggled out of the country. Eventually, however, the cat became established in Europe, but with considerably less status than that which it had enjoyed in Egypt. The Greeks were too rational, and the Romans too practical to elevate a cat to the status of a deity.

The route by which the Egyptian cat reached Europe is uncertain. From 2000 B.C. onwards, Phoenicia (present-day Syria and Lebanon) was trading briskly with Egypt. Its ships may have carried the cat – and its cult – back to home ports. Remains of animal sacrifices – including cats – have been found at the ancient Phoenician city of Byblos. Phoenician traders probably used Egyptian cats as rat-catchers on their ships and sold the creatures as 'exotic' but useful novelties in Crete, Greece and Italy.

According to one legend, the Greeks rather than the Phoenicians brought the cat to Europe. Greek traders, eager to acquire cats for their home market, offered to buy some from the Egyptians. When the Egyptians refused to consider a god the object of a commercial transaction, the Greeks stole six pairs and sailed back to Greece. After the first litters were born, the breeders carried the cats to Italy and Gaul (modern France). The cat's natural prolificacy ensured survival and gradual dispersal throughout Europe.

Throughout the ancient Mediterranean, semi-domesticated weasels and skunks, and small snakes, were used to catch mice. (The mongoose was also popular for this purpose.) The Greeks may have planned to replace these smelly beasts with clean, refined cats. If so, their plan failed. They soon came to care for cats as companions and put little value on their mouse-catching skills.

During the 6th century B.C., Aesop, the Greek author of moral fables, used cats to satirise some of the worst human characteristics – dishonesty and deceit.

For these young Greeks, who have just discovered the dog-cat antipathy, the cat is still a novelty, an exotic animal from Egypt. This illustration appears on a Greek funerary stele in the National Archaeological Museum, Athens.

*A domestic cat and orna-
mental birds depicted on a
Roman mosaic, now in the
British Museum, London.*

*In this detail from a Greek
vase, two women watch as a
cat leaps up in an attempt
to seize a bird.*

Herodotus (485-430 B.C.) described the Egyptian cult of
the cat – a curiosity from the Greek perspective – in
the second of his *Histories.* There are also references
to cats in two literary works of the 4th century B.C. –
Aristophanes' comedy *Archanians* and Callimachus's
History of the Animals. Two centuries later, the poet
Theocritus, who lived in Alexandria, then a Greek city,
praised cats in the *Dialogue of the Syracusans.*

The cat plays an important role in Greek and Roman
myth. Apollo, the sun god, created the lion; his sister,
Artemis, the cat. Artemis personifies the moon. This
was the beginning of the legend that the moon gave
birth to the cat. The Greeks identified Artemis with
the Egyptian cat goddess Bastet. Later the Romans connected Bastet-Artemis with their goddess Diana.

From the 5th century B.C. onwards, there is increasing evidence in Greek art that the cat has become a
domesticated animal. A Greek funerary stele from this
period, now in the National Archaelogical Museum at
Athens, shows a confrontation between a cat and a
dog, which are held on leashes by two youths.

During the 1st century B.C., the Roman statesman
and orator Cicero was the first to write about the
Egyptian cat. By the following century, the cat was still
relatively rare in Rome and the rest of Italy. But in the
ruins at Pompeii, which was destroyed in the erup-
tion of the volcano Vesuvius in A.D. 79, the surviving
mosaics show images of cats, including one of a spotted feline killing a chicken. A woman trapped in the
Vesuvian lava was found clutching the remains of a
cat. Pliny the Elder, who observed the terrible erup-
tion, wrote about the Egyptian cat in his *Natural
History,* one of the great works of Latin literature.
Pliny noted the stealth with which a cat hunted birds
and mice.

The Romans saw the cat as a symbol of liberty.
Although the cat was domesticated, it was not easily
restrained. Therefore, it was seen as representing

Roman independence. Its image decorated the flags of the legionaries who served in far-flung reaches of the Empire. The goddess of liberty – Libertas – was usually shown with a cat lying at her feet.

At the beginning of the 4th century A.D., when the Roman Empire entered its long decline, eastern religions were introduced into Italy. One of these religions was that relic of ancient Egypt – the cult of the cat goddess Bastet. At Portici, near Naples, a painting shows a woman devotee – with a sistrum – worshipping a cat. In the same century, Palladius published *De re rustica,* an agricultural treatise that recommended cats as a means of getting rid of moles in gardens.

By the end of the Roman Empire, the cat was part of the everyday life of the capital and its environs. But, in the distant provinces, it was a rarity – a pet of Roman officials or local aristocrats.

Names of the cat

In ancient Egypt, the cat's first home, the animal was called mau, presumably because of its miaow.

The Greek historian Herodotus, who lived in the 5th century B.C., translated cat by the Greek word *ailourus,* which means 'the waving ones' – a reference to the cat's tail. Today, cat lovers and haters are *ailourphiles* and *ailourphobes.* Another Greek word – *gale* – is sometimes translated as cat or 'weasel'. The word appears in the writings of Homer, Aristophanes, Theocritus and other classical Greek authors.

The earliest Roman term for cat – *felis* – was also used to describe martens and weasels. The first specific use of *felis* for the domesticated cat appears in the 1st century B.C. in the writings of the Roman orator Cicero.

The Latin term *cattus* or *catus,* source of our English word, appears in a 4th-century agricultural treatise by the Roman Palladius. This word identifies the cat in many European languages: *chat* (French); *katze* (German); *gato* (Spanish); *katta* (Swedish); and *kat* (Dutch and Danish). Originally it may have come from the Byzantine Greek *katos,* which has roots in the Arabic *qatt,* the Syrian *qatì* and the African *kadis.* The Berbers of Morocco use another variant of the African word – *kadiska.*

Mediaeval documents, religious or judicial in content and invariably written in Latin, use the terms *musio, muriceps,* or *murilegus,* meaning 'mouse-catcher', rather than *cattus*, when referring to the cat.

This Gallo-Roman stele, found at Alise-Sainte-Reine in the Côte-d'Or region of France, shows a young boy holding a cat.

35

The cruel Middle Ages

The cat's long and comfortable relationship with man – at least in western Europe – received a major setback with the fall of Rome. The city was little more than an impoverished backwater when the barbarians seized control in A.D. 476. Cats shared a harsh and precarious life with their masters in the last outposts of Roman glory, the decaying communities and the isolated country estates of Italy and France. Even in the Roman world, the cat had been a rarity. Usually it was the pet of an aristocratic family. During the Dark Ages – roughly the period from the 6th to the 10th century – cats survived, but numbers were few relative to other animals. Excavations in northern France at the village of Brébières – founded during this period – reveal two cats to every six dogs.

The cat and the law

In parts of the post-Roman world, the cat disappears altogether from the archaeological record during the Dark Ages. But in Britain it was a familiar creature, highly valued as a mouser. The laws of the Welsh king Hywel the Good, who died in 950, list the price of kittens: a penny, from birth until its eyes open; twopence, when it first kills; fourpence, after four kills.

Hywel's laws also required sellers to ensure that ears, eyes, claws and teeth were in perfect condition. If a tom was a poor mouser or a female an inadequate mother, a third of the initial price had to be refunded. Stealing or killing a cat carried a fine of one ewe with her lamb, or enough wheat to cover a cat, when hung by its tail with its jaw touching the ground.

The cat was also known in Germany, Scandinavia, Ireland and other regions that had escaped Roman rule. In Norse mythology, the cat – probably the wildcat and the lynx – is associated with the goddess of fertility and wealth, Freyja, who introduced the arts of magic to the gods. She is usually shown riding in a chariot drawn by two cats. Even today, the cat holds a privileged place in Scandinavian homes.

In Ireland, a cat-headed god was worshipped as early as the 1st century A.D. According to folklore, the 6th-century Saint Ciaran killed a King of Cats, known as Iruscan.

In the First Phase of Cruelty, *the 18th-century English artist Hogarth showed that cruelty towards cats was as common in his time as it had been during the Middle Ages.*

A 17th-century engraving taken from the Recueil des plus illustres proverbes.

During the Dark Ages, the monasteries opened their doors to cats, who protected the grain supplies against mice. Saint Patrick, the 5th-century patron saint of Ireland, reared cats. Thereafter, the Irish monks became active breeders of cats. One of the great achievements of the Irish monks was the creation of magnificent illuminated – that is, illustrated – manuscripts, which the copyists sometimes embellished with the images of their cats. One of the copyists, whose companion was a beloved cat, left behind a poem, which compares their tasks:

I and Pangur Ban my cat
'Tis a like task we are at;
Hunting mice is his delight
Hunting words I sit all night...

When the monks adopted cats as companions, they followed the example of Pope Gregory the Great (c. 540-604), who organised the early Church. At the end of his life, Gregory retired from the papacy to a monastery, where his only worldly possession was a cat. A mediaeval theologian, John the Deacon, reported Gregory 'liked stroking his cat better than anything else.' In the late Middle Ages, anchoresses – women who lived secluded religious lives – were permitted to have a cat as their sole companion.

Many saints of the early Christian church, such as Saint Martha, who lived during the 1st century A.D., had cats as companions. In some instances, the cat was a symbol of a saint's virtues or concerns – just as it had been for pagan deities such as Bastet and Freyja. According to legend, Saint Agatha, the 2nd-century saint, appeared as an angry cat to scold women who worked on her saint's day. Even today, she is known as Santo Gato – Saint Cat – in the Pyrenees Mountains of northern Spain. The 7th-century Saint Gertrude of Nivelles is the patroness of gardeners, widows, travellers – and cats. The 11th-century Saint Ives, the patron of lawyers, is frequently depicted with a cat, the symbol of justice.

Mediaeval cats

Until the 10th century – the beginning of the Middle Ages – the cat enjoyed the protection of the Church. The image of the cat appeared in carvings and other architectural features of mediaeval churches and as a decorative element on church furniture.

Outside the monasteries, the cat was admired as an aggressive mouser by the owners of barns, granaries and warehouses. Nevertheless, its value was less than that of other domestic animals – cows, pigs, sheep and horses – which supplied food, leather, wool and driving power for ploughing and other agrarian tasks. Even the dog earned greater esteem because of its important role in the hunt.

In northern Europe, where the winters were colder and harsher than they are today, the soft, warm and inexpensive fur of the cat was used to line and decorate garments. (Lawyers often had their gowns trimmed with cat fur.) In times of famine, the flesh of the cat was sometimes added to the soups and stews of hungry farming folk.

PUSS IN BOOTS

In 1697, the French fairy tale writer Charles Perrault published his collection *Le Maître Chat ou Le Chat Botté* (The Teacher Cat, or Puss in Boots). In the title story, the clever feline secures a fortune and a royal princess for his penniless young master, who has assumed the title of Marquis of Carabas. The tale dates back to Italian, Arabic and Sanskrit sources.

Puss in Boots is a 'magician cat' which, in European folklore, brings luck and good fortune. In southern France, the cat is a *matagot;* in Brittany, it is called a 'silver cat'. The English variation of this magical creature is Dick Whittington's cat, who rids an eastern potentate's realm of rats and enriches his young master.

Mediaeval attitudes

In mounting its persecutions, the Church played on widespread superstitions about the cat. Common folk associated it with the predatory wildcat and lynx, and believed sorcerers could change themselves into cats. Moreover, they saw the cat as a plaything of the old nobility, whose paganism was discredited and condemned as evil.

The cat's behaviour fed these fears. The animal submitted to no one; it showed affection spontaneously and without invitation; and, just as suddenly and unpredictably, it lost interest and went on its way. Its freedom and lack of fidelity were troubling to people who lived within the closely knit and rigidly organised society of the Middle Ages.

Cats depicted in a 16th-century engraving, after M. G. Brugense.

Cats and crusades

During the 11th and 12th centuries, the Crusaders, returning to western Europe from their conquests in the Middle East, brought back the black rat in the holds of their ships. The cat was called upon to battle the new scourge, which had a voracious appetite for cereals and fruit. For two centuries, the cat fought the black rat, renewed the admiration of its supporters, and earned itself a period of respite from persecution.

In the early 13th century, the Church launched a crusade against the Albigenses and the Waldenses, two powerful heretical sects in southeastern France. One of the accusations brought against the sects was participating in religious rites involving cats.

The Albingensian crusade, which lasted from 1208 to 1229, laid waste the region and its flourishing culture. In 1233, Pope Gregory IX declared that the sects had worshipped the devil in the form of a black cat. Another of his acts also established the Inquisition, which for more than seven centuries ruthlessly pursued those accused of being in league with the devil.

The devil in the shape of a cat

In the early Middle Ages, the devil was represented with a human form. Saint Bernard, in the 12th century, associated it with night and the powers of darkness. Gradually, the devil assumed different animal shapes – dog, goat, monkey, toad or wolf – but its most enduring form was the black cat.

The cat was depicted as scraggy and hairy, with cloven hoofs, claws, horns in his forehead and, sometimes, with cat's ears. According to Gregory IX, the devil's followers ritually kissed the black cat's genitals or rump before embarking on indescribably lascivious orgies.

In the mid-13th century, the Church hurled the accusation of cat-devil worship at the renewed cult of the goddess Freyja in the German Rhineland. At the beginning of the 14th century, the same charge was brought against the Knights Templar – a rich military order of the Crusades. In both instances, the Church emerged victorious and, in the case of the Knights Templar, considerably wealthier.

From 1347 to 1350, the Black Death – also known as the bubonic plague – swept Europe. After a century of fanatical decimation, there were too few cats to kill the rats infested with the disease-carrying bubonic fleas. As a result, more than a quarter of Europe's population died.

Fire festivals

During the Middle Ages, the Church encouraged the revival of pre-Christian fertility and purification rites. One of the rites was the fire festival – at the beginning of Lent and on St John's Eve in June – where the public burning of cats occurred.

In Paris, the St John's Eve fire was held at the Place de Grève. A basket, barrel or sack full of a dozen or so live cats was suspended from a pole or tree trunk above a huge pile of kindling. After the fire, the Parisians gathered the ash and charred wood as tokens of good luck. In 1648, Louis XIV, wearing a crown of roses, set the fire ablaze, danced and later banqueted. But the event was the last of its kind in Paris. It was abolished by the king, who may have found its mediaeval brutality distasteful. Fire festivals outside Paris, however, remained popular events throughout rural France. They were finally prohibited in 1796 during the period of the French Revolution known as the Directory.

A 16th-century illustration depicts a cat in the company of witches.

Cats and witches

Towards the end of the 15th century, Pope Innocent VIII stepped up the war on heresy with a condemnation of witchcraft. The document unleashed three centuries of persecution, in which 300,000 to 1 million people went to their deaths due to suspected association with the devil. Witches were usually outcasts or misfits, whose eccentric behaviour was seen as the result of demonic possession. In many cases, the witch's only companion was a cat – or 'familiar' – which onlookers took to be the devil's representative. It was also widely believed that a witch could take a cat's shape. At witchcraft trials, cats sat beside their owners in the dock. Both were tortured for 'confessions' and burnt alive. In those troubled times, even a passing fondness for a cat was enough evidence to persecute.

The tribulations of the cat were complicated by the Reformation, which split Europe into warring factions. In England, during the reign of Mary Tudor (1553-1558), who was also known as 'Bloody Mary', cats were burnt as a sign of Protestant heresy. Her successor, the Protestant Elizabeth I (1558-1603), matched her predecessor's cruelties by burning a cat-filled effigy of the pope as a highlight of her coronation procession. According to accounts of the event, live cats caged in a wicker frame 'squalled in a hideous manner as soon as they felt the fire'. The screeching was 'the language of the devil within the Holy Father'.

In later centuries, cat massacres lost all magical and religious significance, and acquired secular overtones. During the 1730s, a crowd of impoverished, unemployed youths in Paris rampaged through the streets and broke into the houses of the wealthy, where they seized pampered pet cats and slaughtered them.

A mediaeval mouser carved in the choir stall at the Cathedral of Saint-Pierre, Poitiers, France.

A Cat Washing Itself. *From a 13th-century album by Villard de Honnecourt.*

The prophet's cat

The fear and hatred of the cat in Europe was unknown in Africa and Asia. The cat may have crossed from Egypt to the Arabian Peninsula, where it became a revered animal among desert tribes. In the early 7th century, the prophet Muhammad founded Islam and united the tribes into a world-conquering force.

In the Koran, the cat is described as a pure animal, whereas the dog is said to be impure. Because the cat possessed the *baraka,* or blessing, it was always cherished by Muhammad's followers. A 13th-century caliph of Egypt bequeathed a small garden to the homeless cats of Cairo. Legacies and charitable donations provided funds to buy meat and offal for the cats.

Even Muhammad had a favourite cat called Muezza. According to legend, the creature once fell asleep on the sleeve of his master's *gellaba* or robe. When the time came for Muhammad to go to pray, he cut off the sleeve rather than disturb the cat's sleep.

Islamic folklore credits the cat's origins to the work of the biblical Noah, who feared the Ark might be overrun by mice. To solve the problem, he passed his hand over the lion's head three times. The lion sneezed forth a cat that kept the mice in check.

In India, the earliest mention of cats dates from 200 B.C. Fables about cats appear in the Indian epics, the *Ramayana* and *Mahabharata,* which date from 500 B.C., but they may be interpolations from a later date. The Indians have a feline deity – Sastht – whose attributes are similar to those of Bastet, the cat goddess revered by the ancient Egyptians.

Oriental cats

Some experts claim that the cat reached China as early as 2000 B.C., but this is doubtful. The cat may have been shipped by caravan along the great trading route – known as the Silk Road – which, from Roman times, linked the Mediterranean with the Orient. Once the cat reached China, it was appreciated as a mouser, and became the symbol of good fortune, peace and beauty.

According to Chinese folklore, the cat's ability to see in the dark is a sign of its power to keep evil spirits at bay. Chinese dwellings are often adorned with images of cats. Small lamps with slit-like apertures – resembling cat's eyes – are lit at dusk to ward off evil night spirits.

In the Far East, Buddhists admire the cat's meditative powers. Yet the cat is not mentioned in Buddhism's original sacred

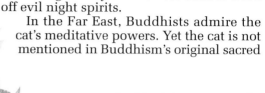

In this 13th-century psalm book illustration, dog and cat share the hearthside.

texts. According to legend, the cat's description was excluded because the creature fell asleep during the Buddha's funeral.

According to Gaston Phébus (1331-1391), 'cats are hunted infrequently and only by chance'. This illumination of wild cats is from an early 15th-century edition of Phébus's book on hunting.

Cats at court

Legend says cats first reached Japan in A.D. 999. On arrival, they became pampered guests at the imperial court in Kyoto. The Japanese treated cats as beloved companions – to be fondled and nourished like lap-dogs – rather than as hunters. (To combat the swelling numbers of mice, the Japanese decorated dwellings with sculpted and painted images of fierce-looking felines.) As a result, the Japanese cat lost its mouse-catching skills. Only in the 17th century, after centuries of spoilt existence, were cats again permitted to hunt freely.

In Japanese folklore, the cat is usually described as a benevolent animal. But the Japanese, like the Europeans, also thought some cats had sinister, magic powers. For example, they believed long-tailed cats assumed human shapes and cast spells on innocent people. In one Japanese tale, a demon cat sucks the blood of a beautiful maiden and assumes her shape in order to deceive her suitor, who is a prince. Eventually, the demon cat is hunted down and slain by the prince. The maiden is released from the magic spell, and restored to her human shape and her suitor.

Cat lore and legend

During the Middle Ages, cats were often used in fertility rites that dated from pre-Christian times. In parts of Europe, they were buried in furrows of newly ploughed fields to improve yields. Sometimes a cat was buried in a field to clear weeds, or at the foot of a tree to ensure growth. The cat was a protective presence while crops ripened. Parents warned children against going into cultivated fields 'because the cat sits there'.

At harvests, the reapers cut off the paws of a cat with the last swathe of the scythe. (In earlier times, people may have used wildcats, bears, foxes or dogs.) In some parts of Europe, the cat was cooked and eaten to ensure future fertility.

In France, cats were burnt in bonfires on the first Sunday of Lent and, again, on St John's Eve in late June. As the fires blazed, local people leaped over the flames or forced domestic animals through the smoke.

CATS IN ENTERTAINMENT

Concert of amateurs. A 19th-century lithograph.

Throughout history, the cat has rarely appeared on stage or in the circus. A relatively small creature, the cat can never thrill audiences as the mighty lion can. Moreover, the cat is as difficult to train as the lion, although obviously less dangerous. A cat can be taught tricks, but it may be unwilling to repeat them on demand in public.

The cat's lack of commitment and its unexpected displays of temperament have always been drawbacks to its career. An entertainer offered to put on a show with his acrobatic cat for the French king Henry IV (1553-1610). Despite its ability to perform a thousand tricks, the cat was banished from the stage for fear it might attack the monarch.

According to legend, monkeys have been used to conduct cat concerts. A remarkable attempt to tap feline vocal talents was the cat pipe organ created by the citizens of Brussels for a procession honouring Charles V (1500-1558), who held the titles of King of Spain and Holy Roman Emperor. The pipes of the organ were replaced by narrow boxes, in which cats were hidden. The tails, sticking through holes in the boxes, were tied by strings to a keyboard. When a performing bear pressed the keys, the strings pulled the cats' tails. The cat organ was played in London and Paris. The last appearance of this musical curiosity was in 1796.

Cats have been more successful in film, where a carefully coaxed performance once captured on celluloid need not be repeated. In 1951, *Rhubarb,* a comedy about a ginger alley cat that inherits a fortune, won the first Patsy (Picture Animal Top Star Award Film) for its eponymous feline hero.

The Audrey Hepburn classic, *Breakfast at Tiffany's* (1962), based on Truman Capote's novel, and Paul Mazursky's *Harry and Tonto* (1985), which starred Art Carney, are memorable cat movies. Cats have also figured in horror films, such as Val Lewton's *Cat People* (1942). The Japanese *I Am a Cat* film tells a story from a cat's perspective. Film animators have captured the comic and rambunctious side of the felines in *Felix the Cat* and *Tom and Jerry* cartoons.

There followed torchlight parades through fields, gardens and meadows. Shaking the sparks from the torches on cultivated ground was thought to improve crops. The Lenten fires were believed to ensure the growth of spring crops and the fires of St John's to protect crops against storms and droughts. The fire ceremonies – and the burning of the cats – continued until the end of the 18th century.

Early farmers said the cat was fat or lean when they described the size of the harvest. The cat was used to predict future harvests. It was a tradition to throw a cat off the top of a church. If the cat landed on its feet, there was hope for a good harvest. In 1938 and again after World War II, the tradition was revived (with a stuffed velvet cat replacing the live animal) at *Kattefest* (Cat Fair) in Ypres, Belgium. The fair, held annually in May, features a parade with floats dedicated to Bastet, Freyja and other cats of lore and legend.

Guardian spirits

From earliest times, the cat was seen as a benevolent guardian spirit. For example, the ancient Egyptians believed the cat goddess Bastet protected them from contagious diseases. It was the custom to inject offspring with a few drops of blood from a sacred cat.

In the Middle Ages, some folk thought of the cat as the protector of their house. The custom of immuring the animal in walls or burying them alive in the foundations was an early kind of house insurance. After the Italian poet Petrarch (1304-1374) embalmed his dead cat 'in the Egyptian manner', he had it interred above the doorway to prevent evil spirits from threatening his house.

The traditional way to keep a new cat at home was to rub its paws in butter and to sharpen its claws on the outside of the chimney. It was bad luck to let an adult cat be carried away from the house or carried into a house. (The cat should be allowed to walk into a house by itself.) Three-coloured cats were said to protect houses from fire.

Other traditions have also persisted for centuries: if a black cat visits, good luck may follow; if it stays, bad luck. In England, it is said that a black cat in a house can save a sailor from danger at sea. In Germany, France, and parts of the United States, black cats are seen as followers of the devil and, therefore, bad luck. In some parts of France, people still think a black cat with a small white tuft will bring good luck.

A legendary figure is the magic cat that brings good luck in return for a share of his master's wealth. In Germany and eastern Europe, a kindly household sprite or goblin was said to appear in the form of a black cat. The traditional children's story of Puss in Boots – the tale of a poor boy who becomes rich by following the crafty advice of a cat – is a well-known example of the notion. In Italy, cats received first portions of every meal in the expectation of good fortune. In Brittany, someone who suddenly acquired riches had found 'the silver cat'.

It was said that cats had the power to foresee death. If a cat jumped on to a sick person's bed, death was imminent. However, some swore the sick person would die if the cat jumped off the bed. In Belgium and

OVERCOMING FEAR

It's hard for cat lovers to understand that there are people who are terrified of cats. The fear may begin during childhood when a cuddly kitten suddenly scratches or bites. After the incident, all cats may be seen as threatening.

The fear may also be caused by an anxious parent who shouts in panic when a cat jumps on a new baby. The parent may be afraid the cat will smother the baby, although it is unlikely that the animal would sit for long on a squealing, squirming infant. If the episode recurs, the parent may communicate a sense of panic about the cat to the child.

Cats are often drawn to individuals who suffer from cat phobia. In the presence of a cat, the individual may become paralysed with terror. The cat may misread the stillness as an invitation to jump on a welcoming and comfortable lap.

Desmond Morris, author of *Catlore* (1988), offers a step-by-step procedure for victims of cat phobia. The first step is to show the individual cat photos and cat-like objects such as toy cats. The second step is to place the victim in a room with a cat. Initially, the cat is in a wicker cage at the opposite side of the room. Gradually, the animal is moved nearer and nearer, until the victim can comfortably pick it up. According to Morris, the procedure works within a few months.

Count Georges de Buffon (1707-1788). The great naturalist did not like cats, but the caricaturist has mischievously inserted one at lower right.

France, families tied a small black ribbon around their cat's neck when someone died at home. When a dying cat senses its own death, it may leave the house. This was considered a bad omen for the house or someone in the family, because the protective power of the cat was gone.

The cat was a symbol of sacred and profane love. In Belgium, a girl who cherished a cat was sure to marry. But it was a bad omen if the cat sat by the doorstep before the wedding as it was thought to be reproaching the young bride for neglect.

If a girl was uncertain about marrying her suitor, she might 'leave it to the cat'. Three hairs from a white cat's tail were placed in a folded piece of paper, which was placed under the girl's doorstep. Next morning the paper was unfolded carefully. If the hairs were found to cross each other, the girl should accept her suitor's offer. If not, she should reject him. When a young bride refused a suitor, she was said 'to have given him the cat'.

In Scandinavia, if the sun shone on a bride at her wedding, she was seen 'to have fed the cat well' – that is, she was a good housekeeper. Someone who wished to harm the newlyweds might mistreat a cat during the wedding ceremony. In the Balkans, it was customary to bring the newlyweds a cradle with a cat to ensure healthy offspring.

A second marriage was often treated with suspicion or derision. In Egypt and parts of Europe, a cat might be hung outside the door as a sign of neighbourly disapproval. Burning the cat – the guardian of the marriage – was said to destroy its protective power. A cat was the symbol of illicit love. An adulteress was put into a sack of terrified cats that clawed her to death.

From head to tail

The superstitious believed a cat's head belonged to the devil and the rest of the body to God. According to legend, when God created the cat, the devil said: 'Make the cat if you like, but its head shall be mine.'

A cat's head was thought to be the seat of magical powers, sometimes good, sometimes evil. When eaten warm, it made a person invisible. Although it was often used in health-giving remedies, it could also cause madness.

Cat Concert. Engraving after Pieter Brueghel (1564-1638).

Cat Concert or Charivari:
*Moritz von Schwind
(1804-1871).*

In a fable by the French writer Countess d'Aulnoy (1650-1705), a wicked fairy transforms a princess into a white cat. The prince cuts off the cat's head and tail, and throws them into a fire. His act breaks the spell, and the princess regains her human shape.

The cat's tail was thought to be dangerous because it moved even while its owner slept, suggesting the presence of an evil force. Stepping on the tail was considered unlucky. For example, if a bride-to-be stepped on the tail, she might have to delay her wedding for a year. On the other hand, if a cat's tail was cut off, it could be used as an antidote for poisons and as protection against snakes. Also, it could prevent an animal from becoming a witch. Clipping the cat's ears was said to stop the animal from attending a witches' sabbath; clipping the tail improved the cat's domesticity.

Fiction and fact

The Greeks were the first to describe cats in literature. Aesop, who may have lived in the 6th century B.C., used cats in his fables. But Aesop's cats usually embody some of the worst human traits – craftiness and dishonesty. This unflattering image also appeared in the works of other writers.

An objective view might have been expected from a man of science, but this was not the case with the French naturalist Buffon (1707-1788), whose *Histoire naturelle* was one of the most widely read 18th-century works. According to him, the cat is a 'fawning and adaptable knave' with 'a deceitful character, a perverse nature that grows worse with age and which education only disguises'. But another French scientist, Louis Pasteur (1822-1895), eventually reversed the harsh judgments of Buffon and others by praising the cleanliness of cats.

THE LAW VERSUS CAT

In 1949, a bill that would confine cats to their owner's property was tabled in the Illinois State legislature. But Governor Adlai Stevenson, who was in office from 1948 to 1952, vetoed the proposed law with this speech:

'I cannot agree that it should be the declared public policy of Illinois that a cat visiting a neighbour's yard or crossing the highway is a public nuisance. It is the nature of cats to do a certain amount of unescorted roaming. Many live with their owners in apartments or other restricted premises, and I doubt if we want to make their every brief foray an opportunity for a brief game hunt by zealous citizens – with traps or otherwise.

'I am afraid this bill could only create discord, recriminations and enmity. Also consider the owner's dilemma: To escort a cat abroad on a leash is against the nature of the cat, and to permit it to venture forth for exercise unattended into a night of new dangers is against the nature of the owner.

'Moreover, cats perform useful services, particularly in rural areas, in combatting rodents – work they necessarily perform alone and without regard for property lines.

'We are interested in protecting certain varieties of bird. That cats destroy some birds, I well know, but I believe this legislation would further but little the worthy cause to which its proponents give such unselfish support. The problem of cat versus bird is as old as time. If we attempt to resolve it by legislation, who knows but we may be called upon to take sides as well in the age-old problem of dog versus cat, bird versus bird, or even bird versus worm.'

Cat lovers and haters

Throughout European history, the cat has had many enemies. Famous cat haters include Napoleon, and such dictators as Mussolini and Hitler. Queen Elizabeth I of England disliked them, and Henry III of France was terrified of them. Some early cat haters included scientists, such as the 16th-century French surgeon Ambroise Paré, who described cats in a chapter on poisons in a 1583 medical treatise.

During the 17th century, there was a renewed appreciation of the cat's intelligence and serenity, particularly among the powerful, wealthy and educated. The French cardinal and statesman Richelieu (1585-1641) was fond of the kittens that kept him company during his long hours at his desk. At his death, he asked his guards to care for the kittens but, in keeping with the widespread anti-cat prejudice of the period, they burnt the animals instead.

Cats as heirs

The 17th-century rehabilitation of the cat had its comic side. Wellborn ladies decked cats with jewels and bequeathed them their worldly goods, much to the despair of human heirs. In 1678, Madame Dupuis, a celebrated French harpist, left the greater part of her fortune to her cats. Her will obliged the other heirs, a sister and a niece, to ensure the cats were properly

The Ball of Wool: *Jean-Baptiste Greuze (1725-1805). In the 18th century, cats often appeared as companions in portraits.*

cared for. She stipulated that, if the relatives died before the cats, 30 sous a week should be spent on the cats 'in order that they may live well'. But the relatives contested the will, which the courts overturned. What happened to the cats is not recorded.

Cats and writers

In general, writers, painters and musicians have been the cat's best allies. Writers maintained a fondness for the cat, even when it was an object of witch-hunts, burnings and other cruelties. The 14th-century Italian poet Petrarch publicly declared his love of cats. The remains of his beloved cat are still preserved at a Padua museum honouring the poet.

Another Italian poet, Torquato Tasso (1544-1595), wrote a sonnet to a cat. The 16th-century French essayist Montaigne was intrigued by the cat's independence. He asked: 'When I play with my cat, who knows if I am not a pastime to her more than she to me?' The Spanish dramatist Lope de Vega (1562-1635) composed *Gattomachia* (Battle among cats), in which he praised cats and ridiculed people. In Act III of *Romeo and Juliet,* Shakespeare celebrates the fabled longevity of cats with this exchange:

Boy with His Cat: *John Hoppner (1758-1810).*

Tybalt: *What wouldst thou have of me?*
Mercutio: *Good king of cats, nothing but one of your nine lives.*

Hodge and Jeoffrey

During the 1800s, various English literary figures wrote about the cat. Dr Samuel Johnson's *Dictionary* (1755) offers the following definition: 'a domestic animal that catches mice, commonly reckoned by naturalists the lowest order of the leonine species'. Despite the objectivity of the entry, Dr Johnson showed great affection for his own cats. His biographer, James Boswell (who was a cat hater), records how Johnson fed oysters to one cat called Hodge. When the cat jumped up on his chest, Dr Johnson said: 'I have had cats whom I liked better than this,' then, as if perceiving Hodge to be out of countenance, adding, 'but he is a very fine cat, a very fine cat indeed.'

Other 18th-century English poets who celebrated the cat include John Gay, William Cowper and Thomas Gray, who wrote an *Ode on the Death of a Favourite Cat Drowned in a Tub of Gold Fishes.* Christopher Smart is still remembered for 'Consider my cat Jeoffrey', a passage from his strange poem *Jubilate Agno.* Smart was briefly an inmate in an asylum, where his only companion was a cat. A popular phrase dating from this period – 'not enough room to swing a cat' – first appeared in Tobias Smollett's 1771 novel, *The Expedition of Humphrey Clinker.*

Woman with a Cat:
*Edouard Manet
(1832-1883).*

Some Victorian cats

The English and American writers of the 19th century were among the cat's warmest admirers and staunchest defenders. They included William Wordsworth, Robert Southey, Joanna Baillie, John Keats, Alfred Tennyson, Algernon Swinburne, Matthew Arnold, Thomas Hardy, Mark Twain and Henry James. Rudyard Kipling added *The Cat Who Walked by Himself* to the world of cat lore. The early Victorian playwright and antiquary James Robinson Planché (1796-1880) is remembered for a single line: 'It would have made a cat laugh.'

Edward Lear (1812-1888), the artist and writer of nonsense verse, created the Runcible Cat and the famous Pussy-Cat that went off with the Owl in the beautiful pea-green boat. Lewis Carroll (1832-1898), who wrote *Alice in Wonderland* and *Through the Looking Glass,* invented the Cheshire Cat, who 'vanished quite slowly, beginning with the end of the tail, and ending with the grin, which remained some time after the rest of it had gone.'

The Victorian novelist Charles Dickens (1812-1870) was not particularly fond of cats. However, the household cat, Williamina, gave birth to kittens and carried them into his study, showing the instinctive attraction to writers common in cats. Dickens asked his daughter to remove cat and kittens. But Williamina returned with them, and again Dickens ordered them removed. A determined Williamina returned a third time, depositing her kittens at Dickens' feet and beseeched 'him with such an imploring glance that he could resist no longer'. The kittens stayed and an erstwhile enemy of the cat was vanquished.

*Colette (1873-1954)
by M. Vertès.*

Admirers past and present

Under the spell of the Romantic movement, which swept through art and literature in the first half of the 1800s, writers considered themselves outcasts of society, marginal and solitary. Some saw the cat as a symbol of their own social status. The German E.T.W. Hoffmann wrote in the first person as his favourite cat Murr. Another writer of this period fascinated by the cat's mystery was Edgar Allen Poe, who endowed the creature with eerie power in his tale, *The Black Cat.*

The cat also had numerous French admirers. The French poet Charles Baudelaire (1821-1867) wrote:

'Both ardent lovers and austere scholars, when once they come to the years of discretion, love cats, so strong and gentle, the pride of the household, who like them are sensitive to the cold, and sedentary.' The French poet Théophile Gautier (1811-1872), who lived in a house full of cats, said: 'God has created the cat to give man the pleasure of caressing the tiger.' Gautier described their habits in *La Nature chez elle et la Ménagerie intime* (Innate nature and the intimate menagerie). Virtually every major French novelist of the 19th century had an attachment to a cat. George Sand (1804-1876) drank from the same cup as her cat; Victor Hugo (1802-1885) built a chair in the shape of a throne for a cat. Alexandre Dumas *fils* (1824-1895), who had his own small zoo, was described as the 'defence lawyer of cats around the world'.

In the 20th century, writers from W. B. Yeats to T. S. Eliot have added to the treasury of fiction and poetry about cats. Hector Munro, otherwise known as 'Saki' (1870-1916), told the tale of the talking cat *Tobermory*. Don Marquis (1878-1937) is best known for his creations 'mehitabel the cat' and her typewriting friend 'archy the cockroach'.

Ernest Hemingway (1899-1961) was an ailourophile, who crossed imported Cuban cats with American varieties, believing that he was creating a new breed. His house in Key West, Florida, now a museum, still swarms with cats.

Other modern writers who certainly can be counted as cat lovers include Raymond Chandler, Olivia Manning, Compton Mackenzie, Walter de la Mare and the Czech playwright and novelist Karl Capek. Truman Capote made Cat a character in his book, *Breakfast at Tiffany's* (1959).

Two 20th-century French writers had high praise for cats. Jean Cocteau commented: 'I love cats, because I love my home, and after a while they become its visible soul.' However, the last word on cats undoubtedly belongs to the French novelist Colette (1873-1954). She said: 'Our perfect companions never have fewer than four feet.' Cats appear in many of her stories, which take pride of place on the bookshelves of cat lovers. There is a pair of Siamese cats in her libretto for Maurice Ravel's pantomime-opera-ballet, *L'Enfant et les sortilèges* (The Child and the Magic Spells) (1925). She herself played the part of a cat – *La Chatte amoureuse* – on the stage in 1912. When her beloved cat – 'La Chatte dernière' – died in 1939, she refused to replace it out of respect to its memory.

Cats and artists

In ancient Egypt, anonymous craftsmen created cat amulets and charms, and sculpted feline heads representing the cat goddess Bastet. The Greeks and Romans bequeathed statues, mosaics and frescos with images

The White Cat: *Pierre Bonnard (1867-1947).*

The novelist Colette, famous for her stories about cats, played a feline role, La Chatte amoureuse, *on stage in 1912.*

The French playwright, artist, and filmmaker Jean Cocteau (1889-1963), shown with his Siamese cats.

The cat and advertising...

49

Cat at a Window: Hiroshige *(1797-1858). This short-tailed cat sits contemplating a view of the Japanese city of Edo (now Tokyo).*

of cats. In the Middle Ages, builders adorned cathedrals with carvings of cats.

From the Renaissance onwards, the image of the cat occurs with greater frequency in European painting. The Italian artist Leonardo da Vinci (1452-1519) painted the *Virgin of the Cat.* Other Renaissance and late 16th-century Italian and Flemish masters who depict the cat on their canvases include: Domenichino, Pinturicchio, Tintoretto, Titian and Veronese. The cat figures in the work of the Flemish master Rubens (1577-1640) and the fantasies of the Dutch Hieronymus Bosch and the Brueghel family.

The cat is a regular feature of 17th-century paintings of Dutch domestic life. In the following century, the animals often appear as pets in portraits of children. Two delightful portraits of this kind are *La pelote de laine* (The Ball of Wool) by the French artist Jean-Baptiste Greuze and *Boy with His Cat* by the Englishman John Hoppner (see page 47). Other important 18th-century Italian and French artists who included cats in their paintings are Giovanni Tiepolo, Jean-Baptiste Chardin, François Desportes, Jean Fragonard and Jean-Baptiste Oudry. Jean-Antoine Watteau (1684-1721) left behind sketches of cats (see page 46) and the painting *The Sick Cat.*

The 19th-century French impressionist Edouard Manet included a black cat in his 1863 painting, *Olympia,* now in the Louvre, Paris. Manet also prepared cat illustrations for Champfleury's *Les Chats,* the first major book about cats, which was published in 1870. The painters Renoir, Bonnard and the American-born Mary Cassatt depicted cats in domestic scenes.

Funny felines

At the turn of the century, the French graphic artist Alexandre Steinlen (1859-1923) featured cats on his posters advertising tea and coffee. Steinlen also published *Images sans paroles,* an illustrated collection showing a cat raiding a fish bowl, playing with a ball of wool, and other comic episodes. Steinlen loved cats, and his home became known as 'Cat's Corner'.

In the 20th century, the cat has inspired quite a few popular cartoons. George Herriman introduced *Krazy Kat* (and his brick-slinging chum Ignatz Mouse) in 1913. A recent comic cat is Jim Davis's Garfield.

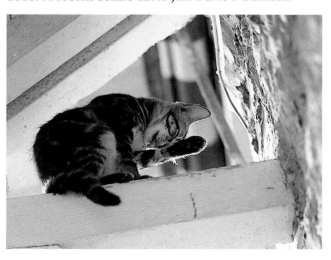

Cat lovers appreciate the animal for its character and independence.

Musical cats

During the 18th century, the cat was rhapsodised in *Fuga del Gatta* by the Italian composer Domenico Scarlatti. In the 1800s, another Italian, Rossini, wrote *Duetto Buffo due Gatti*, a musical depiction of two cats miaowing in tuneful ecstasy. The 19th-century Russian composer Tchaikovsky included music for the figures of Puss in Boots and the White Cat in the ballet *The Sleeping Beauty.*

The best-known modern musical tribute is Andrew Lloyd Webber's 1981 show, *Cats*, whose lyrics are based on *Old Possum's Book of Practical Cats.* This collection of poems about colourful cat characters, such as the Rum Tum Tugger and the Old Gumbie Cat, was originally written by Anglo-American poet T. S. Eliot (1888-1965) for the amusement of children.

Cat's progress

Throughout history, the domestic cat has been both venerated and persecuted. In ancient Egypt, the mightiest pharaoh and the humblest farmer deified the cat; in the mediaeval world, the Church persecuted the cat as being a demon incarnate or a creature associated with the devil and witchcraft. Cats were sometimes valued only as mousers or as guardians who bestowed protection and good fortune. But even in the darkest days, a few individuals cherished the cat as a companion. During the 17th century, cats found their niche in the family household. The paintings of Dutch interiors from this period depict the cat creating a bit of domestic havoc, filching food from the kitchen table and so on.

In the next century, the cat assumed its role as a beloved pet – a role it still plays in our lives. The 18th-century portraitists often show children with cats, a notable example being William Hogarth's portrait of the Graham children, which is in the Tate Gallery, London. But Hogarth also depicted the vicious attacks on street strays in his etching *The First Phase of Cruelty* (see page 36). Country cats of these times fared little better. Many were barely fed in the belief that hunger made them better mousers. They suffered from mange – a skin disease caused by a parasitic mite – and other diseases.

The cat's progress was significantly furthered by two important Victorian developments: an improvement in the treatment of domestic animals and an enthusiasm for exhibiting and breeding cats.

Show cats

The first cat show was organised by the Victorian artist and author Harrison Weir, in London, on 13 July 1871. The setting for Weir's cat show was the Crystal Palace, the great glass hall originally built to house the Great Exhibition of 1851 and re-erected in 1853 in the south London suburb of Sydenham.

Weir's show attracted about 160 cats for display or competition. Its success sparked a fashion for showing pedigree cats. Two years later shows were held at Alexandra Palace in north London, and another was staged at Birmingham. In 1875, 325 entrants appeared at Crystal Palace, and more than 550 entrants were shown at a show in Scotland's capital, Edinburgh. These early shows exhibited mainly short-haired specimens, but imported breeds were introduced in the 1880s. Two Siamese cats – a gift from the King of Siam (present-day Thailand) to Owen Gould, the British consul general in Bangkok – were exhibited in 1885.

During the late 1880s, the enthusiasm for breeding and exhibiting cats began to spread abroad. The British breeders exported their finest specimens, which formed the basis of overseas breeds. The breed standards established by Harrison Weir were widely adopted. France, Belgium and Holland became the first European countries to organise cat shows. The first American show was staged at Madison Gardens in New York in 1895.

Modern status

Today countless organisations encourage an interest in the cat, although they often disagree about breed standards. Cat shows around the world continue to attract large, eager crowds of fans. There are now more than 50 recognised breeds, and numbers are growing. Some new breeds – such as the Sphynx – get a lot of publicity, but receive only guarded recognition. But the biggest news, though, is that the cat has overtaken the dog as the world's favourite pet.

ARTHUR THE TV CAT

Arthur has been a star of British television since the mid 1960s. This green-eyed white British shorthair first became familiar to viewers when he appeared in advertisements for a popular brand of cat food. He became famous for his endearing habit of lifting the food out of the tin with his paw. The original Arthur died in 1976 and the pet-food manufacturer Spillers launched a nation-wide search for a successor. Eventually the new Arthur was found at the Wood Green Animal Shelter. His trainer immediately recognised star quality in the thin and bedraggled feline. A few months of good food and top quality veterinary care restored Arthur to health. With sensitive training, this natural performer was ready once again to appear on national television.

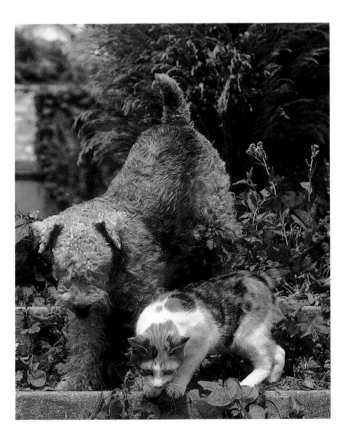

With proper supervision, a dog and a cat can forget their ancestral aversion, and happily share a home.

YOUR CAT'S ANATOMY

Anatomical features

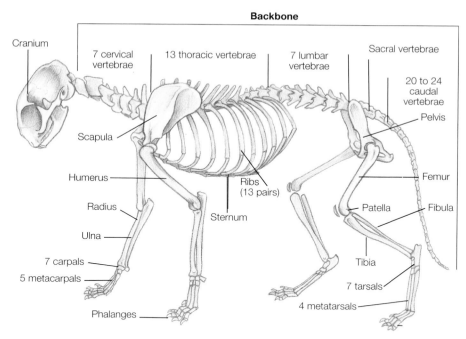

Backbone

Cranium

7 cervical vertebrae

13 thoracic vertebrae

7 lumbar vertebrae

Sacral vertebrae

20 to 24 caudal vertebrae

Pelvis

Scapula

Humerus

Radius

Ulna

7 carpals

5 metacarpals

Phalanges

Ribs (13 pairs)

Sternum

Femur

Patella

Fibula

Tibia

7 tarsals

4 metatarsals

The feline skeleton

A knowledge of the cat's anatomy helps us understand how its body functions and how its system can get out of balance when it is ill. The cat, a carnivore, has a skeleton of approximately 240 bones, bound by a powerful network of muscles forming a small, very lithe mammal.

The head

Most of the cat's sense organs and nerve centres are inside its head. The cat has a short, broad face for the size of its skull. Its very wide, forward-facing eyes give it binocular (three-dimensional) vision. The bony structures forming the cat's cheeks, the zygomatic arches, project far to the side of the skull to accommodate the powerful jaw muscles. These enable the cat to grab and tear off bites of its meaty prey. These muscles are anchored on either side of the skull, and extend down to the lower jaws, or mandibles. The large masseter muscles attached to the zygomatic arches raise the lower jaw and, together with the temporal muscles, allow the cat to close its teeth tightly on its food.

At the opening to the broad, front-facing nasal cavities, cartilage gives the nostrils their shape. The cavities are almost completely filled with cone-shaped nasal turbinates, each consisting of a very thin, curled layer of bone. Before it enters the trachea and lungs, air is heated and moist-

ened by a mucus membrane, rich in blood vessels, that covers the labyrinthian folds of the turbinates. When a cat develops an upper respiratory infection, swelling of the mucus membrane or accumulations of mucus and pus can easily block the tiny openings of the nasal turbinates, forcing the cat to breathe through its mouth. Air-filled spaces – the sinuses – in the bony walls of the cat's face are connected to the nasal cavities.

In the wild, the cat's survival certainly owes a lot to its sense of smell, but the domestic cat's olfactory sense is also highly developed. Even cats who have no need to hunt for food use their noses to inves-

Cross-section of the head

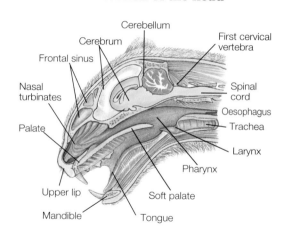

Cerebellum

Cerebrum

Frontal sinus

Nasal turbinates

Palate

Upper lip

Mandible

First cervical vertebra

Spinal cord

Oesophagus

Trachea

Larynx

Pharynx

Soft palate

Tongue

tigate food, to sniff for traces of other cats, and generally keep tabs on their domains. And even a whiff of catnip (*Nepeta cataria*) may transport a feline to seventh

Bones of the head

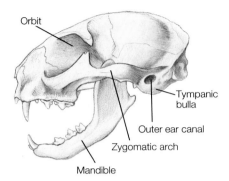

heaven, as the scent of this plant powerfully excites most cats.

A cat's mouth opens very wide. The mucus membranes of the cheeks, lips and palate often show natural patches of dark colour. These may look especially strange if black. However, they are normal.

Five or six lateral ridges cross the palate. The thin, mobile tongue is covered not only with taste buds, but also with hard, cone-shaped papillae that point backwards and are rough to the touch. The tongue's texture is ideal for grasping food and especially for grooming; when a cat neglects its grooming for a few days, its coat will appear dull and dirty. Located in folds of tissue at the back of the throat, near the base of the tongue, are the tonsils. They are composed of lymphoid tissue and they swell and become reddish if inflamed. The role of the tonsils, as in humans, is to help resist disease.

The tongue is suspended beneath the back of the skull by two parallel chains of bone, much like the seat on a swing. You can feel this extended structure, called the hyoid apparatus, by putting your hands on either side of the cat's throat.

The cat's teeth are especially suited to handling the carnivorous diet typical of all predatory mammals. The long, pointed canines are especially effective for biting. These are flanked by sets of much smaller incisors and premolars. Another carnivorous adaptation is that the third molars on both the lower and upper jaw – called the carnassial teeth – are sharpened like scissor blades; these teeth are used to slice and cut – rather than to grind – chunks of meat.

Kittens are born without teeth. Deciduous or milk teeth, 26 in all, begin to appear when the kitten is two or three weeks old. Fourteen teeth (six incisors, two canines, and six premolars) occur in the upper jaw; 12 (six incisors, two canines, and four molars) in the lower.

These are replaced by adult teeth when the kitten is between three and seven months, thus providing a temporary clue to a cat's age. Though tartar builds up during the cat's lifetime and its teeth become worn, both are unreliable indicators of a cat's age because the state of a cat's teeth will often depend on its diet.

The first adult teeth begin to protrude from the upper jaw at about three months, starting with the inner incisors, then the outer incisors, and finally, when the kitten is five or six months old, the canines. The kitten's milk teeth, which are much smaller, finer, and more pointed, may stay alongside the adult teeth for a while, but if they do not fall out of their own accord within a few weeks, they will cause eating problems. For this reason, they should be removed.

Tooth development in adults: left teeth seen from the outside

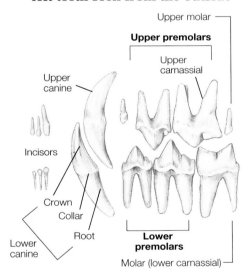

The adult's full set of teeth numbers 30. There are six incisors, two canines, six premolars, and two molars in the upper jaw and six incisors, two canines, four premolars, and two molars in the lower. By the time the animal is seven months of age, all the teeth should be fully developed and the kitten should be eating like a fully developed cat. Basically, the cat's teeth are designed to tear and bite at its food rather than to chew it. However, the carnassial teeth do chop the food into digestible chunks. Accordingly, a cat will usually tear off a piece of meat and swallow it whole, leaving it to the strong digestive juices of its stomach to transform the food into energy.

Eyes

A cat's vision is its most important sense, followed closely by its hearing. Its eyes, adapted over the years for night vision, can detect the faintest glow. Cats have a wide angle of vision, up to 285 degrees. With some 130 degrees of their visual field binocular vision (compared to 120 degrees for humans), they can judge distance more accurately than people can.

The eye's front surface is a wide aperture – the transparent cornea – that lets in lots of light. The rest of the eye is a nearly spherical fibrous shell called the sclera. Its visible front is the 'white' of the eye, a thick, solid wall which is the eye's outer casing. An opening in the back of the eye leads to the optic nerve.

which occupies more than a tenth of the eye's volume. Cats' eyes are wide and quite large compared to those of other mammals. The crystalline lens is held in place on its outer edge by muscles that can contract to vary its curve, ensuring that a focused image is projected onto the retina. After passing through the cornea, the front chamber, the pupil, and the crystalline lens, the light travels through another transparent filling, the gel-like vitreous humour, and forms an inverted image on the retina.

The retina is attached to the surface of the choroid. This light-sensitive coating is an extension of the optic nerve, which transmits nerve impulses. Two kinds of cells, rods and cones, convert light into nerve impulses that are then carried into the brain. The cat's retinas have a lot of

Cross-section of the eye

Pupil size and shape vary according to lighting

Behind the transparent cornea is the iris, which opens and closes the pupil to adjust the amount of light reaching the retina. In darkness, the cat's pupil can dilate fully, forming a circle. In moderate lighting, the pupil flattens to an upright oval shape, while in direct sunlight or harsh lighting it contracts to a vertical slit. This slit protects the highly sensitive retina, though the cat can still see perfectly well. The iris is blue in young kittens but, with few exceptions, changes to green, yellow or orange as the kitten matures. In cats that are white or mainly white, one or both eyes may remain blue, and cats that have Siamese coat colour also have blue eyes.

The iris is simply the visible portion of the choroid, a layer of tissue containing many blood vessels. The choroid membrane covers the internal surface of the sclera. A clear liquid called the aqueous humour fills the eye's front chamber, the hollow space between the iris and the cornea. Eye pressure is maintained as this fluid is secreted and drained.

Behind the iris is the crystalline lens

rods, which means it has superior night vision. Humans, on the other hand, have a comparatively large number of cones, giving them better daylight vision. The cones in human eyes also distinguish colour, but researchers are uncertain as to whether cats can see colour.

Behind the cat's rod-rich retina is a mirror-like layer of highly reflective cells that collects light from dim sources. It is this layer, called the tapetum lucidum, that makes cats' eyes glow when light shines on them – when they are caught in a car's headlights, for example, or in photographs taken with a flash.

As with other animals, the back of the cat's eye can be examined for vision impairment by dilating the pupil with special eye drops – something which should be done only by a vet.

Like most vertebrates, the cat has three eyelids. The third, called the nictitating membrane, is a sheet of pale white tissue that lies at the inner corner of the eye. This third eyelid is a good indication of feline health: if you can see it, the cat is not well. The inner surface of the eyelids and the visible part of the sclera are covered with a membrane, the conjunctiva, that is kept moist by tears and cleaned by the opening and closing of the eyelids. Tears exit through two tiny holes, the lachrymal puncta, at the inner corner of the eye, and flow down a channel, the lachrymal canal, or tear duct, to moisten the nostrils. (The nostrils are also moistened by normal nasal secretions.)

Kittens' eyes are shut at birth; the lids open after about two weeks, but often much earlier in some pedigree breeds.

Ears

Cats' ears have three sections: the external, the middle and the inner ear.

The external ear consists of the pinna and the outer section of the canal that leads to the eardrum. The pinna, a triangular flap of cartilage and skin, stands erect except in a few breeds in which the ears fold over. Perhaps today's best example of

Cross-section of the ear

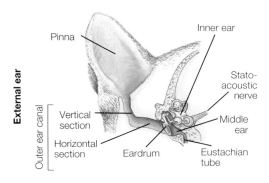

External ear

Outer ear canal

Pinna

Vertical section

Horizontal section

Eardrum

Inner ear

Stato-acoustic nerve

Middle ear

Eustachian tube

this is the Scottish Fold; a similar Chinese breed has become extinct. In some cats, such as the American Curl breed, the ears curl backwards. Cats' highly manoeuvrable ears are attached to the scutiform cartilage, a cartilaginous disc that is controlled by a set of muscles at its base. These enable the cat to swivel its ears to locate a source of sound quickly, or to pin back its ears to express worry or fear.

The outer ear canal consists of cartilage folded into what looks like a pipe with a bend in the middle. The vertical, visible section leads down to a horizontal section, at the end of which is the eardrum. The outer section of this ear canal is covered with a hairless skin that is rich in sebaceous glands, which sometimes produce thick wax.

The middle ear is a complicated cavity inside the skull. It contains a chain of tiny bones – the hammer, the anvil and the stirrup – that transmits and amplifies vibrations from the eardrum to the inner ear. The middle ear is linked to the throat by way of the eustachian tube.

The inner ear contains the cochlea, a spiral tube where sound vibrations are transformed into nerve impulses, a cavity known as the vestibule, and three semicircular canals that gauge the position of the head in relation to gravity. These canals give the cat its incredible sense of balance. Auditory impulses from the cochlea and sensations of movement and gravity from the semicircular canals are transmitted to the brain by the vestibulocochlear nerve, sometimes called the stato-acoustic nerve. This name reflects both roles it plays in the cat's daily life: hearing and balance.

The cat has excellent hearing when young and can hear sounds in the ultrasonic range that humans cannot hear. But many cats begin to lose their sharp sense of hearing from the age of five. Some white cats are deaf from birth in one or both ears.

Neck and torso

The backbone, or spine, is composed of many individual, cylindrical bones called vertebrae. A solid but highly flexible stem, this backbone is the skeleton's central axis and extends from the skull at one end of the cat to the tip of the tail. Running the length of the backbone is the spinal canal, which is occupied by the spinal cord.

Seven cervical vertebrae form the neck; they are connected to 13 thoracic vertebrae each supporting a pair of ribs which, together with the breastbone, make up the rib cage. Owing to their length, the seven lumbar vertebrae between the rib cage and the pelvis make the backbone especially flexible. Three fused vertebrae which form the sacrum, the last bone of the spine, are firmly anchored to the three pelvic bones – the ilium, the ischium and the pubis – to create the rigid cup of the pelvis.

Behind the sacrum are 20 to 24 tail bones, called caudal vertebrae. These give the cat's long tail the flexibility necessary to act as a counterbalance. This becomes important when the animal is climbing a tree or walking along the top of a fence. In some breeds, these caudal vertebrae have atrophied, resulting in a kinked or bobbed tail. One breed, the Manx, has no tail at all yet still manages to maintain a good sense of balance.

The ligaments that run the length of the spine connecting the vertebrae are relatively small and leave considerable room for muscle. This makes the backbone flexible, allowing the cat to stretch its back and propel itself forward in a series of leaps and bounds. The cat is a sprinter, and a domestic cat in good shape can reach a maximum speed of 48 kilometres (30 miles) an hour.

Inside the rib cage, or thorax, which extends to the diaphragm in the rear, are the two lungs, the heart and the large blood vessels, as well as part of the oesophagus, the tube that carries food from the throat to the stomach. Air enters the lungs through the trachea, commonly called the

Thoracic and abdominal organs
(front leg, torso wall and diaphragm removed)

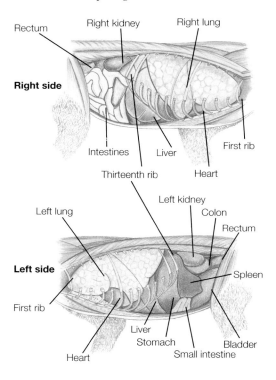

Rectum · Right kidney · Right lung

Right side

Intestines · Liver · First rib · Thirteenth rib · Heart

Left kidney · Colon · Rectum

Left lung

Left side

First rib · Spleen · Liver · Stomach · Bladder · Small intestine · Heart

windpipe. Above the heart, this separates into two large bronchial tubes that enter the lungs, subdividing repeatedly until they become tiny air sacs called alveoli. This is where oxygenation of the blood takes place – and at a much higher rate of exchange than in humans. The cat's heart beats 110 to 140 times a minute, which is about twice as fast as a human heart. During physical exertion or when a cat is excited, the heart rate can increase to 240 beats per minute.

Each lung is enclosed in a kind of double-walled membrane, called the pleura, whose inner wall is joined to the lungs and whose outer wall lines the thorax. A small quantity of liquid in the space between these two thin sheets allows the

outer surfaces of the lungs to slide against the thoracic wall as the cat breathes. The presence of too much of this liquid can compress the lungs.

The egg-shaped heart lies almost on top of the breastbone, its point facing the rear. Just in front of the heart, in the space between the right and left pleural sacs between the lungs, is the thymus; this gland gets smaller with age, but can become massive in a cat with thymic lymphosarcoma, a cancer that is often seen in young cats.

The abdominal cavity is bounded by the abdominal muscles, the sublumbar muscles and the diaphragm, with the pelvic cavity behind.

At the front of the abdominal cavity and just below the diaphragm are the liver, the stomach, the pancreas and the spleen. In the sublumbar region near the backbone, but not tightly attached to the body wall, are the kidneys, the adrenal glands and, in the female cat, the ovaries. The bladder is close to the entrance to the pelvis. The abdominal region also contains the intestines, and, in the female cat, houses the uterus as well.

Most of the abdomen's internal organs are enclosed in the peritoneum, a double-walled membrane resembling the pleural sacs. One side of the membrane fits closely around the organs and their blood vessels; the other is attached to the wall of the abdomen. Inflammation of the peritoneum causes accumulation of fluid within the abdomen and a dangerous condition called peritonitis.

The digestive tract includes all the organs that perform digestion, and these are not concentrated solely in the stomach. Digestion starts in the mouth with the salivary glands and continues into the pharynx, or throat, which leads through the oesophagus to the stomach. A cat's stomach can hold about 350 millilitres (12 fluid ounces).

The digestive juices in the stomach break down the food which moves slowly through to the intestines – the small intestine, 1 to 1.5 m (3-5 feet) long and consisting of the duodenum, the jejunum and the ileum, and the large intestine, 20 to 40 cm (8-16 inches) long and comprising the cecum, the colon and the rectum.

The duodenum receives secretions from two very important auxiliary organs: bile from the liver and digestive enzymes from the pancreas. The liver and the pancreas also serve as endocrine glands, secreting substances into the blood that are crucial for regulating the level of sugar in the cat's bloodstream.

The digestive process is completed in the small intestine, where much of the liquid is removed. The remaining semi-solid waste travels into the large intestine and is then expelled through the anus. Two anal sacs are located on either side of the anus. Researchers think the liquid discharged from these sacs by healthy cats serves to mark out a cat's territory, but there is as yet no scientific proof of this. Occasionally these sacs become blocked, causing discomfort to the cat.

Female urogenital apparatus, front view

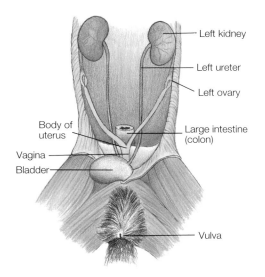

- Left kidney
- Left ureter
- Left ovary
- Body of uterus
- Large intestine (colon)
- Vagina
- Bladder
- Vulva

The urinary tract contains organs concerned with the formation and excretion of urine. The urine itself is produced by the kidneys, a pair of yellowish, bean-shaped organs, each weighing approximately 20 g ($\frac{3}{4}$ ounce). Their main function is to filter waste products from the blood and eliminate them with any excess water in the body. The urine travels down the ureters to the bladder, where it remains until forced out through the urethra during urination. In the female, this canal leads to the base of the vulva, while in the male it extends into the penis.

The genital apparatus includes the reproductive organs. The gonads are glands that produce sex hormones as well as ova in the female and spermatozoa in the male. These unite during fertilisation. The female gonads, or ovaries, are two almond-shaped bulbs about 8 mm ($\frac{1}{3}$ inch) long located directly behind the kidneys. In the male, the gonads are the two testicles, which are carried in a pouch, the scrotum, in the perineal region under the anus. These appear in the same location as the ovaries in the embryo, and then migrate through the abdomen and its muscle wall to their final position within the scrotum.

In some cases, the testicles may fail to descend, remaining instead inside the abdomen, a condition called cryptorchidism. When this happens, they cannot produce sperm but continue to generate the male hormone, testosterone. Castration, in these cases, requires removal of the testicles that are inside the abdomen. If these retained testicles are not removed they are likely to develop cancer due to the higher temperature inside the abdomen.

In the female, the genital tract begins with the fallopian tubes that are attached to the ovaries from which they collect ova. This is where fertilisation, the union of the sperm and the ovum, occurs after mating. Each tube leads to a Y-shaped uterus, a 5- to 8-cm (2- to 3-inch) long, 3-mm ($\frac{1}{8}$-inch) diameter canal that expands considerably during gestation to accommodate

Male urogenital apparatus, left side view

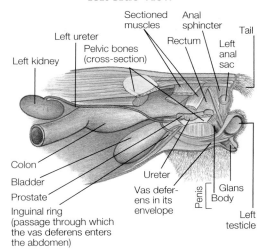

- Sectioned muscles
- Anal sphincter
- Tail
- Left ureter
- Pelvic bones (cross-section)
- Rectum
- Left anal sac
- Left kidney
- Colon
- Bladder
- Prostate
- Inguinal ring (passage through which the vas deferens enters the abdomen)
- Ureter
- Vas deferens in its envelope
- Penis
- Glans
- Body
- Left testicle

the foetuses. A cylindrical cervix links the uterus and vagina. The female's external genitalia – the vulva, consisting of two skin folds called labia, and a small erect clitoris – guards the vagina.

Puberty most often occurs in the female cat when she is about nine months old, though she may have her first heat (see page 159) as early as four months of age. The cat's usual gestation period is about 65 days, and kittens born before the 57th day are very unlikely to survive. At the other extreme, though, live kittens have been born after the 72nd day.

In the male, spermatozoa from the testicles move up a duct called the vas deferens, which enters the abdomen where it connects to the urethra. The prostate gland, which produces part of the fluid found in semen, is located here. The cat's prostate is small and does not entirely surround the urethra. This might explain why these animals rarely have prostate problems, a common affliction of aging human males. A more likely reason is that most male cats are neutered when quite young. Cats also have bulbo-urethral glands that produce fluid, which is added to the semen.

The penis, the male organ of copulation, is towards the rear, and contains two erectile tissues reinforced with cartilage. During erection, these fill with blood so that coitus can take place and the sperm can be deposited in the female's genital tract. The head of the penis, the glans, bristles with hooked spines, or papillae, that disappear after castration.

The female usually has four pairs of teats, two on the chest and two on the abdomen; these are occasionally supplemented by a fifth pair located in the fold of the groin. Males also have teats.

Limbs

Except for a few specific adaptations, the cat's front legs have the same bone structure as human legs.

The collar-bone is reduced to a bony vestige that lies concealed within the muscles, though it is visible in frontal X-rays of the shoulder. As in most quadruped mammals, the front legs are not rigidly attached to the torso. The thorax (chest) is suspended between the front legs by serrated muscles, which provide effective shock absorption when a cat lands from a potentially jarring jump.

The paw consists of a number of bones, tendons and ligaments that together help give the cat its superb agility. The wrist, or carpus, of each front paw has seven bones – five metacarpals in the palm and a pollex, or dew-claw, with two bones. Each of the four toes consists of three bones called the first, second and third phalanxes. The paw's highly developed muscles allow the toes to spread, while the radius is hinged on the ulna inside the front leg so that the palm can rotate as it does in humans. Just watch a cat play with a mouse or climb a tree and you will see how it uses its front legs. Each hind paw has a tarsus with seven bones, including five metatarsals; and four toes, each with three phalanxes.

The cat walks on the tips of its toes, using only the four digits of each front paw, since the short dew-claw, or thumb, does not reach the ground. The underside of the paw has skin pads of elastic fibre and fatty tissue.

These are hairless, but are covered with a tough outer skin, which may be pig-

Front right paw, bottom view

mented. These pads have a lot of nerve endings and are highly sensitive to pressure. They also contain eccrine sweat glands so that when a cat gets agitated, its paws, like a nervous human's hands, become sweaty. If the cat walks on a clean surface, the pads will leave visible wet spots in their path.

Each front paw has seven pads, five with digits, one larger, heart-shaped metacarpal (palm) pad, and one carpal pad located higher up the foreleg. Each digit is tipped by a claw, a curved hollow spike extending from the final (third) phalanx and held in place by a section of skin which produces the claw, and is called the germinal epithelium. As the claw

The claw-sheathing mechanism

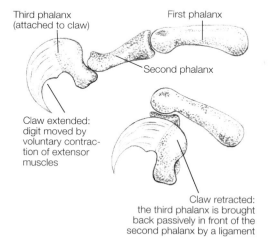

grows, it produces overlapping and flattened cones that curve downwards to a sharp point. These are regularly shed through wear or when the cat sharpens its claws on something rough. The outer part of the claw falls off like a scale, leaving a new claw with its sharp point. Unlike the tough, thick nails of the dog, the cat's claws do not get worn down by scraping the ground when it walks because they are completely retractable.

A flexible ligament connects the upper surfaces of the second and third phalanxes of each digit, allowing the third one to tilt upwards and retract in front of the second one, where it is hidden in a deep sheath of skin. The claws are extended only when the cat pulls on digit-connecting muscles. Since this is a voluntary contraction, the cat can extend or sheathe its claws at will.

The back legs are firmly attached to the pelvis by a ball and socket joint at the top of the femur and extend like springs when the cat leaps or runs. The back legs have fewer claws – four, because there is no dew-claw – and only five pads.

The function of the claws in the back legs is limited to supporting the cat during climbing. Compared to the sharper claws in the front legs, they are less retractable, duller and much shorter.

Skin

The cat's skin is thin and pliable and in some places hangs loosely from the body, but it may be very thick over the head and neck of adult males. It is made up of many elements: the hair, whiskers, sweat and sebaceous glands, and anal sacs. Like the skin itself, the hair and whiskers contain microscopic granules of melanin, a brownish-black pigment. Variations in colour come from the amount of melanin present in skin and hair. Generally speaking, the more melanin, the darker the cat: the less melanin, the lighter it will be. (The fur takes on the colour of the skin.)

Cat skin in cross-section

Guard hair

Sebaceous gland

Epidermis

Erector muscle

Dermis

Hypodermis

Awn hair

Apocrine sweat gland

However, light and temperature influence the degree to which melanin is activated. If a cat is genetically disposed to be white, for example, its coat will contain light-reflecting elements that interfere with full activation. Accordingly, the cat may be lighter than the concentration of melanin would suggest.

Cat hairs are produced in tiny cutaneous cavities called hair follicles, which receive secretions from the sebaceous and apocrine sweat glands. Tiny muscles are attached to the base of some hairs, and these erector muscles can bristle and puff up the fur when a cat is scared, preparing for a fight or wants to intimidate an adversary. The cat has three kinds of hair: down hair, the soft, crinkled hair that forms the undercoat; guard hair, the topcoat, which is the longest; and awn hair, which is not as long as guard hair, but is denser depending on where it is on the cat.

Fur colour

The coat may be classified as solid (self-coloured), tabby, shaded, smoke, pointed or other non-selfs. A coat is solid (self) when all hairs, from root to tip, are the same basic colour – black, blue, chocolate, lilac, cinnamon, caramel, fawn, red, cream, apricot or white.

Tabby coats are determined by two sets of genes: the tabby gene is responsible for determining which pattern the cat will be – blotched (classic), striped, spotted or ticked, as in the Abyssinian – and is possessed by all cats; the agouti gene determines whether or not this pattern will show up and make the cat a tabby cat. The orange gene which produces red, cream or apricot cats, will also show up the underlying tabby pattern.

Shaded cats are tabby cats in which the base of the hair is light with a darker end; in silver shadeds the undercoat is almost white. In some breeds the lighter shadeds are known as tipped or shell. Smoke cats are silver versions of solid or tortoiseshell cats, in which the lower part of the hair shaft is silvery-white.

Pointed cats have a pale body colour with darker hair on what are called the points – mask (face), ears, paws and tail. Siamese, Colourpoints and Birmans are among the pointed breeds. The colour distribution is linked to temperature. Kittens of these breeds are born almost white and, as they mature, the points become cooler than the body and therefore darker. After clipping – in preparation for surgery, for example – the new body hair grows darker. However, it does not take very long to lighten again.

Non-self cats may be tortoiseshell, a patchwork of solid colour and orange. When the tortoiseshell colour is combined with the tabby pattern the cat is known as a tortie-tabby or torbie. Tortoiseshells are usually females but may, very rarely, be males which have two different X chromosomes. Tortoiseshells without white tend to have rather mingled patches of colour, but when white is present the patches are larger and more distinct. Bi-coloured cats are those where part of the coat is white; these are usually solid colours with white, but in some breeds may be tabby, smoke, shaded or pointed with white.

The blue Maltese dilution is a recessive characteristic that dilutes black to blue, chocolate to lilac and red to cream. In non-dilute cats, melanin is distributed uniformly along the hair; in a cat with blue dilution, melanin granules are clumped irregularly along the hair shaft.

The large variety of colourings in cat breeds today is due to the interchange of colour genes between breed groups. The Governing Council of the Cat Fancy now recognises 193 coat varieties in Orientals alone, while Tiffanies may be found in over 300 colour schemes.

The Rex: no topcoat. Only the rippled undercoat is present

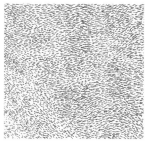

Sphynx: near complete absence of hair

Smooth hair (short or long)

Fur texture

Coats may be soft and silky or thick and coarse, depending on the fur type – short-haired, long-haired, curly or wire-haired. There are hairless varieties, too, but even these cats have fur on their faces, ears, paws and tails.

Short-hair is genetically dominant in cats, long-hair being a recessive trait. In short-hair cats, the longer guard hairs may measure almost about 5 cm (2 inches), while the coat of a good show Persian can be 12.5 cm (5 inches) long.

The so-called hairless Sphynx is not really hairless, but has a short, extremely fine, almost suede-like coat. Curly hair occurs in two major breeds: the Devon Rex and the Cornish Rex. Wire-hair breeds are characterised by rough coats that are irregularly frizzy or barbed.

The cat's fur protects it from excessive heat and cold. When the weather is hot, the cat is able to raise its fur away from its body to allow the circulation of some cooler air. A cat that feels threatened may also raise its fur.

Cat whiskers, or vibrissae, are stiff and very long. The nerve endings at the roots of the cat's moustache and eyebrows make these whiskers very sensitive organs, much like antennae. Cats use their whiskers to sense the location of prey or of obstacles in the dusk. Cats can also use their whiskers like a distant-early-warning system to tell them if there is danger nearby. A cat on the lookout will swivel its ears, use its wide-eyed vision and push its whiskers forward, ready to spring into action – or to head back into a safe place if it senses too much danger. Small whiskers are also found on the cat's front legs behind the carpus, or wrist.

The sebaceous glands produce an oil, called sebum, that forms a film on the skin to keep it from dehydrating. When spread on the fur by grooming, the sebum makes the hairs supple and brilliant. The sebaceous glands are concentrated under the chin, between the toes, where the skin meets the mucous membrane, and under the tail.

Cats have two different kinds of sweat glands. They differ according to how they secrete and where they are. Apocrine glands are found in the same locations as sebaceous glands; eccrine glands are found only on the paw pads. Both types of sweat gland are fairly insignificant because sweat plays no role in cooling the feline body, as it does in the case of horses and humans.

THE CAT ALBUM

Preface

What does an Egyptian Mau look like? What colour will my Persian's kittens be? Is there such a thing as a Red Point Burmese? Where does the hairless cat come from? Why is the Siamese's nose so long and the Persian's so short? What is a cobby cat? These are some of the questions this section attempts to answer.

The Album opens with a catalogue of common and recognised breeds, introduced by a pictorial table of contents. For fast, easy reference, this catalogue of breeds has been arranged alphabetically. (Note, however, that the Cymric and the Nebelung, although not recognised breeds, are shown with the Manx and the Russian Blue respectively because of their close relationship with those breeds.) This section also includes some breeds whose increasing popularity is likely to result in recognition being granted in the near future. The page, or spread, on each featured cat outlines the origins and history of that particular breed, describes the breed conformation and ideal coat, has a chart showing how championship points are allocated, tips on what reduces a cat's competitiveness at shows, and information on the genetic makeup and cross-breeding possibilities. Characteristics are based on standards of the Governing Council of the Cat Fancy (GCCF). Accompanying each featured cat are an illustration of a typical specimen and seven small squares that identify countries where the breed is registered and/or recognised by at least one cat association. Countries are identified by the following abbreviations: AUS for Australia, CAN for Canada, EUR for mainland Europe, NZ for New Zealand, SA for South Africa, UK for the United Kingdom and USA for the United States of America.

Fourteen pages of rare and overseas breeds follow the main alphabetical section of the catalogue. Although some are common in their country of origin or development, these breeds are not recognised by the GCCF.

Sections on genetics and colours provide detailed information on the standards and characteristics for all parts of the body, on colours, on outcrossing, and on genetic anomalies. The album ends with a glossary that defines the technical terms used regularly by cat lovers, breeders, judges and vets.

Cat breeds are generally subdivided into three categories of coat:
• the Shorthairs, the largest group, which includes British Shorthairs, Abyssinians, Rexes, Burmese and Siamese;
• the Semi-longhairs, with flowing coats, such as the Birman, Turkish Van, Somali, Maine Coon and Norwegian Forest Cat;
• the Longhairs, actually the many different colours of a single breed – the magnificent Persian.

All these categories and colours will become familiar as you read about the wide range of breeds. They differ in their characters, their appearance and their origins; a desirable feature in one breed may prevent another from winning, but some structural abnormalities will bar any cat from winning a certificate or any award (see page 246). Many breeds are closely related, but a mating which is acceptable for producing one breed may not be acceptable for the other.

Common and Recognised Breeds

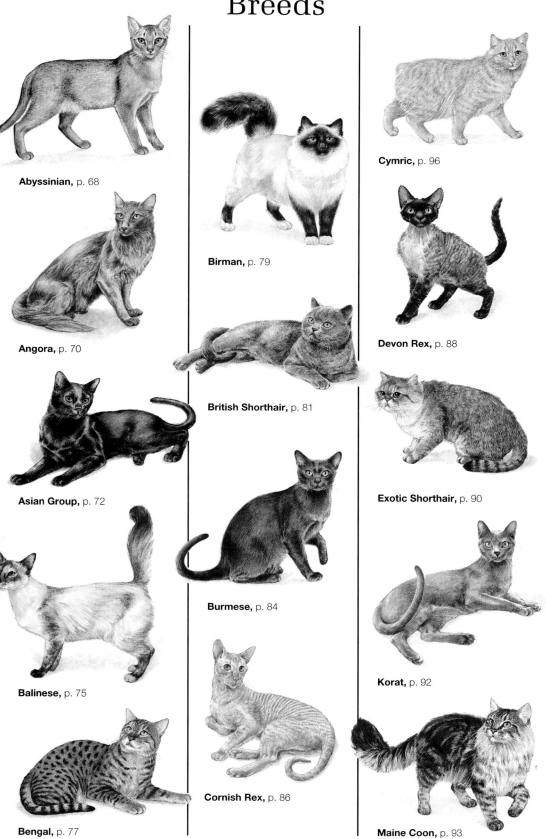

Abyssinian, p. 68

Angora, p. 70

Asian Group, p. 72

Balinese, p. 75

Bengal, p. 77

Birman, p. 79

British Shorthair, p. 81

Burmese, p. 84

Cornish Rex, p. 86

Cymric, p. 96

Devon Rex, p. 88

Exotic Shorthair, p. 90

Korat, p. 92

Maine Coon, p. 93

Manx, p. 95

Persians p. 104

Singapura, p. 117

Nebelung, p. 113

Ragdoll, p. 110

Somali, p. 118

Norwegian Forest Cat, p. 97

Tiffanie, p. 120

Ocicat, p. 99

Russian Blue, p. 112

Oriental Shorthair, p. 100

Siamese, p. 114

Tonkinese, p. 122

Turkish Van, p. 124

Rare and Overseas Breeds

American Bobtail, p. 126

American Curl, p. 126

American Shorthair, p. 127

American Wirehair, p. 128

California Spangled Cat, p. 129

Chartreux, p. 130

Egyptian Mau, p. 130

German Rex, p. 131

Havana Brown, p. 131

Japanese Bobtail, p. 132

Japanese Bobtail Longhair, p. 132

Munchkin Cat, p. 132

Ojos Azules, p. 133

Oregon Rex and Ohio Rex, p. 133

Peke Face, p. 133

Scottish Fold, p. 134

Selkirk Rex, p. 135

Siberian Cat, p. 136

Snowshoe, p. 137

Sphynx, p. 137

Turkish Angora, p. 138

York Chocolate, p. 139

Abyssinian

The Abyssinian comes first in this catalogue because of the alphabet, but its position is well merited. An imposing appearance, striking carriage and lively intelligence have earned the Abyssinian a foremost place in the feline hierarchy. Its rich, warm colours and long, agile body make this beautiful cat an obvious cousin to the cougar and the puma.

By temperament though, the Abyssinian is gentle and friendly. It is also lively and athletic, and therefore less suited to living in a flat than other breeds. Devoted to its owner, it may be cautious in the company of strangers.

Ancestor of them all?

Documents and mummified animal remains from ancient Egypt have convinced many people that the Abyssinian is the ancestor of the domestic cat. Whether this is true or not, the characteristics of the breed have changed scarcely at all since it was first recognised in Britain in 1882. Initially, its basic colouring was similar to that of a hare. Since then, breeders have developed many other colours, giving the Abyssinian a wide-ranging palette of subtle shades.

This medium-sized cat – the male is larger than the female – shows a fine but firm muscular development and athletic look. Its legs are long and it moves with grace and fluidity.

AUS	CAN	EUR	NZ	SA	UK	USA
•	•	•	•	•	•	•

The Abyssinian is active, curious and as well balanced physically as it is psychologically. This exceptionally energetic animal requires plenty of space if it is to develop as it should.

GCCF Standards	Points
Head and ears	15
Ears	10
Eyes	5
Body	15
Legs and feet	10
Tail	5
Body colour	20
Markings and ticking	20

Characteristics

Head: Viewed from the front, a modified wedge with rounded contours. In profile, showing gently curved transition between brow, nose, and muzzle with no flat planes. Rise from the bridge of the nose to the forehead with no sharp break. Of ample length, in balance with the rest of the cat, and gently curved from the forehead over the skull into an arched neck. Muzzle gently contoured to conform with the head. Chin very firm and rounded, neither projecting nor receding. Allowance made for jowls in adult males.

Ears: Large, alert, moderately pointed, broad, cupped at base, and arched forward as though listening. Hair on ears short, preferably tufted.

Eyes: Almond-shaped, large, brilliant and expressive, set well apart. Amber, hazel or green in all colours of Abyssinian.

Body: Medium long, lithe and graceful, showing well-developed muscles without coarseness. Solid to the feel. Rounded rib cage without flat sides, back slightly arched. Proportion and general balance more important than size. Legs proportionately slim, long, and well muscled. The Abyssinian stands well off the ground. Feet oval and compact when standing, giving the impression of being on tiptoe. Long, tapering tail.

Coat: Close lying, short and fine.

Pattern: Each hair showing two or three bands of each colour. The darker colour shows at the tail tip, forms a ring around the eyes, and extends up the back of the hind legs. Any shading on spine to be the darker colour. No bars on legs, chest or tail. Tendency to white on lips and lower jaw but no white locket or belly spot.

Colours: There are eight standard colours plus Silvers and Torties. In Silvers and Torties the base hair and nose leather and paw pads should be appropriate to the standard colour.
Usual: Rich, golden brown ticked with black. Base hair ruddy orange or apricot. Paw pads: black. Nose leather: brick red.
Sorrel: Lustrous copper brown ticked with chocolate. Base hair bright apricot. Paw pads and nose leather: pink.
Chocolate: Rich coppery brown ticked with dark chocolate. Base hair rich apricot. Paw pads: chocolate. Nose leather: pinkish chocolate
Blue: Soft warm blue ticked with deeper steel blue. Base hair pinkish mushroom. Paw pads: mauvish blue. Nose leather: dark pink.
Lilac: Warm dove grey ticked with deeper shade. Base hair pinkish cream. Paw pads and nose leather: mauvish pink.
Fawn: Warm powdery fawn ticked with deeper shade. Base hair fawnish cream. Paw pads and nose leather: pink.
Red: Warm red ticked with deeper shade. Base hair reddish apricot. Paw pads and nose leather: pink.
Cream: Soft, warm cream ticked with deeper shade. Base hair cream. Paw pads and nose leather: pink.
Black Silver: Clear silver ticked with black.
Sorrel Silver: Cool silvery peach ticked with chocolate.
Chocolate Silver: Cool silvery brown ticked with dark chocolate.
Blue Silver: Silvery blue grey ticked with deeper steel blue.
Lilac Silver: Silvery dove grey ticked with dove grey.
Fawn Silver: Silvery fawn ticked with fawn.
Red Silver: Silvery red ticked with red.
Cream Silver: Silvery cream ticked with deeper cream.
Usual Tortie: Rich, golden brown ticked with black and reddish apricot ticked with red.
Sorrel Tortie: Lustrous copper ticked with chocolate and reddish apricot ticked with red.
Chocolate Tortie: Rich, coppery brown ticked with dark chocolate and reddish apricot ticked with red.
Blue Tortie: Soft, warm blue ticked with deeper steel blue and soft, warm cream ticked with deeper shade.
Lilac Tortie: Warm dove grey ticked with deeper shade and soft, warm cream ticked with deeper shade.
Fawn Tortie: Warm powdery fawn ticked ith deeper shade and soft, warm cream ticked with deeper shade.
Usual Silver Tortie: Clear silver ticked with black and silvery red ticked with red.
Sorrel Silver Tortie: Cool silvery peach ticked with chocolate and silvery red ticked with red.
Chocolate Silver Tortie: Cool silvery brown ticked with dark chocolate and silvery red ticked with red.
Blue Silver Tortie: Silvery blue grey ticked with deeper steel blue and silvery cream ticked with deeper cream.
Lilac Silver Tortie: Silvery dove grey ticked with dove grey and silvery cream ticked with deeper cream.
Fawn Silver Tortie: silvery fawn ticked with fawn and silvery cream ticked with deeper cream.

Withhold all awards: White markings. Cobby or Oriental type, coarse or small. Aggressive temperament.

Withhold certificates: Incorrect ticking or markings. Lack of slight nose break. Weak chin. Whip tail. Excessive yellow in silvers.

Basic genetic makeup of a homozygous usual Abyssinian:
AA BB CC DD LL $T^a T^a$ *(see pages 140-151).*

Mating authorised with other breeds: No.

Angora

The Angora is the semi-long-haired version of the Oriental Shorthair and is available in all the Oriental colours and patterns (see pages 100-103) with the same green eye colour. A white Angora may have green eyes, blue eyes like its Foreign White equivalent, or one green and one blue eye.

Although some long-haired cats at the turn of the century were known as Angoras, these were assimilated into the Persians and today's Angoras are completely unrelated to these early cats. They are also distinct from the Turkish Angora, a separate breed that is recognised by various associations in the United States and on the continent.

In Britain in the early 1970s a mating between a Siamese and a Sorrel Abyssinian that happened to carry a longhair gene introduced the cinnamon colour and the longhair gene into an Oriental line and from this the modern Angoras were developed. New lines have been produced by mating Orientals to Balinese, and by mating cats from the original Angora line out to Balinese, Orientals and Siamese. They have been bred in a wide variety of colours. Although technically always semi-longhairs, Angoras are shown with their close relatives, the Orientals.

Confusingly, this breed is known by many different names in different countries or even by differing registering associations within the same

AUS	CAN	EUR	NZ	SA	UK	USA
●	●		●	●	●	●

∗ In some countries the Angora may also be known as the Oriental Longhair, Javanese, or Balinese.

country. In the United States it is known as an Oriental Longhair, while in Europe it is called a Javanese by FIFe and a Mandarin by the independent associations. It is sometimes even classified as a Balinese.

The Angora has a fine silky coat, often only medium length on the body, but long on the tail to produce an elegant plume. Lively, energetic and intensely curious about everything and everyone, the Oriental Longhair makes an excellent pet. It is easily groomed, devoted to its owner, yet gets along well with other household pets.

Characteristics

General description: A semi-long-haired cat with distinctive long tapering lines. It is svelte, refined and very lithe, but strong and muscular. The coat should be fine, silky and lie close to the body. The tail plume should be long and feathery. The head and neck should both be long. The cat's overall condition should be excellent.

Head: Long tapered wedge, neither round nor pointed, that flares out in straight lines from tip of nose to tips of ears, forming a triangle with no whisker break. Long straight profile from top of head to tip of nose. Fine muzzle, strong chin, long, slender neck.

Ears: Large, pricked, wide at base, giving an alert look.

Eyes: Oriental shape, slanting towards the nose in harmony with lines of wedge. Neither too large not too small and deep-set. No less than the width of an eye between the eyes. Green eyes are required in all colours of Angora except the white, where they may be green, blue or one of each.

Body: Medium size, long and svelte, a combination of fine firm bones and firm muscles. Legs slim, the hind legs slightly longer than the front ones. Paws small and oval.

Tail: Narrow at the base, thin, long and tapering to a fine point, with no kink.

Coat: Medium long, fine, silky and glossy, with no woolliness or knots. It tends to lie flat along the body. The tail is plume-like and the ears may be tufted.

Colours: White. Black, blue, chocolate, lilac, cinnamon, fawn, caramel, red, cream. All seven tortie colours. All 16 colours of smoke, tabby, silver tabby, shaded and silver shaded. The requirements for coat, paw pads and nose leather colour are as in the Oriental Shorthair but some allowance is made for slight lightening at the base of the longer hair and for lack of clarity of pattern. Pointed colours are also produced but are not eligible for showing.

Withhold all awards: Visible kink. White markings anywhere.

Withhold certificates: Weak chin and/or uneven bite. Woolly or coarse coat. Incorrect eye colour or coloured flecks in eyes. Incorrect coat pattern.

Basic genetic make-up of a homozygous black Angora: aa BB CC DD ll (see pages 140-151).

Mating authorised with other breeds: Yes, with Oriental Shorthairs, Siamese and Balinese. The shorthaired kittens from matings with Siamese or Orientals are called Angora variants.

GCCF Standards	Points
Head and neck	15
Ears	5
Eye shape and setting	5
Body	15
Legs and paws	5
Tail	5
Eye colour	10
Coat colour and pattern	20
Coat length, texture and condition	20

Asian Group

Bombay

The Asian Group is a breed category based on outcrossing Burmese cats to produce animals of Burmese type in a variety of coats and colours.

The Bombay was first produced in the United States in 1958 by outcrossing Burmese with Black American Shorthairs. It was admitted to championship shows there from 1976. The cat was named after the city of Bombay because it looked like a small Indian black leopard.

In Britain the Bombay was developed from a black half-Burmese, mated back to Brown Burmese until the breed is now a Burmese in everything but its coat: this is dense, sleek, jet black and so shiny as to look like patent leather.

In 1981 an accidental mating between a Lilac Burmese and a Chinchilla produced a litter of four silver shaded female kittens of surprisingly good Burmese type. Baroness Miranda von Kirchberg, the owner of the cats, saw the potential for a new breed, as did many others who saw them on exhibition. Further matings followed as other breeders joined in and a breeding programme was drawn up; by mating back to Burmese in every other generation, the required Burmese type and coat quality were maintained, but various other coat colours and patterns were also produced.

In addition to the black tipped silver coat of the original kittens, blue, chocolate, lilac and

AUS	CAN	EUR	NZ	SA	UK	USA
•	•	•			•	•

Although it looks like a small black panther, the Bombay is a particularly affectionate and gentle cat. It has a healthy appetite and a soft voice. It is also confident, a good hunter, active, inquisitive and patient.

Burmilla

caramel tipped cats were produced in both silver and standard shaded colours, as well as red, cream, apricot and all five tortie colours. Other patterns, too, were soon produced: the non-agouti smokes and selfs and all four tabby patterns, again in the whole colour range. Some kittens had inherited the longhair gene from their Chinchilla ancestor and longhaired kittens were also produced; these were named Tiffanies (see pages 120-121).

In 1990 the GCCF granted preliminary recognition to a wide variety of shaded, smoke and tabby colours, including Burmillas (tipped and shaded), Asian Smokes and Asian Tabbies. Bombays and Tiffanies were granted similar recognition. All these varieties were grouped in a single category – the Asian Group.

The Asians have proved both popular and successful and, in June 1994, the Burmillas, Asian Smokes and Asian Tabbies were promoted to provisional status. As well as Bombays, other self-coloured cats soon appeared in Asian litters. The regular matings to Burmese ensured that blues, chocolates, lilacs, reds, creams and torties arrived in increasing numbers, together with the caramel and apricot colours. Many breeders were keen to develop these attractive cats. At last, in October 1994 the other self colours achieved preliminary recognition by the GCCF.

Before any other Asians were developed in Great Britain, Mrs Yolande Smyth's "Carnelians", appeared on exhibition at many shows. This strain started with a non-pedigree cat with each generation being mated back to Burmese. In this way, she developed her own line of Burmese-type cats with very dark red coats. Few other breeders had been interested in developing these self-red cats so Mrs Smyth persevered to perfect her new breed on her own. Unfortunately, the line was almost lost when she died.

Characteristics

General description: An elegant cat of medium foreign type, like that of the Burmese. There must be no tendency to Siamese or British type.

Head: Wide and gently rounded. The wedge is short and the profile shows a distinct nose-break. Chin firm.

Ears: Medium to large with a rounded tip, set well apart. In profile they tilt slightly forward.

Eyes: Full, expressive, set well apart, neither round nor almond-shaped although the set is slightly slanting. The eyes may be any colour from yellow through chartreuse to green, although green is preferred in silver colours.

Body: Medium, neither cobby nor rangy, well muscled with a straight back. Females smaller and daintier than the males. Legs medium length with paws round to oval.

Tail: Medium to long, medium thickness, tapering to a rounded tip.

Coat: Short, fine and close-lying.

Colours: Black, blue, chocolate, lilac, caramel, red, cream, apricot and the five tortie colours are accepted in selfs. All 13 of these colours and their equivalent Burmese colours are accepted in smokes, standard and silver shaded, and standard and silver ticked, spotted, mackerel and classic tabbies.

Withhold all awards: Poor condition, underweight or undersize. Extreme aggressive temperament.

Withhold certificates: White markings. Cobby or oriental type. Long coat.

Basic genetic makeup of a homozygous Chocolate Silver Burmilla with Burmese colour restriction: AA bb $c^b c^b$ DD ll LL WbWb (see pages 140-151).

Mating authorised with other breeds: Yes, with Tiffanies, Burmese and Chinchillas. All short-haired Burmese look-alikes are called Asian variants.

GCCF Standards	Points
Head	15
Ears	5
Eye shape and set	5
Body	10
Legs and paws	10
Tail	5
Coat colour and pattern	20
Eye colour and rims	10
Coat length and texture	10
Overall condition and temperament	10

Chocolate Smoke
Asian

Balinese

Some people have compared the Siamese cat to a graceful, scantily clad ballerina. The Balinese resembles another exquisite dancer, one whose elegance is masked by delicate silk veils. The reference, of course, is to the exotic Balinese dancers of Southeast Asia.

In the same way that the Somali is a long-haired Abyssinian and the Exotic a short-haired Persian, the Balinese cat is a long-haired Siamese. The Balinese is a svelte and dainty breed with all the elegance of a fashion model.

A struggle to be recognised

In the past, Siamese litters occasionally included a kitten with longer-than-average fur, especially around the ruff and hindquarters. Some breeders considered these long-coated 'sports' worthless and gave them away as pets. Others, however, saw them as 'miracles of mutation'. In fact, Balinese are neither, but rather the product of two carriers of the longhair gene, present among certain Siamese who have a long-haired ancestor many generations back. During the 1940s, US breeders strove hard to get the breed recognised, but it was not until 1968 that the Balinese Club was finally formed.

A Blue Point Balinese, Verdes Blue Warrior of Davina, and his variant daughter were imported to Britain and, in 1974, the first British Balinese

AUS	CAN	EUR	NZ	SA	UK	USA
✱	●	●	●	●	●	●

✱ In Australia the Balinese may also be known as Oriental Longhair. Check with local associations.

The character of the Balinese is very similar to that of its Siamese cousin. It is active, curious, lively, friendly, expressive and loyal. Above all, it loves company, whether feline, canine or human. It tends to fix its magnificent eyes of Mediterranean blue boldly on the face.

GCCF Standards	Points
Head	15
Ears	5
Eye shape and setting	5
Body	15
Legs and paws	5
Tail	5
Eye colour	15
Points colour	10
Body colour	10
Coat length and texture	15

were born. The early cats were mated out to Siamese, but after a brief delay other Balinese were imported as the breed gained popularity on this side of the Atlantic. In 1983 they were granted provisional recognition, and in 1986 they finally achieved championship status with the GCCF. Balinese now compete very successfully with Siamese in the Grand classes, often taking the top honours.

In Britain all Balinese are judged together but in some US associations only seal, blue, chocolate and lilac points are recognised as Balinese, the reds, creams, torties and tabbies being called 'Javanese'.

The standards for the Balinese are identical to those for the Siamese and elegance is the essential feature. They are often outcrossed with Siamese; the kittens from these unions are short-haired but when they are interbred or mated to Balinese, the long fur reappears in the new litter.

Like the Siamese, the Balinese thrives on attention and enjoys constant human companionship.

Characteristics

General description: The Balinese is unmistakably a Siamese in a longer coat, its colours corresponding to those of its short-haired relative.

Head: Long tapered wedge, neither round nor pointed, that flares out in straight lines from tip of nose to tips of ears, forming a triangle with no whisker break. Long straight profile from top of head to tip of nose. Fine muzzle, strong chin, long, slender neck.

Ears: Large, pricked, wide at base, giving an alert look.

Eyes: Oriental shape, slanting towards the nose in harmony with lines of wedge. Neither too large nor too small and deep-set. No less than the width of an eye between the eyes. The eyes must be clear, bright blue, varying slightly with the coat colour.

Body: Medium size, long and svelte, a combination of fine firm bones and firm muscles. Legs slim, the hind legs slightly longer than the front ones. Paws small and oval.

Tail: Narrow at the base, thin, long and tapering to a fine point, with no kink.

Coat: Medium long, fine, silky and glossy, with no woolliness or knots. It tends to lie flat along the body. The tail is plumelike and the ears may be tufted.

Colours: As in the Siamese, the body is pale, the points darker. Balinese are recognised in seal, blue, chocolate, lilac, red, cream, seal tortie, blue tortie, chocolate tortie and lilac tortie points, plus all 10 of these colours in tabby points.

Withhold all awards: White toes.

Withhold certificates: Abnormal bite or very weak chin. Cast in one or both eyes. Eyes tinged with green or green rimmed. Incorrect paw pad or nose leather colour.

Basic genetic makeup of a homozygous female chocolate tortoiseshell Balinese: aa bb $c^S c^S$ DD ll Oo (see pages 140-151).

Mating authorised with other breeds: Yes, with pure-bred Siamese. The short-haired kittens from matings with Siamese are called Balinese variants.

Bengal

The Bengal is a hybrid, the result of crossing domestic cats with the Leopard Cat of Asia. It is one of the most recent breeds to be created, but its conforming standards have already been accepted and recognised in the United States and on the European continent.

This large and powerful cat possesses a long and very muscular body; males can weigh up to 10 kg (22 pounds), females slightly less. The Bengal's likeness to its wild counterpart is obviously an important breeding feature.

A long selection process

In recent years especially, cat fanciers have been extremely ingenious in developing new breeds. One of the biggest successes has been the Bengal. The name is derived from the scientific name of the Asian leopard, *Felis prionailurus bengalensis*, its progenitor. It was with the aim of retaining the beauty of the jungle cat in a domestic setting that the Bengal was developed by cross-breeding the Asian Leopard Cat with domestic breeds such as the American Shorthair. The first kittens were bred with another spotted cat, the Egyptian Mau.

This breeding process took some time. The first hybrids were created in 1963, but the Bengal we know today was created in the late 1970s by Jean Mills of Covina, California. She obtained eight female cats cross-bred from an Asian Leopard Cat and domestic shorthairs by a University of California researcher. She mated them with a feral cat from an Indian zoo, and a domestic tabby shorthair. Some 10 years later there were 200 Bengals in the United States and the breed was recognised by TICA. Several Bengals have been imported into Britain and there is now a very

AUS	CAN	EUR	NZ	SA	UK	USA
●	●	●				●

From its jungle ancestors the Bengal has inherited a rather independent nature. It is a fine hunter and loves to wade in water. It also likes to climb and needs considerable activity–and consequently plenty of space. When playing, the kittens feint and prowl just as if they were really hunting, and attack their toys like prey.

The Bengal is not as vocal as some other breeds, but its voice, although not harsh, is strangely reminiscent of a wild animal's call. Though the breed is easy to care for, requiring the same amount of attention as any other domestic cat, take care when choosing a kitten. Temperaments vary; study its character carefully so that the kitten integrates well into the family group. If care is taken, you can become the proud owner of a friendly, miniature leopard.

enthusiastic group of breeders working to develop the breed here. The gene pool has been enlarged by selective outcrossing. Bengals may be seen on exhibition at most shows.

Characteristics

General description: The goal of the Bengal breeding programme is to replicate the appearance of the wild leopard cat while maintaining the loving, dependable temperament of the domestic cat. In competition, the Bengal must be unchallenging; any sign of challenge will disqualify. It may exhibit fear, seek to flee, or complain aloud, but it must not threaten to harm. Bengals are confident, alert and friendly.

Head: Broad with rounded contours, longer than it is wide. Allowance made for jowls in adult males. Slightly small in proportion to the body, but not taken to extreme. In profile, face curves gently from forehead to bridge of nose, which extends above the eyes. Nose has a slight concave curve and must be large and wide with a slightly puffed nose leather. Muzzle full and broad, with large, prominent whisker pads and high, pronounced cheekbones.

Ears: Medium small and short, with a wide base and rounded tips; set as much on the side as on the top of the head. Ears follow contour of face and point forward alertly. Light horizontal furnishings inside ears are acceptable, but lynx tipping undesirable.

Eyes: Oval; may be slightly almond-shaped. Large but not bugged. Set back into the face, on a slight bias towards base of the ears. Any colour is acceptable except blue or aquamarine.

Body: Long and substantial, neither oriental nor foreign. Not quite as large as the largest domestic breeds. Bones are robust, never delicate. Muscular body, legs and neck, especially in males. Medium-length legs are slightly longer in back than in front. Feet large and round. Thick tail tapered at the end, with a rounded tip.

Coat: Short to medium in length; kittens may have a slightly long coat. Thick, luxurious, and unusually soft to the touch.

Pattern: Spots should be random, or aligned horizontally. Rosettes formed by a circle of spots around a distinctly redder centre are preferable to single spotting. Contrast with ground colour must be extreme, with distinct pattern and sharp edges. Strong, bold chin strap and mascara markings are desirable. Blotchy horizontal shoulder streaks also desirable. The belly must be spotted.
• **Marbled pattern:** Markings must be unique, with as little bull's-eye similarity as possible. Pattern should be random, giving the impression of marble. Vertical-striped mackerel pattern undesirable. Preference given to cats with three or more shades: ground colour, markings and dark outlining.

Colour: All variations of the brown spotted tabby are allowed; however, yellow, buff, tan, golden, or orange ground colours are preferred. Spots may be black, brown, tan or shades of chocolate or cinnamon. White ground colour on whisker pads, chin, chest, belly and inner legs desirable. Smoky undercoat not a fault. Rims of eyes, lips and nose should be outlined with black, and centre of nose brick red. Paw pads and tail tip must be black.
Seal lynx point: Spots can vary in colour from dark seal brown to light brown, tan or buff. Ground colour should be ivory to cream. There should be little difference between body colour and point colour. Tail tip must be seal brown and may be as dark as black. Eye colour blue.
Sepia or seal mink tabby: Ground colour should be ivory, cream or light tan with pattern clearly visible. Pattern may be various shades of sable brown to dark chocolate. Ivory cream spectacles encircling the eyes and ivory cream whisker pads and chin are desirable, giving a wild appearance. Little or no difference between body colour and point colour. Paw pads dark brown, with rosy undertones allowed. Tail tip dark chocolate through sable brown to black. Eyes copper to blue-green.

Subject to penalty: Spots forming a mackerel tabby pattern. (Smoky undercoat permitted.)

Disqualifying fault: Tail tip not black. Belly not spotted. Rose-coloured paw pads. Aggressive behaviour that threatens to harm.

Basic genetic makeup of a homozygous brown spotted tabby Bengal:
AA BB CC DD LL TT (see pages 140-151).

Mating authorized with other breeds: No.

TICA Standards	Points
Head	10
Ears	10
Eyes	5
Neck	5
Body	10
Legs	5
Feet	5
Coat	10
Colour	10
Pattern	30

Birman

One of the most beautiful cat legends comes from Burma, now known as Myanmar. There, the local people built a temple and dedicated it to a beautiful golden goddess with sapphire eyes, Tsun-Kyan-Kse, who watched over the transmigration of souls. The temple was said to house 100 white cats. Mun-Ha, a most respected, white-haired priest, often meditated before the statue of the goddess with Sinh, one of the handsome white cats, always at his side.

One night Mun-Ha was attacked by bandits raiding the temple. As the priest lay dying, Sinh leaped on to his master's head and turned to face the goddess. His white fur immediately became as golden as the radiant light beaming from Tsun-Kyan-Kse, and his eyes became as blue as hers. The cat's legs, mask and tail turned a velvety earth-brown; only his feet, still touching the dead priest's snowy head, remained white, conjuring up the old man's pure spirit. Next morning it was discovered that all the other white cats had undergone the same transformation. From then on, the cats were regarded as sacred and were protected.

At the turn of this century, the same temple was attacked again and a number of priests were killed. Two foreigners, Major Gordon Russell and Auguste Pavie, helped several priests and their sacred cats escape to Tibet. The two men were told about the legend and, when they returned to France in 1919, they were given a pair of sacred

AUS	CAN	EUR	NZ	SA	UK	USA
•	•	•	•	•	•	•

The Birman is a very faithful creature, devoted to its owner and very attached to all family members. Its silky coat and soft voice may give the impression that this is a docile animal. In reality it has a lively temperament and can become a real presence in the household. The Birman is well balanced both physically and psychologically, and its gaze gives it a gentle, calm and dignified demeanour.

BIRMAN AND SIAMESE

Since these two breeds come from the same part of the world and are similarly shrouded in legend, it seems logical to assume that they are closely related. Today, however, the two breeds are quite different.

cats by the priests they had saved. The male cat died on the journey, but the queen proved to be pregnant. Thanks to her, the breed survived, flourished, and was formally recognised in 1925.

The Birmans were further developed in France and it was there that the standard for the breed was established and accepted by the rest of the world. Birmans are still exported from France, where breeders have produced different colours.

Birmans became scarce during World War II, and did not reappear until 1955. At that time they began to be exported to Britain, other European countries, and North America. Seal and Blue Point Birmans were officially recognised in Britain in 1966 and now have championship status in a range of colours.

Characteristics

General description: The Birman is an imposing long-haired colour pointed cat with white feet.

Head: Strong, broad and rounded with a medium-length nose, a slight dip in the profile, rounded cheeks and a full chin.

Ears: Medium sized and spaced well apart.

Eyes: Blue, the deeper the better, almost round in shape but not bold.

Body: Long and massive with sturdy, medium-length legs.

Tail: Medium length.

Coat: Long with a silky texture, slightly curly on the stomach. There is a ruff around the neck and the tail is bushy.

Pattern: Gloves and gauntlets: front paws have white gloves ending in an even line where paws meet legs; back paws have white gauntlets covering the paw and tapering up the back of the legs, ending just below the hock.

Colours: In all colours the gloves and gauntlets must be white. The colour of the paw pads is irrelevant.
Seal point: Body pale beige with a slightly golden glow, points seal brown. Nose leather: deep seal brown.
Blue point: Body cold bluish-white, points blue-grey. Nose leather: slate grey.
Chocolate point: Body ivory, points milk chocolate. Nose leather: chocolate.
Lilac point: Body magnolia, points pinkish grey. Nose leather: pinkish lilac.
Red point: Body pale warm cream, points orange-red. Nose leather: pink.
Cream point: Body warm off-white, points cream. Nose leather: pink.
Seal Tortie point: Body fawn, shading unevenly, points seal brown mingled with shades of red. Nose leather: seal brown and/or pink.
Blue Tortie point: Body off-white, shading unevenly, points blue mingled with shades of cream. Nose leather: blue and/or pink.
Chocolate Tortie point: Body ivory, shading unevenly, points milk chocolate mingled with shades of red. Nose leather: chocolate and/or pink.
Lilac Tortie point: Body magnolia, shading unevenly, points lilac mingled with shades of cream. Nose leather: pinkish lilac and/or pink.
Tabby point: All the above colours are also recognised in tabby points, with tabby markings on the mask, legs and tail and thumb prints on the ears. The body colour and the colour of the tabby markings corresponds to that of the solid and tortie points. The nose leather may be pink outlined with colour or may match the points.

Withhold certificates: Coloured spots in white areas. White spots elsewhere on the body. Missing gauntlet or badly unmatched feet. Streaks of white (runners) extending from the front gloves. Persian or Siamese head type.

Basic genetic makeup of a homozygous seal tabby Birman: AA BB $c^S c^S$ DD II TT (see pages 140-151).

Mating authorised with other breeds: No.

GCCF Standards	Points
Head and ears	20
Eyes	15
Body, legs and paws	20
Gloves and gauntlets	20
Tail	5
Coat colour and condition	20

British Shorthair

British Blue
Shorthair

This British vagabond or alley cat acquired its pedigree in the show ring. The standard was established to distinguish it from non-pedigree household pets.

AUS	CAN	EUR	NZ	SA	UK	USA
●	●	●	●	●	●	●

A long history

The ancestors of the British Shorthair were brought to Northern Europe, and later to Britain, by Roman soldiers almost 2,000 years ago. For a long time they lived wild, multiplied rapidly, and bred without control. In the 19th century, the English author and artist Harrison Weir, appreciating the sturdiness and intelligence of these street cats, began breeding the most outstanding specimens. Weir wrote the first standards of cat-show judging and his favourites, the shorthairs, were among the cats on show at the exhibition he organised at London's Crystal Palace in 1871.

Like its ancestors, the British Shorthair is a sturdy, powerful animal, and a particularly good hunter. Calm, patient and good-natured, it can be entirely self-sufficient and independent, even rather distant. It is truly a problem-free pet.

Blues always popular

Blues were especially popular among the numerous British Shorthairs appearing in shows in the late 1800s. At Weir's bidding, a special category was established for British Blues. At the time they were compared to the Chartreux Blue. Breeders then began to work towards differentiating the two breeds, crossing the British Shorthairs with Persians to make them heavier and with a rounder head. This is the type that has persisted. More recently, matings to Persian were used to develop the British Tipped and the Colourpointed British Shorthair, both of which are now established British Shorthair breeds.

Although outcrossing to Persians is still permitted, it is discouraged because the short-haired cats produced from such matings tend to have rather long, soft, fluffy coats instead of the short, firm coat typical of the British Shorthair and their head shape is often reminiscent of an Exotic Shorthair; in most colours of British Shorthair these first generation crosses may not be shown.

British Shorthairs are now bred in a wide range of colours and patterns. Some breeders prefer to concentrate on the traditional blues, blacks, whites, torties or tabbies, some prefer bi-colours or smokes, while others are working hard to improve some of the newer colours such as red and tortie silver tabbies or the Golden Tipped. A few breeders have even made selected crosses to Oriental Shorthairs to introduce the cinnamon gene and are now breeding towards the day when the cinnamon and fawn British Shorthairs will be recognised.

The British Shorthair was not recognised in North America until 1970, and then only blue cats of this breed were accepted – under the name of British Blue. Now all coat colours are accepted.

No matter what its colour, the sturdy British Shorthair, with its smiling face and calm, pleasing disposition, is always popular both on the show bench and as a family pet.

Red Mackerel Tabby
British Shorthair

GCCF Standards	Points
Selfs	
Head and ears	20
Eyes	10
Body, legs and paws	25
Tail	10
Coat length and texture	20
Coat colour	15

GCCF Standards	Points
Non-Selfs	
Head and ears	25
Eyes	10
Body, legs and paws	20
Tail	5
Coat length, texture, colour, pattern	40

Black Silver Spotted
British Shorthair

Characteristics

General description: Compact, powerful, muscular, medium to large in size. A well-balanced cat, with a generally rounded look.

Head: Round face, full cheeks, broad skull and rounded forehead. Nose short and straight with a definite nose break which is not too pronounced. Strong chin. Neck short and thick.

Ears: Small, rounded at the tip, set wide apart, not distracting from the roundness of head.

Eyes: Round, large, well opened, set well apart. In most coat colours the eyes must be copper, orange or deep golden yellow.

Body: Medium to large, cobby and massive, not rangy. Legs short and strong with round paws.

Tail: Medium length, thick, especially at the base, with a rounded tip.

Coat: Short, dense and crisp.

Colours: Each self-colour is judged separately. All colours are judged together in Bi-colour, Smoke, Tipped and Colourpointed categories.
Selfs: White, black, blue, chocolate, lilac, red, cream. The coat should be sound and there must be no white markings. In white British Shorthairs, the eyes may be copper to gold, blue or one of each. Nose leather and paw pads: appropriate to coat colour. Each self-colour is judged separately.
Tortoiseshell: Black with red, blue with cream (known as a Blue-Cream), chocolate with red, lilac with cream. There should be a balanced mixture of colours over the whole cat, with no large patches of one colour and no white markings. Nose leather and paw pads: appropriate to coat colour and/or pink.
Bi-colour: Any self-colour accepted in British Shorthairs with white: between one-third and one-half of the cat should be white. Nose leather and paw pads: appropriate to patching colour and/or pink.
Tortoiseshell and White: All four tortie colours with white, showing as clear patches of solid colour; between one-third and one-half of the cat should be white. Nose leather and paw pads: appropriate to the colours and/or pink.
Smoke: Any colour accepted in British Shorthairs, with a silver undercoat. Nose leather and paw pads: appropriate to coat colour.
Tabbies: Classic and mackerel tabby patterned British Shorthairs are judged together. Markings: black (known as brown tabby), blue, chocolate, lilac, red, cream and the four tortoiseshell colours, in standard and silver tabbies. Nose leather and paw pads: appropriate to coat colour. In black silver tabbies the eyes are green or hazel. Only the brown tabby, red tabby and black silver tabby have championship status.

Spotted: Judged separately from the other tabbies. The colours and eye colours are as in the other tabbies. The brown spotted, red spotted and black silver spotted each has its own class, with blue, chocolate, lilac and cream spotted judged together as AOC spotted. The other silver colours and the tortie spotted have preliminary recognition only.
Colourpointed: Points colour seal, blue, chocolate, lilac, red, cream, all four tortie colours, all 10 tabby colours. Body colour pale, showing good contrast. Nose leather and paw pads: appropriate to points colour. Eyes: blue.
Tipped: Coat silvery white, tipped with any recognised British Shorthair colour, including the tortoiseshells. Evenness of tipping is more important than degree of tipping. In black tipped cats the eye colour is green. Nose leather: brick-red, outlined with colour appropriate to tipping colour, may be mottled in torties. Paw pads: appropriate to tipping colour, mottled in torties.
Golden Tipped: The non-silver version of the black British Tipped, the coat is a rich golden apricot tipped with black. Eye colour: green. Nose leather: brick red, may be outlined black or dark brown. Paw pads: black or dark brown.

Withhold certificates: Long or fluffy coat. Pronounced nose stop, flat face. Uneven bite. Colour and pattern faults particular to individual colours.

Basic genetic makeup of a homozygous blue tipped British Shorthair: AA BB CC dd II LL WbWb (see pages 140–151).

Mating authorised with other breeds: Yes, with selected colours of Persian. Any long-haired kittens are called British variants.

Burmese

Few breeds of cat are as well documented in their origin as the Burmese. All are descended from one small brown queen named Wong Mau. In 1930, she was imported to the United States from Yangon, Myanmar (formerly known as Rangoon, Burma).

In San Francisco, Dr Joseph Thompson, a retired ship's doctor, first mated Wong Mau to a seal point Siamese tom. Some of the resulting kittens were Siamese, the others were dark brown. When the brown kittens were mated to each other, or when one of the brown males was bred back to Wong Mau, they produced the even-coloured, darker kittens we now call Burmese.

A rocky road to acceptance

The breed was established with great difficulty and was not allowed to compete in Cat Fanciers' Association shows until 1956, although other associations recognised them far earlier.

In 1949 the first Burmese, a male and two females who were as unrelated as possible, were imported into Britain. They were joined, in 1953, by a second male, Casa Gatos Darkee, who, in addition to being a particularly healthy cat, happened to carry the dilute gene (see page 142). When, in 1955, one of Darkee's daughters was mated back to him a blue kitten was produced, much to the surprise of everyone as no blues had been reported by American breeders at that time.

Chocolate Burmese, known as champagne in the United States, were imported later and lilacs

AUS	CAN	EUR	NZ	SA	UK	USA
•	•	•	•	•	•	•

The Burmese, though quite a reserved animal with a gentle and even timid nature, has retained the loud voice it probably inherited from its Siamese ancestors. This cat is intelligent, active and a playful companion. As a kitten it is a hell-raiser. Burmese cats like to stay comfortably at home, and are faithful to their owners.

were soon produced. Red, cream and tortoiseshell Burmese were developed in Britain by a strictly controlled programme of matings to introduce the sex-linked orange gene.

In Britain, breeders have felt no need to change the Burmese breed so today's cats bear a very close resemblance to the original US imports. In the United States, however, many breeders have concentrated on changing the type to produce a cobbier cat with a much shorter nose.

In 1981 a Burmese queen helped to start another new breed when she was mated with a Chinchilla, thus producing the first four Asian kittens. Burmese are also mated to Siamese to produce Tonkinese.

Characteristics

General description: A medium-size, elegant cat of foreign type, neither elongated nor cobby. Good muscular development and surprisingly heavy for its size. Lively and alert.

Head: Slightly rounded on top, broad between the ears, with wide cheek bones and jaw, tapering to a short blunt wedge with a firm chin. Distinct nose break followed by straight nose.

Ears: Medium size, set well apart following the lines of the face. Tips slightly rounded.

Eyes: Set well apart, large and lustrous. The upper line slanting towards the nose, the lower line rounded. Colour from chartreuse to amber, golden yellow preferred, in all coat colours.

Body: Medium length, strong, chest rounded and back straight. Legs slender and in proportion, paws oval.

Tail: Medium length, tapering slightly to a rounded tip.

Coat: Fine and short, like satin.

Colours: Brown (genetically black), blue, chocolate, lilac, red, cream and four colours of tortie. All these colours are affected by the Burmese gene (see page 151).

Withhold certificates: Oriental or British type. Small or dainty adults. Lack of weight or condition. Eyes showing more blue than yellow. White markings. Extreme aggressive behaviour.

Basic genetic makeup of a brown Burmese: aa BB $c^b c^b$ DD LL (see pages 140-151).

Mating authorised with other breeds: No.

GCCF Standards	Points
Head and neck	20
Ears	10
Eye shape and set	5
Body	20
Legs and paws	5
Tail	5
Eye colour	5
Body colour	10
Coat texture	5
Condition	10
Temperament	5

Cornish Rex

The Cornish Rex has a very distinctive appearance and is well known for its delightful nature. Lively, inquisitive and very friendly, it makes an ideal companion.

This unusual breed is of genuine Cornish origin. On 21 July 1950, in a farmhouse on Bodmin Moor, a perfectly ordinary tortoiseshell cat named Serena gave birth to a perfectly normal litter, except for one frizzy little 'ugly duckling'. Serena's owner, Nina Ennismore, was a breeder of curly-haired Astrex rabbits and realised immediately that she had something unique on her hands. The wavy coat was confirmed as being a true recessive mutation. The name was easy: Cornish for the kitten's birthplace, and Rex for its wavy fur's resemblance to that of the Astrex rabbit.

A new breed that almost disappeared

The mutant kitten, a cream tabby male with curly hair, was named Kallibunker. Because the wavy-haired gene was recessive, geneticists advised his owner to mate him with Serena, his tricolour mother. (To have the wavy hair reappear, a kitten would have to inherit two copies of the gene that produced it – one from each parent. In this case both mother and son carried the wavy hair gene.) In 1952 Serena had another litter consisting of one female with a normal coat and two Rex toms. One of the toms died while still young; the survivor, a blue tabby, was named Poldhu.

Later Poldhu was accidentally rendered sterile, and the new breed seemed in danger of disappearing. Kallibunker had already died, and only one of his descendants, a cream and white male

AUS	CAN	EUR	NZ	SA	UK	USA
●	●	●	●	●	●	●

TWO TYPES

The British Cornish Rex is a cat of medium foreign type with a medium-length head not too unlike that of Kallibunker, the first of the breed. The American Cornish Rex is lighter, more fragile, with an oval head, enormous ears, and the lean look of a long-distance runner.

GCCF Standards	Points
Head	15
Ears	10
Eyes	10
Whiskers and eyebrows	5
Body and legs	20
Tail	5
Coat	35

called Sham Pain Chas, was left. In efforts to save the mutant gene, this tom was outcrossed to British Shorthairs and Burmese. This outcrossing also avoided inbreeding, provided a wider colour range, and helped establish the future standard for the Cornish Rex.

In 1957 a daughter of Poldhu, Lamorna Cove, was exported to America. She soon had four kittens and launched the breed on a new continent.

Cornish Rex in the United States and Canada were mated to Siamese and Orientals, producing a more elongated, fine-boned version of the breed. Riovista Kismet, a descendant of Lamorna Cove, was imported back to Britain from Canada and helped to counteract the rather heavy type of Cornish Rex that was developing on this side of the Atlantic.

Cornish Rex were mated to Orientals and Siamese in Britain too, increasing the range of colours and producing the colourpointed Rex. They were also mated to Russian Blues with great success, producing some excellent cats. The smooth-coated kittens from these outcrosses are known as variants and may be used for breeding Cornish Rex, but not for mating back to their other parent breed.

A good Cornish Rex coat has amazingly neat waves and, lacking the guard hairs found in a normal coat, is very soft to the touch. The curly eyebrows and whiskers add to the unusual effect. Some lines of Cornish Rex carry the longhair gene and now and then a long-haired kitten is produced, with a very untidy, shaggy coat; these cannot be shown and are usually sold as pets.

> The Cornish Rex, a well-co-ordinated, athletic cat, is a born acrobat with a lively intelligence. It is happy and affectionate, has a sweet but persistent voice, and eats like a horse despite its delicate appearance. It is no more demanding than any other cat, and requires no special care. The breed is unlike any other in the UK, with traits that make it unique: curly hair all over its body, including the legs and tail, in regular waves like a crimped coiffure; even the whiskers and eyebrows are wavy. At birth the Cornish Rex is curly, like an astrakhan lamb.

Characteristics

General description: A curly-coated elegant cat, standing high on its legs.

Head: Medium wedge, one-third longer than its maximum width, narrowing to rounded muzzle. In profile the flat skull curves gently at the forehead and continues straight to the nose tip. Strong chin.

Ears: Large, with rounded tips, set rather high.

Eyes: Medium sized, oval in shape. Any colour allowed.

Body: Medium length, slender yet hard and muscular. Long straight legs, small oval paws.

Tail: Long, slender, tapering.

Coat: Short, silky and plushy. Must curl, wave or ripple, especially on back and tail.

Colours: All combinations of colours and patterns are allowed, including any degree of white with any coat pattern.

Withhold certificates: Long or shaggy coat. Bare patches. Head round or too long. Low-set ears.

Basic genetic makeup of a homozygous white and black smoke Cornish Rex: aa BB CC DD ll LL rr SS (see pages 140-151).

Mating authorised with other breeds: Yes. Straight-coated kittens are called Cornish variants (registrations of Devon Rex crosses and longhair crosses are labelled as carrying these genes).

Devon Rex

A pixie, a clown, an extraterrestrial, a cartoon cat – everyone has a special description for the Devon Rex. It sports bat-like ears, the curly hair of a poodle or a lamb, has a lively intelligence, and an endearing expression.

In 1960 Beryl Cox of Buckfastleigh in Devon took in a stray tortie and white cat; in an abandoned tin mine locally there was a strange curly coated feral cat with whom her stray played and, in due course, a litter of kittens arrived. One of these kittens was like his father and Mrs Cox kept him as a pet, naming him Kirlee. As the Cornish Rex had been found a decade previously in the neighbouring county, this new cat was presumed to have the same gene.

Kirlee went to live with Brian Stirling-Webb, who had helped to develop the Cornish Rex, and was mated to a rex descendent of Kallibunker but all the kittens had straight coats. The mating was repeated and Kirlee was mated to other Cornish queens, but still only straight-coated kittens were produced and it was realised that, although both genes were recessive and produced much the same result, this was a new rex gene.

Breeders tried to separate the two breeds but by this time there were many cats which carried both rex genes and even some which were both Cornish and Devon genetically. However, by selective matings the two rexes developed as distinct

AUS	CAN	EUR	NZ	SA	UK	USA
•	•	•	•	•	•	•

The Devon Rex might be described as a 'poodle-lamb-puss'. Attractive, intelligent, playful, loving, agile, and lively, it has an extraordinary coat. However, the most seductive characteristics of this creature are its bat ears and pixie face.

breeds. Devons were mated out to other breeds, including Burmese and Siamese, to increase the gene pool.

The Devon Rex coat is slightly less silky than that of the Cornish as guard hairs are present, although they are very short and have a tendency to break off. The whiskers and eyebrows, too, are often broken off almost as soon as they appear. The coat, although curly, rarely shows the 'marcel wave' of the Cornish, and Devons have an unfortunate tendency to baldness, especially underneath: a very poorly coated cat may have a furry face, legs and tail, 'muffs' at the base of the ears and a 'suede finish' body – striking in appearance but incorrect.

Devon kittens have an appeal unlike any other breed: their coats are often sparse and, with their enormous ears and wrinkled foreheads, they look like little Devon pixies.

Characteristics

General description: An alert and active cat, the Devon shows a lively interest in its surroundings. Its large eyes, short muzzle, prominent cheekbones, and huge low-set ears create a characteristic elfin look. Viewed from the front, the head is delineated by a narrowing series of three distinct convex curves: the outer edges of the ears, cheeks, and whisker pads.

Head: Wedge shaped with full cheeks and a whisker break and a strong chin. Forehead curves to flat skull. Nose has a well defined stop.

Ears: Large, very wide at base, set low and wide apart. Ear muffs and tufts may or may not be present.

Eyes: Large, oval and wide-set. Opening should slope towards the outer edge of the ear. Any colour allowed.

Body: Slender and of medium size, hard and muscular. Neck slender, chest broad. Legs slim with body carried high and length of hind legs emphasised. Small oval paws.

Tail: Long, fine, tapering and covered with short fur.

Coat: Very short, fine and soft, wavy, curly, may be rippled. Eyebrows and whiskers crinkled and rather coarse.

Colours: All combinations of colours and patterns are allowed, including any degree of white with any coat pattern, there being no points for this feature.

Withhold certificates: Straight or shaggy coat. Bare patches in adults (many have down on the underparts, which is not bareness). Round, long or narrow head. Small or high-set ears. Straight profile.

Basic genetic makeup of homozygous brown mackerel tabby Devon: AA BB CC DD LL rere TT (see pages 140-151).

Mating authorised with other breeds: Yes, all except Sphynx. Straight-coated kittens are called Devon variants (registrations of Cornish Rex crosses and longhair crosses are labelled as carrying these genes).

GCCF Standards	Points
Head	20
Ears	10
Eyes	5
Body, legs and neck	20
Tail	5
Coat	40

Exotic Shorthair

A Persian in a short coat, the Exotic Shorthair is both a popular show cat and an excellent pet. A gorgeous plush coat is no doubt part of its charm. But many of its fans find the endearing expression of its round, snub-nosed face to be equally captivating.

This breed was acknowledged officially in America in 1967 after considerable debate within various cat associations about just how a well-bred Exotic Shorthair should be received. Prior to this, many breeders had obtained Exotic Shorthairs accidentally, when Persians mated with short-haired cats, or when they were trying to create a new colour of Persian.

In Britain, 'Exotics' had been produced for many years from matings of British Shorthair to Persian, but had been registered and shown as British Shorthairs although their head type and coat quality were, in many cases, incorrect. With the increasing popularity of Exotics overseas, breeders here became interested in developing them as a distinct breed and, as well as breeding their own lines, imported some from America. Exotic Shorthairs were recognised in 1986.

In order to ensure that the distinction between Exotic and British Shorthairs does not become blurred, the breeding programme is carefully controlled: a Persian may be mated to a British to produce a new Exotic line, but from then on all matings must be back to Persian or to other Exotics, with no further outcross matings, thus preserving the Persian type and the soft plushy

AUS	CAN	EUR	NZ	SA	UK	USA
●	●	●	●	●	●	●

The Exotic Shorthair has the Persian's gentle nature together with some of the liveliness and playfulness of the shorthair breeds. It loves comfort, peace, and quiet, but it is more playful, active and inquisitive than the Persian. Many of its admirers consider it to be the perfect indoor cat.

coat. Long-haired kittens from these matings are considered to be Exotic variants, not Persians, and may be used for breeding Exotics.

Classifying the newcomer

Although, theoretically, Exotics should be in the shorthair section of shows because of their coat length, they did not fit into any existing shorthair category – British, Foreign, Burmese, Oriental or Siamese – and their numbers were certainly not sufficient to warrant a section of their own. However, in everything but coat they are Persians, so they were placed in the longhair section, to be judged with cats of their own type. Although it might sound contradictory to have short-haired 'longhairs', the reverse was already normal practice as the Balinese had moved out of the long-hair section to be judged with their short-haired cousins, the Siamese.

In competition, a Persian's coat can hide faults: an over-long body or too-big ears. But adroit combing of the long coat can mask these problems. Similar camouflage is impossible in the Exotic Shorthair. Grooming will not hide flaws from the judges.

Characteristics

General description: Persian in type, with a round head, cobby body and neat legs and tail, but with a plushy coat.

Head: Broad, round and massive with a short, broad nose, full cheeks and muzzle, strong chin and broad jaws. The nose has a stop and the nose leather should be fully formed.

Ears: Small, round-tipped, set wide apart and low on the head.

Eyes: Large, round and bold, set well apart. The eye colour corresponds with the coat colour as in Persians and British Shorthairs.

Body: Large or medium, well-muscled, cobby and low on the legs with a deep, broad chest and massive shoulders and rump. Legs short and thick with large round paws.

Tail: Short and in proportion to body length.

Coat: Slightly longer than other shorthairs but not flowing. Dense, soft and plushy, standing out from the body.

Colours: All Persian colours and patterns are accepted, plus several additional colours and patterns: mackerel and spotted tabby patterns in brown (black), blue, chocolate, lilac, red, cream and black/silver; classic and mackerel pattern tortie-tabbies; all colours of silver tipped; blue silver shaded. All colours are judged together.

Withhold certificates: Upper edge of nose leather above lower edge of eye. Various colour faults individual to specific colours or patterns.

Basic genetic makeup of homozygous white Exotic Shorthair: BB CC DD LL WW (see pages 140-151).

Mating authorised with other breeds: Yes, with Persians. Longhaired kittens produced are called Exotic variants.

GCCF Standards	Points
Head, including eyes and ears	30
Body, including legs and tail	20
Coat	20
Coat colour	20
Eye colour	10

Korat

One of the oldest natural breeds, the Korat dates from 14th-century Thailand. The Thais regard this cat they call Si-Sawat (pronounced *see-sah-what*) as a symbol of good fortune, and often presented a pair to a bride to ensure wedded bliss. Two cats sent to the United States in 1959 were the first true Korats to reach the West.

Many US-bred Korats were exported to other countries and further cats were imported from Thailand. Although their ancestors probably mated with other colours in their native land, Korats have not been crossed with other breeds since they left Thailand.

AUS	CAN	EUR	NZ	SA	UK	USA
●	●	●	●	●	●	●

GCCF Standards	Points
Head breadth	5
Profile	6
Breadth between eyes	4
Ear set and placement	5
Eyeshape and set	15
Body	15
Legs and feet	5
Tail	5
Coat length	4
Coat texture	4
Close lying	2
Coat condition	5
Body colour	2
Eye colour	5

Characteristics

General description: A semi-cobby cat of medium size, with a silvery blue coat that is rather longer than the other Foreign shorthairs, and particularly luminous eyes.

Head: Heart shaped from the front, broad across the eyes, curving gently to a well developed muzzle, neither pointed nor square. Forehead flat, with slight stop to short, downward curving nose. Strong chin.

Ears: Large, rounded tip, flared at base, set high.

Eyes: Large and luminous, oversized for the face, well rounded but set at slight slant. Colour brilliant green, with amber cast allowed. Yellow or amber eyes acceptable up to 2 years old.

Body: Medium size, strong and muscular, with back carried in a curve. Legs in proportion to body, paws oval. Females daintier than males.

Tail: Medium length, heavier at base, tapering to rounded tip.

Coat: Short to medium length, fine, glossy, close lying, but inclined to break over the spine when the cat moves.

Colour: Any shade of blue, tipped with silver to give a silvery sheen which intensifies as the cat matures. Paw pads and nose leather: dark blue or lavender.

Withhold all awards: White markings. Weak chin.

Withhold certificates: Scattered white hairs. Incorrect eye colour. Tabby markings.

Basic genetic makeup of a homozygous Korat: aa BB CC dd LL (see pages 140-151).

Mating authorised with other breeds: No.

Maine Coon

Admirers use superlatives to describe the Maine Coon Cat, the oldest American breed. To its fans, this is the big one, the head honcho, the boss cat. One story maintains that this impressive beast is descended from matings between raccoons and wildcats of the North American forests. (Even though early specimens had tabby in their coats and round ring markings on their tails — something like those of the raccoon — geneticists say such a mating is biologically impossible.) Fuelling this legend is the fact that the Maine Coon Cat has large snowshoe feet with large, round and well-tufted paws, which help it cross the winter snows that fall in abundance in Maine and other parts of the northeastern United States.

Another legend endows the breed with French blood from Marie-Antoinette's Angora cats. She is said to have given some to the Marquis de Lafayette on one of his trips to the New World during the American War of Independence (1775-1783). Once in America, the Angoras mated with local cats.

The first 'purebred American'

In fact, the Maine Coon is the result of inter-breeding between Angora cats imported by British sailors and the semi-wild cats of Maine's forests. Thus, it is the first truly American breed. Maine Coon cats were appearing in shows as early as 1860 and became immensely popular. A brown tabby Maine Coon took Best in Show at Madison Square Gardens, New York in 1895. With the

AUS	CAN	EUR	NZ	SA	UK	USA
●	●	●		●	●	●

Elegant yet rugged, gentle yet wild, the Maine Coon is also loving, faithful and self-confident. It has a noble bearing, is extremely healthy, and is an excellent family cat. Even though it enjoys being indoors, it needs access to a garden or other open space where it can romp. The Maine Coon has a soft voice.

A MIGHTY HUNTER

The Maine Coon is not afraid of water, and hunting is its favourite occupation. It can fend for itself when necessary — proof that it has not forsaken its free-roaming ancestry, and that breeders were wise to adhere to its original size and build. Good specimens often weigh as much as 14 kg (30 pounds).

arrival of Persians, Siamese and other 'pure-breds' in the New World, however, the Maine Coon's glory went into eclipse for almost 50 years. But in the early 1950s a Maine Coon club was founded, followed in 1976 by the formation of the International Society for the Preservation of the Maine Coon. As a result, the breed has regained all of its former prestige.

North American farmers always recognised the Maine Coon's hunting skills. In so doing, they helped to conserve the breed. The Maine Coon can adapt to any climate and to the toughest terrain, and is an exceptionally powerful cat. The legs are long and heavily muscled, ending in paws that are almost like hands, with very long, widely spaced toes that are astonishingly prehensile.

Maine Coons were introduced to Britain in 1983. Here they soon proved to be a popular breed, both on the show bench and as pets, and were granted championship status in 1994.

Characteristics

General description: The Maine Coon was developed as a 'working cat' that could fend for itself in rough, woody terrain and endure extreme climatic conditions. Today it is a show cat, but a sturdy-looking one with an amiable disposition. Maine Coons are large with big ears, broad chest, substantial boning, a long, hard muscled, rectangular body, and a long flowing tail. Good muscle tone and density give the cat the appearance of power. Females are significantly smaller than males and can weigh about 2.5 kg (5 1/2 pounds) less.

Head: Medium length, width slightly less than length. Cheeks slightly full with prominent cheek-bones. Nose uniform width. Square muzzle and firm chin. Slight concave curve at nasal bridge but no stop.

Ears: Large, tall, wide at base, tapering to appear pointed at tip. Set high but well apart.

Eyes: Full, round, set wide apart at slight slant. Colour green, gold or copper with any coat colour. Whites may have blue or odd eyes.

Body: Large to medium, solid and muscular. Chest broad. Long back and square rump. Legs substantial and in proportion to the body to give rectangular appearance. Large round paws.

Tail: At least as long as back, wide at base, tapering towards the tip.

Coat: Waterproof and natural. Undercoat covered by substantial glossy top coat. Not fluffy. Shorter on head, neck and shoulders, longer down back, flanks and tail, with full ruff, breeches and belly fur. Tail fur long, full and flowing, not bushy. Ears well feathered and preferably tufted. Paws well tufted.

Colours: White, black, blue, red, cream, tortoiseshell and blue tortoiseshell, in self, smoke, tabby (classic or mackerel), silver tabby and shaded. White allowed with any colour or pattern but not more than one-third of cat to be white. Coat colour and markings less important than coat type and quality.

Withhold certificates: Cobby body. Fine bones. Definite nose stop. Blue or odd eyes except in white cats. More than one-third of fur white. Even-length coat. Untufted paws.

Basic genetic makeup of a homozygous brown and white classic tabby Maine Coon: AA BB CC DD II SS t^b t^b (see pages 140-151).

Mating authorised with other breeds: No.

GCCF Standards	Points
Head	35
Body	35
Coat length and quality	20
Coat colour and pattern	10

Manx

The Isle of Man is world famous for its tailless cats. According to one legend, the Manx slipped on to Noah's Ark just as the door was closing – in time to sail, but too late to save its tail. Another says that a few tailless cats escaped from some of the ill-fated Spanish Armada's stricken galleons, which were wrecked offshore in 1588. The cats sheltered on what is now called Spanish Rock until low tide, then made their way to the island. Restricted to that small space, with little opportunity for intermingling with other cats, they bred among themselves. Thus, the gene causing their taillessness was widely propagated.

What is much more likely is that tailless cats began as a natural mutation of the island's domestic breeds. Since the responsible gene is dominant – it can be passed on even if only one parent has it – one mutant cat could easily have founded a whole strain of look-alikes in that isolated island environment.

It runs like a hare

The Manx has a distinctive gait; it runs like a hare. This is due to long hind legs, and not as another myth claims that it mated with rabbits. The homozygous (see p. 140) Manx gene is lethal, the foetuses dying before birth, so when Manx are mated together the litter size is reduced. As well as lack of tail, the heterozygous gene causes a spinal abnormality, which results in a lack of flexibility that produces the hopping gait. Manx may also suffer from spina bifida (failure of the spine to form properly) and from lack of anal control.

AUS	CAN	EUR	NZ	SA	UK	USA
●	●	●	●		●	●

The true Manx has a hollow or dimple where a tail would ordinarily grow, and is known as a Rumpy. An apparently tailless Manx may have one or two tail vertebrae and is known as a Rumpy Riser. One with the remnant of a tail is called a Stumpy. As all viable Manx are heterozygous (see p. 140), tailed cats are also produced from Manx matings.

In order to reduce the problems, Rumpy Manx are usually mated to tailed Manx or, sometimes, to British Shorthairs; all the kittens are registered as Manx – Rumpy, Stumpy or Tailed – and are only used for breeding Manx. Only Rumpy Manx may be shown in competition.

The Manx was one of the earliest show breeds, with its own classes prior to the turn of the century. If the mutation had only been discovered recently, it is very doubtful if the Manx breed would be recognised, or even registered, in view of its inherent deformity.

Non-pedigree cats without tails may be seen everywhere. Many, of course, have lost their tails in accidents, but others are genetically tailless and have an ancestor from the Isle of Man. Although these cats may be as tailless as any pedigree Manx, they lack the true Manx double coat which is another important feature of the breed.

Characteristics

General description: The essential feature of the Manx is its complete lack of tail, the rump being rounded and slightly higher than the shoulders.

Head: Large, fairly round, with prominent cheeks. Muzzle strong, not pointed. Nose medium length, broad and straight with no break. Chin firm.

Ears: Fairly tall, open at the base and tapering to a narrow rounded tip. Set rather high.

Eyes: Large and round. Colour preferably in keeping with coat colour.

Body: Solid and compact. Broad chest, deep flanks and short back ending in a round rump. The rump is higher than the shoulder. Substantial legs, short and well set in front, longer at the back with powerful thighs.

Taillessness: The rump should be completely rounded, with no bone or cartilage interfering with this.

Coat: Double coated: short, very thick undercoat with slightly longer overcoat, giving a well padded quality. This coat quality is far more important than colour or markings.

Colours: All colours and patterns are allowed, except pointed. They are only taken into account if all other points are equal.

Withhold certificates: Definite bone or cartilage interfering with roundness of rump. Any anatomical abnormality.

Basic genetic makeup of a red and white Manx: BB CC DD LL MxMx SS (see pages 140-151).

Mating authorised with other breeds: Yes, with British Shorthair. Rumpy Manx are mated to Stumpy and Tailed Manx. All offspring are registered as Manx, whether tailed or not.

GCCF Standards	Points
Head and ears	20
Eyes	5
Body, legs and paws	30
Taillessness	25
Coat texture	20

Cymric

The Cymric is simply the long-haired version of the Manx. It is a relative newcomer, first appearing in litters of pedigreed short-haired Manxes in Canada in the 1960s. When the new long-haired cats were bred together, the breed held true.

The standard Cymric is affectionate, intelligent, happiest when active, and is identical in every respect to its forebears, except for the coat.

The fur of the Cymric is long, soft, silky and double, with a thick undercoat. The ruff and hind legs are thickly furred, and the cat sports distinctive tufts of hair on both its cheeks and its ears.

Although long-haired Manx are produced occasionally, they are not recognised as a breed by the GCCF.

Norwegian Forest Cat

Norse legend describes this sturdy cat as mysterious and enchanting. Known in its native land as Norsk Skogskatt (Norwegian Forest Cat), its ancestors were Angora cats adopted by Viking sailors in the Near East to serve as rat-catchers, pets, and sometimes as ships' mascots.

The early Norwegian cats lived wild in Norway's rugged forests. According to a legend, Thor, strongest of all the Norse gods, was unable to lift one off the ground. A pure white pair pulled the chariot of Freyja, the goddess of battle, death, fertility and love.

Life in the wild

As protection against Norway's heavy winter snows and harsh winds, the Norwegian has a double coat – the undercoat thick and woolly, the guard hairs long and water-resistant. Like any good insulation, it keeps the cat warm in winter and cool in summer. Its water-repellent guard hairs, which are 12 cm (5 inches) long, can dry out 15 minutes after being soaked. These cats are solidly built and well proportioned, strong walkers and skilful climbers, qualities guaranteed to ensure their success as hunters.

Norwegians were first exhibited in Norway in the 1930s, but because of a ban on their export they were not recognised internationally for another 40 years, when the Fédération Internationale Féline admitted the Norwegian Forest Cat to championship competition in 1977. Unlike their ancestral owners, Norwegian Forest Cats were slow to invade Britain but when they did it was not long before they were, in 1989, granted preliminary recognition. They are now extremely popular, with excellent entries at most shows.

AUS	CAN	EUR	NZ	SA	UK	USA
●	●	●	●		●	●

The Norwegian Forest Cat is affectionate, confident and calm, and has a faithful nature. It loves the outdoors and is an effective hunter. The 'Wegie', as it is sometimes called, is hardy and self-sufficient and, if an outdoors cat, can endure the extremely cold temperatures of Norway's harsh northern climate.

SUMMER AND WINTER COATS

When showing these cats, the changing seasons must be taken into account. The length and thickness of the fur vary considerably depending on the temperature. In summer, the only really long fur that remains is on the tail and the tufts in the ears and between the toes.

The coat of the Norwegian Forest Cat is so dense that you need a generous amount of shampoo to make sure the lather gets through the water-repellent guard hairs. The thicker hairs on the back make it almost waterproof. In winter, the undercoat is extremely thick.

Characteristics

General description: A Norwegian Forest cat is large and elegant, standing high on its legs to give a rather square outline rather than rectangular. The cat should be firm and muscular, with a distinctive double coat. Slow to mature, a Norwegian Forest Cat may take up to 4 years to develop fully.

Head: Triangular, with a strong chin. The profile is long and straight from top of forehead to tip of nose, with no break.

Ears: High, with good wide base. Set high on the head, with less than the width of an ear between the ears, so the line of the outer edge of the ear follows the line of the head down to the chin.

Eyes: Large and well opened, set slightly oblique. All colours are permitted, regardless of coat colour.

Body: Big and strong with solid bone structure. Neither cobby nor delicate. Long body set high on the legs, with hind legs higher than front legs.

Tail: Long, reaching at least to the shoulder blades and preferably to the neck.

Coat: Semi-long with a woolly undercoat covered by a smooth waterproof topcoat. The glossy topcoat covers the back and sides. A cat in full coat has a shirtfront, ruff and knicker-bockers but in summer the coat is considerably shorter. The ears have tufts and feathering. The toes are tufted and the tail is bushy.

Colours: White, black, blue, red, cream, tortoiseshell and blue tortoiseshell, in any pattern – self, smoke, tabby, silver tabby, shaded – but not pointed. Any amount of white allowed on any coat pattern. The coat colour may appear to change as the cat matures.

Withhold certificates: Cobby, small or delicate build. Profile break. Round or square head. Short legs. Short tail. Dry knotted coat.

Basic genetic makeup of a homozygous brown and white classic tabby Norwegian: AA BB CC DD ll SS t^b t^b (see pages 140-151).

Mating authorised with other breeds: No.

GCCF Standards	Points
Head	20
Ears	10
Eyes	10
Body and legs	25
Tail length and fur	10
Coat quality, length and texture	25

Ocicat

This wild-looking animal possesses a temperament that seems almost half-cat, half-dog. Its 'doggy' half can be trained to fetch, sit and respond to human commands; it will eagerly go for a walk on a lead.

As a pet, the Ocicat is loyal, affectionate, playful and even-tempered. It combines the liveliness and speed of the Abyssinian with the gentleness of the Siamese – minus the harsh voice.

The first Ocicat appeared in the United States in 1964 during experiments to create Abyssinian-pointed Siamese. The successful litter also produced one spotted kitten that breeder Virginia Daly called Tonga. Her daughter, seeing the resemblance to an ocelot, called him an ocicat. Tonga was sold as a pet, but news of him awakened cat fanciers' interest and the mating that produced him was repeated.

Several Ocicats have been imported to Britain from the United States and the breed is being developed here by an enthusiastic group of breeders, using matings to Abyssinians to increase the gene pool. Ocicats may often be seen on exhibition.

AUS	CAN	EUR	NZ	SA	UK	USA
●	●	●	●			●

Characteristics

General description: The Ocicat is a large, well-spotted cat of moderate type. It displays the look of an athletic animal, being powerful, well-muscled and solid, graceful and lithe, yet with a fullness of body and chest. It is alert to its surroundings and shows great vitality. The Ocicat is bred in many colours.

Head: The head is a modified wedge. In profile, there should be a gentle rise from the bridge of the nose to the brow. The well-defined muzzle should have a suggestion of squareness; in profile it shows good length. Ears are moderately large. The neck should be arched.

Eyes: Almond-shaped, wide-set, the opening angled slightly upwards towards the ears. All eye colours allowed except blue; there is no relationship between coat and eye colours.

Body: The large and substantial body is semi-foreign in length. The chest is deep. The tail should be fairly long, medium-slim and have a slight taper with a dark tip. Legs should be medium-long, well-muscled and with a substantial bone structure. Oval feet should be in proportion to the legs.

Coat: The coat should be long enough to carry several bands of ticking, and should be fine, thick, tight, and close-lying.

Basic genetic makeup of a homozygous chocolate spotted tabby Ocicat:
AA bb CC DD LL TT (see pages 140-151).

Mating authorised with other breeds: Yes, with Abyssinians.

Oriental Shorthair

Havana

Oriental shorthairs are the close relatives of Siamese, with the same elegant shape and silky coat, their inquisitive character and their persistent loud voice. The difference is, of course, in the colour: whereas the Siamese is only coloured at the points and has blue eyes, the Oriental has a full colour coat and green eyes. There have always been self-coloured Siamese. The first 'Siamese Cat Register', published in 1924, lists three cats, all born before the turn of the century, as 'Col., black'; one had unknown parents but the other two purported to be produced from a seal point mated to a blue point – a somewhat unlikely event.

A chocolate surprise

Black, tabby and tortoiseshell half-Siamese undoubtedly appeared over the years, but never caused any excitement. However, when Chocolate-pointed Siamese were recognised, a group of breeders set to work to produce a self chocolate cat. A seal point was mated to a Russian Blue and the resulting black kittens were mated back to Siamese; the planning worked and, in 1953, two chocolate males were born.

Meanwhile in 1952, Susanna, a half-Siamese who had been mated to a seal point, produced, somewhat to the breeder's surprise, Elmtower Bronze Idol, the first 'Havana', and a repeat mating

AUS	CAN	EUR	NZ	SA	UK	USA
✱	●	●	●	●	●	●

✱ In Australia the Oriental Shorthair may be called Oriental or solid-coloured Siamese. Check with local associations.

Lively, curious and intelligent, the Oriental Shorthair does not like to be left alone. It demands attention by draping itself around the feet or neck.

The Oriental Shorthair has the enduring muscle strength of a long-distance runner. These cats mature quite early, breed easily, and produce larger-than-average litters.

produced the first female. Some early Havanas descended from these cats were exported to the United States and from them the Havana Brown breed was developed (see page 131).

More Siamese breeders joined in, more 'Havanas' were produced and, in 1958, the breed was recognised as the Chestnut Brown Foreign; eventually, in 1970, the name was changed to Havana, as the breeders wanted in the first place.

Self lilacs, too, cropped up quite early in the breeding programme, but did not excite such interest. Later, however, a group of breeders concentrated on developing the breed and the Foreign Lilac gained recognition in 1973.

Blacks and blues were also produced right from the earliest days of the Havana, and were even slower to catch on, but eventually became breeds in their own right.

Spots before the eyes

When a Havana queen was mated with a Chocolate Tabby Point Siamese the results proved interesting: the magnificent litter included Havanas, lilacs and very striking spotted tabbies. Many breeders were interested and, before long, spotties were being bred all over the country. Because of their resemblance to the early Egyptian cats, their devotees called them Egyptian Maus (see page 130).

Before long other tabby patterns were produced and breeders introduced the sex-linked red gene

GCCF Standards	Points
Tabbies	
Head and neck	15
Ears	5
Eye shape and setting	5
Body	15
Legs and paws	5
Tail	5
Eye colour	10
Coat colour (pattern & ground)	15
Pattern shape & clarity	20
Coat texture	5

GCCF Standards	Points
All except Tabbies & Whites	
Head and neck	15
Ears	5
Eye shape and setting	5
Body	15
Legs and paws	5
Tail	5
Eye colour	15
Coat colour and pattern	30
Coat texture	5

Brown Spotted Oriental Shorthair

White Oriental Shorthair

to produce tortoiseshells so the number of different Siamese type breeds was increasing rapidly. It was decided that the self colours would be known as 'Foreign' and the patterned cats 'Oriental', so it was as the Oriental Spotted Tabby that the 'Mau' became an official breed in Britain.

Pastel shades and rainbow colours

A chance mating of a chocolate point Siamese to a Chinchilla produced some most attractive short-haired silver kittens. Mated with Siamese to improve the type, these kittens were the foundation of the Oriental Smokes and Shaded. Originally called 'Pastels' because of their attractive pale silvery colours, these cats appeared at shows in the late 1970s but relatively few were shown until recent years, and it was not until 1994 that these breeds were ready to press towards full recognition.

With the traditional self colours, the various tabbies, the smokes, shaded and tortoiseshells, not to mention the reds and creams that came along too, you would think there was enough variety for any breed, but further colours were to emerge.

The mating of Siamese to Sorrel Abyssinian that led to the first Angoras (see pages 70-1) also introduced the cinnamon gene, leading to the first self cinnamons who were followed soon after by their dilutes, the fawns. It was also realised that strange brownish grey kittens were being produced from some lines, especially those descended from the Chinchilla, and this new colour was given the name caramel.

What's in a name

As some matings could produce a wide variety of colours, it was really rather confusing that one litter could contain a Havana, a Foreign Blue, a Foreign Red and an Oriental Tortoiseshell, especially since 'Foreign' was also used to describe

GCCF Standards	Points
Whites	
Head and ears	20
Eye shape and setting	5
Body	15
Legs and paws	10
Tail	10
Eye colour	15
Body colour	15
Coat texture and length	10

an assortment of other breeds, including two other 'foreign' blues – the Russian and Korat. To simplify matters, in 1991 the names were all changed to Oriental with the exception of the Havana, the original breed whose name caused no such confusion, and the Foreign White.

The Siamese in a white overcoat

While others worked to develop the coloured Orientals, a group of breeders set out to produce a white Siamese. Starting with white shorthairs, they mated to Siamese in each generation, so that the breed became pure Siamese under its white coat, with the deep blue Siamese eyes, so unlike the blue eyes of other breeds.

When all the other colours became 'Orientals' the White retained its name in order to distinguish it from the green-eyed Oriental Whites bred overseas.

No matter what their colour – and there are certainly plenty to choose from – Orientals are delightful characters and life with them is never dull.

Characteristics

General description: A lithe, svelte cat with long tapering lines. It should be hard and muscular with no indication of fat or emaciation – in fact, it should have an appearance of health and vitality. Its coat should be short, fine-textured, glossy and lie close to the body.

Head: Long tapered wedge, neither round nor pointed, that flares out in straight lines from tip of nose to tips of ears, forming a triangle with no whisker break. Long straight profile from top of head to tip of nose. Fine muzzle, strong chin, long, slender neck.

Ears: Large, pricked, wide at base, giving an alert look.

Eyes: Oriental shape, slanting towards the nose in harmony with lines of wedge. Neither too large nor too small and deep-set. No less than the width of an eye between the eyes. Green eyes are required in all colours of Oriental except the Foreign White, where they must be blue.

Body: Medium size, long and svelte, a combination of fine firm bones and firm muscles. Legs slim, the hind legs slightly longer than the front ones. Paws small and oval.

Tall: Narrow at the base, thin, long and tapering to a fine point, with no kink.

Coat: Short, fine, glossy and close-lying, with no sign of dandruff.

Colours: White. Black, blue, chocolate, lilac, cinnamon, fawn, caramel, red, cream. All seven tortie colours. All 16 colours of smoke, spotted, mackerel, classic and ticked tabby and their silver versions, shaded and silver shaded. The self colours must be sound to the roots and the smokes have a clear silver undercoat. The ticked tabby should have a well ticked coat, but show tabby markings on head, legs and tail; the spotted, mackerel and classic tabbies must have clear patterns, whereas only a very indistinct pattern, if any, should show on the shaded. Paw pads and nose leather: appropriate to the individual colours.

Withhold all awards: Visible kink. White markings anywhere.

Withhold certificates: Weak chin and/or uneven bite. Any bony tail abnormality. Long, coarse or open coat. Incorrect eye colour or coloured flecks in eyes. Colour and pattern faults for individual breeds.

Basic genetic makeup of a homozygous fawn Oriental Shorthair: aa $b^l b^l$ CC dd LL (see pages 140-151).

Mating authorised with other breeds: Yes, with Siamese. Foreign Whites and other Orientals may not be mated together.

Persians

A Calico or Tortoiseshell-and-White Persian

Persians or Longhairs, the most numerous and most prized of all pedigree cats, are descended from various breeds introduced to Europe from Afghanistan, Iran, Turkey and Russia from the 1600s on. Before the Italian traveller Pietro della Valle (1586-1652) brought several pairs from Persia (present-day Iran) to Italy in 1620, there were no long-haired breeds in Europe. Other early imports were by French scholar and politician Nicholas-Claude Fabri de Peiresc (1580-1637), who brought cats from Angora (present-day Ankara), Turkey, to France. (When this breed appeared in England, Britons called it the French cat.)

By the late 1800s, British cat owners had begun selective breeding of the various strains and colours. In the 1889 Standard of Points of Excellence and Beauty, as specified by Harrison Weir, who wrote the first standards for cat shows (see page 32), there are three colour-groupings of longhair – 'White Long-haired Cat', 'Black, Blue, Grey, Red or Any Self Colour Long-haired Cats' and finally 'Brown, Blue, Silver, Light Grey and White Tabby Long-haired Cats' – all of which included Persians, Angoras and Russians. The descriptions of head, eyes, ruff or frill, fur, size shape and condition and colour made no distinction between the breeds and it was only under 'Quality of Fur and Tail' that differences were described, the coat being fine and silky in the Persian, slightly woolly in the Angora, and still more so in the Russian.

By the turn of the century, however, the Angora, Russian and other long-haired breeds had virtually disappeared, rating barely a mention in Frances Simpson's 1903 *Book of the Cat*, and the Persian reigned supreme.

AUS	CAN	EUR	NZ	SA	UK	USA
✶	●	●	●	●	●	●

✶ In Australia Persians may be known as Longhairs. Check with local associations.

A ROYAL CAT

In the early 1600s, Italian traveller and writer Pietro della Valle returned home with a species of cat never before seen in Europe. They had long, grey silver hair and came from the Chorazan Province of Persia (present-day Iran). Ordinarily these cats were reserved for the aristocracy. Eastern rulers sent some as gifts to French notables, including King Louis XV.

The Persian retains its 'aristocratic' connections, continuing to be associated with luxury, silken cushions and high living. Even in less illustrious households, it relinquishes none of its regal habits. It also has acquired a wide range of coat colours.

The Persian remains one of the breeds most affected by changes in fashion and, as a result, has been much altered over the years. Its appearance can be modified easily in only a few generations.

Black Smoke Persian

Blue was one of the most popular shades. Even Queen Victoria had a blue pair, and 100 blues were exhibited at the London Cat Show of 1899. Whites, too, were very popular, especially those with blue eyes. Tortoiseshells, Tortie and Whites and Smokes put in an appearance on the show bench, as did the newer Chinchillas which were probably bred initially from very poorly marked silver tabbies. In some early shows, tabby and white cats were shown alongside tabbies, but they were soon relegated to Any Other Colour classes with the other Bi-colours and an assortment of cats which did not fit any accepted breed.

Breeders soon started clubs to cater for the different colours and patterns. The cats were sometimes called Longhaired, sometimes Persian, but when the GCCF was organised in 1910, it ruled that Persians would be called Longhairs and that each colour type would be a different breed. The name Persian is, however, retained in the titles of the Blue Persian and White Persian Clubs and is still commonly used for these cats.

For many years Longhairs predominated at shows, together with a good entry of Siamese, but remarkably few other shorthairs. Most breeders concentrated on perfecting the existing colours and patterns and few cats were shown in the Any Other Colour class. Blue-Creams existed from the early days, but were used almost solely as a step to breeding Creams, being regarded by many as unattractive. It was not until 1930 that they were recognised as a breed in their own right.

There was another long gap before any other new Longhair breeds appeared, but in the 1950s a group of breeders started work to introduce the Siamese pattern into Longhairs. Their careful breeding programme was successful and the Colourpoint became the first genuinely new longhair breed for half a century; these cats are true Persians in every way, but have the striking colour

GCCF Standards	Points
Smokes	
Head and ears	20
Eyes	10
Body	15
Tail	5
Coat texture and condition	10
Colour	40

Blue Persian

Red Shaded Cameo
Persian

GCCF Standards	Points
Cameo and Pewter	
Head and ears	25
Eyes	10
Body and legs	15
Tail	10
Coat texture and condition	10
Colour	30

contrast of the Siamese, with blue eyes. For some time there were only seal, blue, chocolate and lilac points. Then the seal tortie and red points joined them, followed by the other colours of tortie and the cream points, and finally, in the 1980s, the entire range of tabby points.

In the meantime the Bi-colour, shown in a variety of colours at the earliest shows, had been recognised as a breed in its own right in the 1960s, although only as self colours with white; it was another 20 years before the tabbies and white and the Van pattern longhair, both of whom existed at the turn of the century, reappeared on the British show bench.

Tortoiseshell Persian

DAILY CARE IS VITAL

A Persian's grooming must never be neglected. Tangles and knots form easily and can be impossible to remove. To prevent this happening, the coat must be combed and brushed every day. A thorough brushing needn't be a chore, however. It can serve as a time of pleasant closeness between an animal and its owner. The eyes, which weep easily, must also be cleaned daily.

Before welcoming such a marvellous bundle of fur into the home, potential owners should realise that keeping this magnificent cat happy, clean and at ease in its luxurious coat lies entirely in their hands. However beautiful it may be to start with, however proud and majestic, an animal of this breed can soon become an unattractive mess. There is no more pathetic sight than an ill-kept Persian.

Grooming for exhibition can take hours. All breeders have their own secret tips for making their animals look their very best on the judge's table.

106

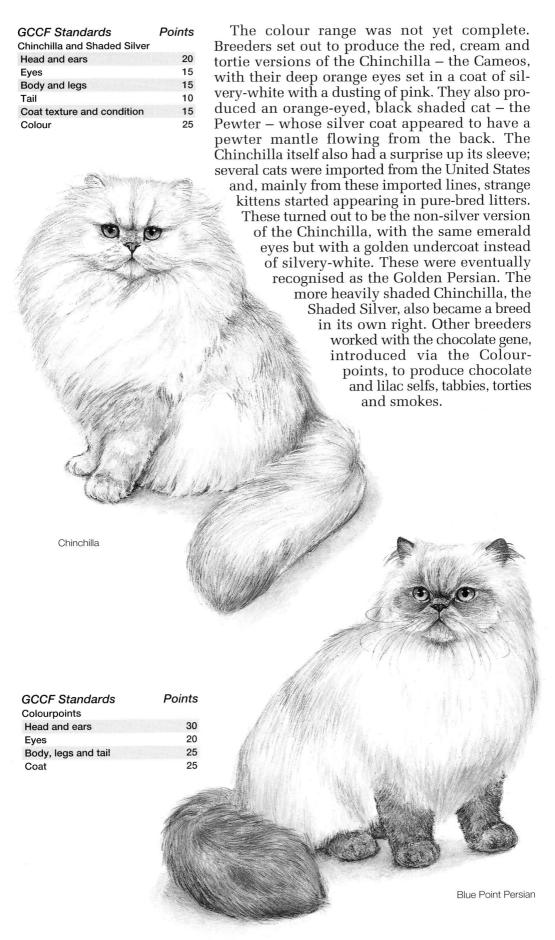

GCCF Standards	Points
Chinchilla and Shaded Silver	
Head and ears	20
Eyes	15
Body and legs	15
Tail	10
Coat texture and condition	15
Colour	25

The colour range was not yet complete. Breeders set out to produce the red, cream and tortie versions of the Chinchilla – the Cameos, with their deep orange eyes set in a coat of silvery-white with a dusting of pink. They also produced an orange-eyed, black shaded cat – the Pewter – whose silver coat appeared to have a pewter mantle flowing from the back. The Chinchilla itself also had a surprise up its sleeve; several cats were imported from the United States and, mainly from these imported lines, strange kittens started appearing in pure-bred litters. These turned out to be the non-silver version of the Chinchilla, with the same emerald eyes but with a golden undercoat instead of silvery-white. These were eventually recognised as the Golden Persian. The more heavily shaded Chinchilla, the Shaded Silver, also became a breed in its own right. Other breeders worked with the chocolate gene, introduced via the Colourpoints, to produce chocolate and lilac selfs, tabbies, torties and smokes.

Chinchilla

GCCF Standards	Points
Colourpoints	
Head and ears	30
Eyes	20
Body, legs and tail	25
Coat	25

Blue Point Persian

107

Red Tabby
Persian

GCCF Standards	Points
Selfs, Tabbies, Patched	
Head and ears	25
Eyes	15
Body, legs and tail	20
Coat (inc. pattern)	40

Placid, good-tempered and extremely easy-going, the Persian is upset by virtually nothing. It is indeed a charming and decorative addition to any household. A modern Persian is not adapted for hunting and its coat soon becomes matted with brambles and burrs, so a cat that is neglected or strays is a very sorry sight indeed. Persians tend to be expensive, largely because they achieve sexual maturity relatively late and often have small litters.

Despite the comparative vast increase in the range of colours and patterns over the past 20 years, longhair breeders in Britain have been very restrained; only the black versions of Silver Tabbies, Chinchillas and Pewters are recognised, although 'Blue Chinchillas' appeared in Any Other Colour classes decades ago. As yet, no attempt has been made to produce caramel longhairs or to introduce the cinnamon gene or the Burmese colour restriction, so perhaps the next 20 years could see a further increase in the number of colour schemes available.

Although the written description of the breed has altered relatively little, the type has changed quite dramatically over the decades. The Persians of the 1900s could be mistaken for Norwegian Forest Cats or Maine Coons, whereas today's cats have short noses which fit neatly into their beautifully rounded heads and some even have virtually flat faces.

The longhair breed has proved equally popular in the United States, where it is known as the Persian, with all colours except the pointed cats being judged as colour varieties of one breed; the colourpointed cats, known as Himalayans, are

Lilac and White
Bi-Colour Persian

considered to be a separate breed by some associations. US breeders produced a cat with a chunkier build, shorter body and a rounder head. This is how the Peke Face (see page 134) came into being, but whereas it may be encouraged in North America, most British breeders tend to regard it as a deformed breed, preferring the more 'open-faced' type.

GCCF Standards	Points
Golden	
Head and ears	20
Eyes	15
Body and legs	10
Tail	10
Coat texture and condition	15
Colour	30

Characteristics

General description: The Longhair, or Persian, is a medium to large, cobby cat with a round head, sturdy legs and a neat tail. The coat should be long, dense, silky and groomed to perfection.

Head: Round, massive, with a broad skull, rounded forehead, broad cheeks and a full muzzle. Nose short and broad with a stop. Strong chin, broad jaws and short neck.

Ears: Small, round at the tip, well furnished, set wide apart and fitting into the rounded head shape.

Eyes: Large, round and full, bold and not deep-set. Deep orange to copper in most colours, blue in Colourpoints, green in Chinchillas, Goldens and Shaded Silvers, hazel to green in Silver Tabbies. Whites may have copper to orange, blue or one of each.

Body: Large or medium, cobby and muscular with massive shoulders and rump. Short sturdy legs.

Tail: Short and bushy.

Coat: Long, thick and silky, not excessively woolly. Frill over shoulders and between front legs.

Colours:
Selfs: White, black blue, chocolate, lilac, red, cream. Sound, with no white markings. Nose leather and paw pads: appropriate to coat colour. Each self colour is judged separately.

Patched colours:
Tortoiseshell: Black with red, blue with cream (known as a Blue-Cream), chocolate with red, lilac with cream (Lilac-Cream). The black and chocolate torties should be well broken with shades of red. The blue and lilac-creams should be well mingled with no patches. Nose leather and paw pads: appropriate to coat colour and/or pink.
Tortoiseshell and White: All four tortie colours' with white, showing as clear patches of solid colour; between one-third and one-half of the cat should be white. Nose leather and paw pads: appropriate to patching colour and/or pink.

Bi-colour: Any self or tabby colour accepted in Longhairs, with white: between one-third and one-half of the cat should be white. Nose leather and paw pads: appropriate to patching colour and/or pink.
Van Bi-colour and Tri-colour: Basically white with any of the self or tortie colours on the ears, head and tail.

Tabbies: Classic pattern only. Markings black (known as brown tabby), blue, chocolate, lilac, red, cream and the four tortoiseshell colours; black only in silver tabbies. Nose leather and paw pads: appropriate to coat colour although brick red nose preferred in black silver tabby.

Colourpoints: Points colour seal, blue, chocolate, lilac, red, cream, all four tortie colours, all 10 tabby colours. Body colour pale, showing good contrast. Nose leather and paw pads: appropriate to points colour.

Smokes: Any colour accepted in Longhairs, with a silver undercoat. Nose leather and paw pads: appropriate to coat colour.
Cameo: Coat as white as possible, shaded or tipped with red, cream, tortoiseshell or blue-cream. Paw pads: pink, mottled in torties.
Pewter: Coat silvery-white evenly shaded with black.
Chinchilla: Pure white delicately tipped with black to give a sparkling effect. Paw pads and eye rims: black. Nose leather: brick red.
Shaded Silver: As in the Chinchilla, but evenly shaded, up to a third of the hair being black.
Golden Persian: The non-silver version of the Chinchilla, the coat is a rich golden apricot tipped with black or dark brown. Nose leather: brick red outlined in black or dark brown. Paw pads and eye rims: black or dark brown.

Withhold certificates: Various colour or pattern faults individual to the breeds.

Basic genetic makeup of a homozygous black Persian: aa BB CC DD II (see pages 140-151).

Matings authorised with other breds: No. Within the Longhairs different matings are authorised for different breed groups, for example, Colourpoints may not be mated to silvers, shaded or bi- and tri-colours.

Ragdoll

The name aptly describes this docile cat's most renowned characteristic – its propensity to lie limp and relaxed in its owner's arms, just like a rag doll. This semi-long-haired breed was developed in California in the 1960s, the progeny of Josephine, a White Persian queen, and her mate, Daddy Warbucks. According to breeder Ann Baker, the pregnant Josephine was hit by a car and all kittens in the subsequent litter exhibited the limpness for which the breed is named. A similar trait did not occur in Josephine's pre-accident kittens. Geneticists, however, dismiss the accident theory, and attribute the trait to the breed's gentle, even-tempered nature, the result of selective breeding.

Another Ragdoll myth is that they have a high tolerance to pain. British breeders were worried that the limpness and reputed high pain tolerance might imply that the breed suffered from a genetic nervous system disorder. Cats were taken to veterinary specialists for full check-ups including thorough neurological examination; this revealed that Ragdolls had perfectly normal nervous systems with perfectly normal reflexes. They were just ordinary cats with a different type and coat pattern and a placid nature.

The Ragdoll rivals the Maine Coon in size, length and strength. It is a tall cat with a long, muscular body, with the hind legs longer than the front. It does not reach full size until it is four years old. Although Ragdolls are usually very

AUS	CAN	EUR	NZ	SA	UK	USA
●	●	●	●		●	●

The Ragdoll is the essence of sweetness and gentleness. Cats of this breed seem to have perfect self-control, rarely showing the slightest sign of aggression or impatience.

placid they can, like any other cat, be upset by teasing or bad handling and with their size and strength can defend themselves effectively.

Ragdolls are bred in four colours – seal, blue, chocolate and lilac – and three different patterns. Although their origin is shrouded in myth, their genetic makeup suggests that different breeds were used in their development.

The basic pattern is that of a pointed cat with blue eyes, the colourpointed Ragdoll. To this is added the white spotting gene, and possibly the Birman gloving gene, to produce the Mitted Ragdoll with white feet, white chest and belly and possibly some white on the nose. The third pattern, the bi-colour Ragdoll, is the most spectacular, with white legs, chest and belly and a large triangle of white on its nose.

It was some time before Ragdolls were imported to Britain, but a few breeders were interested and a good number were shown at the first Cat Association show in 1983. The breed was viewed with some suspicion because of its mysterious origins, but serious breeders worked hard to prove that these were perfectly normal healthy cats, well able to look after themselves should the need arise and, in 1990, the breed was granted preliminary recognition by the GCCF.

GCCF Standards	Points
Head	20
Ears	5
Eyes	10
Body and neck	20
Legs and paws	10
Tail	5
Coat length, texture and condition	10
Markings	20

Characteristics

General description: The Ragdoll is a long, large, heavy cat, muscular not fat, but takes 3 to 4 years to reach full maturity.

Head: Medium to large, flat between ears. Well-developed cheeks tapering to rounded muzzle and strong chin. Nose medium length with very gentle break.

Ears: Medium size, broad at the base with a rounded tip, set wide on the skull with a slight forward tilt. Medium furnishings.

Eyes: Large, oval, neither round nor oriental, set at a slight slant. Blue in colour.

Body: Short strong neck, broad chest and long muscular body. Legs medium length with medium-heavy bone. Hind legs slightly longer than front. Large, round, tufted paws.

Tail: Long and bushy, slightly tapered towards the tip.

Coat: Silky and dense. Medium length on the body and hindquarters. Shorter over head and shoulders, longer round neck to frame the face.

Pattern: Basically colourpointed. Three degrees of white are recognised.
Colourpointed: No white anywhere.
Mitted: Chest, chin and underbody white. Front paws white. Back legs white to hock. Some white permitted on nose.
Bi-colour: Inverted white V on nose, starting on forehead, covering nose, whisker pads and chin. White chest, front legs and underbody. Back legs white to the hock. A limited amount of white allowed on body.

Colours: Seal, blue, chocolate or lilac pointed in all three patterns, body colour corresponding to points as in other colourpointed breeds.

Withhold certificates: Fine boned legs. Short body. Narrow head, pinched muzzle or pronounced stop. Round, oriental or pale eyes. White on colourpointed cats.

Basic genetic makeup of a homozygous seal point bi-colour Ragdoll: BB $c^S c^S$ DD ll SS (see pages 140-151).

Mating authorised with other breeds: No.

Russian Blue

The origins of the Russian Blue are uncertain, but it is believed that sailors docking at Archangel on the White Sea collected grey cats for sale in Britain. Cats similar to today's breed were often seen at British shows in the late 1800s. They had yellowish eyes, were heavier and bigger than the modern Russian Blue, and were known not only as Russian Blues but also as Archangel cats and Maltese cats.

At the turn of the century all blue short-haired cats were judged together. The Russians of those days had deep orange eyes and were distinguished by having longer heads, larger ears and rangier bodies than the 'British' blues. In most cases they were beaten by the cobbier cats, many of whom had been bred from crosses between Russians and Persians, and the breed almost disappeared. In 1912 the Russian Blues were granted their own classes and the breed reappeared, but this time with green eyes.

Two world wars led to the breed's decline in Europe. In Britain after World War II, the cats that remained were often mated to Siamese, and even to British Blues, to revitalise the breed. It is hardly surprising that the Russian Blue almost degenerated into a Siamese type blue self. Around the same time, US breeders imported Russian Blues from Britain and Sweden, and this combination produced graceful cats with silver blue coats, but with ears set far apart like a Siamese, a characteristic that the American cats have to this day.

AUS	CAN	EUR	NZ	SA	UK	USA
∗	●	●	●	●	●	●

∗ In Australia the Russian Blue may be known as Russian, Russian Black, Russian White or Russian Red. Check with local associations.

Timid, reserved, soft-voiced and easily upset, the Russian Blue is affectionate, but needs quiet. It attaches itself to one person only, and will wait for that person for hours without budging. Towards other animals, however, it is demonstrative and friendly.

Breeders in Britain bred selectively to return the Russian Blue to its former glory, with true double coat and upright ears, their success resulting in a vast difference between the breed here and in the United States.

This elegant cat has a gentle expression. Its fur is short, thick, and lustrous – like a seal's pelt but in a shimmering pale grey with a silvery cast. Stroking one is like stroking a piece of silk, and to see one is to fall under the spell of its intense green eyes.

GCCF Standards	Points
Head and ears	20
Eyes	15
Body and tail	20
Coat	30
Colour	15

Characteristics

General description: A graceful cat, with a moderate foreign head, upright ears, prominent whisker pads and a gentle expression in its green eyes. One of its most distinctive features is its blue double coat; this should be so dense that it can be dented by finger-tip pressure.

Head: Short wedge from nose-tip to eyes. Distance from eyes to ears equal or slightly longer. Skull apears flat between ears. Prominent whisker pads. Strong chin. In profile the flat plane of the forehead meets that of the nose at the upper level of the eye, forming the characteristic angle. No stop, nose bump or straight profile.

Ears: Large and pointed, wide-based. Set vertically to the head.

Eyes: Almond-shaped, set well apart, not small or deep set. Colour vivid green.

Body: Long, graceful and well-muscled with medium-strong bone. Not cobby or heavy. Legs long, feet small and oval.

Tail: Fairly long, tapering and in proportion to the body.

Coat: The double coat is fine, short and soft with a dense undercoat. It must not be harsh.

Colours: Clear blue to the roots, which may be slightly paler. Medium blue preferred. No banding or tipping although the tips of the hairs may be transparent, creating the distinctive silvery sheen. Free from tabby markings in adults, although ghost markings may show in kittens. Paw pads and nose leather: blue. Pads may be less blue than nose and pinkish in kittens. Russian Black: jet black to roots; paw pads and nose leather black. Russian White: pure white, but head smudge permitted in kittens; paw pads and nose leather pink.

Withhold all awards: Extreme aggressive temperament.

Withhold certificates: Flat coat. Oriental or cobby type. White anywhere. Incorrect adult eye colour.

Basic genetic makeup of a homozygous Russian Blue: aa BB CC dd LL (see pages 142-151).

Mating authorised with other breeds: No.

Nebelung

The Nebelung is essentially a long-haired, American-type Russian Blue. The coat is semi-long, double and very soft to the touch, the colour being a pale blue grey with a silver sheen. White Nebelungs are also being bred.

In the early 1980s a black non-pedigree cat chose to mate with a blue who looked very like a Russian Blue. The ensuing litter included a blue long-haired male who was named Siegfried. In the next litter was Brunhilde, a blue long-haired female. The two were mated together and produced three kittens, the image of their parents; they were so enchanting that the breeder decided to create a new breed, the Nebelung – 'creature of the mist'.

As these cats were obviously too closely related to be mated together, they were mated with Russian Blues and a breeding programme was developed. Other breeders became interested and so the breed slowly progressed in America.

Although at least two Nebelungs have been imported into Britain, to date there has been no interest in developing the breed here.

Siamese

Seal Point Siamese

Once a wild cat of the Far East, the Siamese cat was refined at the royal court of Siam (now Thailand). Its earliest depiction appears in the manuscript of the *Cat-Book Poems*, a Thai literary treasure, now preserved in the National Library at Bangkok. The poems describe a feline with the features of today's seal point – a white body, and dark ears, feet and tail. The manuscript survived the destruction of the ancient Thai capital, Ayuthia, by Burmese invaders in 1767. The great age of the manuscript, thought to date from the 1500s or earlier, suggests the Siamese was centuries old even in 1767.

Cats of palace and plain

According to Thai tradition, only royalty were permitted to own Siamese cats. The tradition began with an early Thai monarch, who was so entranced by the cats that he threatened to execute anyone who attempted to steal one. His successors honoured his wish to preserve the purity of the breed and confined the cats within the palace walls. They became cherished pets, and according to Buddhist belief, the inheritors of the souls of dead royalty. To obtain one of the revered cats was difficult: to receive one as a royal gift was a great honour.

The Siamese was also seen in regions far from its hot, humid homeland in southeast Asia. A German naturalist, Peter Simon Pallas (1741-1811), observed the cat while travelling across the plains of Russian central Asia during the 1770s. Pallas described the colour of its body as light chestnut,

AUS	CAN	EUR	NZ	SA	UK	USA
•	•	•	•	•	•	•

A ROYAL TALE

A kinked tail is considered a flaw in a Siamese cat. But legend says the flaw is a sign of service to royalty. Before Thai princesses bathed, they put their jewels on the tail of their favourite cat, which curved the tip to keep the rich burden from falling off.

rather than white, with dark extremities. Some experts wonder whether the cat was a genetic oddity. Others believe it may have been the offspring of an imported cat, in which case, the colour difference was due to the colder, harsher climate of central Asia. (As a rule, outdoor exposure during the winter darkens the colour of a Siamese cat.)

Lilac Point
Siamese

A gift of royal cats

The first genuine 'Royal Cats of Siam' appeared in Britain at the London cat show of 1885. They were a pair of seal points – known as Pho and Mia – presented by King Chulalongkorn to Owen Gould, the departing British consul general in Bangkok. (Chulalongkorn, Thai ruler from 1868 to 1910, was the son of Mongkut, whose story is told in the Rodgers and Hammerstein musical play, *The King and I.*) Gould gave the pair to his sister, a Mrs Veley, who exhibited them with success.

Unfortunately, later imports were too sickly to survive in their new home. Some British cat fanciers of the 1890s wondered whether the Siamese would ever become popular. By the decade's end, once breeders had resolved the rearing problems, the cats were proliferating.

For many years the seal point was the only desirable type of Siamese; despite the fact that a blue point was born in 1894 and produced three more in 1898, they did not get official recognition until 1936. The chocolate point followed in 1950 and the lilac point a decade later. Chocolate points had certainly existed from the early days but were considered 'poor seals', and with both blue and chocolate points in the Siamese population, lilacs must surely have been produced.

The other colours of Siamese had also existed for some time: the first 'official' red point appeared in 1948, from a tortoiseshell half-Siamese, although red points had existed in the 1930s. These cats, and their seal tortie point sisters, were shown as Any Other Variety shorthairs for many years while their breeders tried again and again to get them recognised as Siamese. It was not until tabby points, the offspring of tabby half-Siamese, joined them in the AOV classes in the early 1960s that attitudes changed and in 1966, all three breeds were officially recognised as Siamese. They were joined by blue, chocolate and lilac tortie points in 1971, red, cream and tortie tabby points in 1973, and finally the cream points achieved full status in 1977.

Some breeders did not consider these newer colours to be 'proper' Siamese since they had not been bred from pure Siamese lines, but today they take top honours, frequently beating the tradi-

A ONE-OWNER CAT

The Siamese is characterised by a frank, steady gaze, accurate, and controlled movements, unequalled flexibility and grace, and such steadfast loyalty that an animal can become ill if it is abandoned. The Siamese is a one-owner cat, but owners must be wary, because it can easily take control of the household. The cat adores children, treating them with gentleness and patience. Its charm and lively intelligence quickly win admirers. However, it is extremely vocal, and its ear-splitting voice may strike some as disagreeably strident. Sometimes Siamese talk noisily to their owners, who seem to understand perfectly. The blue eyes are also very expressive. Siamese get on well with other cats. But with their lively nature, they invariably dominate such relationships. The females are reputedly highly sexed and in heat more frequently than those of other breeds. They are efficient, attentive mothers.

tional colours. In the United States, however, they are known as colourpoint shorthairs, only the four original colours being recognised as Siamese.

In the early 1970s, when cinnamon was introduced into the Orientals, Siamese cinnamon points and their dilutes, fawn points, were also produced. Caramel points cropped up in many Siamese litters and were usually considered to be poor lilacs; the gene had probably been introduced with the early tabby points. Interest in these new colours increased and in 1993 they achieved preliminary recognition as Siamese.

Whatever its colour, the Siamese is a firm favourite. Its intelligent and affectionate nature, as well as its beautiful blue eyes, lithe body and graceful movements, ensure its continuing popularity.

GCCF Standards	Points
Head	15
Ears	5
Eyes	5
Body	15
Legs and feet	5
Tail	5
Eye colour	15
Colour of points	10
Body colour	15
Coat texture	10

Characteristics

General description: The ideal Siamese is svelte, graceful, refined, of medium size with long tapering lines. It should be in excellent condition, very strong, lithe and muscular.

Head: Long tapered wedge, neither round nor pointed, that flares out in straight lines from tip of nose and to tips of ears, forming a triangle with no whisker break. Long straight profile from top of head to tip of nose. Fine muzzle, strong chin, long, slender neck.

Ears: Large, pricked, wide at base, giving an alert look.

Eyes: Oriental shape, slanting towards the nose in harmony with lines of wedge. Neither too large nor too small and deep-set. No less than the width of an eye between the eyes. Vivid blue eyes are required in all Siamese colours.

Body: Medium size, long and svelte, a combination of fine firm bones and firm muscles. Legs slim, the hind legs slightly longer than the front ones. Paws small and oval.

Tail: Narrow at the base, thin, long and tapering to a fine point, with no kink.

Coat: Short, fine, glossy and close-lying.

Colours: In all colours the points should contrast well with the body, any body shading to tone with the points.
Seal point: Points seal brown, body cream, shading to fawn. Paw pads and nose leather: seal brown.
Blue point: Points light blue, body glacial white. Paw pads and nose leather: blue.
Chocolate point: Points milk chocolate, body ivory. Paw pads and nose leather: chocolate to pinkish chocolate.

Lilac point: Points pinkish grey, body magnolia. Paw pads and nose leather: pinkish grey.
Cinnamon point: Points warm cinnamon brown, body ivory. Paw pads: pink to cinnamon brown. Nose leather: cinnamon brown.
Caramel point: Points brownish grey, body magnolia. Paw pads and nose leather: pinkish grey.
Fawn point: Points warm pale rosy mushroom, body magnolia. Paw pads and nose leather: pinkish fawn.
Red point: Points bright red gold, body warm white. Paw pads and nose leather: pink.
Cream point: Points cool powdery cream, body creamy white. Paw pads and nose leather: pink.
Tortie points: All seven colours: seal, chocolate or cinnamon with red; blue, lilac, caramel or fawn with cream. Points colour patched or mingled with appropriate colours. Body colour as in appropriate colours; any shading may be patched or mingled. Paw pads and nose leather: as in basic colour and/or pink.
Tabby points: All 16 colours, including tortie tabby points. Points appropriate colour, showing clear tabby markings. Body appropriate colour, may show shading in any tabby pattern.

Withhold all awards: White markings.

Withhold certificates: Very weak chin. Cast in one or both eyes. Green tinged eyes. Incorrect colour of nose or paw leather. No contrast on head.

Basic genetic makeup of a homozygous cinnamon point Siamese: aa $b^l b^l$ $c^s c^s$ DD LL (see pages 140-151).

Mating authorised with other breeds: Yes, with Oriental Shorthairs except for smoke, silver or shaded varieties.

Singapura

This rare breed hails from Singapore, where it roams the city streets. Following its new-found popularity abroad, the Singapura has now been proclaimed a national mascot by the Singapore government.

The rise of the Singapura breed has been remarkably swift. An American couple discovered the cats in the Singapore streets and, in 1975, brought three back to the United States for breeding purposes. The breed was recognised by the Cat Fanciers Association in 1982, with championship status granted in 1988.

Singapuras were imported into Britain in the late 1980s and were put on exhibition in 1989. The breed then languished in obscurity, but four years later there was renewed interest, Singapuras re-appeared at shows and a breed club was formed.

The perfectly proportioned Singapura cat is small to medium in size, with an average adult weighing only about 3 kg (6½ pounds). In contrast to the dainty body, the ears and eyes are strikingly large, as might be expected in an animal whose senses must be keen for nocturnal foraging. The preferred eye colours – essential for the show-class Singapura – are hazel, green or yellow. The silky, short coat has an old or yellowed ivory background colour with dark brown ticking.

Singapuras are intelligent, people-oriented cats, quite at home with strangers or at parties, where they look for a welcoming lap. From kittenhood to old age they retain their playful nature and delight in toys and games.

AUS	CAN	EUR	NZ	SA	UK	USA
●	●	●				●

Calm, even-tempered, quiet, and alert, the Singapura possesses a beautifully soft voice that it hardly ever uses. It makes itself understood through the candid expression of its large eyes. When it comes to hunting, this charming animal has the speed and talent of a judo expert.

Although the Singapura is one of the smallest breeds, it is a sturdy cat. Breeders are aware that there will always be people who wish to create the extreme, so they emphasise that the breed is medium to small and discourage any thought of 'smallest is best'.

117

Somali

The wild-looking Somali is a long-haired Abyssinian that was bred in the United States in the 1960s. Although some Abyssinians in Britain carried the recessive longhair gene, 'long-haired Abyssinian' kittens were not shown and the breed was not developed here, whereas in the United States it went from strength to strength. In 1980 a group of British breeders combined resources to import the nucleus for a breeding programme here and in 1982 the breed was recognised by the GCCF.

More cats were imported from the United States, France and Australia, and Somalis were mated with Abyssinians to increase numbers without inbreeding. Although, at first, only usual and sorrel Somalis were accepted, one or two of the original imports carried the dilute gene and soon blue Somalis arrived. Silver was introduced by matings to silver Abyssinians and the spectrum of colours was increased. These Abyssinian matings also brought in chocolate, so that chocolates, fawns and lilacs were soon to be seen, together with silvers in all of these colours.

Somalis attracted many dedicated breeders who were determined to retain the breed's moderate type, sweet expression and superbly ticked coats. Careful breeding produced excellent results and

AUS	CAN	EUR	NZ	SA	UK	USA
•	•	•	•	•	•	•

Playful, active and highly interested in everything that is going on around it, the soft-voiced Somali is a lively, muscular and intelligent cat, as well as gentle and easy to handle. It is also a fine hunter.

in 1991 the usual and sorrel Somalis attained full championship status, followed, two years later, by provisional recognition for the other colours and acceptance of the newly-introduced sex-linked range of colours.

Like Balinese, Angoras and Tiffanies, Somalis started their show career as 'shorthairs', being judged in the same section as their short-haired relatives, the Abyssinians. A club referendum showed that the majority of Somali breeders wished to change, and so, in 1994, permission was given for them to join the semi-longhair section of breeds.

With their rich colouring and their charming squirrel tails, Somalis are a delightful breed; playful and intelligent, like the Abyssinians they are impatient of restraint, preferring to leap round the furniture or bound through the long grass with tails held high.

Characteristics

General description: The Somali is a well-proportioned, foreign type cat of medium size, lithe and muscular, with a medium-length coat. It is alert, lively and active.

Head: Moderate wedge, all lines showing a gentle contour. Muzzle rounded, not sharply pointed, with a shallow indentation, not a pinch. Forehead gently rounded with a slight nose break. Firm chin.

Ears: Comparatively large, set well apart, broad at base, pricked and tufted.

Eyes: Almond-shaped, neither round nor oriental, set well apart. Colour amber, hazel or green, deep and rich.

Body: Medium size, with legs in proportion. Feet oval, with toe tufts.

Tail: Length to balance with torso, thick at the base and slightly tapering. Full brush.

Coat: Very soft, dense and fine. Medium length, preferably with ruff and breeches, but shorter over shoulders.

Pattern: Hair shows at least three bands of ticking. Darker shading on spine and top of tail. Dark tip of tail and ear tips, dark between toes and up back of hind legs. Dark eyelids with lighter 'spectacles', dark lines above eye and extending from eye towards ear. Underside free of markings.

Colours: As in the Abyssinian: usual (black), sorrel (cinnamon), blue, chocolate, fawn, lilac, red, cream and six tortie colours and all 12 silver colours.

Withhold all awards: White markings. Incorrect nose leather or paw pad colour. Any skeletal abnormality or tail kink.

Withhold certificates: Cobby or Siamese type. Pinch. Cold or grey coat colour. Unbroken necklaces, leg bars or tabby stripes on body or tail.

Basic genetic makeup of a homozygous fawn Somali: AA $b^l b^l$ CC dd ll $T^a T^a$ (see pages 140-151).

Mating authorised with other breeds: Yes, with the Abyssinian. Short-haired kittens from Abyssinian matings are called Somali variants.

GCCF Standards	Points
Head (skull and muzzle)	10
Ears	10
Eyes (shape, colour and set)	10
Body – torso	10
Legs and feet	5
Tail	10
Coat colour	10
Ticking	10
Coat texture	5
Coat length	10
Condition	10

Tiffanie

When, in 1981, the first Burmillas were produced in Britain from a mating between a
Burmese and a Chinchilla, the basis for the development of the Tiffanie – the long-haired Asian –
was established. The breeders concentrated on
the Burmillas at first, then on the other short-
haired varieties of what was to become the Asian
group (see pages 72-73), but attractive long-haired
kittens often cropped up.

Because the American Tiffany was believed to
be a long-haired Burmese, this new breed was
given a similar name. When in 1990 the Asian
Group were given preliminary recognition, the
Tiffanies appeared on the show bench with their
short-haired counterparts.

The Tiffanie comes in a vast range of colours
and patterns – selfs, smokes, standard and silver
tabbies and shaded and the Burmese colour versions of all of these, making 312 in all, but its
essential feature is that it has the Burmese shape
under its semi-long coat, together with the delightful nature of all the Asians.

With the longer coat, correct colour and pattern become more difficult to achieve. The coat
tends to pale a little towards the roots and a black
Tiffanie will never have the polished patent leather
look of the Bombay. In addition, the spotted, classic and mackerel tabby patterns can never be as
clear on the longer coat where the hair tends to diffuse the pattern. However, the smoke and silver
shaded Tiffanies, with their greater length of silver undercoat, can look far more dramatic than
their shorthaired cousins.

Unlike the other breeds in Britain where long-
haired and short-haired versions exist, Tiffanies

AUS	CAN	EUR	NZ	SA	UK	USA
•	•	•	•	•	•	•

In the United States and Canada
a breed known as the Tiffany has
existed for many years. It was
believed to be a long-haired
Burmese because one of its permitted colours is brown and its
basic shape is similar to old-style
Burmese, but tabby and cinnamon Tiffanies also exist. Breeders
have now established that it probably derived from Siamese-
Abyssinian crosses in the same
way as our Angora, but has been
selected to have a different shape.

and short-haired Asians may be mated together. Such a union often produces a mixed litter of long- and short-haired kittens, all of which, with one exception, can be shown. The exception is the kitten that looks like a Burmese. All short-haired Burmese look-alikes from any Asian mating are registered as Asian variants and not as Burmese, in order to protect the parent breed.

Tiffanies are delightful, happy, inquisitive characters who will converse with you and answer back. Their semi-long coat is easy to keep groomed as it lacks the woolliness of the Persian or the thick undercoat of the Maine Coon.

Characteristics

General description: An elegant cat of medium foreign type, like that of the Burmese. There must be no tendency to Siamese or British type.

Head: Wide and gently rounded. The wedge is short and the profile shows a distinct nose-break. Chin firm.

Ears: Medium to large with a rounded tip, set well apart. In profile they tilt slightly forward. Ear tufts are acceptable.

Eyes: Full, expressive, set well apart, neither round nor almond-shaped although the set is slightly slanting. The eyes may be any colour from yellow through chartreuse to green, although green is preferred in silver colours.

Body: Medium, neither cobby nor rangy, well-muscled with a straight back. Females smaller and daintier than the males. Legs medium length with paws round to oval.

Tail: Medium to long, medium thickness, tapering to a rounded tip.

Coat: Semi-long, silky and fine, not woolly. Longer on the tail and around the neck.

Colours: Black, blue, chocolate, lilac, caramel, red, cream, apricot and the five tortie colours, and their equivalent Burmese colours, are accepted in selfs, smokes, standard and silver shaded, and standard and silver ticked, spot-ted, mackerel and classic tabbies.

Withhold all awards: Poor condition, underweight or undersize. Extreme aggressive temperament.

Withhold certificates: White markings, Cobby or oriental type. Coat too short, shaggy, woolly or badly groomed.

Basic genetic makeup of a homozygous blue tortie Tiffanie with Burmese colour restriction: aa BB $c^b c^b$ dd ll Oo (see pages 142-151).

Mating authorised with other breeds: Yes, with Asian Shorthairs, Burmese and Chinchillas. All short-haired Burmese look-alikes are called Asian variants.

GCCF Standards	Points
Head	15
Ears	5
Eye shape and set	5
Body	10
Legs and paws	10
Tail	5
Coat colour and pattern	10
Eye colour and rims	10
Coat length and texture	20
Overall condition and temperament	10

Tonkinese

Neither a natural breed nor a true random mutation, the Tonkinese is the result of complex genetics, and the product of mating Siamese to Burmese. Developed in the 1960s by Margaret Conroy, a Canadian cat fancier, it is the first pedigree breed to originate in Canada. In 1965, the Canadian Cat Association recognised it as a separate breed with its own standard. For the first few years, these cats were called Golden Siamese. In 1972, the now defunct US Independent Cat Federation admitted Tonkinese for championship competition and other cat registries followed.

In Britain 'Tonkinese' have been produced since Burmese came into the country in 1930, but were always considered to be pets, not show cats. However, breeders in the 1980s developed these 'in-between' cats, and in 1991 the breed gained preliminary recognition.

In every respect the Tonkinese is part-way between Burmese and Siamese – shape, coat colour and eye colour. Its type is kept this way by careful selection, but its coat colour is produced by being genetically half-Burmese, half-Siamese. All the kittens from a pure-bred Siamese crossed to a Burmese are Tonkinese, although they may not have the ideal type or colour, but from then on things get more difficult; if two Tonkinese are mated together only half of the kittens will be the correct colour, a quarter being Siamese-coloured and the other quarter Burmese-coloured.

AUS	CAN	EUR	NZ	SA	UK	USA
●	●				●	●

A nicely balanced cat in all respects with quite beautiful colouring, the Tonkinese is also a very lovable animal. Intelligent, lively and devoted to its owner, it has all the good traits of both its ancestors, and seems to have escaped their small faults.

In the United States there is a great difference between the Siamese and the Burmese: the Siamese is more slender than the Siamese we know in Britain, and the Burmese is stockier. In Britain because the two breeds are closer in build, it is more difficult to establish an 'in-between' breed that cannot be mistaken for either.

People who like the older pet-type Siamese, with rounder heads and sturdy bodies, are often attracted to Tonkinese. This extremely inquisitive cat is also one of the most affectionate. An excellent traveller, it seems to enjoy looking out at the passing scene. It enjoys play and outdoor exercise, and enough attention from its owner to be assured that its affection is returned. It needs little grooming; a rub with a dampened gloved hand is usually sufficient to keep its soft shiny coat looking its best.

The Tonkinese is a healthy cat with a long life expectancy. However, its curiosity and interest in people leads it to investigate moving cars, which can lead to tragic results.

Characteristics

General description: A medium foreign type cat half-way between Burmese and Siamese, well-proportioned and well-muscled.

Head: Moderate wedge, neither pointed nor square muzzled, with definite whisker pinch. Slightly rounded top of head with width between ears. Profile shows slight nose-break. Chin medium depth.

Ears: Medium size with outer line following line of wedge. Broad base, slightly taller than wide, with oval tip. Held pricked forward.

Eyes: Medium size, set well apart. Top line oriental, slanting towards nose, lower line rounded. Colour blue-green to greeny-blue.

Body: Medium to long, firm and muscular. Neck medium length. Legs slim and well-muscled, hind legs longer than front. Paws oval.

Tail: Neither thick nor whippy, preferably reaching to shoulder.

Coat: Short, close-lying, fine and silky.

Colours: Brown, blue, chocolate, lilac, red, cream and the four tortie colours plus the tabby versions of all 10 colours. The points are a noticeably darker shade of the body colour,

merging into it gently without sharp contrast. Self colours unbarred except reds and creams.

Withhold all awards: Siamese or Burmese coat pattern. Miniaturisation. White markings.

Withhold certificates: Orange, yellow or bright blue eyes. Round eyes. Barring on body in brown, blue, chocolate or lilac.

Basic genetic makeup of a Tonkinese homozygous for brown: aa BB $c^b c^s$ DD LL (see pages 140-151).

Mating authorised with other breeds: Yes, with Burmese and Siamese. Burmese and Siamese look-alikes from Tonkinese breeding are called Tonkinese variants.

GCCF Standards	Points
Head	15
Ears	5
Eyes	5
Body	15
Legs and Feet	5
Tail	5
Eye colour	10
Coat pattern and colour	20
Coat texture	10
Temperament	10

Turkish Van

In 1955 Laura Lushington and Sonia Halliday returned to England from a Turkish vacation with a couple of cats from the Lake Van area. Four years later, they brought home two more. The cats' white kittens with auburn markings launched the Turkish Van. Miss Lushington bred the cats under the prefix 'Van' to commemorate the region from which they had come. Shown first of all in Any Other Colour Longhair classes, with other unrecognised breeds, the Turkish, as it was then known, was granted full recognition in Britain in 1969, but was not recognised in North America until 1985.

Some of the early cats were very heavily marked with auburn (as the red colour is known in this breed), but selection over the years has produced the cat we know today, with, ideally, a white body, legs, head and ears, an auburn tail and an auburn spot either side of the top of its head extending towards the eyes. This came to be known as the 'Van' pattern. Cats of other colours and patterns existed in Turkey and some had been exported so, in October 1985, the breeders asked for the breed name to be changed to Turkish Van to distinguish it from any other Turkish breed.

At first only the amber-eyed auburn and white cat was recognised as a Turkish Van, any kittens with blue or odd eyes being considered 'mismarked'. However, in 1982 some cream and white kittens were born to pure Turkish Van parents, to be followed by more over the next couple of years, so it was obvious that the dilute gene had been present in at least one of the original imports. This colour variety was recognised in December 1985, to be followed in 1989 by the blue-eyed and odd-eyed Turks. These new varieties of Turkish

AUS	CAN	EUR	NZ	SA	UK	USA
✳	●	●	●	●	●	●

✳ In Australia this breed may also be known as the Turkish.

The Turkish Van's temperament has been modified by breeders. Once an aggressive cat, it is now friendly and very faithful. It is also called 'the swimming cat', as it delights in going for a swim.

Van have never been very numerous on the show bench, but their quality has always been equal to that of their amber-eyed, auburn litter-mates and they were due to be given Provisional status classes of their own in 1995.

Most breeders in Britain were content with these six varieties of the Turkish Van, but on the Continent Vans are bred and shown with black, tortie or tabby markings as well as the traditional colours; some of these cats were imported but although they are acknowledged to be Turkish Vans, these colours have not yet been recognised for competition so may only be seen on exhibition here.

'Turks', with their silky coats, require little grooming and, for a breed which enjoys playing in water, bathing is more a pleasure than an ordeal. They are now a very popular and successful breed.

Characteristics

General description: A solidly built, semi long-haired cat with a seasonal coat, and great breadth to chest and hips. The strength and power of the breed can be seen in the substantial body and powerful legs. The breed also has unique pattern, an assertive temperament, and affectionate nature. Males are large and imposing, females medium-to-large.

Head: Short wedge. Long nose with a barely perceptible profile dip.

Ears: Large and well feathered. Set high on the head and fairly close together.

Eyes: Large and oval. Colour either light amber, blue or one of each.

Body: Long, sturdy, particularly muscular in males. Medium-length legs, with neat, well-rounded, tufted feet.

Tall: Full brush, in balance with length of body.

Coat: Long, silky and soft with no woolly undercoat. The winter coat is long and heavy, but the summer coat much shorter. Immaculately groomed with no stain, grease or tangles.

Pattern: The face markings must not extend below the eyes or past the back of the ears, and must be separated by a white blaze. The ears and nose must be white. The whole tail must be coloured, the colour being allowed to extend a short way up the back. Small 'thumbprints' of colour elsewhere on the cat should not necessarily disqualify an otherwise good exhibit.

Colours: White with auburn or cream markings.

Withhold certificates: Siamese, Persian or British type.

Basic genetic makeup of a homozygous auburn and white Turkish Van: aa BB CC DD II OO SS (see pages 140-151).

Mating authorised with other breeds: No.

GCCF Standards	Points
Head and eye shape	25
Ears	10
Eye colour	10
Body and tail	25
Colour and coat	25

RARE AND OVERSEAS BREEDS

American Bobtail

If this animal were to bear a label, it would read 'Made by hand in the United States of America'.

In the 1960s, an American family named Sanders was holidaying in an Arizona motel near an Indian reservation. There they spotted a wild-looking yet friendly male kitten with an unusually short, upraised tail. Since the animal appeared homeless, they adopted him, naming him Yodie. The new pet soon became friends with Mishi, the family Siamese, and the two animals mated before there was time to have Yodie neutered.

Some kittens from the resulting litter were black, the rest tabby; some had the short tail of their father, others the long one of their mother. A few kittens from the litter found homes with friends of the Sanders family, but others began to live on their own in the wild.

Standards proposed

Soon afterwards fate intervened in the shape of a cream point and white cat. It mated with one of Yodie and Mishi's offspring, and the result was a litter of white and colourpoints with quite short tails. A neighbour of the Sanders,

Mindy Schultz, was charmed by these kittens and drew up a possible list of characteristics for the breed she called the American Bobtail. At the time – the 1970s – she described the breed as a colourpoint with a shortened and knotted or slightly curled upraised tail, showing white on the paws and breast, and with a white blaze on the nose.

Originally the breed's fur was short, but crossing with colourpoint Persians, eventually resulted in a very dense, semi-long coat. The animal was also crossed with other breeds, and some lines resulted in litters that had no tails at all – kittens similar to the variety known as the Manx. In fact, the Bobtail is the result of the same genetic mutation that had given rise to the Manx a century before; varying lengths of tail among this group are quite usual.

> The ideal American Bobtail should resemble a small lynx sporting its winter coat. It is a strong, stocky cat. Good-tempered, calm, gentle, and patient, it is a breed that adapts well to other animals. An excellent hunter, it can run extremely fast for short periods. It prefers keeping to the ground to scrambling up trees, and its most favoured spots are the soft cushions of its owners' living-room furniture.

American Curl

This animal's name makes its origins clear: American because it was first discovered in Lakewood, California, and Curl because of its attractively curled ears.

Set on the outer corners of the head, the ears curve back in a smooth arc away from the face, pointing towards the centre of the skull. The insides of the ears are full of tufts of fur that stick out like antennae. Firm cartilage makes the ears quite hard to the touch. This cat's unique ears are the result of a spontaneous mutation rather than of genetic engineering – the product of a

natural mating of non-pedigree domestic cats.

Shorthair and longhair

The American Curl is a medium-sized cat, well-proportioned, solid, and surprisingly heavy for its size. By the time it is fully mature, between 2 and 3 years of age, it weighs from 3 to 5 kg (7-11 pounds).

In the long-haired variety, the coat is moderately long and smooth, without an undercoat, and not at all woolly. The coat has a glossy shine and a silky texture that is very pleasing to the

Breeders debate whether the Curl should be more cobby (that is, more sturdy and rounded), or have a finer shape, whether it should be long-haired or short-haired, and so on, but there is universal agreement about the ears. Three angles of inclination are permitted: in the first and least admired, the ear is hardly turned back at all; in the second, it is a little more curved; and in the third and most preferred curl, it forms a complete crescent shape.

Since the gene that transmits this curvature of the ear is dominant, the peculiarity need only be present in a single parent to be passed on.

The cartilage of the ear does not start to curve or harden until the fourth day of life, and the curvature does not take its final form until the fourth month.

touch. The Shorthair American Curl has a thick, non-woolly coat, also very soft and silky.

As is the case for many new breeds, the conformation of the American Curl is still being developed. Only after much deliberation, and many votes by cat associations and breeders to recognise the breed and decide on its standards did the Curl earn its place in the well-bred cat world.

A NEW BREED WITH A SHORT HISTORY

In 1981, a black female stray kitten with unusual curled ears was found by a Mr and Mrs Joe Ruga. The couple called her Shulamith. Later that year, she gave birth to four kittens, two of which displayed the same ears as their mother. Shulamith was entered in a show in California. Judges, breeders and the general public all proved enthusiastic, and in 1985 the breed was officially registered by TICA as the American Curl.

American Shorthair

This cat, a descendant of domestic cats brought to North America by European settlers, was originally simply called the Short-hair. As short-haired breeds increased on the continent, breeders decided a more specific name was required, and so this cat became the Domestic Shorthair. The first of the breed to be registered in a stud book was a male orange tabby from Britain called Champion Belle of Bradford. Belle was born on June 1, 1900. The first to become a show champion was a white female with blue eyes, born in April 1948 and called Nor Month' Angelique.

Cat fanciers vacillated about the breed for several more years. The cats often competed in household pet categories of shows, since championship classes frequently offered no rosettes or trophies for Domestic class winners. But some breeders persevered, continuing to show their animals at every opportunity. In 1966 they renamed the breed the American Shorthair.

A perfect balance

The breed's reputation then improved dramatically, thanks largely to a male silver tabby called Shawnee Trademark winning the 'Best Cat of the Year' award in 1965. Despite the resulting surge in popularity, breeders have respected the animal's unsophisticated charm and allowed the processes of natural selection relatively free rein, rather than weakening the strain by inbreeding. The American Shorthair remains a well-proportioned and strong cat, the fine hunter it was on its arrival in the New World.

The American Shorthair is medium to large in size. It has a firm, powerful body, the males showing a particularly well-developed chest and hindquarters. The head is broad, with cheeks especially developed in males. The nose and face are medium short, the eyes and ears set wide apart, and the muzzle squarish but not foreshortened. No part of the cat should look out of balance with any other part. It must appear solidly built, and above all symmetrical – of a shape, in other words, that gives an impression of agility and strength.

A working cat

The American Shorthair is the working cat par excellence. It combines patience, stamina, and the qualities of a great hunter with total self-control. It is constantly aware of its own capacities and potential.

Its long, powerful limbs make the American Shorthair something of an all-terrain animal, while its solid muzzle pushes forward just enough to make grasping its prey in its firm, solid jaws an easy business. Its fur adapts well to all kinds of weather, being dense enough to protect it from cold, rain, wind, and minor injuries, but short and fine enough to avoid getting easily tangled.

American Wirehair

The Wirehair is a spontaneous mutation of the American Shorthair, in which the original breed's soft fur has become rough, springy, or hooked, and almost prickly to the touch. The tip of the guard, or primary, hairs is bent. All three hair types are present, resulting in a full coat which should be short to medium short. In other respects, including colour, the breed is very similar to its parent breed, the American Shorthair.

The Wirehair appeared originally in 1966 in Verona, New York. The first male kitten to display this unusual rough fur was called Adam, and all members of the breed currently registered are descended from him. The Wirehair gene is recessive; only two Wirehairs or a Wirehair and a carrier of the gene can produce Wirehair kittens. This explains their extreme rarity.

California Spangled Cat

Like the Bengal, this new breed dates from the 1970s. It was then that American breeder and scientist Paul Casey, on a visit to Tanzania, was impressed by sightings of magnificent wild leopards and determined to create miniature domestic replicas.

Not yet fully accepted

Although the first Spangled Cat was not created in a test tube, it was the result of careful calculations. Casey used eight different breeds, each chosen for certain characteristics, to establish the bloodline. Abyssinians were used for their leopard-like qualities and Siamese contributed their svelte and muscular characteristics, but even cats of no specific breed added personality or physical traits to the gene pool. By 1986 TICA had accepted the breed for registration in the New Breed category. In 1991 the American Cat Association followed suit.

A complex pedigree

Although the Spangled Cat is often confused with the Bengal, the look is very different. While both breeds are large and well muscled, their body structure and facial characteristics are quite different. As well, Bengal breeders work towards green eyes; Spangled breeders favour brown eye tones that complement most of the nine accepted coat colours. Only the leopard coat is favoured in the Bengals.

'Spangled' is an ornithological term meaning spotted, an apt description of this cat. California is part of its name because that is where the first such spangled cat was born.

> The Spangled Cat, which looks exactly like a miniature leopard, is slender, elegant and graceful, but also highly muscled, athletic and well-proportioned. At first glance it looks like a wild creature, a hunter, and gives the impression of being bigger than it actually is. The males, considerably larger and more muscular than their mates, weigh up to 7.5 kg (16½ pounds), while the females weigh up to 5 kg (11 pounds).
> This intelligent and energetic but gentle animal is renowned for its sociable, affectionate nature.

Chartreux

Also known as the Monastery Cat or the Blue Cat of France, the Chartreux is the natural breed of France, descended from one of the earliest breeds. It is also the subject of many legends. One claims that in 1558 Carthusian monks were already breeding the cats because of their hunting skills. The animals were also needed to protect the abbey's stores of wheat from hungry rodents. The Chartreux has scarcely changed since this time, a rare phenomenon in the world of animal husbandry.

Originating in the Middle East, the Chartreux probably arrived in Europe on merchant ships some 450 years ago. The breed was much exploited by the fur trade, since Chartreux coats could be cut and dyed to look like otter pelts.

Confusion with British Blues

Even though the Chartreux owes a great deal to French writer Colette (1873-1954), whose frequent references aroused new interest in the breed, the first breeders of record are the Léger sisters of Brittany. They discovered a large population of cats on Belle-Isle-sur-Mer off Brittany, and in 1931 became the first to exhibit these cats in France. In the 1940s, the war caused many pedigree cats to go homeless: during those lean years some Chartreux were undoubtedly killed for food; others may have died because their plush coats could be sold.

Breeders in the 1950s outcrossed Chartreux to Blue Persians to achieve a paler shade of blue, more intensely gold eyes, and a sturdier bone structure. This explains why Chartreux were confused with British Blues, and why the hybrids were later crossbred to them. A single litter may contain British, Chartreux and long-haired kittens. American breeders, however, who only began to take an interest in the Chartreux in 1970, are more purist than the Europeans. They maintain two distinctly different standards, and never cross Chartreux with British Blues. In recent years, French breeders have followed suit.

A Chartreux is big, but supple and less cobby than the British Shorthair. Although it must be blue-grey in colour, the shade may vary from ash-grey to slate-grey.

Egyptian Mau

Mau meant cat in ancient Egypt. This animal is the descendant of the legendary cat of the pyramids, which was deified and worshipped in ancient times.

Today's Egyptian Mau looks extraordinarily like its ancestors, depicted in papyri, sculptures and frescoes dating from the age of the pharaohs. Few breeds can boast such nobility or such a glorious past. This cat was the constant companion to Cleopatra, enjoyed the protection of the temples, was an integral part of the Egyptian culture, and held pride of place in every home in that ancient civilisation.

A princess and the ambassador's cat

Despite its long history, however, the Mau's contemporary reputation dates from 1953 in Rome, where Russian Princess Natalie Troubetskoy became the first modern admirer of the Mau. Entranced by a Mau belonging to Italy's ambassador to Egypt, she obtained a female named Baba.

The ambassador's cat and Baba produced a bronze-coloured male, who was later mated with his mother to produce Lisa. This female was shown in Rome in 1955.

In 1956, the princess took her three Maus to the United States. There, in 1957, Baba was the first of the breed to be exhibited in North America.

The Egyptian Mau is a medium-size cat of medium type, neither cobby nor oriental, its distinctive feature being its spotted tabby pattern. It is sometimes confused with the Oriental Spotted Tabby (see page 102) which was also called 'Egyptian Mau' in the early stages of its development. The two breeds are, however, distinct.

German Rex

In 1951, Dr Rose Scheuer-Karpin adopted a stray cat that was wandering around the Hufeland Hospital in what was then East Germany. The black curly-haired cat had a couple of unspectacular litters sired by local toms. But when she was bred to one of her sons, two of the four kittens in the litter that resulted had their mother's wavy hair.

The kittens' astrakhan-style coats fascinated French cat fancier Étienne Letard, who imported one to France.

For a time, Professor Letard and Dr Scheuer-Karpin continued developing German Rex kittens, unaware that English breeders were also experimenting with Rex cats (see pages 86 and 88). Despite their efforts, the German Rex is almost unobtainable today. The type has remained the same over two decades: fairly heavy bone structure, roundish head, wide-set ears and a thick tail. The fur is dense, longer than that of the Cornish Rex, and curls all over.

Havana Brown

Havana Browns are descended from Havanas (see page 100) that were exported to the United States during the early years of the breed's development. While British breeders mated their Havanas to Siamese and other Oriental shorthairs so that the type is identical, the American breeders retained the heavier body type of the original imports.

The Havana Brown is a cat of foreign, rather than oriental, build. The head has a square muzzle, a profile with a definite stop and round-tipped ears, quite unlike the Havanas in Britain which, in the United States are known as Chestnut Orientals. The lilac dilute is also seen.

The Havana Brown is a shy cat that prefers to have only one owner. It usually dislikes being handled by strangers and appreciates quiet and comfort.

Japanese Bobtail

Despite its name, this breed originated in China, migrating to Japan centuries ago. It appears in numerous ancient works of Japanese art — statues, prints, and paintings. The breed is said to have once saved the Japanese silk industry from hordes of rodents who were devouring its silkworms. Japanese Bobtails reached the United States in 1968 and breed standards were set there in the 1970s.

A medium-sized cat, with long, lean body and legs, the Japanese Bobtail has a strong short tail which is usually carried upright; the tail hair is slightly longer than that on the body and fans out to form a pom-pom. The face is distinctive also, with large upright ears and large oval eyes set at a pronounced slant.

The colour pattern most sought after in the Japanese Bobtail is known as the *mi-ke* (pronounced *mee-kay*), which consists of large red and black patches on a white background.

Japanese Bobtail Longhair

The first recorded instance of a long-haired version of the Japanese Bobtail was in Japan in 1954. However, the longhairs existed in Japanese street cat populations, especially in the northern provinces, long before that.

Even though the Longhair may seem bigger than the traditional Bobtail, the animals are exactly the same except for the hair length. Newborns of both breeds tend to be exceptionally large.

> Friendly, easy-going, intelligent, charming, both kinds of Japanese Bobtails have soft voices and a wide range of tone. Some people say that they sing.

Munchkin Cat

The latest American novelty cat could well be called the dachshund cat. Based on non-pedigree stock, it is characterised by very short legs. It began with a spontaneous mutation in a cat's genetic code that introduced a gene similar to the one that produces dachshunds, basset hounds and corgis. The Munchkin is therefore a product of nature that appeared without any help from man. Since the gene is dominant, any cat carrying it will produce short-legged offspring.

The first Munchkin Cat was discovered at a TICA show in 1991. The Munchkin Cats presently registered all come from Louisiana. All are descended from a black queen called Blackberry.

Unlike the short-legged, long-backed dog breeds, Munchkin cats are reputed not to have had back problems so far, but they obviously lack the supple grace which is one of the most attractive features of any normal cat. The breed is unlikely to be recognised by British cat associations.

Ojos Azules

Despite its lovely Spanish name, the Ojos Azules (Blue Eyes) is an American cat of recent vintage. This comparatively rare breed dates from 1984 when Cornflower, a tortie female, was discovered in New Mexico.

Cornflower's most remarkable characteristic was her blue eyes. Dark pools of intense blue, they were such that even the bluest blue-eyed Siamese might envy.

A puzzle for the geneticists

Geneticists do not yet fully understand how the genes responsible for eye colour sometimes do the unexpected. For example, from a genetic standpoint, only white cats with white or colourpoint genes can have blue eyes. Yet one can find black, auburn, tortie, blue, silver and blue cream cats with blue eyes. Is it then possible to produce a jet-black cat with dark-blue eyes, an auburn cat with blue-green eyes, or a tortoiseshell with sapphire eyes? Such unusual colour combinations would indeed be staggeringly beautiful. Research carried out on the Ojos Azules did not yield these answers. It did reveal that the cat's blue eyes resulted from a spontaneous mutation. Since the responsible gene was dominant, all Cornflower's kittens had magnificent blue eyes.

The standard for Ojos Azules has not yet been fully defined. Only about 10 of the breed had been registered in 1992.

GOOD HEARING AND NOT A SQUINT IN SIGHT

Although some blue-eyed white cats are deaf, to date no Ojos Azules has had this handicap, and while some Siamese have a pronounced squint, no Ojos Azules is cross-eyed.

Oregon Rex and Ohio Rex

Mutations produced both these cats, one born in Oregon, the other in Ohio, in 1944. In each case, the mutation is believed to be similar to that which produced the Cornish Rex in England some six years later. These American cats resembled the British mutant in type and colour (see page 86). But World War II overshadowed 1940s life, and few people took any interest in developing the feline oddities. Inevitably the Oregon Rex and the Ohio Rex disappeared from the cat show scene.

Peke Face

The Peke Face Persian, a spontaneous mutation of the Red Persian, is named for its resemblance to a Pekingese dog. Controversy surrounds the breed, which tends to have skin problems, and because its facial features – deformities some say – contribute to eating and breathing difficulties. Some breeders have pushed experiments with the breed so far that the cats' faces have a piggy look.

The Peke Face has a Persian's long coat, but has long legs and a long body. Most differences between it and other Persians relate to the head. The head is square rather than round; the jaw long, narrow and very undershot. Poor occlusion of the jaws makes it hard for the cat to chew and swallow.

An ultra-snub-nose

The Peke Face's snub-nose, set back in a furrowed muzzle, is so short that it is practically nonexistent; narrow nostrils are level with the eyes. Breathing through such a nose is hard work at the best of times, and almost impossible if the animal has a cold.

Because of its squished facial features, the skull seems flat, and the round, tufted ears, set not on the sides of the head but on top of the skull, seem disproportionately big and flat, the eyes tend to be particularly prominent, or may appear deep-set and half-closed. Weeping eyes are often a problem because the eye ducts may be distorted. There is a distinct indentation, almost a hole, between the eyes. It is particularly prominent in young cats.

Most British breeders consider the breed's compressed features a deformity and have relegated it to the ranks of those to avoid. It is still encouraged in North America.

An affectionate, sociable cat, the Peke Face prefers an indoor life. Generally calm, it usually gets along well with other cats. Its thick, silky fur, with red or red tabby colouring, requires the same daily grooming as for Persians.

Scottish Fold

At first glance, the Scottish Fold looks owlish, teddy bearish even, with its saucer-like eyes and rounded head set off by forward-folding ears. It first came to attention in Perthshire, Scotland, in 1961, when Susie, a white

kitten with folded ears, the result of a spontaneous mutation, was born on a Tayside farm belonging to the McRae family. Two years later, the mutant Susie had an identical kitten, which the McRaes gave to William and Mary

Ross, a local shepherd family that had long been enamoured of Susie. They named their kitten Snooks.

From Scotland to England to the United States

Within a few years, the Rosses were taking their unusual cats – by now Snooks had produced Snowball, a white male kitten with folded ears – to local shows. They caught the eye of English breeder, Pat Turner, who introduced the Folds to England. It became evident that when Folds are bred to cats with straight ears, half the litter will have folded ears. Matings of Fold to Fold, however, can produce kittens with epiphyseal dysplasia which produces severe skeletal abnormalities such as fused tail vertebrae and thickened legs with abnormal cartilage around the joints.

In 1970, several Scottish Folds arrived in Massachusetts. One of the cats was given to Sally Wolfe Peters, a Pennsylvania breeder. She produced Wyola Jed Gallant, the first Fold registered in the United States (1973). Five years later, Scottish Folds were admitted to championship competition.

In Britain the GCCF was initially concerned that Fold's ears would be more prone to infections and ear mites. This worry delayed the registration of any of these cats. Further breeding, carried out under veterinary supervision, revealed the crippling bony abnormalities found in the homozygous Fold, and occasionally in the heterozygote too, and sealed the fate of the breed: it would not be recognised, or even registered, by the GCCF. In 1983, the Cat Association of Britain added the breed to its register, thus enabling British breeders to register this cat. FIFe (Fédération Internationale Féline), like the GCCF, does not recognise the Scottish Fold and the Cat Association of Great Britain only registers folded-eared kittens if one parent has pricked ears and both parents have normal tails. Unfortunately, the breed is recognised by some organisations without any such restrictions.

Experience has shown that this breed can be treated for ear mites in the same way as any other breed, but there is a real difficulty associated with the skeletal problem of this breed.

A long-haired version of the Scottish Fold, sometimes known in Europe as the Coupari, also exists.

Selkirk Rex

Looking like an animated stuffed toy, the Selkirk Rex is another of the rare curly-haired breeds, the result of spontaneous mutation. Cat fanciers say that the Cornish Rex looks like a greyhound, the Devon Rex like the lovable alien in the Steven Spielberg film, *ET*, and the Selkirk Rex like an ordinary cat that got too close to the fire and ended up singed and frizzy.

A sheep in cat's clothing?

Each hair on the Selkirk Rex is curly, giving it the look of a poodle. And because the top coat, the awn hairs, and the down hairs are affected, the coat appears extremely thick. But it is not just the coat that curls: no part of this cat's body is smooth. Brow tufts, whiskers, and ear tufts are all curly. No wonder some people call it a 'sheepcat'.

The Selkirk Rex first appeared in the United States in 1987 and was not at first recognised officially by any cat association. However, The International Cat Association has given it provisional recognition, a first step on the road to registration as a separate breed. Some of the independent European registering bodies also accept the Selkirk Rex, so it may occasionally be seen at shows on the Continent.

Chance mating

Until a curly-haired kitten arrived (it became known as Miss Pesto), there was nothing exceptional about the straight-haired founding queen of the Selkirk Rex. Miss Pesto was the result of a chance mating in Wyoming with an unknown tom. Jeri Newmann, a Montana breeder of Persians, adopted Miss Pesto and mated her to Photo Finish, a black Persian. On 4 July 1988, Miss Pesto produced six kittens. Three of them had curly hair: a black-and-white tom, a black female, and a tortie female. In all three, their curly coats were thick, soft and beautiful.

Inbreeding was necessary to produce more curly-haired kittens, since this is the only way to fix a type or a gene. A year later Miss Pesto was pregnant by one of her sons. Of the four kittens in the litter, three had beautiful curly coats, and the breed came into being.

According to geneticists, the gene that produced these cats is dominant; a single Selkirk parent produces Selkirk kittens. The responsible gene is quite different from three other curly-haired breeds.

Siberian Cat

This rarity from the Russian Federation takes its name from the Asian part of the country that extends from the Ural Mountains to the Pacific Ocean.

From St Petersburg to Berlin

The first registered members of the breed came from the city of St Petersburg (formerly Leningrad). The names of the pair were Mussa, a red-and-white tabby female (born in 1987 and discovered in a Leningrad market), and Tima, a tom of the same age from the same city.

Both cats arrived in Berlin in September 1987. Several months later, they produced a litter of five kittens: three males, a red tabby female and a cream female. The litter was eventually moved to Plettenberg, near the city of Wuppertal, in what was then the Federal Republic of Germany. By April 1990, five males and nine females were registered in different European countries. Most of the offspring had been born in what was once East Germany.

The only Russian club with an accepted birth registry for the Siberian breed is the Kotofej in St Petersburg. If you are offered a Siberian cat, be wary, and check for identification papers showing the cat's pedigree and Russian ancestry.

The Siberian cat is similar to Norwegian Forest and Maine Coon cats, which also hail from wooded northern regions. The resemblance to these breeds may explain the reluctance of the clubs to accept Siberians in championship classes.

As a protection against the cold, harsh climate, the Siberian has long, dense fur, which thickens in winter. Another distinguishing characteristic is its powerful bone structure.

A GENTLE GIANT

The Siberian cat has charm, quiet strength and gentleness. Its soft voice is in tune with its slightly shy nature. It is a big, powerfully built cat: females can weigh almost 6 kg (13 pounds) and males almost 11 kg (24 pounds). Despite their weight, Siberian cats are agile, lively, and good hunters.

Snowshoe

Another new and still rare North American breed, the Snowshoe, was developed in the late 1960s by breeding Siamese with bicoloured American Shorthairs. Its striking physical features are Siamese-type points and bright blue eyes combined with sparkling white feet and white face markings. It blends the grace, elegance, and refinement of the Siamese, with the muscularity and coordination of the Shorthair. Medium to large in size, the Snowshoe is well-boned and muscular with long legs, a medium to long tail and a triangular-shaped head.

Although the Seal Point and White is most frequently seen, the Snowshoe may be produced in any of the Siamese colours and a wide variety of colours are now being bred. However, the most striking combination remains the original, especially when the seal mask shows a white triangle on the nose. Snowshoes have been developed in the United Kingdom, but the breed is not recognised by the GCCF.

> The Snowshoe has inherited a positive personality and a gentle and friendly nature from its ancestors. It is a lively creature and a good hunter, affectionate and faithful, and fond of the company of humans.

Sphynx

The public is divided in its opinion of the Sphynx. Some people find it attractive and fascinating. Others recoil with shock, possibly because the Sphynx runs counter to their idea of what a cat should be.

Soft, pliable and warm

The Sphynx is said to be hairless. However, its wrinkled skin – with a texture as soft and pliable as suede or chamois leather – has a covering of short, fine down. There should also be short, tightly packed soft hair at the extremities – the ears, feet, muzzle and testicles. A tiny tassel of hair may appear at the end of the tail. Whiskers and eyebrows – either whole or incomplete – may also be present. The skin can have any recognised coat colour or pattern; the colour of the eyes should complement that of the coat.

Despite the lack of a thick, insulating fur, the Sphynx is warm to the touch. The unprotected creature has a system that compensates by producing body temperatures that are considerably higher than those of other breeds.

Unlike other breeds, the Sphynx sweats and, with no thick coat to absorb natural oils, it must be bathed or sponged often. It is best kept indoors at all times, because it responds poorly to changes in temperature.

The Sphynx's temperament is a blend of gentleness, gallantry, intelligence and mischief. It is sociable and affectionate, although it does not like to be clasped or cuddled.

The road to recognition

The modern Sphynx appeared in an otherwise normal litter of short-haired kittens in Canada in the late 1960s. Efforts to gain recognition for the breed have not met with complete success. The Cat Fanciers' Association (CFA) gave provisional status in 1970. In the early 1990s, The International Cat Association (TICA) was the only registry in North America with championship classes in which the Sphynx could compete.

Today the Sphynx is still rare outside North America, but is being bred in many European countries. The GCCF will register Sphynx in order to record them and to monitor the variants produced from matings with other breeds, but will not recognise the breed for showing.

Turkish Angora

T he Turkish Angora, famous for its long, thick silky coat, came to Europe from Ankara (then called Angora), Turkey, in the early 1600s. The breed helped create the Persian (see page 104), which became so popular that the Angora became all but extinct in Britain and the United States. It became a protected animal in its native Turkey. Revived in the United States after World War II, the Turkish Angora made a strong come-

For many years, the Angora was considered aggressive, difficult to handle and anti-social. However, these disagreeable traits were the result of poor selection and excessive inbreeding. Today, these problems have been rectified, and the animal is now a good companion – quick-witted, lively, playful, mischievous and friendly.

back there in the 1960s, when a breeder, Liesa Grant, imported a pair, Yildiz (Star) and Yildizcik (Starlet), from the Ankara zoo.

Turkish Angoras are bred in many European countries. Originally only the white was recognised, but it is now bred and shown in a wide range of colours.

A medium to small cat, it has a rather small wedge head with high-set, tufted ears. The coat is medium long, silky and fine, with a slight undercoat.

York Chocolate

This is a newcomer to the world of the purebred cat. The breed takes its name from New York State, where it first saw the light of day (in 1983) on a farm belonging to Janet Chiefari. The second part of its name celebrates the rich brown colour of its semi-long coat.

Cool reception

This new American cat was a spontaneous mutation – that is, a naturally occurring specimen. However, the breed has received a cool welcome from cat fanciers and geneticists. By late 1994, it had not received full recognition. Some cat associations want to see more examples of the York Chocolate before making a decision about the breed's future. Moreover, many geneticists consider the breeding programme unacceptable.

Siamese background

The parents of the first York Chocolate kittens were household cats with a trace of Siamese in an otherwise uncertain ancestral background. The sire was a long-haired black cat, and the dam a long-haired black-and-white. The Siamese ancestry common to both of the parents introduced the chocolate-coloured gene that has become the defining factor in the breed's makeup.

The cat comes in a wide variety of chocolate colours, including solid chocolate, chocolate and white, solid lilac lavender, and lilac lavender and white. The colouring of the cat develops slowly, the kittens being much lighter than the adults. The kittens may have a few tabby markings or tipping. However, these defects are acceptable under the age of 18 months.

Some Chocolate traits

The York Chocolate is bigger than the Siamese. An adult York weighs between 7 and 8 kg (15-17 pounds). However, the structure of the head and of the body is similar to the Siamese.

By the early 1990s, there were only about 100 York Chocolates in existence. A programme of interbreeding guarantees a 100 per cent pure York Chocolate pedigree.

Cheerful and lively, agile and healthy, the York Chocolate is also very attentive to its owner's wishes. It is enthusiastic, energetic, playful and a good hunter.

Elements of feline genetics

Genetics is the part of biology that deals with heredity – the transmission of characteristics via genes from parents to offspring. Genetics applies to all living things, including cats.

Genes are contained within the nucleus of a cell. They direct the manufacture of proteins, which build the body's cells and tissues, and enzymes, which are essential for the body's growth and function.

Cells

A domestic cat's life starts with a single fertilised sex cell – or zygote – too small to be seen without a microscope. That cell contains a structure called the nucleus. Within the nucleus are 38 tiny structures called chromosomes, which contain the genes. These genes are arranged in a predetermined order and position – or locus – along the length of the chromosomes.

The physical differences between cats – eyes, hair type and colour – are caused by differences in the genes controlling the development of these traits. These genes may be dominant or recessive.

Half of a cat's genes come from its father, the other half from its mother, by way of the sperm and egg respectively. Each parent provides different genes, and this accounts for each cat's different characteristics, whether in appearance (phenotype) or in health.

If the offspring received identical genes from both its parents, the genetic makeup of the offspring would be pure (denoted by the symbols AA or aa) and the kittens would be called homozygotes. If one parent contributed a dominant gene and the other a recessive gene, the offspring would have a mixed genotype (Aa) and would be called heterozygotes.

Two recessive genes for a characteristic are required before the characteristic can express itself. Either the dominant or the recessive gene can be passed on by a heterozygotic cat to its progeny. A recessive gene can be carried for several generations without being visibly expressed.

The gene for a characteristic that can be seen in a heterozygotic kitten is dominant; it is symbolised by the capital letter (A). The other gene for that characteristic has no effect on the kitten's appearance when combined with the dominant gene; it is recessive, symbolised by the small letter (a).

Determining the sex

The domestic cat carries 38 chromosomes, 19 of which come from the father via the sperm and the other 19 from the mother via the egg (ovum). When the egg is fertilised by the sperm, it therefore carries 19 pairs of chromosomes. Each chromosome of a pair carries genes at identical loci to its mate. Eighteen of these pairs are identical, but one pair, the sex chromosomes, is different in the two sexes. This different pair decides a kitten's sex. Females carry two X chromosomes, males carry an X and a Y chromosome. A kitten inherits one of its mother's X chromosomes and either an X or a Y from the father. If it inherits two X chromosomes, it is a female; if it receives an X and a Y, it is a male.

Pattern and shade

Some genes located at different loci on the chromosomes often interact and modify each other's expression. These are called polygenes and modifiers. They have a strong influence on traits such as colour and appearance, or conformation. They are the cause of variations of pattern and shade in the cat's fur.

Epistatic or masking genes prevent or mask the expression of other genes in the same cat. For instance, the dominant white gene (W) prevents colour cells from reaching the skin and masks the presence of the pigments eumelanin, which appears as black and brown, and phaeomelanin, which appears as red, orange and yellow.

Pigmentation

Melanin

Melanin is a pigment produced by cells called melanocytes that are spread throughout the top layer of the skin and the hair follicles. It gives colour to the hair, skin and eyes.

There are two types of melanin: eumelanin and phaeomelanin. Granules of eumelanin, which are spherical in shape, absorb almost all light. Granules of phaeomelanin, which are longer and oval, refract light in the red-orange-yellow range. Depending on the variety of enzyme in the melanin, the colour will change in heat and light. The less sensitive the enzyme is to heat and light, the darker the colour will be. So a black coat will be less sensitive to heat than a chocolate one.

Intensity of pigmentation

Density of pigmentation is determined by a pair of dominant (DD) genes or recessive (dd) ones. The fur of cats with the dominant genes absorbs light across the whole surface, resulting in a darker colour, such as black, chocolate, or cinnamon (for skin containing eumelanin) and red (for skin with phaeomelanin). The dd genes cause a scattered pigmentation. Light is less well absorbed, resulting in a lighter colour, such as blue, lilac or fawn for eumelanin, and cream for phaeomelanin.

Agouti

The agouti (A) gene is responsible for the banding or ticking that produces the tabby pattern. Each hair has alternate bands of light and dark colour, ending with a dark point.

The presence of the non-agouti (aa) gene prevents the yellow band from being produced on the hair, and so allows an uninterrupted distribution of eumelanin on the hair shaft. This gives the cat a solid-coloured coat.

It is practically impossible to obtain a solid red or cream coat, however. All red or cream cats have a tabby pattern to a greater or lesser degree.

Colour expression

The C gene is responsible for a coat that is coloured all over, whether it is self, tabby, tortoiseshell or smoke. All full-coloured cats have at least one C gene. A lack of colour can be caused by more than one genetic arrangement, one of which is the absence of a C gene at the C locus.

Various mutant forms of the C gene are known, including the c^b gene. This gene reduces the colour more on the body (in a graduated way) than on the points (mask, ears, legs and tail) and produces the Burmese colour distribution. The c^s gene reduces the body colour far more, producing a coat pattern where almost all colour is restricted to the points, as in the Siamese, Colourpoint Persian or Birman.

Both of these genes are recessive to the full colour C gene, but the Burmese c^b gene is incompletely dominant over the Siamese c^s gene. The combination of c^b and c^s produces the Tonkinese coat pattern which is intermediate between the two.

Also in this genetic series is the c^a gene, which produces an albino cat with blue eyes. When the c gene occurs homozygotically (cc), it produces an albino cat with red eyes. This combination was believed to be fatal. However, occasionally an albino with red eyes does survive.

White spotting

The white spotting gene, symbolized by the letter S, is responsible for coloured coats with a varying degree of white. These white areas contain no pigment cells, or melanocytes, at all. White spotting takes various forms, from small white spots on the chest and belly, through the bi-colour pattern to Van patterned cats (coloured only on head and tail).

However, the white feet seen in Birmans are produced by a different gene, the recessive white gloving gene – g.

Dominant white

Unlike the white spotting gene, the dominant white gene, represented by the letter W, masks all other colours and patterns and produces completely white fur. The fur of cats carrying the W gene has no pigments because there are no melanocytes in the skin. The white is therefore not a colour, but an absence of colour. It is impossible to tell what other colour genes a white cat has unless its full pedigree and breeding history are known.

Silver

The silver colour is due to a dominant inhibiting gene that eliminates yellow pigmentation from the hair shaft and influences the amount of melanin deposited at the tip of the hair. Its symbol is I.

Breed-specific mutations

Various recessive mutant genes have been selected by breeders to establish special breeds. A good example of the true breeding genotype is the Siamese, $c^s c^s$.

However, some dominant mutant genes have also been used to establish breeds. For example, the American Curl carries a dominant gene that affects the shape of the ears, causing them to curl towards the back of the head. And taillessness, as in the Manx breed, results from the dominant M gene. This gene is lethal in the homozygous form, since it prevents proper development of the spinal cord.

GENETIC SYMBOLS

Wild type		Mutation	
A	Agouti	a	Non-agouti
B	Black pigment	b	Chocolate
		b^l	Cinnamon
C	Full colour	c^b	Burmese
		c^s	Siamese
		c^a	Blue-eyed albino
		c	Pink-eyed albino
D	Dense pigmentation	d	Dilute pigmentation
dm	Normal pigmentation	Dm	Dilute modifier
fd	Normal ears	Fd	Folded ears
G	Normal colour	g	White gloving
i	Normal pigmentation	I	Silver (inhibited) pigmentation
Hr	Normal coat	hr	Hairless
L	Short hair	l	Long hair
m	Normal tail	M	Manx taillessness
o	Normal colour	O	Sex-linked orange
R	Normal coat	r	Cornish Rex
Re	Normal coat	re	Devon Rex
s	Normal colour	S	White spotting
T	Mackerel tabby	T^a	Ticked tabby
		t^b	Blotched (classic) tabby
w	Normal colour	W	Dominant white
wb	Normal pigmentation	Wb	Wide band
wh	Normal coat	Wh	Wirehair

Colour descriptions

Obvious and hidden colours

When breeding cats, it is important to remember that a cat of a certain colour may carry genes for other colours. A black cat, for example, may genetically be BB (having two dominant genes for black), or Bb or Bb^l (in which chocolate and cinnamon respectively are carried by the recessive gene). This means that a black cat bred to a black cat may produce black, chocolate or cinnamon offspring, depending on the colour genes they carry.

A black cat may also carry d – the recessive dilute gene that is responsible for paler colours. If this cat is bred with another black cat carrying the dilute gene, their kittens may be black or blue. If they both carry b or b^l as well, their kittens may be lilac or fawn. This same genetic principle applies to any other recessive colour or pattern genes and means that each of the basic colours may appear in practically any breed.

When colour descriptions are written in genetic terms, sometimes the capital letter of the dominant gene is paired with a hyphen rather than with a letter, for example: A- . The hyphen indicates that there must be another gene accompanying the dominant one. This second paired gene may be either dominant or recessive.

Eumelanin (black-based) colours

Black (B-, C-, D-)

Most standards require a lustrous jet-black coat, black from roots to tip, with no reddish shading and no white or grey hairs. This coat is difficult to maintain, because both the sun and the cat's saliva tend to redden the colouring somewhat.

Black Persian kittens are born with a grey ruff that is often so pale they are taken for smokes. The grey disappears with moulting, and is not considered a fault in young cats. In adults, the head, front legs, top of the back and tail are shiny black, while the ruff, hind legs and belly are more mat, since these areas are woollier.

Some black cats, in particular Orientals and Bombays, can have a coat that is so intensely jet black that it looks blue-black.

The eyes of black cats range from gold to orange to deep copper, except for Orientals where green is the colour required by the breed standard. The nose leather, lips and paw pads in all breeds are a deep charcoal or brownish black.

Blue (B-, C-, dd)

This colour is quite common. In fact, blue is included as an accepted colour in many breeds of cats. The shade varies depending on the length and thickness of the fur, although some standards do not take into account these differences. As with black fur, the sun and saliva both have a reddening effect on blue coats.

Blue kittens are born a very pale blue, but darken a little with age, especially on the back, head, and upper surface of the tail. The woollier lower leg areas remain pale. Short-haired breeds display a more even blue colouring than long-haired ones. Tabby ghost markings may be visible in young blue cats.

The eyes are gold, except for Orientals, Korats and Russian Blues, in which they are green. The nose leather, lips and paw pads are slate grey.

Chocolate (b-, C-, D-)

The shade of chocolate required by the standard varies from breed to breed but should be as even as possible with no ghost markings. In Persians, the thickly furred areas are paler. The colour is more common among Orientals where it should be chestnut brown. In short-haired breeds, the brown is very shiny and smooth.

The eyes vary from gold to orange and deep copper. They are green in Orientals. The nose leather, lips and paw pads are a similar shade to the fur but with a slight rosy flush.

Cinnamon (b^{l}b^l, C-, D-)

This very warm and attractive colour is found mostly in Orientals, Abyssinians and Somalis. It has different shades, from a medium, reddish-brown, lighter in colour than chocolate, to terracotta or burnt sienna.

The eyes are amber, hazel, or green for sorrel Abyssinians, and green for Orientals and Somalis. The nose leather, lips and paw pads are a pinkish tan.

Lilac (b-, C-, dd)

This colour ranges from an even frost-grey or dove to light grey. Adults should have no ghost markings, although these are seen in kittens.

The eyes are gold to orange or deep copper, but green in Orientals. The nose leather, lips and paw pads are lavender pink.

Fawn (b^{l}b^l, C-, dd)

Fawn can be a warm rosy mushroom colour to a warm pinkish buff. Abyssinians and Somalis may have amber, hazel or green eyes; green is required in Orientals. The nose leather, lips and paw pads can vary from dusty rose to pink.

Caramel (--, C-, dd, Dm-)

In Caramels the blue, lilac or fawn is converted by the dilute modifier gene to a brownish-grey colour which, in caramel tabbies, shows a distinct metallic sheen. The eye colour is yellow to green in Asians and green in Orientals. The nose leather, lips and paw pads are pink to bluish fawn. The dilute modifier gene, although dominant, has no effect on black, chocolate, cinnamon or red, so breeders may be unaware that the gene is present in their cats until they produce a dilute kitten of this interesting colour.

Phaeomelanin (red-based) colours (OO)

For a red to be solid, both genes must be dominant and homozygous (OO). If they were Oo, the cat would be a tortie. Although the colour standards for most breeds require an even, deep warm, clear solid red or cream, this is in fact almost a genetic impossibility. Tabby markings are almost always evident in reds and creams.

Red (--, C-, D-, OO)

All shades of red are accepted, but richer, deeper colours are preferred. Red may be black, chocolate or cinnamon based. The eye colour is gold to orange and copper except for Orientals, in which the eyes are green. The nose leather, lips and paw pads are pink.

Cream (--, C-, dd, OO)

A very pale beige, or buff cream, this colour rarely occurs naturally. Creams may be blue, lilac or fawn based. The colour standard requires a pale, uniform, sound cream colour. Tabby markings may be more visible on short-haired breeds.

The eyes are gold to orange and copper, but green for Orientals. The nose leather, lips and paw pads are a rosy pink.

Apricot (--. C-, dd, Dm-, OO)

The dilute modifier gene transforms cream to apricot, a colour with the same powdered look as the cream, but with a rosy glow. The eye colour is yellow to green in Asians and green in Orientals. The nose leather, lips and paw pads are pink.

Dominant white (W-)

White is the most difficult colour to achieve. This is because the standard requires that it should be absolutely pure. But saliva and tears (particularly in Persians) tend to tint the fur a yellow-brown, and the genital area, feet and hocks all tend to become discoloured.

Many white kittens are born with a patch of colour on the head. This is a trace of the genetically masked colour of which they are carriers, and it disappears with age. It is not penalised in kittens and young adults.

The eyes may be gold to copper, blue or odd-coloured. The nose leather, lips and paw pads are pink.

Genetically speaking, white is not considered a colour, but a factor that masks another colour. In order to determine the possible colours of the future offspring of a white cat, it may be necessary to consult its pedigree. This will not necessarily reveal much, because recessive genes may be in the pedigree many generations back. They may not show up on a common five-generation pedigree. Breeding a white cat to a white cat may produce any colour or pattern the cats are carrying.

Tortoiseshell (Oo)

The tortoiseshell colour combination may be seen in full-coloured, Burmese, Tonkinese and pointed cats (as well as in Tabbies, Smokes and Shadeds). The nose leather and paw pads should be the same colour as either or both of the two solid colours, and often a mottled pattern is seen on the pads.

Tabby markings may be seen in the red or cream areas if these are large. If the eumelanin patches have any tabby patterning the cat is a tortie-tabby.

Red and black tortie (aa, B-, C-, D-, Oo)

This unusual colouring, found mostly in females, consists of a mosaic of small patches of red and black. There are two opinions about torties: British standards require a perfect and regular mixture of red and black, whereas some American standards accept a less uniform appearance. The ideal coat consists of red and black patches of colour. Brindling, or scattered red and black hairs, may be allowed in certain breed standards in which the type and quality of the coat are more important than colour.

The eyes are gold to copper, except for Orientals, in which they are green. The nose leather, lips and paw pads are mottled pink and black.

Blue tortie (Blue cream) (aa, B-, C-, dd, Oo)

This is a dilution of a red and black tortie, in which the red has become cream and the black has become blue. In Persians and British Shorthairs the colours should be pale and softly intermingled, whereas the distribution and proportion of the different colours in other breeds is less important.

The eyes are gold to orange to deep copper, except for Orientals, in which they are green. The nose leather, lips and paw pads are a mottled pink and grey.

Chocolate tortie (aa, b-, C-, D-, Oo)

A combination of chocolate-brown hairs and red hairs creates this very warm colour.

The eyes are gold to orange to deep copper, except for Orientals, in which they are green. The nose leather, lips and paw pads are a mottled brown and pink.

Cinnamon tortie (aa, b^{l}b^l, C-, D-, Oo)

Cinnamon and red, with a marked tint-on-tint effect, produce this rare colour.

The eyes are amber to green in Abyssinians and Somalis, and green in Orientals. The nose leather, lips and paw pads are a mottled red and cinnamon.

Lilac tortie (Lilac cream)
(aa, b-, C-, dd, Oo)

This pinkish beige is a subtle blend of cream and lilac, which produces a very delicate tint-on-tint look.

The eyes are gold to copper, except for Orientals, in which they are green. The nose leather, lips and paw pads are a mottled pink and pale grey.

Fawn tortie (aa, b^{l}b^l, C-, dd, Oo)

This very delicate and rare colour is a dilution of cinnamon tortie, which has become fawn and cream.

The eyes are amber to green in Abyssinians and Somalis, and green in Orientals. The nose leather, lips and paw pads are pink speckled with a pinkish brown-grey.

Caramel tortie
(aa, --, -C, dd, Dm-, Oo)

The dilute modifier gene converts the blue, lilac or fawn tortie to a mixture of brownish grey and apricot. The eye colour is yellow to green in Asians and green in Orientals. The nose leather, lips and paw pads are pink to bluish fawn.

Tabbies

Four tabby patterns are recognised: ticked, mackerel, classic and spotted. Like tortoiseshells, tabbies exist in all colours and in all gradations, from full colour to Burmese, Tonkinese and pointed. If the colour of the tabby is in question, the colour on the tip of the tail should determine the accurate colour. Only the patterns are described here.

In long-haired cats, the markings are always less obvious than in the short-haired cats because of the length and thickness of the fur, which tends to blur the pattern slightly. The markings are clearer on the head, legs and along the tail, where the fur is shorter.

The tabby markings are the same colour as the equivalent solid colour, the ground colour in between consisting of banded hairs as seen in the ticked tabby. Although most colours of tabby are described in the same way as their self equivalent (blue tabby, cinnamon tabby, and so on), the black tabby is not: in Abyssinians and Somalis the black version is known as 'usual' and in other breeds as 'brown tabby' due to its rich brown background colour. Tabby cats have a paler chin colour, but this paler area should not extend down the neck.

The nose leather is either the same colour as the marking colour or may be pinkish towards the centre and outlined in the marking colour. Lips and paw pads are the same shade as the marking colour.

Whatever the pattern or the colour, the goal is to achieve the greatest contrast between the markings and the ground colour.

Ticked tabby (A-, T^a-)

Abyssinians and Somalis are excellent examples of the ticked tabby. Each hair (with the exception of those on the belly and the inside of the legs) is marked with a band of yellow that separates the darker band of eumelanin colour. The yellow band in these two breeds has become apricot (or rufused), giving these cats a reddish-brown appearance.

In other breeds, the yellow band may or may not be rufused, and separates eumelanin or phaeomelanin pigment. What we see is a yellow band alternating with a coloured band repeatedly. The tip of the hair should be coloured with the marking or indicative colour, with the lower part of the hair shaft ending with a paler yellow band. The more bands of colour there are on an individual hair, the better.

The belly and inside of the legs are not ticked or banded. Tail rings, leg bars and unbroken necklaces are considered faults in Abyssinians and Somalis. In these breeds the coat should be evenly ticked, although they must have dark tail tips, dark markings behind the back legs, and tabby markings around the eyes. Oriental ticked tabbies, however, should have distinct tabby markings on the head, legs and tail.

Mackerel tabby (A-, T-)

The legs and tail should be evenly marked with fine rings and there should be at least one complete necklace. The M on the forehead, the frown marks extending between the ears and down the back of the neck, and the spine lines should all be continuous, close together and parallel. The flanks, shoulders and haunches show either markings like the rib bones of a fish (hence the name 'mackerel tabby') or fine, regular parallel lines. The belly should show rows of the spots of the dark marking colour.

Classic tabby or blotched tabby (A-, t^{b}t^b)

The rings encircling the tail and legs are quite broad and well spaced, and wide necklace tracings appear on the neck. The M on the forehead and the parallel head lines should also be broad. The swirl on the side of the body should be an unbroken circle centred with a spot of marking colour surrounded by the ground colour.

The spine lines consist of three broad parallel stripes running from the base of the neck to the tip of the tail. The shoulders are marked with a pattern like a butterfly with open wings. The belly should be spotted.

Spotted tabby (A-, T- or t^{b}t^b)

The legs and tail are barred with fine, close lines, and there should be necklace tracings. The forehead should be marked with an M, and the head and neck lines should be parallel and close together.

The back, flanks, shoulders, legs and belly are marked by spots which follow the lines of the mackerel or classic pattern; the spots may vary in size and shape, but the standard prefers them to be round, evenly distributed and quite distinct.

Tortie tabby or torbie (A-, Oo)

A tortie that has been tabbied is called a tortie-tabby. All the torties, if they have the agouti gene (A-) instead of the non-agouti (aa), can appear in any of the four tabby patterns. The colour combinations remain the same, but the tabby pattern is now visible over the whole of the cat instead of being restricted to the red or cream areas.

Silver tabby

All the colours and patterns of tabby previously mentioned can exist in silver. In this case the tabby markings are exactly the same, but the ground colour (including the chin and lips) must be a brilliant silver white, which should be as pure as possible. The contrast should be extremely sharp, so that the markings are very clear. The silver ground colour usually shows a slight hint of the pattern colour and although the dilute colours have a delicate beauty, the black silver tabby has the most dramatic effect. The paw pads and nose leather should be the same shade as the marking colour.

Green is the preferred eye colour, but the eyes may appear gold-green in kittens and young adults, as full green pigmentation is slow to develop.

Silver tabbies are highly valued, especially those with the spotted and classic patterns, which make the cat look as if it had been handpainted. Silver classic tabbies are seen in Persians, silver classic, mackerel and spotted tabbies in British Shorthairs, silver ticked tabbies in Abyssinians and Somalis, and all four patterns of silver tabby in Asians and Orientals.

Shaded

Shaded (A-, Wb-)

Shaded cats are produced by the presence of the wide-band gene in an agouti cat of any of the four tabby patterns. This gene has the effect of widening the yellow bands on the agouti hairs, pushing the darker colour towards the tips of the hairs and diffusing the tabby pattern. The result is a cat with a pale undercoat, dark hair tips and, to a greater or lesser degree, some tabby pattern on the head, legs and tail.

The degree of colour reduction varies considerably and may change seasonally in an individual cat, the shading looking more intense when the cat has moulted and the shorter new hairs are growing through. It is a pattern that develops with age; almost all shaded kittens show a tabby pattern when tiny and may not develop the full shaded effect until they reach adulthood. The effect is more dramatic in long-haired breeds where the more lightly shaded cats are referred to as 'tipped' and the more heavily marked as 'shaded'.

Silver shaded (A-, I-, Wb-)

The presence of the inhibitor gene, which removes yellow pigment, enhances the shaded effect. The undercoat becomes silver, as in the ground colour of silver tabbies, and the amount of shading is reduced.

The most extreme example of a silver shaded cat is the Chinchilla. By selecting only the most lightly tipped cats, breeders have produced a silvery-white longhair with the tiniest of black tipping to the hairs – just enough to give a sparkling effect to the coat. Sometimes a more heavily shaded Chinchilla is produced and this is known as a Shaded Silver. A very similar long-haired breed, the Pewter, is distinguished from the Shaded Silver by having orange eyes instead of green. Chinchillas and Shaded Silver and Pewter longhairs are at present only recognised in black/silver by the GCCF, although other colour combinations do exist and are recognised elsewhere.

The red and cream silver shaded longhairs are known as Cameos; the shaded Cameo has a delicate mantle of red or cream over its silver undercoat, while the lightly tipped version, known as the Shell Cameo, has sparkling red or cream tips to its hair. Tortie and blue-cream Cameos are also recognised, but here they are not divided into shell and shaded, any depth of shading being acceptable.

On a short coat the distinction between shaded and tipped is less obvious than with long-haired cats, and in the shorthairs varied degrees, from light tipping to medium shading, are permitted within a single breed. Several colours are recognised in the Exotic shorthair, and the silver shaded British Shorthair – the British Tipped – includes all British Shorthair colours, although the black tipped is the most commonly seen. The Asian shaded is known as a Burmilla, reflecting its origins from a cross between Burmese and Chinchilla, and may be any of the myriad of colours found in Asians, including the tortie colours. The whole colour range for the Orientals is available in the silver shaded pattern. Most of these cats also have a Chinchilla a long way back in their ancestry.

In Chinchillas, shaded silvers, black-tipped British Tipped and all silver shaded Orientals the eye colour is green, whereas among the pewters, cameos and the other colours of British Tipped it is copper to gold. In Asians the eyes are yellow to green although green is preferred in silver Burmillas. The nose leather, lips and paw pads in silver shadeds are basically the same as those of the equivalent colours of silver tabby, although in Chinchillas, shaded silvers, pewters and British Tipped cats, a brick red nose leather is preferred.

Standard shaded (A-, ii, Wb-)

Standard shaded are less dramatic than their silver counterparts, showing less contrast between shading and undercoat colours. The shading itself is darker because there is no inhibitor gene to reduce it. They usually take even longer to develop their true adult colour; standard shaded kittens, especially in the very short coated Asians and Orientals, often look like indistinct tabbies. Fewer standard shaded than silver shaded breeds are recognised, apart from the Asians and Orientals where, again, standard shaded are produced in the whole colour range of the breed group. The pattern also occurs in the Golden Persian, a cat with a rich golden undercoat and black shading, the non-silver version of the Chinchilla, and its British and Exotic counterparts. The eye colour of standard shaded cats is the same as in their silver shaded relatives, as are the colours of the nose leather, lips and paw pads.

Smokes (aa, I-)

A Smoke is produced by the effect of the inhibitor gene on a non-agouti cat. Smoke points are not recognised in Britain by the GCCF, although they are in some other countries. The combination of Smoke and the Burmese colour distribution is recognised only in Asians.

The base of the hair is a brilliant silvery white for a quarter to two-thirds of its length, the remainder being coloured. This coloured portion may be black, blue, chocolate, lilac, cinnamon, caramel, fawn, red, cream or apricot. Tortie Smokes can appear in black and red, blue and cream, chocolate and red, lilac and cream, cinnamon and red, caramel and apricot or fawn and cream.

Long-haired black Smokes are the most striking, because they appear to be a solid colour until they move. Then the hair ripples, revealing the brilliant, white undercolour beneath. For judges, this contrast is extremely important. It is most obvious in long-haired cats. For this reason, Persian Smokes look their best in the winter, when their coat is at

its longest and thickest. In this condition, the best examples show all the desired contrast and good colour proportion.

Ghost tabby markings may appear in kittens and young adults. These should disappear or become less obvious when the cat reaches maturity.

Colour points

This is a restricted colour pattern in which the pigmentation is confined to the points only – the ears, mask, legs and tail – and the body colour is a paler shade of the indicative colour. This colour pattern is seen in Siamese, Balinese, Colourpoints, Birmans, Colourpointed British Shorthairs and Ragdolls.

The eye colour must be blue – the deeper the better. This blue colour is caused by the effect of the Siamese gene on the eye colour. It is not related to the blue eye colour seen in cats with the dominant white gene, so blue-eyed cats with this coat pattern are not prone to deafness.

Solid point

In these cats, the ears, mask, tail and legs are dark, well-defined and contrast with the body colour, which is much lighter. Body shading should harmonise with the point colour. In longhairs, the chest and ruff may be paler than in shorthairs.

Seal point (aa, B-, c^{s}c^s D-, oo) This is the best known, best loved, and most common of the Siamese varieties. The body colour should be an even pale fawn or cream, shading gradually into a lighter colour on the belly and chest. The points should be a dense, deep seal brown. Adult seal points tend to darken very markedly over the back.

The nose leather, lips and paw pads are seal brown.

Blue point (aa, B-, c^{s}c^s, dd, oo) The points should be a cool, grey-blue. The very pale body should show only a very light blue shading in adults.

The nose leather, lips and paw pads are dark blue-grey.

Chocolate point (aa, b- c^{s}c^s, D-, oo) The points are a warm milk-chocolate colour, the body a pale ivory.

The charm of this colour lies in its warmth. The contrast between the points and the body is marked and should persist even in adulthood. However, 'spectacles' of paler hairs outlining the eyes are frequent. The eyes are as dark a blue as possible, with a rosy aura (with a tendency towards violet in the Siamese and Birmans).

The nose leather and lips of chocolate points are a burnt rose, and the paw pads are a salmon pink colour.

Cinnamon point (aa, b^{l}b^l, c^{s}c^s, D-, oo) The points should be an extremely warm, reddish, cinnamon brown. The pale body colour ranges from buff to ivory. As in the chocolate point, there is generally a marked contrast between the body and the points. This is an extremely rare colour that is recognised only by the GCCF in the Siamese.

The eyes are the darkest shade of blue possible. The nose leather and lips are a burnt rose, and the paw pads are a salmon-pink colour.

Lilac point (aa, b-, c^{s}c^s, dd, oo) The points should be a lilac-grey or pinkish tone, the pinker the shade the better. The body colour ranges from milk-white to an extremely pale old ivory; there is a marked tint-on-tint effect, which gives a rather 'dull' but very delicate look.

The eyes are as dark a blue as possible. The nose leather, lips and paw pads are coral pink.

Caramel point (aa, c^{s}c^s, dd, Dm-, oo) The points are a brownish grey. It is important that the colour should match on all points since the tendency in Caramel points is for them to appear more chocolate in some places and greyer in others. The body colour should be off-white. The eyes should be a deep blue and the nose leather, lips and paw pads are pinkish-grey.

Fawn point (aa, b^{l}b^l, c^{s}c^s, dd, oo) The body should be an even milk-white, rather like a magnolia shade. The points should be a pale dove to light taupe-grey and may have light fawn tones or a pinkish lavender cast. The eye colour is the darkest shade of blue possible.

Paw pads are an ash-rose to lavender-pink, and the nose leather is a lavender-pink to lavender-grey.

Red point (aa, c^{s}c^s, D-, OO) The points should be a deep orange-red, a 'hot' colour, the deeper the better. The body should be a warm, even shade of white, with delicate pale red shading on the back.

As all red points show some tabby markings, the standards make allowance for this. These markings cannot be totally eliminated as the red gene reveals the tabby pattern. The eyes are as dark a blue as possible, the nose leather, lips and paw pads hot pink; black spots are common on the lips and nose.

Cream point (aa, c^{s}c^s dd, OO) The points may be any shade of cream, from deep cream to pale cream but should always have a powdery look. The body should be an even white all over; the overall colour should be sufficiently 'dull' to distinguish it from the red point.

The eyes are deep blue, as dark a blue as possible, and the nose leather, lips and paw pads are rosy pink.

Tortie point (aa, c^{s}c^s, Oo)

The tortie point is a mixture of eumelanin and phaeomelanin: seal, chocolate, cinnamon and red pointed colours; blue, lilac, caramel or fawn, and cream pointed colours. These colours appear on the points only. The red or cream areas may show tabby markings, but stripes elsewhere mean that the cat is a tortie-tabby point. The body in a mature cat may have the mottled pattern of the tortie, which may be only a shade lighter than the points. This colouring is found in Siamese, Birmans and Colourpoint Persians among others.

Tabby point (A, c^{s}c^s, OO, Oo or oo)

The tabby point is the agouti equivalent of any of the other colours of pointed cats, including the red point, cream point and all colours of tortie point. The mask shows the same markings as in a tabby cat, the tail is ringed and the legs show stripes which may be very faint in the paler colours such as red, lilac and fawn, especially in kittens. The ears often show a pale central 'thumbprint'. The markings and body colour should be the same as in the equivalent solid pointed cat, but as the cat matures the body often shades to show tabby markings which may be any of the four tabby patterns. Silver tabby points are not recognised by the GCCF. The eye colour should be as deep a blue as possible. The nose leather, lips and paw pads are the same as in that solid-pointed colour, except that the nose leather may be pink with a coloured rim.

Particolour points (c^{s}c^s, Ss or SS with any pointed colour and/or pattern)

The ears, mask and tail of particolour points are of the marking colour. If the cat is bicolour, it may have an inverted V or a white blaze running from the point of the nose to between the eyes. The body, legs and feet may have white patches, which indicate the presence of the white spotting gene. If there are spots of white on the body, the body may be only slightly paler than the points.

The action of the white spotting gene causes the body shade to be darker than in most colourpoint cats. If the white spotting gene is not present, the body colour will be a very pale version of the points.

The nose leather, lips and paw pads may be in the indicative colour, mottled, or pink.

The breed standards for Ragdolls and Snowshoes specify the exact placement of the white.

Gloved points (c^{s}c^s, gg)

The recessive gloving gene, responsible for the white feet of the Birman, may be found in any solid, tortie or tabby points colour except for cinnamon, caramel and fawn.

Particolours (Ss or SS)

These are cats that have the white spotting gene, which creates white areas of various sizes, mixed with one or more other colours.

There are three levels of white: mitted (a low grade of white and a colour and/or pattern), bicolour (a medium grade of white spotting and a colour and/or pattern), and harlequin or Van (a high grade of white spotting and a colour and/or pattern).

For all particolours, the nose leather, lips and paw pads are either pink (because of the white gene), mottled, or the same as the indicative colour.

Mitted (Ss)

This is a predominantly coloured cat with the white limited to the paws, the back legs, belly, chin and chest. Mitted cats are typically about one-quarter white.

Bicolour (Ss)

A bicoloured cat has a coloured head, back and tail, with white on its legs, feet, underside and lower flanks. A white blaze such as the inverted V pattern is often seen. Various markings of white and pigment may occur, but the cat is generally one-third to two-thirds white.

Harlequin or Van (SS)

This is a predominantly white cat with coloured patches. The coloured patches are usually found on the head and tail with two or three separate patches permitted on the back. The Van pattern (below) has a coloured cap and tail and is an extreme expression of the white spotting gene. In Turkish Vans the ears should be white, with coloured patches at their base. In addition, they should have coloured markings on the tail.

Tortoiseshell and white (aa, Ss or SS, Oo)

When white spotting is added to tortoiseshell, the colour patches are distinct, with large areas of black, chocolate or cinnamon with red, blue, lilac or fawn with cream, or caramel with apricot. The larger the white areas, the greater the colour separation, so that in a Van patterned cat each spot may contain only a single colour.

Dilute calico or blue tortie and white (aa, B-, C-, dd, Ss, Oo)

Blue and cream patches of colour surrounded by white define these attractive cats.

BODY TYPES

Cobby
Short, sturdy: Persian, Exotic Shorthair, British Shorthair, Manx.

Semi-cobby
Slightly longer and not as sturdy as the cobby: American Shorthair, Korat.

Long and substantial
Birman, Turkish Van, Maine Coon, Norwegian Forest Cat, Ragdoll.

Foreign
Each breed differs in type, some being quite heavily boned, but none are either cobby or elongated: Abyssinian, Somali, Russian Blue, Devon Rex, Cornish Rex, Burmese, Asian, Tiffanie, Tonkinese, Bengal, Ocicat, Singapura.

Oriental
Long and elegant: Siamese, Balinese, Oriental, Angora.

BURMESE (c^bc^b)

The coat colour is slightly paler than in the full coloured equivalent, often showing slightly darker ears and mask, and a rather paler belly. Any shading should be gradual. Eye colour is any shade of yellow from chartreuse to amber, with golden yellow preferred.

Brown (B-, c^bc^b, D-, oo)
The effect of the gene is most obvious on black, which appears as a rich warm seal brown.
Blue (B-, c^bc^b, dd, oo)
A soft blue-grey, showing a silver sheen.
Chocolate (bb, c^bc^b, D-, oo)
Warm milk chocolate, preferably even in colour all over, although chocolate Burmese often show darker mask and ears.
Lilac (bb, c^bc^b, dd, oo)
Pale delicate dove-grey with a slightly pinkish cast, giving a faded effect.
Red (c^bc^b, D-, OO)
A tangerine colour, preferably free from any tabby barring, although slight markings may sometimes be seen.
Cream (c^bc^b, dd, OO)
Cream, with a distinct powdery bloom.
Tortie (c^bc^b, Oo)
All four colours of tortie are seen – brown or chocolate with red, blue or lilac with cream.

TONKINESE (c^bc^s)

The points are darker than body colour but, unlike the pointed cats, the colour should merge and not show a sharp contrast. Where this colour gene combination occurs in breeds other than Tonkinese, such as Cornish or Devon Rex, the colour is described as 'brown, darker points' and so on. The eye colour may be green to light blue, although pale greenish-blue or bluish-green is preferred.

Brown (B-, c^bc^s, D-, oo)
Warm light brown with darker seal points.
Blue (B-, c^bc^s, dd, oo)
Silver-grey with slate grey points.
Chocolate (bb, c^bc^s, D-, oo)
Light chocolate with darker chocolate points.
Lilac (bb, c^bc^s, dd, oo)
Pale dove-grey with a slightly pinkish cast, with darker grey points.
Red (c^bc^s, D-, OO)
Light red with darker points, although the legs are often no darker than the body.
Cream (c^bc^s, dd, OO)
Rich cream with darker points, although the legs are often pale in colour.
Tortie (c^bc^s, Oo)
All four colours of tortie are seen – brown or chocolate with red, blue or lilac with cream, pale on the body and darker on the points.
Tabby (A-, c^bc^s)
All of the above colours, including red, cream and tortie, also occur in their tabby versions. These show pale tabby markings on the body with darker striping and barring on the points.

Glossary

This glossary gives the definitions of a number of terms used in cat breeding and showing. Words followed by an asterisk (*) have their own alphabetical entry.

Agouti: Hairs 'ticked'* with alternate bands of light and dark colour, ending with a dark tip, or the colouring between stripes. This colour formation creates a tabby* pattern.

Albinism: The total lack of pigmentation and therefore of colour, due to a c gene. This gene is lethal* when carried by homozygous* cats, creating red-eyed albinos that rarely survive.

Alopecia: A condition that causes patchy hair loss.

Anurous: Used to describe a cat without a tail.

Awn hairs: The coarser of two secondary types of hair composing a cat's coat; the awn hairs form an insulating layer of varying thickness.

Balance: A cat's physical and mental balance. A cat is said to be 'out of balance' when the parts of the body are not in proportion.

Best of breed: An award presented in some cat shows.

Bicoloured: Said of a cat showing one of various markings formed by white and another colour (black, blue, red, tabby, cream, etc.).

Blaze: A marking on the centre of the forehead between the eyes and which can run down the nose.

Blotched or classic tabby: One form of the tabby* pattern showing large solid-colour areas on the flanks and broad lines on the back and legs.

Bracelet: The ringed marking encircling the legs in the tabby* pattern.

Brachygnathism: A malformation of the jaws that prevents them from closing properly. The lower jaw is too narrow and set back, and the upper teeth are sometimes actually visible.

Break: An indentation of the nose at about eye level or between the eyes (see also stop*).

Breeches: Longer, thicker hair on the back of upper hind legs.

Brindle (brindled, brindling): A scattering of 'wrong' coloured hairs in a colour (usually in the tail or mask*).

Brown: The colour of certain breeds; genetically speaking, though, it is black.

Calico: Tortoiseshell* and white, showing clearly defined patches of black, red and white.

Cameo (shell or shaded*): The tip of the hair is red, cream or tortie*, the remainder being a brilliant silver white.

Carrier: An animal able to transmit to its descendants a colour, an illness, a fur type, etc., other than those it expresses itself. A heterozygous* animal capable of passing on a recessive* gene.

Cat association/club/federation/society: Non-profit-making organisations that may arrange shows and seminars, keep a stud book or produce newsletters or magazines for their members.

Challenge certificate: An award given to the winner of an open class for entire adults, if the cat is deemed by the judge to be of sufficient quality.

Champion: The name given to a cat who has gained three Challenge certificates* under three different judges.

Chinchilla: The tip of the hair is black, the rest a brilliant silver white; this is the weakest degree of tipping*.

Chocolate: A rich shade of brown.

Cinnamon: A light reddish-brown.

Classic tabby: See Blotched* tabby.

Cloven (Forked): Said of a deformed foot in which the toes are stuck together in twos. It is a disqualifying fault for all breeds.

Cobby: A short, compact, sturdy body with broad shoulders and rump (seen in Persians, Exotics and British Shorthairs).

Co-dominance: The situation in which two colour genes are equally dominant. For example, the Tonkinese, which results from a combination of the c^s Siamese genes and the c^b Burmese genes, constitutes a third breed $c^b c^s$.

Colour point: Coloured only at the extremities, or points*; the eyes are always blue (as in Siamese, Birmans, Colourpoints, etc.).

Cryptorchidism: The obvious absence of a testicle (a disqualifying fault for all breeds). In this condition, the testicle remains within the abdominal cavity.

Curling: The regular crimping of the fur displayed by Rex breeds, especially the Cornish.

Dam: the female parent of a cat.

Depigmentation: A lack of colour in the skin, which causes pink spots on the paw pads or nose leather.

Dilute calico: A colour with patches of blue, cream and white.

Dilution: Caused by pigment granules clumping together in the hair shaft to produce a pale colour. For example, dilute black gives blue, dilute chocolate gives lilac*.

Disqualification: Elimination from a competition due to a breach of rules or for veterinary reasons.

Dome: Rounded forehead.

Dominant: Describes a gene that prevails over another, such as the agouti* over the non-agouti gene.

Double coat: A thick coat in which the awn* hairs are as long as the outer, guard* hairs.

Down hairs: Soft, slightly wavy secondary hairs (around the ears and toes).

Fawn: Dilution* of cinnamon*; refers to a 'coffee and milk', vanilla fudge or warm pinkish buff colour.

Fontanelle: A space above the forehead covered by membrane; the skull, thought to be open while the cat is young, gradually closes due to ossification.

Foreign: A body type characterised by a medium length, elegant shape: seen in Abyssinians, Burmese, etc.

Frill: A ruff that extends down between the front legs.

Fur ball: A collection of dead hairs swallowed by a cat while grooming itself.

GCCF: Governing Council of the Cat Fancy. The Cat Fancy is an organisation that lays down breed standards and runs cat shows in the United Kingdom.

Genotype: The hereditary characteristics of an individual, expressed or not.

Ghost markings: Faint tabby* markings seen in some genetically solid-coloured animals, particularly when young; these marks disappear with age and moulting.

Gold/golden: A golden apricot shade.

Grand Challenge Certificate: An award given to the winner of a special class for Champions only, if the cat is deemed by the judge to be of sufficient quality.

Grand Champion: The title given to a cat who has gained three Grand Challenge Certificates under three different judges.

Grand Premier Certificate: An award given to the winner of a special class for Premiers only, if the cat is deemed by the judge to be of sufficient quality.

Grand Premier: The title given to a cat who has gained three Grand Premier Certificates under three different judges.

Guard hairs: The longest of the three types of hair making up the cat's coat. They form the outer layer, giving the coat its shine and colour.

Hairlessness: This condition is never absolute. Even in the Sphynx breed, there is some hair on the points* and the body is covered with a light down*.

Harlequin: A predominantly white cat with colour patches usually restricted to the extremities, but sometimes with a few body spots, usually on the lower back.

Heterozygous: Possessing two dissimilar genes for a particular trait, one received from each parent. One is dominant*, the other recessive*. In the case of Aa or Bb, the cat shows a dominant colour (black, for example), but is the carrier of a dilution* (blue or lilac*).

Homozygous: Possessing two identical genes for a particular trait. In the case of AA or BB, the cat displays a colour and does not carry a gene for any other.

Hybridization: The crossing of two distinct breeds.

Inhibitor gene: The gene responsible for the inhibition of pigment, and therefore causing smoke, silver tabby or silver shaded cats.

Intermediate Certificate: An award given to the winner of an open class of provisional status breeds, if the cat is judged to be of sufficient quality.

Jowls: Especially developed cheeks in adult males caused by a heavier musculature and a thickening of the skin in this area.

Kink: A deformity of the spine or tail, usually seen as a fixed deviation of the last vertebra of the tail.

Lavender: See lilac*.

Lethal gene: A gene that in the homozygous* state leads to the death of the foetus or newborn.

Lilac: Also known as lavender; a pale pinky-beige shade.

Mackerel tabby: A type of tabby* pattern with fine stripes.

Marbled: A tabby* pattern used only to describe the Bengal cat. The pattern is a variation of the classic* tabby pattern.

Markings: Tabby* markings, such as the frown lines, the 'M' on the forehead, necklaces*, bracelets*, tail rings, and body markings.

Mask: A darker region on the face, including the nose, whisker pads, chin and around the eyes, stopping between the ears.

Masking, or epistasis: The masking of the phenotype*. When a gene masks, or hides, another; for example, the W gene produces a white cat but masks another colour that may appear in that cat's offspring. Masking is more visible in ghost markings*, which appear on solid-coloured cats.

Merit Certificate: This may be awarded to any cat of sufficient quality in an assessment class for breeds with preliminary recognition status.

Monorchism: The presence of only one testicle (a disqualifying fault for all breeds).

Mutation: A sudden change in genotype* having no relation to the individual's ancestry.

Muzzle: The projecting part of the head, including the nose, whisker pads, chin, mouth and cheeks.

Muzzle break: Indentation where the muzzle* is attached to the skull; also a whisker break.

Necklace: Tabby* markings around the neck.

New breed: Used to describe a breed that is in the process of being created and whose standard* has not yet been perfected.

Odd-eyed: Having eyes of different colours: for example, one blue and the other gold, as in white Persians.

Oriental slant: A particular slanted setting of the eye (seen in Siamese and Orientals, for example).

Oriental type: A long, lean body type like that of the Siamese. See also Foreign*.

Particolour: Displaying one or more colours or patterns, and white; for example, black and white, tortie* and white, tabby* and white.

Pattern: Refers to colour distribution that forms a pattern, such as the tabby* pattern, or colour and white distribution such as the mitted*, bicolour*, harlequin* or Van* patterns.

Paw pads: The furless padded area under the feet.

Pedigree: A document or certificate showing the names, breeds and colours of a cat's ancestors; a family tree.

Pewter: A silver shaded* breed with gold eyes.

Phenotype: The physical appearance of an individual.

Points: The extremities of a cat's body: the mask*, ears, tail and legs.

Polydactyly: A malformation in which there are more toes than normal: either six or seven instead of five on the front feet, and five or six instead of four on the back feet (a disqualifying fault for all breeds).

Prefix: a word granted to a breeder to be used as the first part of the name of any cat bred and registered by that breeder.

Premier: The title given to a neutered cat who has gained three Premier Certificates under three different judges.

Premier Certificate: An award given to the winner of a neuter open class, if the cat is deemed by the judge to be of sufficient quality.

Prognathism: A malformation in which the lower jaw juts too far forward; the lower teeth may actually be visible (seen in Persians, etc.).

Recessive: Describes a gene which is usually masked by a dominant* gene; it must be present on both members of a pair of chromosomes in order to be expressed.

Roman profile: Said of a profile that displays a downward curve, as in Birmans and, in a more pronounced form, in the Cornish Rex.

Ruddy: Sometimes used to describe Abyssinians, Somalis or brown ticked tabbies* with a high degree of red in the ground colour.

Ruff: A mass of long, thick fur around the neck.

Runner: A white area seen on the back of the feet in Birmans.

Self-coloured: Solid-coloured.

Shaded or shading: Colour change at the tip of the hair or in certain areas (particularly the upper legs).

Silver: Refers to the silver ground colour of a tipped*, shaded or tabby cat with the inhibitor gene, or the undercoat of a smoke cat; a brilliant silver white caused by the elimination of yellow pigmentation.

Sire: The male parent of a cat.

Smoke: Colouring of 50 per cent to 80 per cent of the hair shaft, the rest being silver*.

Sorrel: A colour name given to Abyssinians or Somalis. A cinnamon* ticked* tabby that has a high degree of red. Sometimes referred to as 'Red', a misnomer in that it is not a true red and does not have OO in the genotype*.

Spectacles: A lighter area surrounding the eyes in a coloured mask* (as in Siamese, Birmans and Colourpoint Persians).

Spotted: A pattern displaying clearly defined spots of a darker colour; a type of tabby* marking.

Spread: The distance between the ears or eyes.

Standard: The detailed description of each breed, describing the ultimate in 'perfection'. Used by judges as the criteria against which to evaluate individual animals.

Sternum: The breastbone. At the rear end is a cartilage, the xiphisternum; if this sticks out and is obvious to the touch it is a withholding fault for all breeds.

Stop: The short incline between the forepart of the skull and the muzzle*, or a concave curve occurring in the nose at or just below eye level; may be slight or very marked.

Stud book: A book of breeds prepared by an organisation that establishes pedigrees.

Tabby or agouti*: Refers to any of the tabby patterns. The agouti gene must be present for full expression of a tabby pattern.

Tabby point: Describes a cat whose points* are coloured with tabby* markings.

Thumbprint: A round mark found on the upper part of the back of the ears in tabbies*; this paler patch actually shows the ground colour.

TICA: The International Cat Association, an international organisation that governs breed recognition and lays down its own breed standards.

Ticked tabby: The most extreme form of tabby;* each hair is banded in alternately dark and light colours.

Tipped: A form of tabby* in which only the tip of the hair is coloured (chinchilla*).

Tortie: See tortoiseshell*.

Tortoiseshell: A mixture of red and black, chocolate or cinnamon, or cream and blue, lilac, fawn or caramel, displayed as a rule only in females, although the rare male tortoiseshell has been produced. A male with this colouring is usually sterile.

Triangle: Used to describe a particular head shape seen in some breeds, such as Siamese and Orientals.

Tufts: The extension of the hairs from the tips of the ears; a desired characteristic in Maine Coons and Norwegians; discouraged in Persians and Exotics.

Undercoat: The woolly or down hairs that are the finest of the three types of hair of which a cat's coat is composed. Also used to describe the end of the hair nearer to the skin in smokes, shaded, and so on.

Van pattern: A particoloured pattern; the most extreme expression of the white spotting gene*. Usually exhibits a coloured cap and tail, although a few small spots may appear on the lower back near the base of the tail.

Whippy: Describes a type of long, slender, flexible tail: seen in the Cornish Rex, Siamese, Orientals and Sphynx.

Whisker pad: The fleshy part of the upper lip on either side of the nose, from which the whiskers grow.

White spotting (S) gene: The gene responsible for white with colour patterns; has incomplete dominance in the heterozygous* form (when it produces mitted and bicolour patterns).

YOUR CAT'S PHYSIOLOGY

How the body functions

Physiology deals with body functions – the activities of the organs and systems, and the way they interact. Physiologically the cat is similar to other mammals, including humans. This section focuses on what is specific to the cat's physiology, and discusses the animal's different body functions in detail.

The senses

Vision

The retina and pupil of the domestic cat's eye, although much the same as those of other mammals, do differ in important ways. All retinas contain light receptor cells: cones and rods. The cones detect colour and fine detail, but require a lot of light to function; they don't react in dusk. The rods, however, give black-and-white vision and are sensitive to dim light.

The cat, a nocturnal animal, has evolved a retina with a greater proportion of rods than most other animals. In addition, layers of reflective cells, the tapetum lucidum, form a mirror behind the rods and cones, which bounces light back to them for a second hit. (This is why we see a cat's eyes glowing in the dark.) Thus the cat's night vision is particularly strong (see page 56).

The cat's vision is perfectly adapted to different light conditions. The pupils are narrow slits in bright light, but become round at night or when the light dims.

When it is dark, the pupil opens into a large circle, letting in whatever glimmer of light there might be. In bright light the pupil contracts – to a tiny circle in most animals – limiting the light that enters the eye. The cat's round pupil shrinks to a thin vertical slit in bright light. The slit pupil closes more completely than a circular one, thus protecting the cat's highly sensitive retina.

The cat's distinctive whiskers are essential to its sense of touch.

Cats have stereoscopic vision. This means that when a cat looks at a bird, for instance, it can judge the distance between itself and the bird accurately. The bird, however, must look at the cat first with one eye, then the other, in order to judge how far away the cat is. By the time the bird has assessed this distance, the likelihood is that the cat will be on it. The cat's comparatively large eyes, deeply set in the sockets, face forward. This means that the cat must move its head, and sometimes its body, to see what is around it.

Touch

Vibrissae or whiskers – large stiff hairs growing in neat rows on either side of the upper lip – play a major role in the cat's acute sense of touch. Rooted in an inner layer of the skin called the dermis, the base of each whisker has many nerve endings that provide instant information about everything it brushes against and even about changes in air currents when anything moves. The cat finds its whiskers particularly useful in dim light or when stalking prey. Using powerful muscles at the whiskers' base, the cat projects them forward to discover obstacles in its path.

The eyebrows, cheek hairs, nose tip and paws are other tactile-sensitive areas.

Smell

Cats generally have a very keen sense of smell, approximately 30 times more powerful than that of a human. This has two practical consequences.

A cat's meal will seem tasty or not depending on its smell, especially since cats have relatively few taste buds – 473 in cats compared to 9,000 in humans. (Cats generally prefer lukewarm food, for example, because it has a stronger aroma. They are especially sensitive to odours of substances such as fish, which contain nitrogen.) A cat with nasal congestion may refuse to eat at all, simply because it cannot smell what is in its dish.

A cat marks out its territory chiefly through the use of smells. Both males and females use urine to make their marks, and sometimes excrement or secretions from the skin around the lips. A cat that rubs its cheeks against an object such as a door or a piece of furniture – or against its owner – is impregnating that object or person with its smell and in this way staking out its private property.

When on the hunt, the cat uses all its senses for maximum effectiveness.

Hearing

Cats have a wider hearing range than humans, especially in the high frequencies, and therefore live in a different world of sound to ours. Like most mammals, cats have highly mobile ears that can turn to detect sounds more clearly and to identify the location of those sounds.

With their highly developed senses of hearing and vision, cats are ideally suited to hunting at dusk and during the night, especially when the moon is shining. This is why even domestic cats are often more active at night than during the day.

Digestion

Cats are carnivores, their organs designed to handle a diet of raw meat. Their teeth are shaped to ready food for digestion: the incisors to grab prey, the pointed canines to kill it, and the premolars and molars to cut and tear it apart, after which it is swallowed in large chunks.

Stomach

The digestive process begins in the cat's mouth, then continues in the stomach. Large amounts of hydrochloric acid secreted there break down food into components the body can absorb.

Intestines

Most of the transformation of food into nutrients and all the absorption of nutrients take place in the small intestine. Fats can only be absorbed after they are converted into an emulsion by fluid from the bile. The enzymes required for digestion are supplied by the pancreas and the intestine, and these go to work in the neutralising process. The stomach's contents are transformed from acidic to alkaline by bicarbonate supplied from large quantities of pancreatic juices.

Since a cat's digestive system is designed primarily for meat, the small intestine is very short. When a cat has diarrhoea, it can quickly become undernourished and lose weight.

Adapted as they are to a carnivorous diet, the digestive enzymes will not absorb vegetable foods properly. A diet too high in vegetable matter can reduce the cat's overall nutrition, and cause diarrhoea and gas production in the large intestine. Most vets recommend a cat be fed high-quality animal protein and fat. Any dietary changes should be made gradually over several weeks because the cat's digestive system is comparatively fragile. When you find the particular diet that your cat thrives on – and likes – it's best to stick to it with little variation.

Metabolism and diet

Metabolism refers to the chemical reactions that make the digested food available for essential cell activities, and transform it into energy.

The prey that makes up a cat's natural diet contains all the nutrients its body requires. If the cat devours skin, muscle, bones and entrails of small animals, it has very little need for other food. Thus the digestive system of the cat has a limited ability for metabolising essential nutrients from carbohydrate or vegetable sources. For proper nutrition, therefore, the domestic cat's food should contain the same nutrients that are found in its natural diet.

Protein requirements

Cats must consume a great deal of protein. In fact protein should provide at least 25 per cent of the cat's energy supply or, in food terms, 25 to 30 per cent of the dry content per serving. A diet of less than 19 per cent protein may cause a deficiency in amino acids, protein's basic structural units. A diet of 19 to 25 per cent protein may lead to overeating as the cat attempts to consume sufficient protein; the result is often an unhealthy weight gain.

The diet of all animals must include 10 essential amino acids. The body cannot synthesise these – they must come from the diet. The amino acids are lysine, leucine, isoleucine, threonine, histidine, tryptophan, arginine, methionine, phenylalanine and valine. Certain of these are of particular importance to the cat.

Arginine is necessary to convert ammonia, which is produced when protein is metabolised, into urea that can be easily eliminated from the body. This process is important in the cat because of its high protein intake. An inadequate supply of arginine can result in acute ammonia toxicity, which can lead to death; consequently it must account for about 1 per cent of dry content in the cat's diet.

Lysine is important for growth. It is found in abundance in animal proteins, but it can be destroyed by overcooking. Taurine is also needed for feline growth – in fact, cats have a greater need for it than other animals, but they cannot synthesise sufficient amounts. A deficiency, over time, can cause irreversible degeneration of the retina, and eventually blindness. Cats fed a diet low in taurine can also develop reproductive problems and a form of heart disease called dilated cardiomyopathy. Plant products are poor sources of taurine, but meat and fish contain high levels of it. Although commercial cat foods are formulated with sufficient amounts of taurine, dog foods are not and should not be substituted for cat food.

Fat requirements

A carnivore can digest fats easily because it can secrete ample bile and lipase, a digestive enzyme produced in the pancreas. Fats can represent between 30 and 40 per cent of its total food.

As with amino acids, there are also fatty acids essential to a cat's health.

Cats have a special need for arachidonic acid, which many other animals can synthesise from linoleic acid, found in many foods other than flesh. Arachidonic acid is found only in animal fats, especially fish oil. Consequently a cat's diet must contain a large proportion of fat, one of the principal components of living cells, and this fat must come from animal sources.

Vitamin requirements

Vitamin metabolism in cats differs from that of other animals in a number of ways. First, vitamin A occurs naturally only in animal tissue. Vitamin A precursors (B-carotene) are found in abundant supply in plants such as carrots. Most other mammals can convert B-carotene to vitamin A, an ability that cats lack.

Cats have a much greater need than most animals for the water-soluble B vitamins. In the case of pyridoxine (vitamin B_6) and niacin, for example, they require four times as much as dogs. They need pyridoxine to convert dietary protein into energy. Niacin is essential in metabolising carbohydrates and fats, and for the general functioning of the digestive system. Yet unlike other animals, cats do not convert tryptophan (an essential amino acid) to niacin.

Feline metabolism

Cats are particularly vulnerable to poisoning. Their livers are unable to metabolise toxins and other chemicals efficiently, so even a small dose of poison is life-threatening. Cats are particularly sensitive to insecticides, preservatives used in food products, and medications. Since even common drugs such as aspirin and paracetamol are eliminated very slowly, they can be toxic. Do not administer any medicines to your cat without consulting a vet.

Excretion

Urine is produced by the kidneys in two stages. A diluted urine consisting of water, urea and various mineral salts is extracted from the blood by the million or so filtering units called nephrons that lie in the outer section of the kidneys. Since the kidneys' main role is to maintain the body's water balance, nearly all of this fluid and some of the other substances are subsequently reabsorbed into the blood. The excess water and other waste products are then transported to the bladder and eventually excreted as urine.

The ancestors of the cat lived in semi-desert areas and rarely drank water. They didn't have to: 60 to 70 per cent of their prey's body weight was water.

Today's cats also drink very sparingly, but unlike their predecessors, their normal diet often contains little water. This can lead to constipation, dehydration and urinary tract problems. Without adequate quantities of water to flush waste matter from the body, for example, mineral salts in the urine will form stones in the urinary organs.

The formation of stones in the bladder can be influenced by other factors, too. When a cat eats, acidic gastric juices are secreted in quantities more or less proportional to the amount of food eaten. The blood becomes alkaline in order to neutralise the acid. Alkaline urine is then created, which can promote the formation of mineral salts and stones. For this reason, your cat may need a diet that does not produce alkaline urine. Ask your vet's advice. It is also essential that the cat have ready access to water.

Residue waste from food is expelled from the anus as faeces.

Reproduction

Puberty and the seasons

In a typical male (tom) cat, the production of reproductive cells, a process called spermatogenesis, begins when the animal is about 5 months old. Although most cats will not yet be capable of fertilisation, reproductive behaviour such as the marking of territory and the mounting of females can start as early as 4 months.

In the female (or queen), puberty is signalled by the first heat, the age varying with the breed. Domestics, Birmans, the Rex and the Sphynx breeds reach puberty around 6 to 9 months. Siamese, Orientals and Burmese are more precocious and their puberty begins at 4 to 6 months. Persians reach puberty later than most cats, when they are 12 months or even older.

The seasons of the year also have an important bearing. If a cat reaches puberty between October and December, it may not go into heat until the following spring.

Sexual activity in cats is largely governed by changes in the length of daylight hours, a phenomenon called photoperiodism. Shorter days will result in sexual dormancy in the female and lowered fertility in the male. Sexual activity peaks from January to October and occasionally stops altogether in the middle of the summer. These variations in sexual activity prevent the birth of kittens during the cold winter months.

Reproductive surgery

As cats reach sexual maturity, they often develop undesirable behaviour. Male cats tend to roam, fight with other cats, spray urine to mark territory, and become more aggressive towards people and other animals. Females will have heat cycles during which they are extremely vocal, and they will deposit urine markings. Early reproductive surgery typically prevents these objectionable behaviours.

Male cats generally are castrated, or neutered, by the removal of both testicles at 5 to 10 months of age. Most vets recommend that a female cat have an ovariohysterectomy, or spay, before her first heat, and before she is 6 months old.

The female cat's cycle

All female mammals who have intermittent sexual activity have a cycle of several phases:
• anoestrus, a period in which the female will have little or no sexual activity;

Sunshine is more than a luxury; the amount of daylight governs the cat's reproductive functions

• prooestrus, a period immediately before heat, which normally lasts about 2 days;
• oestrus, a period when the female is in heat and mates voluntarily, which generally lasts from 5 to 8 days. There is great variety in the length of oestrus, but it may last anywhere from 3 to 20 days.

The female cat's behaviour when she is in heat is unmistakable. She is generally nervous, caterwauls and crouches, flattening her back while arching her pelvis upwards, then kneads with her hind legs and lifts her tail to the side.

In most species, ovulation occurs spontaneously during this phase. In the cat, it is triggered by coitus, which follows a definite pattern. The male sniffs the female's genital region while she crouches, then mounts her, biting her loose neck fur. Penetration lasts only a few seconds. The female emits a dramatic coital 'scream' and breaks the male's hold by turning and striking him with her paws. As the male withdraws, the female rolls and thrashes and licks her vulval area. Ovulation occurs about 24 to 48 hours later.

Sexual cycle of the cat

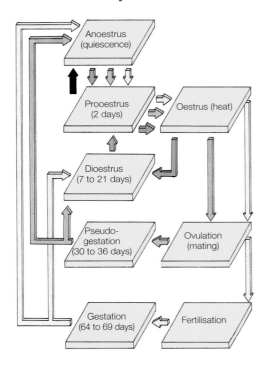

Fewer than 50 per cent of female cats ovulate after a single encounter, so it is recommended that the male and female be left together for several days to ensure pregnancy. Suprafecundation (multiple impregnation) occurs when several toms sire a single litter.

After oestrus, there are three possible outcomes. If coitus did not occur, there will be no ovulation, and the cat will enter the period between two oestruses called

A female cat in heat.

dioestrus. On the other hand, if ovulation occurs without fertilisation, there will be a false pregnancy. If fertilisation is successful, gestation will start.

Dioestrus is the interval between two oestruses when ovulation does not occur. It normally ranges from 3 to 14 days during the breeding season, but may be as long as 30 days.

Infrequently, and most commonly in older cats that have never given birth, a cat may show signs of continuous oestrus. This condition is called nymphomania.

A false pregnancy, which lasts from 35 to 70 days, corresponds to the time during which progesterone, the hormone that supports pregnancy, is secreted by the corpus luteum, a structure that forms in the ovaries when ovulation has occurred.

This is followed by dioestrus, when the interval between two oestruses is extended. Some breeders use this technicality to control reproductive periods by artificially stimulating ovulation.

Gestation lasts from 62 to 70 days, with the average duration between 64 and 66 days, counting the first coupling as the starting date.

Implantation of the embryos within the uterus occurs approximately 13 days after mating. The placenta is the organ that unites the foetus to the uterus by way of the umbilical cord. In the cat the maternal and foetal tissues lie alongside each other and are not intermingled. Therefore the foetus does not receive antibodies from its mother prior to birth. This makes it particularly important for the newborn kitten to receive its first mother's milk, its colostrum, because it is rich in maternal antibodies.

Each foetus has its own placenta, and it is important that each of these placentas, or afterbirths, is expelled as the kittens are born, otherwise the mother may have difficulties with the remaining births.

Pregnancy is usually diagnosed by a direct medical examination of the cat, and cannot be diagnosed by measuring hormone levels as with other species.

After the third week of pregnancy, the cat's nipples often enlarge or become darker pink. During the period between the third and fourth week, a vet should be able

A queen waiting to give birth.

to feel the foetuses, because by now they should be between 1.5 and 2 cm (0.6-0.8 inch) in diameter. Between the 36th and 38th day, the kittens' skeletons will show up on an X-ray or ultrasound scan and the age of the foetuses can be determined from their measurements.

Giving birth

About 12 hours before the kittens are born, the mother cat's rectal temperature drops a few degrees below the normal of 38 to 38.4°C (100.4-101.2°F). The teats will then enlarge and often begin producing milk. But the surest sign that birth is imminent is a distinct change in the mother cat's behaviour.

She becomes nervous and, a few hours before giving birth, washes herself continuously. She may prepare a nest with her claws. She will start panting and, soon after, labour begins.

The first contractions of the uterus are barely noticeable. The mother cat will lie down and begin to purr.

Then the contractions become more violent, with labour lasting from 10 to 60 minutes until the first kitten is born. The afterbirth is expelled up to 15 minutes after each kitten.

As soon as each kitten appears, the mother breaks the amniotic sac surrounding the kitten and licks the newborn. She will usually eat the afterbirth.

The kittens are born at intervals of 5 to 120 minutes. In some cases, kittens may be born half a day or even a whole day after the first ones. These extended delays are no cause for alarm as long as the mother cat seems to be handling the births well and is no longer showing signs of imminent labour.

There is cause for alarm, though, if the mother stops eating 24 hours after giving birth, if she has a temperature above 39.4°C (103°F), or if she will neither groom nor nurse her kittens. If your cat has any of these symptoms after having kittens, you should call your vet immediately.

Nursing begins soon after the kittens are born. The kittens will nurse frequently until they are weaned, about eight weeks after their birth. During this period, the mother eats two to three times more food than normal and needs a great deal of calcium. Cats, unlike other animals, can have heats during this stage, sometimes as early as one week after giving birth.

Although most cats, even first-time mothers, seem to know how to look after their kittens, some cats ignore their kittens totally. Newly born kittens are unable to look after themselves, and those that are rejected should be treated as orphans (see the box on page 178).

Growth of kittens

Kittens are born deaf and blind. From the top of the skull to the base of the tail, they measure about 14.5 cm (5½ inches) and usually weigh between 80 and 110 g (3 and 4 ounces).

The nursing box must be kept warm – a temperature of about 30°C (86°F) is recommended – until the kittens begin to suckle normally. The most frequent causes of kittens dying shortly after birth are hypothermia (a subnormal body temperature) and hypoglycemia (a decrease of sugar in the blood).

Determining the sex of kittens is not always easy. One way is to examine them from behind. The anus and genitals are always farther apart in males than females. At birth, the distance between the two in the male is about 13 mm (one-half inch) and in the female about 8 mm (one-third inch). The scrotum, the external pouch

The newborn kitten needs the mother's 'first milk', or colostrum, immediately after birth.

containing the testes, is more visible when a male kitten is still wet. At birth the testicles are normally in place, but occasionally they will not descend into the scrotum permanently until the 10th or 14th week.

A kitten should gain weight at a rate of 10 g (1/3 ounce) a day, and at three weeks will weigh between 300 and 350 g (10-12 ounces). It should reach 700 to 800 g (24-28 ounces) after six or seven weeks. The fewer kittens the mother has to feed, the faster they are likely to gain weight.

An average litter is four kittens. Some breeds have larger litters. Queens giving birth for the first time sometimes have only one kitten.

Soon after birth, the kittens will suckle 2 to 3 ml (about 0.10 fluid ounce) of milk every three hours. As the days pass, they will suckle less often but will take more milk each time, reaching 10 ml (0.35 fluid ounce) of milk seven times a day at one month of age.

After each nursing session, the mother will lick the kittens' anogenital regions to make the kittens urinate and defecate: she then swallows the results.

Kittens may open their eyes at 1 to 14 days, depending on their breed. In the third week they begin to play and leave the nest and by the fourth week they can start on solid food (see pages 195-198). Weaning is a gradual process and many kittens will continue to feed from their mother for several weeks.

A newly weaned kitten will probably need five small meals a day to keep healthy. As it grows, and its capacity increases, it should have four larger meals each day. When the cat is 9 months old it should be well developed and have two good meals a day of 110 to 140 g (about 4-5 ounces) of high-quality commercial cat food, either canned or dry.

When the average adult cat is fully grown, it will need 50 calories for each 450 g (pound) of body weight daily, although this might vary according to how active the cat is. A nursing mother cat will need more food. Neutered cats generally need less since they tend to be less active.

From this brief survey of a cat's physiology, we can better understand the diseases that afflict them.

General disorders

Organic diseases

The cat is a secretive animal. When it is sick, it displays few symptoms. It concentrates on conserving its strength to fight its illness. Owners, therefore, must watch their cats carefully. Even the slightest change in the animal's activity could indicate that it is sick.

This section explores the disorders that can afflict the cat's internal systems, and how these disorders can lead to disease.

The cat is also prone to infectious diseases, most of them viral. An index at the end of this chapter (page 188) lists some of the common infections.

Cardiovascular system

Heart

The main cause of heart disease in cats is disorders of the cardiac muscle. These abnormalities, called cardiomyopathy, take several forms:
• Hypertrophic, where the ventricle walls in the chamber of the heart thicken and the volume of the cavities decreases;
• Dilated, where the ventricle walls become thin and tend to balloon out under pressure;
• Intermediate, in which the wall of the heart is affected by dilation and hypertrophy (enlargement);
• Restrictive, which scars the inner lining of the heart, making it tough and fibrous.

In all these conditions, the volume of blood pumped into the arteries at each beat of the heart is lower than normal. Blood then pools in the ventricles, which can cause a blood clot, called a thrombus, to form. As the disease progresses, the body compensates for the lack of blood flow by increasing the heart rate. If this does not work, the tissues of the body do not receive enough oxygen. The cat's respiratory rate will increase, and it will tire from even the slightest effort. In many cases, there will be one of two fatal complications. The first is congestive heart failure caused by pooling of fluid in the lungs. The second occurs when the blood clot that has formed within the heart moves into the descending aorta and blocks key blood vessels; this can lead to kidney failure and/or paralysis of the cat's back legs.

Heart disease in cats is often fairly advanced before there are noticeable signs. When treatment is started late in the course of the disease, the response can be disappointing. Unfortunately, the causes of most forms of feline heart disease are not fully understood.

Blood and anaemia

When the quantity of haemoglobin – the oxygen-carrying substance in red blood cells – is below normal, the cat is said to be anaemic. The first outward sign is pale mucous membranes: in cats this shows up on the gums. If the anaemia is severe, the cat will also suffer from rapid breathing (tachypnoea) and an accelerated heartbeat. Many underlying problems can cause anaemia:
• Blood loss due to injury or poisoning by anticoagulants, especially certain types of rat poison;
• Abnormal haemolysis, a widespread destruction of red blood cells within the body. This can be caused by the blood parasite *Haemobartonella felis*, which is spread by biting insects; feline leukaemia virus (see page 184); poisoning; or an auto-immune disorder in which the body creates antibodies that attack its own red blood cells. Many of these conditions can be treated.
• Nonregeneration or inadequate production of red blood cells. This can be caused by chloramphenicol poisoning; by feline leukaemia virus; by a kidney disorder in its final stages (see page 168); by chronic inflammatory diseases, including feline infectious peritonitis; and by the invasion of bone marrow by abnormal cells which may or may not be malignant.

Digestive system

The mouth and pharynx

The most common form of oral disease found in the cat is the gingivitis and periodontal disease caused by plaque and tartar buildup on the teeth. If left untreated, the gumline will become progressively inflamed and painful. In more serious cases cats may refuse to eat, may salivate excessively, and may even become aggressive. In cases of severe periodontal infection, when the gums recede and the roots are exposed, painful root tip abscesses can develop. Most vets recommend routine dental care, which may include home care such as brushing, as well as regular cleanings by the vet.

Possible tooth defects include cervical line lesions, or neck lesions – so-called because they occur at the gumline or neck of the tooth. They resemble human cavities, but do not have the same cause. Teeth affected by neck lesions can be quite painful if the lesion extends to the root. This also weakens the teeth making them susceptible to fracture.

Tooth fractures arising from accidents are also fairly common, especially with the long, narrow canine, or fang, teeth. If the fracture is spotted immediately, the tooth may be saved by performing root canal treatment. Otherwise, the root of the tooth is susceptible to infection. If this occurs, the cat is likely to develop a painful root tip abscess. For this reason, your vet is likely to recommend that any fractured teeth are extracted.

There are other causes of severe gingivitis in the cat that are not completely understood. Feline immunodeficiency virus (FIV) is commonly associated with these very serious cases, as is chronic calicivirus infection. Calicivirus most commonly causes an upper respiratory infection. Most of these conditions seem to be triggered by a deficiency in the immune system. Treatments to make these cats more comfortable range from the administration of anti-inflammatory cortisone-type drugs and antibiotics to the removal of all the cat's teeth.

Less frequently, cats may develop tumours within their mouths or throats. Biopsies should always be performed. Even though such lesions are frequently cancerous, some are benign and treatable. Unfortunately, cats hate having their mouths examined, and growths can become quite large before they are noticed. Often the first symptoms are eating difficulties and excessive salivation, frequently blood-tinged.

Many of the problems a domestic cat has with its teeth are a result of its diet. Cats that eat wild prey have less plaque and tartar and consequently less gingivitis and periodontal disease. Eating commercial dry food helps control the buildup of plaque and tartar.

Gingivitis, causes redness of the gums, inflammation of the mucous membranes in the mouth.

Oesophagus

The oesophagus is a long, narrow, muscular tube that extends from the back of the throat to the stomach. Its purpose is to act as a conduit for food and fluid from the mouth to the stomach.

Because cats are fastidious eaters, the oesophagus is rarely obstructed by foreign objects. However, it is subject to a number of diseases and abnormalities which may make swallowing difficult, or may prevent it entirely.

Chief among those diseases is megaoesophagus. This occurs when food fails to pass into the stomach for whatever reason, and instead accumulates in an ever-ballooning pouch on the wall of the animal's oesophagus.

Common causes include thoracic tumours, failure of the sphincter (the circular muscle between the oesophagus and the stomach) to relax during swallowing to allow food into the stomach, and reflux of the stomach's acidic contents. Cats with this condition are liable to inhale regurgitated food. This in turn can lead to the development of bronchopneumonia.

Disorders of the oesophagus may sometimes require surgery. In some cases, the vet may recommend that you place the cat's food on top of an elevated platform in such a way that gravity aids the passage of food while the cat is actually eating.

Stomach

Gastritis, or inflammation of the lining of the stomach, is a common condition in cats. It may be caused by infection (see page 181), allergies, parasites, or ingestion of rancid food, wild animals, toxic chemicals or a foreign body, such as a toy or a piece of foil. Hair balls swallowed by the cat can become so large that they cause stomach disorders. This is one reason why regular, thorough grooming is important.

In the case of gastritis, frothy, blood-stained vomit is the first symptom you are likely to see. This will be followed by diarrhoea. Be aware that this combination often leads to dehydration.

Vomiting is not always a symptom of any illness. Even healthy cats may vomit as often as once or twice a week, and greedy cats often vomit after eating too much too quickly.

Intestines

The intestinal tract, a major part of the digestive system, has two parts: the small intestine, where nutrients from food are absorbed into the body, and the large intestine where fluid and additional nutrients are absorbed, and subsequently where undigested food residue and other matter are stored until the cat has a bowel movement. Feline disease can affect either or both intestines. Cats with intestinal problems generally suffer from diarrhoea or constipation.

Often, cats will develop diarrhoea after an abrupt change in diet, and the cure may simply be to return to the previous foods. Many cats cannot digest dairy products and will develop diarrhoea when given milk or cheese. This intolerance stems from the lack of lactase, the enzyme that breaks down milk sugar.

Diarrhoea can also be a reaction to antibiotics or other medicines. If your cat develops diarrhoea or begins vomiting after taking medicine, call your vet. Most cases are easily treated by a 24- to 48-hour fast, often in combination with an anti-diarrhoeal medicine. However, some intestinal diseases can be fatal, so be sure to see your vet if the constipation or diarrhoea does not clear up completely within a day or two.

Immediate veterinary intervention is essential in the case of an obstruction of the intestine. This usually occurs when the cat swallows an object that it can neither digest nor pass. Toys, particularly small balls, are common culprits, as are Christmas tree tinsel and yarn. Infrequently, a large hair ball can also cause an obstruction. The diagnosis is usually made with the aid of X-rays, and treatment may include surgery.

Occasionally cats will swallow sewing thread attached to a needle. If one end of this thread becomes looped under the tongue, the cat develops what is known as string foreign body. The swallowed end of the thread will continue to move along with each contraction of the intestines, pulling the loops of the bowel tighter and tighter into an accordion-like mass. If the thread is not removed, necrosis of the bowel, in which tissue weakens and eventually dies, may result. The thread could then actually cut through the bowel and cause the intestines' contents to leak into the abdomen, which could cause a fatal case of peritonitis. Cats that are suffering from a string foreign body will vomit and generally refuse to eat. It is imperative that you do not try to remove the string by pulling as this will worsen the situation.

Sharp objects like sewing needles or toothpicks can perforate the intestines. If you know your cat has swallowed a sharp object, see your vet immediately. Your cat is likely to suffer a punctured peritoneum.

Intestinal diseases can be caused by viral infections such as panleucopenia, fungal infections and bacterial infections such as salmonella and *Campylobacter jejuni*. These diseases cause severe diarrhoea and are particularly dangerous since they can be transmitted to humans.

Cats of 7 years or older that suffer from diarrhoea and weight loss may have hyperthyroidism. This is caused by overproduction of the hormone that controls the cat's metabolic rate. The diagnosis can be made following a blood test, and the disease is treatable.

Intestinal parasites are among the most common causes of intestinal diseases. Those affecting domestic cats include roundworms, hookworms, tapeworms, giardia and coccidia.

Roundworms, often called ascarids, are the most common. Two species, *Toxocara cati* and *Toxacaris leonina*, can infect cats. Infestation occurs if the cat ingests infected eggs which are usually found in the soil where an animal suffering from roundworms had a bowel movement. Kittens can catch the infection from their mother through her milk.

Roundworm eggs hatch into larvae in the intestine, then migrate through the liver and lungs of the infected cats, finally returning to the intestine where they become adult worms. Cats suffering from these parasites may lose weight and suffer from vomiting, diarrhoea and noticeable abdominal distension.

Diagnosis of roundworms is made by spotting the long, spaghetti-shaped worms in the stools or vomit, or by microscopic examination of a stool specimen.

Two species of blood-sucking hookworms, the *Ancylostoma tubaeforma* and the *Ancylostoma braziliense*, infect the cat, though both are rare in Britain. Infection can occur through ingestion of larvae, or through penetration of the skin. The immature larvae migrate through the lungs and eventually inhabit the intestine where a large infestation can consume considerable quantities of blood. This produces symptoms, such as anaemia and blood in the stool, that are related to this

Rice-shaped egg packets around the anus are a sure sign of tapeworms.

blood loss. Diagnosis is made by microscopic examination of the stool.

Most tapeworm infestations occur after a cat ingests an infected flea when grooming itself. Occasionally cats become infected after eating small mammals such as rodents and rabbits. The most noticeable clinical sign is the presence of tapeworm segments in the cat's stools or around its anus. These segments, called proglottids, are not the entire worm but are packets of eggs. Diagnosis is made by spotting the rice-shaped segments or by microscopic examination of the stool.

Giardiasis, an infection that can spread to humans, is contracted when a cat ingests single-celled *Giardia lamblia* found in the stool of infected animals. Giardia cause diarrhoea and weight loss. Diagnosis is made by laboratory analysis of the cat's faeces or by the cat's response to treatment.

Roundworm, or ascarid, coils.

There are several kinds of coccidia that can affect the cat. All are likely to cause diarrhoea. The most serious perhaps is *Toxoplasma gondii*. This infection can be spread among humans and is of particular risk to unborn children. Therefore pregnant women should guard against tooclose contact with their cat if it roams outdoors. Diagnosis of an infestation is made by microscopic examination of a stool specimen.

Cats can also develop cancer of the intestines as well as a number of other diseases that affect their ability to digest and absorb the nutrients in food. They can also suffer from inflammatory bowel diseases.

Liver

The liver has many complex and diverse functions. It manufactures and excretes bile, which is necessary for proper fat absorption, it detoxifies and excretes many potentially toxic substances, and it produces many blood proteins, including those necessary for normal blood clotting.

The most common symptom of severe liver disease, and the most noticeable, is jaundice. Cats that are jaundiced will have a yellowish cast to their skin, gums, and the sclera (white areas) of their eyes. Jaundice can occur with other disorders, but is seen in liver disease because of an increase in the yellow-brown bile pigment bilirubin in the cat's bloodstream. The liver is responsible for excreting bilirubin, a product in the breakdown of red blood cells. When the liver is not functioning properly or if there is an obstruction to the flow of bile, which contains the bilirubin, the pigment will cause the animal to appear jaundiced.

Idiopathic hepatic lipidosis, or fatty liver syndrome, is one of the least understood of the diseases that affect the cat's liver. It usually occurs in obese cats. The most common clinical sign is lack of appetite, which often lasts several weeks. Other symptoms include lethargy and intermittent vomiting and diarrhoea. Treatment requires forced feeding of a balanced cat food diet until the cat will eat on its own. Because this forced feeding may take several weeks, it is often necessary to have a feeding tube placed into the cat's stomach. Even with very intensive treatment, this condition is frequently fatal.

Cholangiohepatitis, simply defined, is an inflammatory disorder of the hepatobiliary system which includes both liver cells and the bile excretory system. The causes of cholangiohepatitis are not well understood, but some cases are probably caused by bacterial infections. The final stage of this condition is cirrhosis. Treatment usually consists of antibiotics and cortisone-type drugs.

Since the liver is responsible for the detoxification of many of the chemicals that enter the body, it is particularly susceptible to injury from these chemicals. Generally, treatment is specific for the poison and the cat's chances of a cure are usually related to the type and amount of toxin involved.

Cats can develop cancer of the liver. Cancer can be either primary, developing from cells in the liver, or it can be metastatic, involving cancer that initially developed elsewhere in the body.

Some cats are born with a congenital abnormality of the blood vessels of the liver called a portosystemic shunt. In this condition the vessels that generally lead into the liver from the intestines bypass the liver and go immediately into the circulation. Because the blood bypasses the liver where detoxification occurs, the kittens suffering from this condition have symptoms related to poisoning such as loss of appetite, excessive salivation, depression, blindness, abnormal behaviour and even seizures. Treatment involves surgery to correct the abnormality.

Bile is excreted from the liver through the bile ducts. Occasionally these will become obstructed. The most common causes are gallstones and sludged bile, which is associated with cholangiohepatitis. Inflammation of the pancreas and bile duct cancer can also cause a bile duct obstruction. Cats suffering from this disorder are very ill, and surgery is the only way to remove the obstruction.

Cats are also subject to a number of less frequently seen liver disorders such as bacterial abscesses, benign cysts, fungal and parasitic diseases, and trauma.

Pancreas

The pancreas is actually two totally separate glands occupying the same organ. The exocrine pancreas produces and excretes digestive enzymes. The endocrine pancreas consists of clusters of cells called the islets of Langerhans. These clusters, dispersed among the exocrine cells, produce insulin.

Diseases of the exocrine pancreas are difficult to diagnose in the cat. Pancreatitis, or inflammation of the exocrine pancreas, is associated with a number of conditions such as cholangiohepatitis, pancreatic fluke infestations and trauma, but the disease is still poorly understood. Symptoms can vary and are usually none too specific. Weight loss, depression and loss of appetite are the most common complaints, with vomiting, increased thirst and diarrhoea occurring less frequently. Some cats have abdominal pain and/or enlarged livers. The diagnosis can generally be made during a surgical exploration of the abdomen, but sometimes it cannot be confirmed until after the cat has died. Treatment is directed at reversing the cause, if known, and at providing supportive and symptomatic care. Fluid replacement, antibiotics and withholding food and water when the cat is vomiting are usually recommended. Some vets believe pancreatitis in cats is far more common than the number of diagnosed cases suggest. Many cats that have cyclical episodes of vomiting and general malaise followed by periods of normal health may have pancreatitis.

Occasionally a cat may develop exocrine pancreatic insufficiency. These cats' bodies lose the ability to manufacture the digestive enzymes produced by the exocrine pancreas. They generally have tremendous appetites, but tend to lose weight and have voluminous stools. Without the pancreatic enzymes, the food eaten by the cat cannot be absorbed and used for nutrition. A diagnosis is usually made if the cat responds appropriately to the treatment, which generally consists of adding pancreatic enzyme supplements to the diet. These supplements 'pre-digest' the cat's food, making it available for the animal's nourishment. Cats are also susceptible to cancer of the pancreas.

Problems of movement

The skeleton

Cats are active, athletic creatures, and this puts them at risk of suffering broken bones. This is especially true of cats that are allowed out of doors.

Luckily, cat bones heal well and quickly. With proper treatment most fractures will heal in 3 to 6 weeks, unless they become infected.

Unfortunately, there are cases where the outlook is not so optimistic. Cats are susceptible to several forms of bone cancer that increase the risk of fractures without preceding injury. Such a fracture, commonly called a pathologic fracture, is usually diagnosed by X-ray. This may be the first indication that the cat has cancer. The disease will interfere with normal healing of fractures.

Kittens fed an all-meat diet may be getting too little calcium and too much phosphorus, and may develop osteodystrophy, or nutritional secondary hyperparathyroidism. Kittens with this debilitating condition have paper-thin bones that can break easily. Deformities of the spinal column and pelvis are also common. Treatment is directed at correcting the nutritional imbalance. Generally the solution is to feed the kitten a good-quality commercial cat food, which should contain all the nutrients essential to healthy bone formation.

Adult cats are also affected by this condition, but they generally do not develop skeletal deformities; instead, they suffer from pathological fractures brought on by thinned bones. Cats with impaired kidney function or renal secondary hyperparathyroidism may also develop symptoms of osteodystrophy.

Cats that are fed a diet composed primarily of liver may be consuming too much vitamin A. They may, as a result, develop exostoses, bony spurs around their joints. Exostoses are extremely painful, but the condition can be stopped by feeding a good commercial cat food. Unfortunately, bony spurs that already exist will remain.

Rickets, seen in animals fed a diet low in calcium, is very uncommon in the cat.

Too much vitamin D on the other hand can be fatally toxic.

Those skeletal diseases related to imbalanced diets can be prevented by feeding a good quality commercial diet. Vitamin supplements should be used with caution and only with a vet's approval.

Muscles

Most muscle disorders are associated with trauma: injuries due to lacerations, punctures and bone fractures are fairly common. Bacterial infections sometimes result from such injuries and may have to be treated with antibiotics.

Drops often must be given for inflammations of the nose, but only on a vet's prescription.

Cats are known to suffer from a disorder called polymyositis in which the muscles become inflamed. Cats that suffer from the disorder exhibit an abnormal head posture, weakness of the limbs, and muscle pain. The cause of this rare disorder is not known, but fortunately most cats do respond well to corticosteroid (cortisone-like drug) treatments.

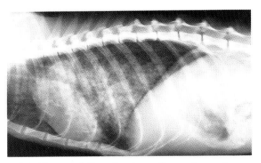

This X-ray of the chest, or thoracic region, reveals lesions in the lung.

Respiratory system

Rhinitis, which causes congestion and excessive discharges from the nostrils, is often seen in cats suffering from upper respiratory infections (see page 181). Nose drops prescribed by your vet may help relieve these symptoms.

Bronchopulmonary diseases

Bronchopulmonary diseases affect the lower airways and involve the pulmonary tissue below the level of the trachea. The most common affecting cats is bronchial asthma. This condition is not a single disease, but comprises a group of disorders with different causes and similar symptoms. One form is a familial immune-mediated disorder which can be passed along from generation to generation. Cats suffering from this disease will squat down, extend their necks and have a coughing fit. Some cats will vomit after an episode. About half of the cats with bronchial asthma have difficulty breathing and some 25 per cent wheeze. Most cats respond well to corticosteroids.

Symptoms of heartworm disease, *Dirofilaria immitis*, a rare cat parasite in Britain, are similar to those of bronchial asthma. Treatment depends on the severity of the disease.

Cats infected with the feline lungworm, *Aelurostrongylus abstrusus*, generally have few if any symptoms. Some cats suffer laboured breathing and require treatment.

Cats with severe upper respiratory disease may develop pneumonia. Unless treated quickly, the condition can be fatal.

Primary lung cancer is not common in the cat, but secondary malignant tumours (metastases) of the lung occur fairly frequently, as a result of primary cancer of some other organ.

Diseases of the pleura and pleural cavity

Inflammation of the pleurae, membranes that envelop the lungs and line the chest wall, produces fluid, called a pleural effusion. This compresses the lungs. (Pleural effusions may affect one or both sides of the chest.) As fluid accumulates in the pleural cavity, breathing becomes more difficult. If the condition is left untreated, the cat will die.

Different pleural effusions give rise to the following conditions:
• Haemothorax: an accumulation of blood in the pleural cavity. The condition is caused by physical injury, but it may also occur in cats suffering from anticoagulant poisoning or cancer;
• Chylothorax: an accumulation of chyle, lymphatic fluid, which can follow from cancer or heart disease;
• Pyothorax: an accumulation of pus caused by a bacterial infection. This usually follows a severe chest wound or puncture of the lung;
• Hydrothorax: an accumulation of watery fluid, following an injury to the lungs, diaphragmatic hernia (see below), heart failure or cancer.

Pleural disease may also occur in cats suffering from feline infectious peritonitis (see page 184).

X-rays are usually used to diagnose pleural diseases. The treatment for all pleural effusions is fundamentally the same. If a cat has difficulty breathing, fluid is removed from the pleural cavity. After the cat's condition has stabilised, further treatment aims to find and cure the underlying disorder.

Diaphragmatic hernia

The diaphragm is a muscle that separates the abdominal organs from the heart and lungs. Its main function is to aid breathing. A cat may suffer a tear, called a diaphragmatic hernia, often as a result of an accident. For example, a hernia may occur when a cat has been hit by a car. The seriousness of the condition depends on the size of the tear, and it may be complicated if the abdominal organs, such as liver, stomach, and intestines, intrude into the thorax. The treatment for a diaphragmatic hernia is surgical repair.

The urinary tract

Kidney disease

The kidneys filter toxins from the blood and maintain the fluid and electrolyte balance within the body. The end product of these functions is urine, which flows down small tubes called ureters into the bladder, where it is stored.

Feline congenital kidney diseases include polycystic renal disease, which occurs when large cysts develop in the kidneys and damage normal tissue, or when one kidney is missing.

Kidney stones occur in cats. The stones may remain within the kidney, or they may move down a ureter into the bladder. This problem becomes critical when the stone lodges within the ureter, stopping the flow of urine. Surgery is then necessary to remove the stones from the kidney or the ureter.

Glomerulonephritis is an inflammation of the kidney's filtering units (glomeruli). Although this condition is uncommon, it can hamper the removal of waste from the body, and cause death.

Infection of the kidneys, called pyelonephritis, can cause fever, lack of appetite, dehydration and weight loss. If not treated with antibiotics, pyelonephritis can lead to renal failure.

Acute renal failure (ARF), characterised by an abrupt deterioration in kidney function, leads to an inability to regulate water and electrolyte balance. This in turn leads to the development of uraemia – a buildup of toxins generally removed from the blood by the kidneys. There are three different forms of ARF:

• Prerenal failure is caused by a reduction of the blood flow to the kidneys. This can occur as a result of a blood clot in the renal arteries, or a severe drop in blood pressure. Treatment of prerenal ARF aims at restoring normal kidney flow (perfusion). If the treatment does not succeed, one or both kidneys will soon fail.

• Intrarenal failure is caused by loss of blood supply and exposure to renal toxins. The most common cause of intrarenal failure in cats is the ingestion of ethylene glycol used in antifreeze.

• Postrenal failure may occur following an obstruction to the outflow of urine or a rupture with leakage of urine into the abdomen. The most common cause in the cat is urethral obstruction associated with feline urological syndrome (FUS), which is described in the next section.

Acute renal failure requires immediate veterinary help to restore the kidneys to their normal functions and to reverse the principal cause. Without this, the cat will undoubtedly die.

Chronic renal failure (CRF), which occurs with chronic interstitial nephritis, is the most common chronic kidney disease of cats. Exactly what causes this condition is not yet known, but what is known is that there is a progressive loss of functional kidney tissue.

Cats in the critical stages of CRF vomit, are indifferent to food, and lose weight; they also drink water and urinate excessively. These cats are usually lethargic and dehydrated when first brought to the vet. Often the owner of a cat that is in the earlier stages of CRF will notice the animal increasing its usual water consumption several weeks or months before other symptoms appear.

This condition is common in cats that are 7 years of age or older. Vets use blood tests and urine evaluation to diagnose CRF. Specifically, two blood tests, called the blood urea nitrogen (BUN) and creatinine, as well as an analysis of the specific gravity or concentration of the urine, are used to determine if CRF is indeed present.

Initial treatment of CRF tries to reverse dehydration with intravenous fluids. When the cat is in stable condition, long-term medical treatment begins. This includes dietary restriction of protein and phosphorus, and the administration of vitamin supplements, sodium bicarbonate, anabolic steroids, and control of vomiting. There are low-protein prescription diets available to help in the treatment of CRF, and these should be given to the cat if at all possible. These diets are often refused by finicky cats but home-made diets may be substituted.

Cats suffering from feline infectious peritonitis (see page 185) may also show signs of CRF.

Diseases of the lower urinary tract

The bladder stores the urine produced by the kidneys. It is subject to a number of disorders that are unique to the cat as well as to those found in other mammals.

Feline urological syndrome (FUS), sometimes called feline lower urinary tract disease (FLUTD), encompasses a number of disorders that produce similar symptoms. Vets have seldom been able to determine the underlying cause of the disease in individual cats.

Those with FUS urinate small amounts frequently, have pain when they do, and scratch themselves extensively whenever they have to use their litter boxes. Often they will not even bother to seek out the litter box, but will urinate wherever

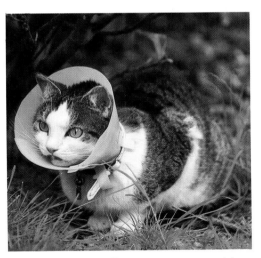

An Elizabethan collar prevents a cat with a bladder infection from licking itself.

they may happen to be, often in front of their owner.

As if to counteract burning or itching, cats suffering from this disorder lick themselves repeatedly.

Cats with FUS may suffer from one or more of the following:

• Urolithiasis, or stones in the bladder, which occurs when substances that are usually excreted in urine precipitate out of solution and form crystals within the bladder instead. This occurs when urine is saturated with various salts and is low in fluids, something that occurs frequently in cats due to their tendency to drink very little water. Most bladder stones are composed of struvite, a combination of magnesium, ammonium and phosphate. Urolithiasis occurs with equal frequency in male and female cats.

• Urinary tract infections (UTI) are most often caused by bacteria, but may also, in rare cases, be activated by fungi and viruses. Bacterial infections can occur alone, or in conjunction with FUS disorders such as urolithiasis.

• Obstructed urinary flow can usually be traced to a urethral obstruction. The urethra is the canal which discharges urine from the bladder and urethral obstruction affects males almost exclusively. The male cat's urethra is much longer and narrower than a female's and so more subject to blockage. Obstruction can be caused by mucus, a blood clot, or sloughed fragments of tissue, but most commonly by struvite bladder stones. Blockage can also occur without the presence of material at the obstruction site. Swelling of the urethra, cancer, scar tissue and prostate disease can interfere with urinary flow. Untreated urinary obstruction can cause postrenal acute renal failure, rupture of the bladder, and death.

Symptoms determine FUS treatment. A urinary obstruction requires emergency care. Most vets will catheterise the urethra to remove the blockage and establish the flow of urine. Then they administer intravenous fluids to promote kidney function. If an infection is present, antibiotics will be prescribed.

Reoccurrences of FUS can be controlled with dietary changes. Although foods themselves do not cause this condition, some contribute to stone formation. Vets have found that by limiting dietary magnesium and feeding cats diets that produce an acid urine, the incidence of FUS episodes can be reduced. Since magnesium is a component of struvite stone production, limiting the cat's intake, and thus decreasing magnesium in the urine, also decreases crystallisation of struvite. Struvite crystals form most readily in a nonacidic environment.

Large bladder stones can be treated by a diet that dissolves them, or they can be removed surgically.

Skin

The most common fungal disease in cats is dermatophytosis, better known as ringworm. Infection occurs when several different fungi called dermatophytes invade

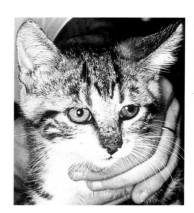

Ringworm, which affects many cats, occurs frequently in kittens.

the outer layers of the skin, the nails and the hair. The results are bald spots, stubbled hairs, and a scaling and crusting of the cat's skin that can cause itching. In severe cases, lesions may cover the whole body. Treatment includes oral and topical medications.

Parasitic dermatosis

Fleas infest cats to suck their blood. Yet most cats can harbour several dozen fleas without suffering anything more serious than itching. This is not the case, however, with kittens or cats already weakened by disease and those that are severely infected. They may develop flea anaemia, which can be fatal. Some cats are hypersensitive to flea saliva; reactions include varying degrees of itching, a reddened skin and scabs. The cat and its surroundings – the entire home perhaps – should be treated with flea-control products.

Mites also cause problems for cats. Notoedric mange, for example, begins with intense and constant itching around the head and neck. The cat may get red scaly bald spots, especially on the ears and neck. Lesions may extend to the face, paws and genitals. This mange may infect a whole litter of kittens.

The parasite *Otodectes cynotis* is the most common cause of external ear disease. Infected cats will get scabs on their ears from scratching. This mite can spread to other parts of the body, causing lesions on the head, neck, rump and paws.

Demodectic mange, though rare, can occur in young and weakened cats. It produces bald spots, possibly with inflammation, scaling, and itching, usually on the head, ears and neck.

Cheyletiellosis is not uncommon. The cheyletiella live on the dead surface of the skin and can sometimes be seen moving along the hairs of the cat; they are called 'walking dandruff'.

The lavae of harvest mites (or chiggers), *Trombicula autumnalis*, may be seen as orange specks, usually on the head, ears and feet. They are very small and are active during summer and autumn. This parasite may cause intense itching and scabs. Ticks, too, are sometimes found on cats, but cause little irritation.

Infestation by lice may sometimes be seen, especially on strays. This may cause itching in some cats, depending on their sensitivity to the parasite.

Allergy problems

Allergies are the main cause of most skin diseases that affect cats. All of them cause itching. Most affected cats suffer itching all over their bodies. In most cases, these cats will scratch themselves so much that their hair will break off or fall out in clumps leaving bare patches.

Your vet may call this hair-loss problem symmetric hypotrichosis, and recommend corticosteroids or the progesterone drug megestrol acetate.

A majority of cat skin disorders are due to an allergic reaction to flea-bites. Other allergies are caused by inhalants, either in the home or in the outside air, and food.

Food allergies, for example, can result in highly itchy skin. If you suspect a food allergy, monitor your pet's diet. Your vet may recommend that you try one of sev-

Harvest mite larvae (enlarged many times) are easily recognised by their orange colour.

eral available hypoallergenic diets for about three weeks.

Vets generally do not recommend home-made diets for cats with allergies, since such diets may not be nutritionally balanced. Ask your vet to recommend one of the foods being produced by cat-food manufacturers specifically for cats suffering from allergies. More and more of these foods are being sold commercially.

Cats suffering from food allergies will respond favourably to the right diet and the symptoms should then decrease, though it may be a gradual process. For a lasting solution to allergy problems, find out what the cat is allergic to and eliminate it from your household or from the animal's diet. This may take some time, so a lot of patience is required.

Other skin diseases

Atopy is a common, hereditary disease that causes cats to itch. Airborne allergens trigger attacks.

Miliary dermatosis is a common feline reaction to food allergies, flea bites, atopy and several other conditions. Cats suffering from this problem have small, seed-like scabs, and inflamed skin on their heads, necks and rumps.

A number of rare autoimmune diseases, known collectively as pemphigus complex, make cats quite ill with fevers, depression, loss of appetite, a discernible weight loss and skin lesions. Biopsies of skin tissue are needed before any diagnosis can be made.

Psychogenic alopecia is the term used for self-inflicted hair loss and skin lesions. Cats that do this may be reacting to pain or physical discomfort of some sort – an arthritic joint, for example – or they may have behavioural problems. Psychogenic alopecia occurs most often in the Siamese, Burmese and Abyssinian breeds. Many cats with this condition are successfully treated with behaviour-modifying drugs on a long-term basis.

Eosinophilic granuloma complex is a relatively common group of skin disorders whose underlying cause is not always evident. They can be divided into three groups:

This angry-looking, pus-filled lesion is the result of eosinophilic plaque.

• ulcers, red-brown sores found mainly in the mouth or on the upper lip;
• Eosinophilic plaques, fiery-red hairless lesions found anywhere, but 80 per cent occuring on the inside of the cat's thighs and on the abdomen. These lesions ooze pus and are likely to cause intense itching (pruritus);
• Linear granuloma, long narrow lesions. Yellow or pink, they tend to form in a row, especially on the back of the thighs. These lesions also occur in the mouth.

Alopecia and acne

Many cats have areas of thin hair between their eyes and ears, a feature which is especially noticeable in Siamese and related breeds. Few cats, however, develop feline endocrine alopecia, a condition characterised by symmetrical areas of abnormally thin hair rather than complete baldness. It occurs in cats that were neutered at a young age – 90 per cent of those affected are males – and is believed to be related to sex hormone deficiencies or imbalances. Thinning of hair occurs in the genital area, the inner thighs and abdomen. The condition does not cause itching nor does it damage the skin, and the cat is otherwise normal. Treatment is by sex hormone injections.

Stud tail (tail gland hyperplasia), another skin disease, is mostly seen in sexually active purebred male cats, although the condition sometimes occurs in castrated males and spayed females. Persian, Siamese and Rex cats are particularly susceptible. (Some experts feel that stud tail affects all breeds equally,

Cats lacking protective pigmentation are prone to sunburn, which can lead to cancer.

but that owners of purebreeds seek treatment for the condition more often than other cat owners.) The condition is characterised by blackheads, scaling, and yellow-to-black waxy debris on the skin and hairs near the base of the tail. It occurs when the supracaudal organ – the preen gland which produces the oily substance the cat uses to groom itself – becomes overactive. There is no particular treatment for the condition, although antiseborrheic shampoos may help.

Feline acne is fairly common. The most likely cause is the cat's failure to clean its chin properly. Affected cats have blackheads on their chin and lower lip and these may become infected. Bacterial infection may be suspected if there is swelling, pain and itching, and antibiotics may be needed to clear it up. There is no particular treatment for the feline acne itself other than cleaning the area with a mild benzoyl peroxide preparation. Changing the cat's bedding may help control the acne. Checking the cat's forelegs might also be in order: a leg injury may have prevented the cat from cleaning its chin properly in the first place.

Cats with white ear tips and nose are susceptible to solar or actinic dermatitis. Without protective pigmentation at these points, they are prone to sunburn. Initially, there is mild reddening of the ear margins and occasionally of the eyelids, nose and lips. As the condition worsens, balding, scaling and pus develop, along with curling of the ears. The lesions are at their worst in summer, then regress, or disappear entirely, during the winter, but return and become progressively worse each summer. This condition can progress into a skin cancer called squamous cell carcinoma, at which time the ear flaps may have to be amputated. Prevention, or treatment at the precancerous stage, consists of limiting exposure to the sun, and applying protective sunscreen before exposure.

After the lungs, the skin is the most common site of feline cancers. These vary greatly in malignancy and any tumour that develops on a cat's skin should be examined by a vet. Squamous cell carcinoma occurs mostly in older cats and in white cats. It generally appears on the head – the ears, lips, nose and eyelids – as an irregularly shaped, crater-like, ulcerated tumour. Surgery or radiation are the most likely therapies.

Older cats are also the most likely to develop fibrosarcoma and the rarer cutaneous lymphosarcoma. Surgery is usually recommended for fibrosarcoma, but the condition may recur. Cutaneous lymphosarcoma, which spreads quickly to other parts of the body, is usually fatal within a few months.

Melanomas, well-defined brown or black tumours of the melanin-producing cells in the skin, may be removed surgically if diagnosed at an early stage of the disease. These tumours also spread quickly to other organs. By contrast, the fat-cell tumours known as liposarcomas seldom occur in cats, are slow to spread to other parts of the body, and can usually be effectively removed surgically.

Endocrine glands

All diseases of the endocrine glands disrupt hormonal production. The most common disorders are diabetes mellitus (sugar diabetes) and hyperthyroidism.

Diabetes mellitus

This disease occurs when the insulin-producing cells in the pancreas become impaired. Insulin is essential for glucose (sugar) metabolism, promoting its absorption into the muscle cells for energy and into the liver for storage. Reduction of insulin production can lead to increased levels of glucose in the blood. Cats younger than 8 years old rarely develop diabetes mellitus, which affects older males and females equally.

Affected cats may be overweight at the onset of the disease, but become emaciated as it progresses. The most common symptoms of diabetes mellitus are excessive thirst and urination, accompanied by an increase in appetite and loss in weight. Other signs include soreness and swelling of the gums and tongue and a thinning of the coat. As the disease progresses, the symptoms become more severe and include weakness, vomiting, even more severe weight loss and, finally, coma and death. One unusual symptom is a weakness of the hind legs. Cats with this disorder will walk with their hocks touching the ground.

Diagnosis can be difficult. Even though a cat with this condition has an abnormally high glucose level, many cats develop unusually high blood glucose when nervous or stressed. Even a routine visit to the vet may bring this about. It may be necessary, therefore, to test not only the cat's blood several times, but also its urine before a diagnosis is made. Normal cat urine should not contain any glucose; it is found only when the blood glucose is at an abnormally high level.

Treatment varies with the severity of the diabetes, and how ill the cat is. Inevitably, this disease makes tremendous demands on the cat's owner. Schedules must be observed. A missed meal or a delayed medication can have serious results. Even in not-so-critical cases, once- or twice-daily injections of long-acting insulin may be prescribed. Many vets also recommend a change in diet; often, cats will require less insulin if they are fed a high-fibre diet.

Constituents of food must be checked carefully. Products with a high sugar content, semi-moist cat food for example, should be avoided. Cats on insulin must also be monitored regularly to make sure they receive the proper dosage. To regulate this, many vets recommend daily to weekly checks of the blood glucose. Once the dosage is regulated, the cat's blood glucose should be monitored every month or so. If the diabetes is well advanced and there is a risk the cat may die, the blood glucose may have to be monitored hourly. Dosages of short-acting insulin can be adjusted to the blood test results and administered after each test. The cat will also require intensive care to survive.

Ordinarily, however, full recovery is possible, provided the disease is diagnosed early, treatment is carried out consistently, and the cat is taken to the vet for regular checkups.

There are many probable causes of diabetes mellitus in the cat. One common cause is long-term use of megestrol acetate, a progesterone drug sometimes used to treat cancer and allergies.

Hyperthyroidism

Hyperthyroidism is an increasingly common disorder, particularly in older cats. The thyroid gland, which is located in the neck, can become enlarged and produce excessive hormones. Hyperthyroidism may also cause enlarged nodules in the thyroid. These are usually benign, but may on rare occasions be cancerous. Cats with hyperthyroidism seem unable to rest and become hyperactive, pacing and grooming constantly. Despite the attention, the coat appears dull and unkempt. Most cats with the disease lose weight even though their appetite may be normal, sometimes even voracious. Other symptoms include tachycardia (increased heart rate), vomiting, diarrhoea, and excessively long nails. As the disease progresses, the cat will become thinner and more run-down.

Hyperthyroidism can also cause congestive heart failure. Heart problems related to the disease disappear once the hyperthyroidism is treated. Conversely, if the cat is left untreated, it will almost certainly die.

Hyperthyroidism is generally diagnosed by a blood test measuring the amount of thyroid hormones in the blood. One or both thyroid glands may be diseased although in nearly all instances of hyperthyroidism, both glands are affected. There are several effective treatments, including oral medication, surgery to remove part of the thyroid gland and a dose of radioactive iodine. The option recommended by your vet will depend on the age and condition of the cat.

Eyes

Eye examination is particularly important because the eyes may present the first symptoms of diseases such as feline infectious peritonitis and feline leukaemia virus. Your vet can examine the inside of the eye with an ophthalmoscope.

Conjunctivitis is quite common in cats.

Diseases of the orbit

The orbit is the bony cavity that protects the eye. Traumatic exophthalmos (abnormal protrusion of the eyeball) is fairly common in cats. It may be caused by an accident or a bite. A cat injured in this way must see a vet quickly.

Abscesses behind the eye are common causes of bulging eyeballs. Often the abscess is due to a bite that became infected. Dental abscesses can also cause ulcers behind the eye. Treatment is essential.

There are also several forms of cancer that can develop within the orbit, especially in older cats. One or both eyeballs protrude gradually as the cancer grows.

Diseases of the eyelids

Coloboma – incomplete formation of the upper eyelid – is a congenital defect. Surgery is usually necessary.

Entropion, a rolling inward of the eyelids, is usually the result of injury. There is also a congenital entropion that afflicts some cats, Persians in particular. When the eyelids roll inwards, the eyelashes rub against the cornea, causing injury and discomfort. Surgery is the usual remedy.

Blepharitis (inflammation of the eyelids) may affect only the eyelids, or may accompany a generalised skin disorder. The underlying cause must be treated.

Lacerations of the eyelid may result from bites, scratches or injuries. Early treatment will avoid complications that could interfere with eyelid function. Always consult your vet about tumours of the cat's eyelids.

Diseases of the conjunctiva and nictitating membrane

The conjunctiva is a thin, semitransparent mucous membrane that covers the surface of the eyelids and the nictitating membranes (semicircular folds of conjunctiva between the globe and the lower lid). Conjunctivitis (inflammation of the conjunctiva) occurs frequently in cats. There are many causes, the most common being upper respiratory viruses and irritants such as dust and chemicals.

The nictitating membrane, also called the third eyelid, provides extra eye protection. The membrane, usually retracted into the corner of the eye, will sometimes protrude and partly cover the eye. This usually indicates that the cat is under the weather. Treatment and prognosis depend on the cause, whether injury, infection, cancer, severe weight loss, dehydration, congenital microphthalmia (smallness of one or both eyes), or a nerve disorder such as Horner's syndrome.

Diseases of the cornea

The cornea is the transparent part of the eye that covers the iris and pupil. This transparency is crucial to normal vision; any reduction is a sign of corneal disease. The cornea is particularly susceptible to injury, the eye being a favourite target when cats scratch each other. Such injuries are very painful, but ordinarily heal quickly.

Superficial corneal ulcers are treated with a topical antibiotic. If anterior uveitis is present (see next page), an atropine ophthalmic ointment may be recommended.

Deep corneal ulcers are serious; as the ulcer becomes deeper, the chances of the globe's rupturing increase. Deep corneal ulcers generally require surgery. Eyedrops containing antibiotics and atropine should be applied for at least two weeks after surgery. Prognosis depends on the severity of the ulceration; some permanent corneal scarring is to be expected.

A form of keratitis (inflammation of the cornea) is seen in cats infected by feline herpes virus. Herpetic keratitis occurs mainly in adult cats and may affect one or both eyes. Some cases display a telltale, irregular, branching ulceration. Treatment consists of a topical virostatic drug.

Cats can develop eosinophilic keratitis, a rapidly spreading corneal disease unique to felines. Raised pink masses appear on the cornea and adjacent conjunctiva. Immediate surgery is needed to remove the masses and the superficial layers of the cornea. A biopsy is essential to check for corneal cancers.

Corneal sequestrum, a black plaque on the cornea, is another lesion seen only in cats. It may be a response to chronic irritation from entropion or ulcerative keratitis. Treatment consists of antibiotics and surgical removal of the plaque.

Diseases of the uvea

The uvea is a pigmented structure consisting of the iris, ciliary body and choroid, and is the middle, blood-vessel-containing layer of the eye. The iris is the thin, coloured membrane that separates the back and front chambers of the eye. The posterior uvea or choroid contains the large and small blood vessels in the back of the eye, and the tapetum lucidum (see page 56). The ciliary body is located between the iris and the choroid, and produces the transparent fluid, called the aqueous humour, that is found in the anterior chamber.

Heterochromia, a two-coloured iris or irregular brown patches in the normal ground colour, may occur. Cysts sometimes develop on the iris at the margin of the pupil.

Uveitis, an inflammation of the uvea, may cause pain, excessive blinking, protrusion of the nictitating membrane, a change in the colour of the iris and blood or protein deposits in the anterior chamber. Causes of uveitis include injury, corneal ulceration, feline leukaemia virus, feline immunodeficiency virus, feline infectious peritonitis and toxoplasmosis. Atropine ointment, which dilates the pupil, will decrease pain and minimise potential adhesion of the iris to the cornea – a condition called synechia. A topical antibiotic and/or corticosteroid is generally prescribed as well.

Glaucoma occurs when the pressure of fluids in the eyeball becomes excessive. Owners may not observe anything amiss until there is irreversible damage. Causes include congenital abnormalities, injury, intraocular cancer and feline infectious peritonitis. With early diagnosis, treatment can be effective. The eye may be removed if glaucoma has led to blindness. Removal of the eye is usually the best solution to most cancers of the uvea. The most common of these, lymphoma, can sometimes be seen on the iris.

Diseases of the retina

The retina is a semitransparent membrane made up of photoreceptors – the rods and cones that are the immediate instrument of vision.

Inherited retinal degeneration is progressive deterioration of both the rods and cones. Blindness is usually complete by 4 years of age.

Taurine deficiency (see page 196) causes feline central retinal degeneration. This is seen in cats fed taurine-deficient diets as well as in cats fed commercial dog food. If caught in its early stages, the condition is reversible with taurine supplementation. Advanced degeneration causes blindness.

Retinal inflammation is a side effect of choroiditis. Owners will notice that their cats, whose sight is failing, are bumping into things. Treatment is directed to controlling the choroiditis.

Retinal bleeding has several causes, including feline infectious peritonitis, feline leukaemia virus, systemic infections and hypertension arising from renal (kidney) disease.

Retinal detachment occurs in cats suffering from feline infectious peritonitis, lymphoma and systemic fungal infections. Blindness may occur if the retina separates completely from the back of the eye.

Reproductive disorders

Except for a few modifications, the feline reproductive system is similar to that of other mammals. Having your pet neutered will avoid problems in this area. With uncastrated cats, the most common problems are failure of toms to produce sperm and of queens to conceive.

Reproductive diseases of the male cat

Male cats are usually born with both testicles in the scrotum. During development, the testes follow a complicated path from inside the abdomen into the scrotum. Occasionally a cat may be born with one or both testicles undescended. A cat with undescended testicles, a cryptorchid, is generally sterile, whereas a monorchid, a cat with one testicle, may be fertile and can transmit its condition to its offspring. Your vet may recommend surgery in either instance. Even sterile monorchids and cryptorchids have all the characteristics of toms, including strong-smelling urine and an urge to mark their territories.

Because diseases may be spread during the close contact of mating, a tom should be tested for feline leukaemia virus and feline immunodeficiency virus before breeding.

Toms can transmit genital bacterial infections to female cats. If the females are suffering from genital discharges or infertility, the tom's semen should be cultured for bacteria and breeding should be suspended until he is free of infections.

A hair ring may form around the base of the penis in long-haired uncastrated male cats. This makes mating difficult and very painful. If the tom does not remove this hair during its normal grooming, it should be removed by a vet.

Some toms refuse to mate when they are under stress, or an inexperienced tom may be intimidated by an aggressive queen. In such cases, time and familiarisation should alleviate the problem.

Poor libido and low sperm production have been linked to malnutrition, obesity, hypothyroidism and hypervitaminosis A, toxicity arising from too much

---

NEUTERING A TOM

A male cat should be neutered when it is 5 to 8 months old, before its male fighting and spraying habits become established. The operation to remove the testes is short, done under a general anaesthetic, and the cat should be able to return home the same day. Recovery should be speedy, but it is a good idea to put shredded paper in the litter box. Litter or earth can get into the wounds and cause infection. Do not use newspaper or any printed paper (see page 199).

---

vitamin A (see page 167). Early diagnosis and treatment of underlying disorders may bring about a return to fertility.

Territorial fighting may result in bites on the scrotum and testes, commonly followed by fever and abscess formation. Proper treatment with antibiotics and surgical drainage of the abscess will generally conserve fertility.

A male tortoiseshell or calico cat is usually sterile, but a few have been reported to be fertile. The orange-and-black genes are found in the X chromosome and are therefore sex-linked. For a cat to have the tortoiseshell colour pattern, it must have two X chromosomes. The majority of tortoiseshell male cats have three sex chromosomes, XXY; these males exhibit small testes, poor libido and are sterile.

Reproductive diseases of the female cat

Prolonged anoestrus (see page 159) can be caused by malnutrition, genetics, hormonal imbalance and disease. Cats that lack exposure to other cats or to at least 12 hours a day of light may not have normal heat cycles.

Precociousness, or early sexual maturity, can occur in kittens as young as 4 months of age. Good nutrition, adequate light, and contact with older cats with normal heat cycles may result in early cycling – going in and out of heat regularly. It is not advisable to breed these very young females: small litter size, difficult labour and birth, and a greater incidence of birth defects are some of the many valid reasons to wait until the kitten is mature enough physically.

Nymphomania (see page 160) may occur in older females that have never had a litter. These cats usually have a disease called cystic endometrial hyperplasia-pyometra complex (see below). Nymphomania is characterised by heat cycles with excessive, frenzied, oestrus-related behaviour.

Pseudopregnancy (false pregnancy) may occur following a sterile mating, stimulation of the vulva of the cat, or spontaneous ovulation.

Because of the risk to the developing kittens, all medications, including vaccines, should be avoided during pregnancy. Griseofulvin, for example, a drug commonly used to treat ringworm, can cause birth defects.

Cats that are otherwise healthy but have recurrent miscarriages at the same point of gestation are thought to suffer from a progesterone hormone deficiency.

Bacterial and viral infections can cause infertility in the queen. Feline panleucopenia (see page 183), feline leukaemia virus and feline infectious peritonitis have all been proven to do so.

The progressive condition called cystic endometrial hyperplasia-pyometra complex occurs in female cats aged 3 to 14. Mostly it affects cats over 5 years old that have never borne kittens.

Cystic hyperplasia, the first disorder of the complex to develop, involves a thickening of the uterus lining and cyst formation; victims usually display no symptoms except for infertility. Endometritis, an inflammation or infection of the lining of the uterus, can develop during or after cystic hyperplasia. Cats with endometritis often have no obvious signs of disease, although a vaginal discharge may be evident in some cases.

Untreated endometritis may develop into pyometra, an accumulation of pus in the uterus. As the disease progresses, the cat will appear steadily more ill. In the final stages, there will be a bloody uterine discharge, depression and an elevated white blood cell count. Finally, infection throughout the body will lead to a rapid death.

The early stages of this disease complex may be treated successfully, but treatment becomes more difficult as the disease progresses. Unless the cat is essential for breeding purposes, an ovariohysterectomy (spay) is recommended.

Chronic infections of the cervix and vagina may cause infertility. A slight discharge may be evident, but is often overlooked due to the cat's normal cleaning habits. These infections usually occur following injury or difficult delivery of large kittens. If not treated, they may cause scarring and even closure of the cervix.

Foetal death and abortion

Foetal loss occurs frequently in cats. If the kittens are lost very early in gestation, the foetuses may be resorbed. Cats who are miscarrying may discharge bloody fluid containing foetal debris or whole dead foetuses. The kittens may appear normal, or may be mummified or decomposed.

The death of a foetus, depending on the cause, is not always followed by abortion. The rest of the kittens in the litter may not be affected and may be carried to full term. It is not unusual for a queen to deliver a dead foetus, in any stage of development, along with her otherwise healthy litter. This is most common when the foetus dies due to abnormalities in its development.

Feline panleucopenia can result in death shortly after birth, mummification, stillbirth, weak newborns and malformations. Cerebellar hypoplasia, a common birth disorder of kittens associated with feline panleucopenia, causes a severe lack of coordination.

Feline viral rhinotracheitis (FVR) infections in utero can result in abortion or miscarriage, foetal death, and congenital foetal infections. Feline leukaemia virus (FeLV) is associated with many reproduction disorders. (Whether FeLV causes these disorders is not known.) Problems include infertility, foetal death and readsorption, abortion, stillbirth, endometritis, and the birth of fading kittens. Fading kitten syndrome refers to kittens that are lethargic and unusually small. They also have dry, lustreless coats.

Feline infectious peritonitis (FIP) (see page 184) is also associated with infertility and foetal death.

An infectious parasite, *Toxoplasma gondii* (see page 185), can cause abortions and miscarriages, and infections resulting in foetal death. The parasite can also affect kittens.

A bacterium, *Streptococcus canis*, can cause kitten death 7 to 10 days after birth. Kittens that acquire umbilical infections at birth, or shortly afterwards, can develop life-threatening infections. Dipping the end of the umbilical cord in iodine immediately after delivery helps prevent this.

Cats used for breeding should be tested for feline leukaemia virus (see page 184), and feline immunodeficiency virus (see page 182). The outward appearance of good health is no guarantee that a cat is free from these diseases.

Cats with access to the outdoors should be kept away from breeding cats, as well as pregnant and nursing queens. Very

---

KITTEN MORTALITY

97.2% of litters are carried to term.

Of these, 10.5% of the kittens are stillborn.

Of the 89.5% that survive:
2.6% die between 1 and 3 weeks
4.6% die between 3 and 6 weeks
3.9% die between 6 weeks and 6 months
0.7% die between 6 months and 1 year.

The mortality rate among cats is high: Including the stillborn, a total of 22.3% of kittens die before they reach one year of age.

---

young kittens should be isolated from other cats, but total isolation may result in behavioural problems.

Reputable breeders have standard procedures for preventing disease among their stock. Such precautions include immunisation programmes and facilities for isolating or quarantining animals as needs arise. Good nutrition, ventilation, and hygiene are other essentials. Being cared for in such an environment will enhance both the general health of kittens and their chances of survival.

Inbreeding with immediate family members or line breeding with grandparents will increase the chance of revealing hereditary abnormalities. Cats with hereditary defects should be neutered and ideally all cats that prove to carry defects should be removed from the breeding programme. If they must be used they should be mated to unrelated cats.

Disorders of parturition (queening)

The birthing process, or parturition, is called queening or kittening. This process starts with the contractions that signal the onset of labour and ends with the expulsion of the last placenta (afterbirth).

Cats, like other mammals, may have difficulty in giving birth. Dystocia, the term for difficult or abnormal labour, can be caused by complications associated with the queen, or the kittens, or both. Healthy queens rarely have trouble giving birth. Inbred, sick, or undernourished queens may experience uterine inertia. They may not have the stamina to push strongly enough or their uterine contractions may be too weak, and they will need help to deliver their kittens.

Primary uterine inertia (not caused by disease) is most common in Persians. The tendency may be inherited, in which case these queens should not be bred again. However, sick or nutritionally deficient cats that have difficulty with one litter may have normal deliveries in future provided that the underlying problem is corrected.

Pelvis size is often a factor in dystocia. A queen 5 months old or younger may be too small to deliver her kittens. Previous injuries or inadequate nutrition can also be a source of trouble. A cat that fractured her pelvis may have sustained a pelvic deformity that makes birthing difficult. This may also be the case if a queen has not been fed properly. In these cases, a caesarean section – surgery to ease delivery of the kittens – is usually necessary.

ORPHAN KITTENS

Sometimes a queen will not live through kittening. When this happens, the kittens must be cared for. Their body temperature must be kept at a precise temperature.

Birth to 7 days: 31-34°C (88-93°F)
8 to 14 days: 27-29°C (80-84°F)
15 to 28 days: 27°C (80°F)
29 to 35 days: 24°C (75°F)
After 35 days: 21°C (70°F)

Occasionally, a uterine torsion may cause dystocia. A cat's uterus is divided into two horns. The twisting (torsion) of one horn a quarter to a full turn can cause dystocia, acute abdominal pain, uterine bleeding or peritonitis. Immediate veterinary attention is necessary to preserve the queen's life.

First litters, particularly in young queens, may have only one or two large kittens. In such situation, it is not uncommon for a cat to have difficulty and require assistance. If a kitten in the birth canal cannot be delivered, it must be removed surgically to save the lives of the queen and remaining kittens.

Dystocia should be suspected if a kitten is not born within 30 minutes of the foetal membrane rupturing, or if two hours of unproductive labour pass. A vet should be consulted immediately. A physical examination and X-rays may be necessary to identify the difficulty. Treatment may

be a caesarean section or an injection of medication to stimulate contractions of the uterine muscles.

Postpartum disorders

Immediately after the birth of her kittens, the queen cleans and nurses her litter. Stillborn and placentas, unless removed, are usually eaten by the queen. Cannibalism is rare but is more likely after a first delivery by a highly nervous queen. Such cats should not be used for future breeding.

There is a normal, bloody discharge for 7 to 10 days after birth. Persistent foul-smelling discharges are signs of uterine infection. Persistent vaginal bleeding after three weeks may indicate a problem with normal uterine healing.

Generally speaking, postpartum disorders are uncommon in a healthy queen. Infections of the uterus associated with dystocia or a retained placenta are the most frequent problems. When one is present, the queen is listless and may be unable to nurse or care for the kittens. There is usually a foul-smelling discharge and a fever. Treatment with antibiotics may control the infection and restore the queen to health. In severe cases, it is necessary to perform an ovariohysterectomy (spay) to remove the infected uterus together with the ovaries.

Occasionally, a postpartum queen develops a uterine prolapse, usually following a difficult delivery. In this condition, the uterus protrudes through the vagina. Uterine prolapse may be partial or complete (the entire uterus is expelled). Cats so afflicted are usually dehydrated and may be in shock. They are frequently restless and continue to strain as if in labour. Immediate veterinary attention is necessary to save the queen's life. The uterus may be salvageable, but an ovariohysterectomy may also be necessary.

Eclampsia, a life-threatening disease caused by an abrupt drop in the circulating calcium in a postpartum queen, is uncommon. The condition develops during the nursing period and usually occurs between two days and three weeks after giving birth.

The most noticeable symptoms are extreme weakness and an increased respiratory rate, followed by muscle tremors and loss of co-ordination. If the queen is left untreated, convulsions, coma and death will inevitably follow. Treatment consists of a slow intravenous infusion of calcium. If at all possible, the kittens should be moved away from the queen and fed by hand.

In most cases, a mother cat will allow kittens to nurse without any fuss.
If not, the kittens must be nursed artificially.

When a queen develops postpartum disorders, it may be necessary to rear kittens by hand for a time. A commercial replacement for the queen's milk must be used. Cow's milk or infant formula does not provide adequate nutrition for kittens. It is also crucial to keep the kittens warm.

Disorders of the mammary glands

Most major disorders of the mammary glands tend to be related to infections or tumours. One infection, mastitis, is usually associated with queening and lactating. It occasionally occurs in pubescent queens, and is characterised by a benign enlargement of the mammary glands.

In bacterial mastitis, there is enlargement, or swelling, of the mammary glands, accompanied by heat, redness and pain. The cat will also suffer from depression, fever and lack of appetite. As a result, the queen may refuse to nurse, and the kittens will cry continuously from hunger and cold. Unless they are taken away from their mother and fed a milk substitute, they will die. They should also be examined for any signs of fever, lethargy, bloating and diarrhoea. If they have been nursed by an infected queen, however briefly, they may need antibiotics. Meantime, the afflicted queen also requires treatment. Antibiotics, drainage of any abscesses, hot packing and surgery may be necessary.

ARTIFICIAL NURSING

If the kittens require artificial nursing, they must be weaned young according to the following timetable:

At birth: 8 feedings a day
At 1 week: 5 feedings a day
At 2 weeks: 4 feedings a day
At 3 weeks: 3 feedings a day
At 4 weeks: 2 feedings a day
At 5 weeks: 1 feeding a day

The kitten must drink the equivalent of at least 25 to 30% of its weight in milk every day.

When bottle-feeding, be sure the kitten swallows properly and does not choke on the milk.

Tumours of the mammary glands are usually malignant. Therefore, any lump or mass should be examined by a vet immediately. Malignancies can spread rapidly to the lungs, liver and other internal organs. Surgery will be necessary to remove the tumour. An ovariohysterectomy (spay) may also be performed, if it has not yet been done.

Megestrol acetate, a synthetic progesterone used to treat skin and behavioural problems, has been linked to benign and malignant mammary tumours. If this drug, or any other similar drug, is being taken by a cat with mammary tumours, discontinue its use.

Tumours of the breasts can spread to the neighbouring organs.

Pathology of the nervous system

Vets usually distinguish between disorders of the brain, spinal cord and peripheral nervous system.

The brain of a cat, like that of humans, is a complicated, even mysterious organ. Since the various regions of the brain have different functions, symptoms of disorders vary widely depending on the area of the brain that is affected.

Symptoms of brain disorders include such behavioural changes as abnormal sleep, aggression, excess docility, changes in litter-box behaviour, walking in circles, blindness, facial weakness or weakness of the limbs, tilting of the head, stumbling, dizziness and episodes of falling. Treatment of these problems and prognosis vary depending on the cause.

Brain disorders may be classified as congenital, infectious, nutritional, metabolic, toxic or cancerous.

Congenital brain disease generally results from a foetal injury, which prevents the normal development of one or more regions of the brain. Cerebellar hypoplasia, a disorder unique to cats, is the result of a foetal infection by the feline panleucopenia virus (see page 183), which prevents normal development of the cerebellum. Symptoms of congenital brain disease include an abnormal gait, tremors of the head and a general lack of co-ordination. There is no treatment for this disorder.

Brain disorders also are caused by feline leukaemia virus, feline immunodeficiency virus, feline infectious peritonitis and rabies. Pseudorabies, sometimes known as Aujesky's disease, is caused by a herpes virus contracted as a result of eating infected raw pork. One symptom is an episode of intense scratching, during which the cat bites its own skin savagely. Unfortunately, death generally occurs within 24 hours, because there is no prevention nor any treatment possible.

Toxoplasmosis (see page 185) causes a parasitic brain disorder.

Occasionally, roundworm larvae (see page 165) may reach the brain and cause neurological disturbances.

Because of their small size and unique metabolism, cats are particularly susceptible to toxic, metabolic and nutritional disorders, such as lead poisoning and thiamine deficiency.

The symptoms and severity of spinal cord disorders, as well as their treatment and prognosis, depend on their cause. Physical injury, malformation of the vertebrae, infection of the intervertebral spinal discs, cancer of the spine and intervertebral spinal disc disease are common causes of spinal cord disorders. Symptoms range from a general weakness to paralysis of the legs, especially the hind legs.

The main symptom of disorders of the peripheral nervous system is a general weakness of the animal. Such disorders include myasthenia gravis, diabetic polyneuropathy and dysautonomia.

Cats suffering from diabetes mellitus (see page 173) develop an unusual walk: their hocks (ankles) touch the ground. Weakness of the tail is another symptom of diabetes.

Feline dysautonomia is a disease of the peripheral nerves. Its cause is unknown. It may now be less common than it was. Symptoms include a rapid onset of depression, appetite loss, constipation, decreased tear production, regurgitation of food and dilated pupils. Unfortunately, the disorder has a death rate of 70 per cent.

Seizures are triggered by an abnormal discharge of energy from the brain. These electrical discharges will result in relatively brief, but disturbing, episodes of unusual activity. These spells may be

Diabetes often causes motor disorders, which may result in the cat walking on its ankles, or hocks.

brought about by feline infectious peritonitis, toxoplasmosis, fungal infections, rabies, cancer, trauma or bacterial abscesses. Epilepsy, which causes multiple seizures, is still something of a mystery to vets.

The severity and frequency of the episodes will dictate the kind of treatment your vet will recommend. Mild seizures and infrequent seizures probably will not require treatment. Extensive grand mal seizures, which may last several minutes, probably will be treated with anticonvulsant drugs.

SAMPLE VACCINATION SCHEDULE

Feline infectious enteritis, viral rhinotracheitis (herpes virus) and calicivirus vaccines

Some makes of vaccine require two doses, given between 2 and 3 weeks apart, usually being completed when the kitten is at least 12 weeks old. Other vaccines may only require one visit provided that the kitten is at least 12 weeks old. It should then receive a booster vaccination annually.

Chlamydia

This vaccine requires two doses given 3 weeks apart, followed by annual boosters.

Feline leukaemia virus

Two doses of vaccine are required, from 15 days to 4 weeks apart depending on the vaccine. Unless the cat or kitten comes from a known leukaemia tested household, a FeLV test is advisable before vaccination. An annual booster is required.

Rabies

Laws for rabies vaccination vary between different parts of the world. At present only animals intended for export are vaccinated in the United Kingdom.

Principal infectious diseases

The most common underlying causes of feline upper respiratory diseases are feline herpes virus, which causes viral rhinotracheitis, and feline calicivirus.

Inflammation of the respiratory tract

Feline viral upper respiratory disease (VURD) usually occurs in kittens that are under 6 months of age. Kittens raised in catteries or in households where there are a number of other cats are particularly vulnerable. The most common method of transmission is direct cat-to-cat contact. But the virus may also be transmitted over short distances when an infected cat sneezes near another cat.

Feline infectious rhinotracheitis is caused by feline herpes virus. The seriousness of the symptoms depends on the cat's immune status. The most acute form occurs in kittens at weaning, when the immunity provided by the queen's colostrum is lost. The disease causes fever, inflammation, sneezing and a clear nasal secretion; bacterial

This 'dry eye' is the result of a severe cold.

Gum disease caused by calicivirus infection.

infection causes a purulent nasal discharge. Irritation and inflammation of the mouth and throat, in turn, lead to anorexia, an inability or unwillingness to eat. Severe conjunctivitis combined with mild keratitis (see page 174) is common. Tracheitis (inflammation of the windpipe) is likely to cause coughing.

The incubation period, the time between exposure to feline infectious rhinotracheitis and the onset of symptoms, is two to six days. If the condition is not treated, side effects such as appetite loss and dehydration may cause blindness, even death. The acute stage of the disease generally lasts from two to three weeks. After that the cat either recovers or develops chronic rhinitis with a nasal discharge. Some cats, though no longer afflicted, remain chronic carriers. It is believed that up to 80 per cent of cats that contract the disease become carriers.

Several strains of calicivirus cause symptoms with varying degrees of severity. The most acute form is seen in 6-month-old kittens.

Calicivirus infection appears as fever, inflammation of the eyes, inflammation and discharge from the nose, and ulcers on the gums and tongue. If kittens catch a virulent strain, they can develop tracheobronchitis and pneumonia, and die quickly. In general, though, the symptoms are less severe than those of rhinotracheitis. Again, most afflicted cats remain chronic carriers and develop a clear, watery inflammation of the eyes and gingivitis (gum disease).

In its mild form, calicivirus causes coughing, which is responsible for the spread of the virus. Because this virus can live outside as well as inside the cat's body, it may survive on surfaces used by other cats, which then become infected.

Chlamydiosis is caused by *Chlamydia psittaci*, a bacterial infection of the respiratory tract. The initial symptoms are an acute, severe conjunctivitis and runny eyes. Frequently, one eye is affected before the other. Other symptoms include sneezing and clear or purulent nasal discharges.

In its chronic form, chlamydiosis causes a thickening of the conjunctiva. The bacteria are generally transmitted from one cat to another by direct contact with infectious secretions.

Treatment of upper respiratory diseases depends on the symptoms. In the acute stage, good hygiene is essential. Gently remove discharges from the nose and eyes, and feed the sick cat by hand, making sure it drinks enough water. If necessary, use antibiotics, antihistamines and decongestants to clear the nose. The treatment needs to be continued as long as your cat is sick. Most cats become chronic carriers, and this cannot be prevented except through prior vaccination (see box, page 181).

To prevent the spread of upper respiratory infection in a household with several cats, a comprehensive vaccination programme must be combined with strict isolation of all new cats and kittens for 2 weeks, and isolation or quarantining of sick cats.

Feline immunodeficiency virus

Feline immunodeficiency virus (FIV) is similar to human immunodeficiency virus (HIV), responsible for AIDS. It has become known only since the onset of the AIDS epidemic. However, FIV cannot be transmitted from cats to humans. Nor can it be easily passed between cats. FIV and HIV are both lentiviruses, which belong to the larger retrovirus family. When this type of virus enters the body, it may become active immediately or remain dormant for long periods.

In its active stage, FIV attacks T lymphocytes, white blood cells, that are essential for adequate immune response.

FIV develops in five distinct stages:

Stage 1 occurs just after infection and is limited to a slight fever that may last a few days or weeks. There may also be lymphadenopathy (enlargement of lymph nodes) for two to nine months. Some cats suffer from diarrhoea and depression. The death rate at this initial stage is low, but despite recovery, virtually all cats remain chronic carriers for life.

Stage 2, the dormant phase of the disease, may also last several weeks or years. There are no specific symptoms.

Stage 3 is characterised by recurrent fever, anaemia and intermittent weight loss. Generally the cat looks thin and scruffy. Stage 3 FIV may last for years before progressing.

Stage 4 is marked by chronic secondary infections. Weight loss is common, and lymph node enlargement and other signs of illness occur. Chronic infections at this stage include: progressive infections of the mouth, upper respiratory tract infections, enteritis, bacterial infections of the kidneys and bladder, and skin disorders.

Stage 5, the final stage, is characterised by opportunistic infections. These are disorders that normally do not cause illness in healthy cats.

Secondary infections include chronic gum disease, inflammation of the mouth (stomatitis), rhinitis, conjunctivitis, enteritis and recurring abscesses.

Opportunistic infections include haemobartonellosis, transmitted by biting insects (see page 163); feline infectious peritonitis (see page 184); systemic fungal infections (cryptococcosis); candidiasis (a yeast infection); toxoplasmosis (see page 185); and parasitic skin diseases (see page 170).

Chronic disorders include fever, loss of appetite and weight, anaemia and autoimmune disorders.

Neurological disorders include: twitching movements of the face and tongue; behaviour disorders, such as excessive shyness or aggression; refusal to use the litter box; and compulsive roaming. Lack of co-ordination, convulsions and tremors may also occur.

Experts believe that there is an increased incidence of certain cancers among FIV-infected cats. These cancers include lymphosarcomas, solid carcinomas and sarcomas.

Feline immunodeficiency virus, like other lentiviruses, cannot survive outside the body of its host. Therefore, direct contact – usually by a bite – is the only known way to transmit the virus. The disease is most common in uncastrated male cats that fight more than neutered cats.

Blood tests are used to detect FIV antibodies. Kittens born to an FIV-positive queen may or may not be infected. Kittens with maternal antibodies will test positive. If the maternal antibodies are eliminated, the uninfected kittens may then test negative. The change from a positive to a negative result is called seroconversion. But this result is rare because the FIV virus causes life-long infection.

Treatment of FIV is limited to symptomatic care of opportunistic and secondary infections. The only effective prevention is to isolate a cat that tests positive. A safe and effective antiviral drug has not yet been made available.

Feline panleucopenia (feline infectious enteritis)

Feline panleucopenia is caused by feline parvovirus, which is excreted in the faeces of infected cats. Outside the body, feline panleucopenia may survive in the faeces at moderate temperatures for several months and is spread by oral contact with infected faeces. It has an affinity for the digestive tract, the lymphoid tissues and bone marrow, where the severest symptoms of the disease appear. The death rate for cats with feline panleucopenia ranges from 50 to more than 90 per cent.

The initial symptoms, which occur four to six days after exposure, are lethargy, anorexia and persistent vomiting. Other symptoms include temperatures of 40°C (104°F) or higher and severe dehydration. Most cats develop diarrhoea and occasionally jaundice. The most important and consistent symptom is profound panleucopenia (an abnormal drop in the number of white blood cells), which begins two or three days after infection. It occurs when the virus suppresses the growth of white blood cells in the bone marrow. The extent of the drop is an indication of the severity of the disease and of its outcome.

Very few diseases can be transmitted from cats to children. (See Zoonoses, page 186.)

Subclinical infections (infection without symptoms of illness) affect adult cats in particular, but also occur in younger or other susceptible cats. In pregnant females, feline panleucopenia causes miscarriage, early neonatal death and malformations.

Another form of this disease, chronic ataxia, occurs in kittens infected before or shortly after birth. The virus affects the kitten's developing cerebellum, the part of the brain concerned with balance and coordination. The disease becomes apparent when the kittens begin to walk at 3 to 4 weeks of age. Their unusually awkward gait is jerky, movements are exaggerated and falls frequent.

There is no specific treatment, only symptomatic and supportive care. This involves maintaining normal liquid intake, antibiotic therapy and treatment for vomiting and diarrhoea.

Prevention of panleucopenia involves routine yearly vaccination. Live-virus vaccine is not recommended for pregnant queens. It may cause foetal deaths or cerebellar hypoplasia.

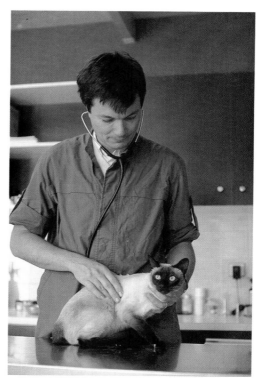

Regular examinations by a vet can help prevent disease.

Feline leukaemia virus

Feline leukaemia virus (FeLV) is caused by a retrovirus which can lead to tumours. Sixty per cent of all cats exposed to the virus develop a self-limiting infection and rarely become ill. About 30 per cent of this group develop a transient viraemia. That is to say, the cat's immune system fights the virus. Five to 10 per cent of exposed cats develop an atypical or sequestered infection. The cats test negative but the virus is, in effect, hiding undetected in their bodies. However, FeLV-related diseases may develop in the future. Persistent viraemia with progressive infection develops in about 30 per cent of exposed cats.

FeLV infection can lead to death within four to eight weeks, particularly in kittens. This is a result of the virus's suppressive effect on the immune system and is most common in kittens. Usually, FeLV-related diseases take months, even years, to develop. FeLV also causes cancerous (neoplastic) or noncancerous (nonneoplastic) disorders. Nonneoplastic disorders include nephritis (see page 168); a number of reproductive disorders such as miscarriage and disorders of the mammary glands (see page 179); disorders of the eye (see page 173); life-threatening anaemias; and chronic diarrhoea.

Neoplastic disorders include the leukaemias and cyto-proliferative diseases. The leukaemias (cancer of the blood cells) are less common. The cyto-proliferative diseases cause cancer of the lymph tissues. Lymphomagenesis is the most common neoplastic disease caused by FeLV. This disease may occur in three areas of the body. Thymic lymphoma occurs in the chest, just in front of the heart. Multicentric lymphoma manifests itself in the lymph nodes throughout the body. The third form, alimentary lymphoma, affects the intestine, intestinal lymph nodes, the kidneys and the liver.

Some cats with FeLV develop neurological problems such as paralysis, behavioural disorders, walking difficulties and general weakness.

FeLV is commonly transmitted to healthy cats by saliva or nasal secretions of infected cats. There is no cure for FeLV, which is more easily transmitted than FIV. Prevention consists of vaccination, and limiting exposure to cats suspected of being infected. Cats with FeLV should not be allowed to roam.

Feline infectious peritonitis

Feline infectious peritonitis (FIP) is caused by a feline coronavirus. The number of cats that become ill with FIP is probably 1 per cent or less. However, it is invariably fatal once a cat becomes ill. The virus is apparently spread among cats by oral exposure to infected faeces, saliva or urine.

FIP is subdivided into two forms based on symptoms: the first, a wet (effusive) FIP, characterised by fluid accumulations in the thorax (chest) and abdomen; the second, a dry (non-effusive) FIP, in which small pyogranulomas (a group of pus cells) develop in the abdominal organs.

The symptoms of wet FIP include poor appetite, weight loss, depression, abdominal swelling and a chronic, recurrent fever that does not respond to antibiotics. If there is fluid in the thorax (pleural cavity), cats will have difficulty breathing.

Cats with dry FIP usually have a fluctuating fever, lethargy and weight loss for 2 to 12 weeks or more. This form of FIP is considered to be a chronic condition. Many cats develop disorders of the eyes (see page 173) and of the nervous system (see page 180).

Diagnosis of FIP is difficult because no reliable laboratory test exists for this disease. The only available test measures the coronavirus antibody, but it cannot distinguish between the different kinds of coronaviruses. Microscopic examination of tissue samples is carried out after death; surgical biopsies before death are rarely performed due to the severity of FIP-related illness.

The fluid in the wet FIP is high in protein, amber in colour, and thick. Many cats with FIP have an increased globulin (antibody protein) level in the blood.

Diagnosis of the dry form of FIP is even more difficult. It commonly goes undetected in weak, lethargic, feverish cats that have contracted minor diseases of the liver or kidneys.

The disease has no effective treatment. Cats that develop FIP-related diseases almost invariably die. Prevention is difficult because no accurate diagnostic test for FIP exists as yet. Therefore, healthy-looking cats with undetected FIP can easily spread the disease. Cats known to be infected should be isolated. The use of proper isolation techniques in catteries helps to prevent the spread of FIP.

Rabies

Rabies is a lethal disease caused by a virus (in the rhabdovirus family) that affects cats, humans and many other animals, including the cat's favourite prey – birds. Most rabies infections result from a bite inflicted by a rabid animal, when saliva containing the virus gets underneath the skin (see *Zoonoses – and how to prevent them*, page 186).

The incubation period varies tremendously depending on the amount of virus transmitted and the area of the body affected. Generally, incubation lasts between 9 and 51 days.

Rabies has three progressive stages: prodromal, furious or dumb, and paralytic. In the first stage, behaviour changes: outgoing cats may hide; shy cats become friendly. In the next phase, which lasts one to four days, unpredictably vicious behaviour predominates with the cat's muscles twitching. The cat becomes irritable, develops a hoarse voice, salivates, and gets progressively weaker. Paralysis, the final stage, lasts one to four days and ends in death. Most cats with rabies die within eight days.

Any cat displaying sudden unusual behaviour should be suspected of being rabid. However, if the affected cat survives more than 10 days, it is unlikely that it

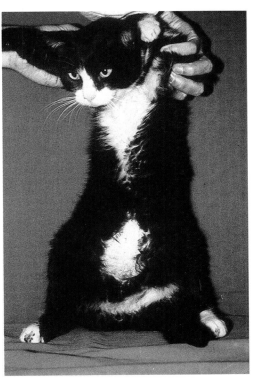

This cat has a swollen abdomen as a result of contracting FIP.

has rabies. If it dies before that, the brain should be examined to confirm diagnosis.

In some countries all cats must be vaccinated against rabies. Regardless of local regulations, routine vaccination is highly recommended if you live in an area where rabies exists.

Toxoplasmosis

Toxoplasmosis is caused by the parasite *Toxoplasma gondii*. A cat is exposed to the parasite when it ingests raw meat or wild prey, such as rodents, whose flesh may be infected. Thereafter, the parasite multiplies in the cat's intestine and lives in its faeces. Generally, the parasite produces few signs of illness. But in severe cases, the parasite spreads rapidly through the cat's system, damaging body tissues. Symptoms, when they occur, depend on the areas affected.

Why some cats become ill, while most others remain well, is not clearly understood. Simultaneous infections, such as feline leukaemia virus, may make cats more susceptible to *Toxoplasma gondii* infection. Common symptoms include anorexia, lethargy and breathing difficulties. Other symptoms include jaundice, vomiting, fever, diarrhoea, uveitis, enlarged abdomen and neurological disorders.

Toxoplasmosis can be diagnosed by a test that measures the antibody level to *Toxoplasma gondii* in blood serum. Infected tissue can also be examined by microscope. The efficacy of drugs to treat toxoplasmosis remains unproven.

An affected cat can be a source of infection for pregnant women. The babies of women infected by the disease while pregnant risk developing severe physical malformations.

Keeping a pet cat indoors and away from hunting wild prey is one sensible method of reducing the risk of exposure. A pet cat should be fed cooked food or commercial pet preparations. The cat's litter box should be emptied daily, preferably by someone not at risk.

The ageing cat

Our present knowledge of the origin and development of many cat diseases is a long way from being complete. In many cases the symptoms that appear on the surface may mask other diseases underneath.

In the end, the cat has only one life – not nine, as folklore would have us believe. Especially as it gets older, the cat needs special attention and care. An elderly cat may want to eat less and drink more, and it may lose weight. A kind and helping hand may be necessary at home. Owners may have to help with grooming, maintain a close watch on diet, keep the cat's favourite spot clean and warm, and enlist a vet's careful attention to keep their animal in good health. The average domestic cat lives into its mid to late teens, and one English tabby queen is on record as living to the ripe old age of 34.

Zoonoses – and how to prevent them

Any infectious or parasitic animal disease that can be transferred to humans is called a zoonosis. Such diseases can be transmitted by insect vectors (mosquitoes), scavengers (rats), and animals used for food (chickens, pigs, cattle) or kept as pets (birds, turtles, dogs, cats). All developed countries have strict food hygiene regula-

Life cycle of *Toxoplasma gondii*

The life cycle of the toxoplasmosis infection is identical in all warm-blooded animals, but it may assume a specific form in cats.

A healthy cat rewards the care given by its owner.

tions to limit infections from animal food sources. Pet owners, however, must rely on their own good sense to make sure they and their families do not catch diseases from the family pet.

There are three routes of infection:
•bites and scratches – bacteria and other microorganisms in the cat's saliva and on its paws may be transmitted this way;
•direct contact – mites and fungi can be picked up from the cat's fur, and fleas can jump from the cat to the owner;
•faeces – worm eggs and parasites may contaminate fingers or food.

All bites and scratches should be washed and treated with antiseptics. Severe bites should always be seen by a doctor. In areas such as North America and parts of Europe that harbour the rabies virus, bites or scratches by a cat behaving abnormally should receive immediate medical attention. If indeed the cat had rabies, the victim will need postexposure immunisation and delay could be fatal.

A small (unidentified) bacterium is suspected of causing cat-scratch fever, an uncommon disease that affects mostly children, mainly in autumn and winter. The cat delivering the bite or scratch is not ill, doesn't need any treatment, and doesn't have to be destroyed.

The child, however, may show symptoms that include swollen lymph nodes or an infected blister near the scratch, fever, rash and headache. Diagnosis is con-firmed by a biopsy and skin tests. A severely infected node or blister may have to be drained. Painkillers may be needed for headaches and other types of discomfort, but the illness usually clears up in about two months.

Bites from fleas occur when fleas jump onto humans to feed. Fleas may have lodged in carpeting and upholstery, which must be treated if the infestation is to end.

Various fungal infections, scalp ring-worm for instance, may be caught from cats. People who develop allergic reactions to debris from a cat's skin may develop hives or suffer asthmatic attacks when a cat is in the house. Cat faeces, or soil or sand contaminated by faeces, may carry eggs that produce infestations of thread-like worms, larvae of which can affect a person's vision.

All zoonoses can be avoided with a few simple precautions:
•Always wash your hands after touching a pet, its toys, dishes, bedding and litter box. Teach children to do this from an early age, and discourage them from playing with pets until such practices have become second nature.
•Do not handle litter boxes when pregnant. Cover the children's sandpit when not in use.
•Make routine worming and flea treatments a regular feature of your cat's regular health care. (See also *Human-cat diseases*, page 205.)

INDEX OF CONDITIONS

THE CAT
AND ITS OWNER

The right cat for you

The Aristocats. © DISNEY. By special permission of The Walt Disney Company.

After living through both its worship as a god-like figure in ancient Egypt and unbelievable cruelty in the Middle Ages, the cat went on to become widely accepted as the world's best mouse-catcher. Today it is generally invited into our homes as a pet, and in recent years has also proved its value as a good companion to the sick and aged. Since the early 1980s, it has been recognised that the company of a domestic animal, particularly a cat, can influence the behaviour of adults and children alike. Stroking a cat's fur can soothe the nerves and reduce blood pressure; having the company of a friendly cat can sometimes speed one's recovery following a heart attack.

Establishing a mutually rewarding relationship with your pet requires certain skills and a little effort. Getting to know something of feline behaviour generally and the characteristics of particular breeds is a good way to begin. Purebred cats are quite predictable in looks and temperament, but cats with less impressive pedigrees, or no pedigrees at all, are just as likely to make delightful pets. The ideal cat should be even-tempered and happy living with humans and possibly with other domestic animals.

Before you get a cat, think about how it will fit into your household. Do you want an affectionate, companionable, cuddly cat or an independent-minded, outdoor feline that will roam the neighbourhood woods at will? Either way, a reputable breeder or knowledgeable cat fancier should be able to suggest a number of breeds that will meet your expectations and requirements.

The best way to see the different breeds is to attend shows and ask exhibitors about their animals. Arrange to visit breeders and look at their stock. This will also give you some idea of prices.

Many people select cats for their looks; others choose a cat over a dog, say, because it is easier to care for in a city. The cat is an ideal indoor pet: it is always clean, does not have to be taken for walks, and can stay at home alone all day. It also costs little to maintain.

You will have to decide whether to get a male or a female, a long-haired or a short-haired cat. Unlike Persians and other long-haired cats, short-haired breeds, such as Siamese and Burmese, do not require grooming every day.

There are certain behaviour patterns, too, which must be taken into account when considering the acquisition of a cat, particularly those related to the cat's sexuality.

Neutering pays off

Pet owners who have their cats neutered at puberty avoid any number of problems. Often owners who intend to keep their cats indoors see no great need for this surgery and put it off indefinitely. But neutering makes sense even if your cat does not go out on the town. Living with an uncastrated male can be quite unpleasant due to its musky odour and the way it marks its territory by urinating on furniture, draperies and clothing. And the wailing of a female cat in heat is likely to bring complaints from neighbours. In the long run, castration or spaying is the only solution.

Acquiring a cat

Kitten or grown cat? Buy or adopt? From shelter or breeder? A registered show breed or the friendly stray that wanders into the garden? Since acquiring a cat will affect the owner's life for a good many years, these are just the minor considerations. The nitty-gritty has to do with the responsibilities of owning a cat, and making a decision that is good for the pet as well as for the household.

Have you the time and temperament to play with the cat? Are you prepared to spend the money pet care requires – on food, veterinary care and even boarding costs from time to time? And do you want a cat, or just a pet? Would you be just as happy with a goldfish?

Adopt or purchase?

Assuming you decide that you and a cat are right for each other, you are now ready to buy or adopt. Either way, you would be wise to first spend some time observing and playing with the cat of your choice. This is particularly important when adopting an adult cat, which already will have a well-established personality.

Adopting from an animal shelter

You can readily adopt a cat from your local animal shelter and this humanitarian act may very well bring you one of the best friends you will ever have. Where there

An example of a clean, well-run boarding cattery.

is a choice, your vet, and possibly local animal groomers and trainers, will be able to direct you to one that is well-run, where you have a good chance of finding a healthy, well-adjusted pet.

Keep in mind, however, that healthy animals may be given to shelters because of serious behavioural problems. This is one reason why you should spend as much time as possible playing with your prospective pet and observing its behaviour. Ask shelter employees about the cat's personality and litter-tray habits. Try to visit a few times before taking the plunge.

Stop off at the veterinary surgery on your way home from the shelter. You have to be sure that the cat is healthy and free from both feline leukaemia and feline immunodeficiency infections, especially if you already have other cats.

Where to purchase?

From a breeder

If you have decided on a purebred cat, your best source is a breeder of the kind of cat you have in mind. Reputable breeders have an established clientele and a reputation to maintain. Some may be happy to put you in touch with their clients so that you can see some adult relatives of the kitten that interests you – a good indication of how the cat will develop.

Where can you find breeders? At cat shows, through your vet or by word of mouth. Cat magazines are also a good source of breeders' names and cats for sale and breeders will often advertise in their local paper. Cat clubs usually have lists of breeders with kittens available. If you wish to own one of the less common breeds you may have to travel some distance or put your name down on a waiting list.

When you have located a prospective kitten, arrange to see it at the breeder's home; you can then check that the kitten is healthy and that you are happy with the temperament of its mother and other related cats. The breeder may ask you to collect the kitten when it is old enough, or may deliver the kitten to you in order to check that your home is suitable.

Pedigree rescue and rehoming services

Whenever possible, the cat clubs rescue and rehome pedigree cats, so that the animal shelters can devote their resources to non-pedigree cats. Your local area club or the appropriate breed club will usually know of an adult cat available, or will put you on their waiting list: many pedigree cats have to be rehomed because of a change in their owner's circumstances, some are picked up as strays and some have to be rescued from unsuitable homes.

Privately

You may find cats advertised in the classified section of a newspaper. But be careful. Always arrange to collect the cat yourself; if it is delivered you will have no opportunity to check out its source, its health or its temperament.

From a pet shop

Impulse, rather than sound reasoning, usually governs pet shop purchases. Often nobody there will know or be willing to tell you where the animals come from. With animals from different sources confined together, disease can spread rapidly. Remember that anyone who has reared their kittens conscientiously will wish to meet their new owners and be sure that the kittens are going to good homes, so would be unlikely to place them elsewhere for sale.

How to choose a cat

Good health should top your list of requirements in choosing a cat. This is no time to become sentimental over an unhappy-looking or sickly kitten. In fact one should avoid all cats from a home or breeder where any cat seems sick. And your two best clues to the cat's good health are the condition of its coat and whether it is active and alert.

The coat should be smooth and without mats, fleas, or other pests. Ruffle the fur gently, watching for any black specks that could be flea droppings, and for scaly areas or fur loss that could indicate ringworm.

The cat should be lively, showing affection and curiosity about the world around it. (If one kitten in a litter bounds over to see you and takes an affectionate interest in your proffered hand, that is probably the one you should buy.) Check its eyes, ears and nose. The eyes should be bright with no sign of the nictitating membrane (see page 55) and the ears and nose should be clean. There should be no discharge from either the eyes or the nose. Examine the anal area for signs of diarrhoea or tapeworm segments. Gently feel the abdomen. Potbellied cats may have worms.

Pedigrees and registration papers

Like all purebred animals, purebred cats vary considerably in price. Show animals, the cream of the breed, are priced accordingly. A 'pet quality' animal from the same litter, one that may be an excellent pet even though it does not meet show standards, may cost less.

When you buy a pedigree cat you must also be supplied with its pedigree. If the cat is registered, you should also receive its transfer document (a copy of its registration certificate, which includes the registered name and details of the kitten), either at the time of purchase or very soon afterwards. Many breeders register all their kittens, some register one or two in a litter and declare the others while some may leave a whole litter unregistered. A kitten that is unregistered or declared may be registered by the purchaser provided that this is done before the kitten is 2 years old.

A breeder may sell a kitten on condition that it is neutered. Such kittens are usually registered on the non-active register, which means that their offspring can never be registered; this should be noted on the pedigree. The precise terms of any other special agreements about the kitten should be spelt out in a contract of sale. Read this carefully before signing, to make sure that you are happy to buy a kitten under such conditions. Many breeders provide insurance that covers the kitten for a few weeks after purchase. However, reputable breeders take all precautions to ensure that they are supplying healthy kittens; if one is found to be in poor health it can usually be returned for a full refund.

Duties

Once you have a cat, you must put some effort into seeing that it doesn't become a danger to itself and a nuisance to others. Ownership requires that we respect the freedom of others. So make sure your new arrival does not inflict itself on those who may not tolerate an animal's company.

Responsible ownership involves looking out for the cat's well-being without imposing on family, friends or neighbours. Set ground rules right from the start. Your cat will not understand why something that was all right yesterday is not permitted today. Say a firm 'No,' as you remove it from off-limits furniture or laps of visitors. Say an equally firm 'No' if it bites or scratches. Don't let it explore your garden if it is to be kept indoors. And if it is allowed outside, keep it leashed at first so that it doesn't go into neighbours' gardens.

The Cat Commandments

Purebred or not, all kittens are lovable.

Ten rules

Follow these ten simple rules to ensure that your new cat settles quickly and easily into its new home. (See also *What will it eat?*, page 195, and *Hygiene*, page 199.)

First rule
Before you bring me home, pick up food and bedding for me

Make sure you have cat food and a place to sleep ready for your new cat. Since it may refuse an unfamiliar food, or suffer digestive problems from eating something new, find out what brand of food your cat was fed previously. The person from whom you're getting the cat may even give you a sample. This will ensure a very gradual transition in the cat's diet over at least a few days. You might also arrange to get some item of bedding that will carry home familiar odours. In this way, the 'orphan' will have a sense of security in its new home.

Second rule
Let me take possession of the house and learn the ropes on my own

Your kitten will want to explore every part of its new domain. But prohibited areas must be shut off from the outset; there is nothing more difficult than teaching a cat not to go somewhere it has already been allowed to explore.

Do not let the arrival of a kitten upset the family routine. There is no point in misleading the kitten into expecting attention all the time, since sooner or later it has to be left by itself. It would not want to sleep alone, either, after having been allowed to sleep on its owner's bed. And it would no longer want to eat alone on the floor after being accepted at table.

Third rule
Bring me into your home quietly

When your kitten arrives home, try not to be overenthusiastic. Undoubtedly everyone will want to get to know the newest member of the household, and as the kitten is passed around, some of the younger members may shriek in delight.

But you should remember that the kitten is likely to be suffering from stress caused by separation from its mother and litter mates. The noise and the strange faces of all these new people may terrify the kitten. So try to make the introductions gradually. Above all, make sure your children do not invite all of their friends to visit the newcomer at once.

Fourth rule
Prepare a place for me to live, sleep and go about my toilet in peace

A quiet room – preferably not the kitchen – should be set aside for the new arrival during the first few days. A cardboard box turned on its side makes a good temporary home. Place the familiar-smelling item of bedding that you brought from the kitten's previous home in or near the box. If the room is cold, a hot water bottle – not too hot – can be wrapped in a towel to provide warmth and help the kitten sleep.

Set out bowls for water and food at the other end of the room and, off in another corner, a litter tray.

Fifth rule
Make sure I have plenty to eat and drink at all times

A kitten eats 8 to 10 times a day and also drinks more than an adult cat. Make sure its food and water bowls are always full. A weighted drinking bowl will prevent spills, or you can weigh the bowl down with a small clean stone. Keep special formula milk – bought from a vet – on hand for any kitten you are weaning.

Sixth rule
Please keep calm and don't rush around too much

The kitten will want to explore everywhere, but is easily frightened. Everyday activities – vacuuming for example – may scare it. And don't forget that even a young child will look like a giant to a tiny kitten. Too much caution in handling the kitten, on the other hand, will make it fearful or aggressive, characteristics that could last for life. Do not keep a kitten cooped up. It must make contact with its new surroundings gradually, even if they frighten the cat at first.

Seventh rule
Stow away potentially dangerous objects so I don't hurt myself

There are any number of objects that are irresistible to kittens – electrical cords and small objects that can be chewed on or swallowed, such as paper clips, drawing pins and coins. Young cats think these objects are their playthings, so never leave them where they can reach them.

Eighth rule
Brush, comb, bathe me, inspect my ears and cut my claws regularly

Even when such attention is not essential for good hygiene, regular grooming makes a kitten easier to handle in the long run. A kitten is more likely to grow up to be docile as a result of the attention. Because of such regular handling, it will be less stressed on veterinary visits and more willing to have its temperature taken when necessary, or to accept pills without a fuss.

The show animals exhibited by breeders in competitions have been accustomed to such attention from birth. These cats have their own distinct personalities, but remain calm when handled. (See also *Grooming*, page 200.)

Ninth rule
Expose me gradually to the rigours of outdoor life

Kittens should not be allowed outside until they have received all their vaccinations (see page 181). After this time, the kitten can be permitted to explore whatever outside territory your home provides. Early outings should be supervised. It is likely that your cat will need to make car journeys from time to time – for example, for visits to the vet. Try to make its first experiences of car travel as agreeable as possible. If those first rides are associated with fear and discomfort, it may be difficult, if not well-nigh impossible, to convince a cat to forget these early associations. On even the shortest car ride, a cat should be safely ensconced in its basket. Left loose in a car, a cat – especially if it is upset or nervous – may distract the driver, or escape through an open window into traffic.

10th rule
Take me to the vet within three days of my arrival

At first, everything is new and wonderful. But almost inevitably some problem will occur. Call your vet as quickly as possible with any questions you may have. Because you've now spent some time with your kitten, you will be able to make sense of the vet's answers and advice. If the kitten has to be vaccinated or wormed, you can take comfort in the fact that at least the acclimatisation period is effectively over.

If particularly troubling symptoms occur, you must arrange to visit the vet immediately, not only for the sake of the kitten, but also because any sale guarantees in the purchase contract are only good for a short time. After the examination, you can discuss health and training problems. By now the kitten should be showing its true character. You can tell whether it will be a lively or a sleepy cat, and whether or not it likes a lot of people around.

What will it eat?

The cat and its food

Strictly speaking, cats are not so much domestic animals as wild creatures that have been tamed. Many habits that set them apart from dogs are relics of their wild past.

This is particularly true in food matters. Cats left to roam outdoors, for example, become hunters, even though they do not always eat what they catch. They remain the carnivorous forest animals they once were – creatures that survived for centuries on living prey. And even though a cat in 'captivity' will eat whatever is available, only meat, fish and animal by-products truly satisfy its protein needs. Here again it differs from the dog, which gets adequate nutrition on half the protein essential for a cat.

However, cats themselves vary considerably both in their eating habits and energy needs. To maintain its weight for example, a small but active cat may require as much food as a much larger sedentary cat. So keep such individual needs in mind when deciding daily food portions and feeding schedules.

You must decide between two types of feeding arrangements: free-choice feeding or scheduled feedings.

Many people who spend the day away from home find free-choice feeding the most convenient. With this method, food is available continuously and the cats can eat when and how much they want. This works well as long as all cats in the home have similar nutritional needs, but it fails if one or more cats in a multi-cat household require a special diet or overeat. And obesity is likely to be a problem if an extremely palatable, high-calorie food is always available to an inactive cat.

Most households have no problem feeding the cat twice a day, and most cats are quite happy with this arrangement. A measured amount of food can be fed at convenient times – typically morning and evening – and this way you can ensure that each cat eats the right food.

Switching from scheduled feedings to a free-choice system is rarely a problem. Doing the opposite may take a little time. Begin by putting down the appropriate rations in the morning, say. After 15 minutes, remove any food that remains. Repeat the procedure that evening, and so on. After two or three days, most cats will adjust to the new routine.

When all cats in a household can tolerate a similar diet, free-choice feeding is a convenient option – especially when family members are out all day.

The cat has an insatiable curiosity and, in a familiar environment, will always try something new. So you should have no hesitation in varying a cat's food as long as you satisfy its dietary needs for fats and animal protein. (Any good-quality commercial cat food will do this.) Change foods, or brands, gradually however. Too abrupt a change may throw the cat off its food or upset its system.

A cat may also refuse to eat in a strange environment. When boarded or caged in a clinic, for example, a cat may not eat for several days.

Never be tempted to make a cat fast so that it will more readily eat a new food. Prolonged fasting can be dangerous – it may lead to hepatic lipidosis, a more or less irreversible fatty degeneration of the liver.

Commercial cat foods come in dry, semi-moist, and canned forms. Dry products are cheapest and will not spoil readily, but some vets feel the higher mineral content may predispose some cats to urinary infections. Not all dry foods are alike, however. Some are specially formulated to actually dissolve some kinds of urinary tract stones.

Choosing the food

Cats have a reputation for being 'difficult' eaters. While they are curious about what is in their bowls and will pick at unfamiliar food, they will only regularly eat what they really like. And true carnivores that they are, their liking is often related to the fat and protein content of what is offered.

To satisfy their nutritional requirements, cat food has to be especially rich. Although dogs can get by very nicely on cat food and on plant protein like soya, cats cannot survive on dog food. They need a diet much richer in fats and digestible protein, one containing larger quantities of amino acids such as taurine and arginine (see page 158). Adapted as they are to a car-nivorous diet, their digestive enzymes can break down only a limited amount of veg-etable matter.

Adult cats can be fed between two and three times a day and be given about 30 calories per 500 g (pound) of body weight a day to keep them healthy.

They need a diet heavy in protein (20 to 25 per cent by weight of the day's total). This can be derived from fish, cheese, poultry and eggs. Milk is also a good pro-tein source, but few adult cats like it and some are milk-intolerant – they cannot drink milk and will be sick if they do. Most kittens, on the other hand, like milk.

Young kittens receive all the nutrients they require from their mother's milk during the first four weeks of life. After that they should be started on solid foods three to four times a day. (See *Balanced diet,* page 198.) Kilogram for kilogram, pound for pound, kittens need twice the nutrition of adult cats. They need a high-er level of protein to develop their mus-cles and coat, and they need more calcium, phosphorus and other minerals than adult cats for their developing bones and teeth. And because they are extreme-ly active, kittens need more energy from their food than adult cats.

Varying the cat's food makes good sense in order to balance the diet and avoid min-eral deficiencies. New items can be added gradually. Experts also recommend mix-ing some of the old food with the new when changing the diet to give the cat the idea of continuity. By and large, though, plenty of meat and fish, whether as dry biscuits or the wet canned food, and chick-en, kidney, heart and other types of meat go down well with the adult cat.

Some cats prefer their food served at room temperature, possibly because the smell and flavour are more intense. They may either refuse cold food or vomit after eating it. Others, however, do not seem to mind cold food in the least and consume it with no problems. Sometimes a cat rejects its food because it has begun to spoil, a fact that is detected by the cat's highly sensitive nose.

Vitamin supplements should not be nec-essary if a cat is fed a properly balanced diet. Exceptions can be anaemic cats or preg-nant or nursing queens. But these or any other medications should not be given with-out consultation with a vet.

A few drops of mineral oil (available as liquid paraffin from pharmacists) added to the food every few days will help pre-vent hair-balls forming in the cat's stom-ach. Long-haired cats are particularly susceptible to these. Commercial hair-ball medication, though more expensive, is also available.

Quantity and quality

The quantity of food a cat needs largely depends on its age and weight. Most cats become accustomed to a certain quanti-ty of food, regardless of its composition or energy value. Therefore, if a cat is over-weight, increasing the cellulose (plant fibre) content in the diet may have posi-tive results. Conversely, increasing the fat content can cause weight gain, although this may not occur with an active kitten, or when the cat is pregnant or nursing kittens.

But whatever the concerns about possible obesity, the cat owner must never lose sight of the fact that a cat's digestive system is designed primarily for meat and, as such, can only handle small quantities of vegetables. Otherwise, it gets inadequate nutrition and suffers from diarrhoea and wind. That being said, vegetables are certainly not off-limits, and in certain circumstances, such as obesity, they may even be desirable. Indeed some medically formulated diets to treat obesity have a high vegetable content.

Even though it is entirely possible to do so, it takes considerable time and effort to produce a well-balanced, home-prepared diet for your cat. If you are determined to do so nonetheless, one rule of thumb is to combine two parts (by weight) of protein foods with one part of vegetable or vegetable and carbohydrate filler. It also simplifies matters that cats like all meats, including offal and fish. Meat, fish and other foods should be well cooked to prevent parasitic infestation and fish should always be deboned before serving.

But it is undeniably simpler, and more reliable, to feed your cat one of today's commercial cat foods. This way you can be sure it is getting a balanced diet. For desirable quantities of dry and canned foods, see page 198.

By nature, cats consume very little water. Domestic cats obtain 70 per cent of the water they need from the meats and canned food they are fed. (Cats in the wild get it from the prey they catch.) Yet they are very demanding about the quality of the water they drink. If it is not clear or fresh enough, a cat will decline to drink, even when very thirsty.

Even though they are not big drinkers, cats must always have free access to their water bowls. But owners should not be alarmed if the water level stays the same for some time. Remember to wash out the bowl and change the water often.

A cat eating dry food will have to drink frequently, about 3 tablespoons per kilogram (1½ tablespoons per pound) of body weight. For the average cat weighing about 4 kg (9 pounds), this means ¼ litre (1 cup) per day.

Common misconceptions

Popular literature and art often portray a cat purring on its owner's couch as it gazes at its saucer of milk and dish of liver out of the corner of its eye. What is interesting about this image is that it depicts exactly what should be avoided in terms of diet if you want to keep your animal in good health.

If they drink milk at all, many cats will develop diarrhoea. This is unfortunate, because milk is an excellent complete food; but many cats, like dogs, are unable to digest lactose.

Other dairy products, however, including yogurt, are quite acceptable, because they have been fermented and contain lactobacteria that assist digestion.

Liver, while remarkably rich in proteins, trace elements, and vitamins, also has a strong laxative effect. Cooking will weaken this effect somewhat. More worrying is the fact that liver contains very high concentrations of vitamin A, making it extremely dangerous for cats. High doses of this vitamin can cause haemorrhagic periostitis (bleeding and inflammation of connective tissue covering bones), as well as painful bony spurs around the joints.

The problem with liver is that cats adore it and have been known to become fixated on it. They may then refuse to eat anything else. Some cats have even been known to go on a hunger strike until they get more liver.

How can you tell if your cat is not eating well? Its coat will become messy and dull, its eyes will be glazed, and its nose will be warm and dry. It will move slowly, appearing completely lethargic, and its breath will smell stale. If these signs continue for more than a few days, consult your vet.

Yes, your cat can eat grass, and no, this does not mean it is sick. Contrary to popular belief, grass is quite good for your cat because it contains vitamins and it also helps the cat to eliminate hair-balls. In fact, if you live in a flat, or if your cat stays inside all the time, it might be a good idea to grow some grass in a pot or window box.

This cat is obese. To prevent or control excessive weight gain it may be necessary to decrease the volume of food, or to feed the cat a special weight-reducing diet.

GENERAL GUIDELINES

Small but frequent meals

Most cats are nibblers. They get by very nicely on several small meals a day. Some cats also do well on one or two larger meals, but others are gobblers, eating a large quantity of food very quickly. This leads to swelling of the stomach in the short run and, eventually, obesity. Obesity can start at a very early age.

Experiments with different foods should be tried when the cat is young. Later, being naturally curious, the cat will taste new dishes, but it will not become completely used to them and may even refuse them. It is therefore important to vary the menus while the cat is still young.

Gradual changes

Any sudden change in food could bring on diarrhoea. If you are planning a change in the cat's diet, do it gradually by varying the foods just a little or alternating meals of different consistencies. If you want to change from canned food, which is very moist (more than 80 per cent water), to a dry food, make sure the cat gets enough liquid, either by moistening the dry food, or getting the cat to drink extra water.

Fresh water

Cats insist on having fresh, clear water. One problem is that most tap water contains chemicals. Many areas have chlorinated water, which the cat does not like and will not drink until the water has settled; this can take 24 hours. This is why many cats refresh themselves from a pond or other body of stagnant water. They also prefer good quality fresh food. For example, they will spurn canned food that is beginning to dry out. Even dry food can become mouldy and unappetizing fairly quickly if it is not properly stored, and then your cat will refuse to eat it.

Balanced diet

A proper diet depends on the cat's age, its size, and how active it is, as well as the energy content of the particular food. Ask your vet's advice.

For serving quantities per day, here are some rules of thumb per 500 g (pound) of body weight: at 5 weeks of age, 125 calories; at 11 weeks, 75 calories; at 17 weeks, 55 calories; at 21 weeks, 50 calories; at 30 weeks, 48 calories; at 50 weeks or maturity, 30 calories.

Most vets recommend dry foods for cats because they have a better energy balance than canned foods. They can also prevent dental problems, and urinary tract infections – a common cat ailment.

In serving commercially prepared foods, estimate about 1 per cent of body weight per day for a 4.5 kg (10 pound) cat, and 1 to 3 per cent of body weight for canned food.

A proper diet of home-prepared food should contain at least 50 per cent of animal meat and fat – beef, chicken and fish – served well cooked, 20 per cent of well-cooked grains, 20 per cent of cooked green vegetables, and 10 per cent of vitamin and mineral complements, oil and dry yeast.

All meats and fish and other foods should be cooked well to prevent parasitosis (see page 165).

Healthy food

A cat's dietary needs are totally different from a dog's, even though a cat may be curious enough to investigate a dog's food bowl. Neither animal's nutritional needs will be met if they eat each other's food. Nor is it a good idea to feed a cat table scraps because most cats do not fare well eating food prepared for people. A cat, unfortunately, has little self-control and is likely to try anything. So it is up to the owner to decide what food is good for the cat.

Make absolutely certain that the cat does eat something if you are denying it certain kinds of food. A cat that does not eat for 48 hours may die. If your cat has not eaten for two days, consult your vet. But remember to check first that your cat is not gorging itself on its favourite foods at a neighbour's.

Always chop up the food

A domestic cat, like its cousins in the wild, does not chew its food, but simply swallows it down in lumps, letting its strong gastric juices break it down. So when putting out your cat's food, eliminate any bones and cut up the rest in small pieces.

A good mix

When a cat eats wild prey, including birds and mice, it swallows a mixture of meat and bone, muscles and internal organs. A domestic cat eating a diet of canned food has to get the equivalent of that same mixture to get the right amount of protein and fat. It needs about 20 to 30 per cent of protein and 40 per cent of fat to stay healthy.

Eat better, live longer

To sum up, if a cat has a good diet, is active and playful, with a shiny coat, regular bowel movements with well-formed stools, correct weight and figure, it is well nourished.

Hygiene

Litter

The cat has been called the 'desert animal' because it needs very little water to survive. Because it consumes so little water, its urine is very concentrated. And because its diet is mainly meat, its urine tends to have a strong odour. So a good litter is very important.

The litter should be both absorbent and deodorising and, since it must not be dangerous to humans or cats, should not contain poisons or powders. Most litter on the market today is clay or plant based.

The litter tray should be made of plastic (wood retains odours) and should be large enough to hold the cat comfortably. It should be about 10 cm (4 inches) deep and the litter itself should be about 4 cm (1½ inches) deep in the tray. This will permit liquids to be absorbed and the cat can bury its solid waste out of sight.

Of the commercial products, dust-free litters are best. With all commercial litters, solid wastes become covered with fine particles, which quickly dry the stools and lock in odours. This is especially true of clumping litter. It has sand-like granules of absorbing ground clay that dries and completely absorbs a cat's liquid wastes.

You will not have to change the litter so often if droppings are removed daily. You can do this with a slotted litter scoop. The box itself should be disinfected regularly, but be careful to choose a disinfectant that is safe for cats. Avoid any with carbolic acid, phenol or coal-tar ingredients.

Plant-based deodorant powders are now available in some stores. The powder, which can be placed under the layer of litter, both deodorises and perfumes the air, making life more pleasant for the cat owner. However, a few cats may be put off by some perfumes and refuse to use their litter. Scented litters, too, should be used carefully for the same reason.

Sand and gravel are not good litter material because cats find them abrasive and they are neither absorbent nor deodorising. They also promote bacterial growth and so are potentially dangerous for both humans and cats.

Sawdust is also unacceptable since it clings to the cat's fur, and the animal may ingest large quantities of it when it grooms. Another concern is the type of wood that created the sawdust. Some woods are treated with chemicals that can be poisonous or allergenic.

Newspapers, too, should be avoided. The chemicals in the ink may interact with urine to produce dangerous gases. Uninked newsprint, however, may be suitable for use in litter trays in some circumstances.

Cats are very finicky about their litter tray. They quickly become accustomed to one type of litter, and often insist on staying with the litter they used as kittens for the rest of their lives.

Cats are generally very clean. If a cat urinates of defecates outside the litter tray, it almost certainly has some kind of problem, and is letting the owner know. The odour may be new or offensive to the cat – or the litter may not be fresh. Sometimes a cat will also avoid using its litter tray if somebody has teased it or handled it roughly or if it has been disturbed while in the litter. Cats are very private animals.

Whenever the cat goes to the toilet somewhere other than its litter box, clean the soiled area very carefully to avoid repeat soilings.

The basic clay-based litter, the most commonly used litter in most countries.

Clumping litter, which causes liquid wastes to form an easy-to-remove lump.

this process helps to maintain a comfortable body temperature.

When it licks itself, a cat swallows a certain amount of hair. This accumulates in the stomach, and from time to time the cat will bring up dark soggy masses known as hair-balls. If these are not regurgitated or excreted with faeces, they can create an intestinal obstruction. In the most

A happy, healthy cat always grooms itself spontaneously.

severe cases, surgery is the only solution.

This is another reason why grooming your cat is so important. Combing not only removes loose hair that might otherwise be swallowed and unsightly mats which cause itching, but it aerates the coat and massages the skin, thus stimulating further hair growth.

A metal comb is better than a brush, since brushes quickly fill up with hair after which they only scratch the surface of the coat. A comb, on the other hand, can penetrate right down to the skin. With a short-haired cat, use a fine-toothed comb and work from head to tail; on the tail itself, use a rubber brush.

For long-haired cats, try a pure bristle brush which does not cause static or break hairs. To remove snarls and tangles that are inevitable in a longhair, use a fine-toothed comb, gently running it upwards through the hair. To finish the job, you will need a toothbrush for the ruff and to smoothe the short facial hairs without getting too close to the eyes.

Although surface mats can generally be removed with blunt-nosed (surgical) scissors, seriously matted hair is another matter. If you try removing it with scissors, you risk cutting the cat's skin. Try to untangle it with your fingers. There are also commercial sprays for removing knotted fur and these can be quite effective. As a last resort, consult your vet about

Grooming

Healthy cats can keep themselves reasonably clean, but a little assistance from their owners can contribute significantly to the cat's coat. A healthy coat will be shiny, neat, and clean, with dead hair and skin cells removed and the skin and circulation toned up. Whether your cat is a short-hair or a longhair, its coat will need regular brushing; you cannot just let it groom itself.

Unlike their wild cousins, most domestic cats shed slightly all year, but have two heavier moults in spring and autumn. Only particular circumstances such as illness, kittening and stress will cause major hair loss, which can look like moulting.

When a cat grooms itself, it combs its coat, untangles its hair, and aerates its fur. It also regulates its body temperature by moistening its coat with its saliva. The air thus trapped in the fur provides thermal insulation, just like fibreglass between roof and ceilings insulates a house. Because the saliva evaporates when the cat is hot, having the cat anaesthetised and shaved. This overall clipping can do no lasting harm, and a new coat, albeit a thicker one, will grow back within a few months.

In any well-groomed cat, long-haired or short-haired, a brisk stroking of the fingertips against the lay of the fur will get out a lot of dead hair without upsetting the animal. Why work against the lay? Because dead hair held in place by the rest of the fur can be removed easily this way, and the coat is fully aerated at the same time.

If you notice your cat grooming one spot of its fur over and over, have a look. More than likely something has become stuck there – a burr or some tar.

Total body clipping may be required for a long-haired cat with severe matting.

Most kittens have learned to wash themselves by the time they are weaned, at which time the owner should get in on the act. The younger the cat when you begin grooming it, the easier it will be in the long run. This is doubly true of long-haired cats, that are not only more susceptible to matting than the short-haired breeds, but also have shorter tongues for doing the job themselves. Long-haired cats should be groomed every day; twice weekly is usually adequate for shorthairs.

From time to time, dust the animal with a flea or tick powder prescribed by your vet. You can clean the cat's fur with household detergent if it has been into some tar, paint or chemicals. Or the fur in the affected area can be soaked in cooking oil until

Shampooing is easier if the cat becomes accustomed to water at a very young age.

the foreign substance loosens enough to be washed off.

Bathing

Even though a few breeds of cat are quite at home in watery surroundings, most cats abhor water. So bath time could be a problem unless you accustom your cat to the practice early in life, preferably in the first few months – and provided you do not mind getting wet yourself! Since exhibitors wash some breeds before shows, good breeders try to get kittens used to water early on. Then, with luck, bath time will not be an ordeal when the cat is fully grown.

Apart from show cats, bathing is not essential on a regular basis. Cats, by their nature, keep themselves clean. But sometimes, whether for medical reasons or because the cat is badly soiled, a bath cannot be avoided.

If this is the cat's first bath, make a game of wetting it gradually, first with a flannel and then a sponge which will work the water into the fur. Use a large washing-up bowl, or the kitchen sink, filled with about 10 cm (4 inches) of lukewarm water, and fitted with a rubber mat so the cat cannot slip out of your grip. Hold the cat firmly, but do not restrain it any more than you have to, otherwise, it will struggle so much that shampooing will be extremely difficult. If possible get someone to help you: one of you can hold the cat, talking to it reassuringly all the time; the other can apply the shampoo. (Make sure you use a cat shampoo: residues from human shampoos, when licked, could poison the cat.) Afterwards rinse thoroughly.

Dry the cat in a warm towel. A good rubdown will be fine for a short-haired cat but may result in tangles if you have a long-haired breed. In that case, blot firmly and confine the cat to some warm area until it is completely dry. Then finish the job with a good combing. Some people find an electric hair-dryer on a low setting useful for drying the cat after its bath. But many cats are simply scared by the noise, which compounds an already highly stressful experience.

Baths are especially helpful in treating parasites and skin disorders. Male cats, for example, often suffer from 'stud tail', an accumulation of sebum under the tail, especially near the base (see page 172). The hair may be so matted that only shampooing can restore its silky smooth appearance.

For those who find giving their cat a bath too much trouble, there is a way out – give your cat a dry bath. Use a standard pet-grooming powder, or a mixture of talcum powder and cornstarch. Shake the powder over the cat's entire coat, spread it around with your hands, and then brush it in using a pure-bristle brush. For a short-haired cat you can use 500 g to 1 kg (1-2 pounds) of dry bran baked at 150°C (300°F) for 20 minutes. Massage the warm bran into the cat's fur, then comb it.

Cleaning the eyes and nose

As a rule, you do not have to wash a healthy cat's eyes. Should an eyewash become necessary, use cool, boiled water, a saline solution, or a product prescribed by a vet.

A cat in good health never has a runny nose, but its muzzle is always moist because it licks itself there often, and its nostrils are moistened by tears flowing from the corners of the eyes down the lachrymal ducts. Therefore a dry or runny nose is a sign that something is wrong. Never tamper with a cat's nose, except on specific instructions from the vet.

Cleaning the ears

The golden rule: the less you touch a cat's ears, the better. Inspect them carefully but do not poke inside with your fingers or cotton swabs. Both ears should be clean and clear, although the base of the pinna (see page 57) may be mildly greasy with cerumen, a yellow or brownish wax.

You can remove this with cotton balls dipped in warm olive or mineral oil and inserted into the outer ear; do not use a water-based cleanser or alcohol. Then pat the pinna with a dry cotton ball to remove the excess grease. Do not use cotton swabs. Although they can absorb much of the grease, they may push more of it back into the ear canal. There it can form a plug, which may have to be removed under general anaesthetic.

Don't be tempted to remove wax buildup too often. Every time you remove

this wax, you exercise the cerumen glands, and in the long run the production of wax will actually increase.

If your cat runs away when you touch its ear, or stays put but is obviously in pain, it may have any number of problems ranging from ear mites and foreign bodies in the ear to middle ear infections. Sometimes the affected cat will actually lean against your hand as you clean its ear, seeking relief from the pain and itching. Deafness, staggering and loss of balance are all symptoms of ear infections that require prompt veterinary attention.

Cleaning the mouth

A cat's breath is always strong, and you must learn to distinguish between strong breath and halitosis (bad breath). Halitosis may be due to bacteria or to wastes that should be excreted by way of the kidneys

DENTAL HEALTH

The cat's mouth must be examined at least once a year by a vet. The mouth is the body's front door, and consequently it can tell a great deal about an animal's general health. It is also the animal's 'hand', its main grasping organ. A cat's teeth are not deeply rooted in the lower jaw and can easily come loose and fall out. They are also prone to disorders such as neck lesions or cervical line lesions. Although these resemble cavities, they are not the same.

These lesions, which develop at a point between the crown and the root, are hidden by the edge of the root and can only be diagnosed after careful examination. If left unattended too long, they eat away at the tooth under the gum, eventually causing the tooth to fracture.

Frequent removal of tartar helps maintain the tooth's support structure, and prevents premature loss of teeth. The short operation is done under a general anaesthetic that poses no danger to the cat, since modern anaesthetics are extremely reliable and risk-free, even for older animals.

Broken teeth can now be repaired, thanks to new procedures in veterinary dentistry.

instead of through the mouth. If a cat's kidneys fail, wastes that would ordinarily be extracted by the kidneys accumulate in the blood. In those circumstances, the cat will have breath that smells like urine. (The breath of a cat in good health merely smells stale.)

Problems with teeth and gums also produce putrid smelling breath. This commonly begins with tartar and food debris accumulating around the cat's teeth and gradually decomposing. Tartar buildup occurs as minerals in the saliva, food debris and proliferated bacteria form a rough coating on the teeth. Older cats and those that are mainly fed soft foods are the most likely victims. Any bacteria or toxins in the mouth eventually find their way to the liver and kidneys. Because these organs are extremely fragile – liver and kidney disorders are the main cause of disease-related deaths in cats – it is easy to appreciate that a clean mouth is a key to good health.

There is no better way to keep a cat's mouth in good shape than by cleaning its teeth. But unless this was begun when the cat was quite young, it is unlikely to sit passively while you attempt it later on. It may work if you use a child's toothbrush and have somebody hold the cat's lips back while you do the brushing. Failing that, try a cotton swab or a strip of gauze bandaging wrapped around a fingertip; ordinary warm water is fine, with a final rinse in salt water. You may wish to use a special cat toothpaste. Never clean your cat's teeth with your own toothpaste: many such products contain detergents that are dangerous to cats. Some cats that are used to regular teeth cleaning may even tolerate having their mouths washed out with a stream of pressurised water. If your cat thwarts all attempts at dental hygiene, you will have no choice but to take it to the vet for an annual descaling. Good saliva circulation can be stimulated by giving your cat frequent opportunities to chew on dried cowhide bones.

Check your cat's mouth regularly to make sure there is nothing stuck between its teeth. Mouth infections sometimes begin when a foreign body, such as a needle or a fish bone, gets lodged between the cat's back teeth. Check its tongue too. Cats are always licking things, and as a result may have adverse reactions to any number of chemicals.

Appetite loss, inflamed gums or tongue, ulcerous sores inside the mouth, and excessive salivating are all signs of mouth infections. If you notice such problems, see your vet without delay. Most such disorders respond well to treatment with antibiotics.

Clipping the claws

One widely held misconception is that cats only strop their claws to sharpen them or to wear them down. Some observers suggest stropping actually produces the opposite effects.

They argue that when a cat 'sharpens' its claws, it is not honing its weaponry at all. It is merely giving notice that it has staked out – marked – the object or territory as its own. This, they point out, is why scratching posts designed to protect walls and table legs may have little effect.

Cats do indeed leave scratch marks as territorial stakes. But it would also seem that cats confined indoors for long periods are beating off boredom, as well as performing a manicure, when they attack your prized draperies or dining-room suite. So put a scratching post at the cat's favourite attack site and thrust the cat at it whenever you find it sacking your home.

You can find all kinds of elaborate models at your local pet store, or you can make your own. (See *Scratching post*, page 205.)

Placing the cat on its back helps relax it. Stroking the stomach will calm the animal between clips.

Even if the scratching post works, you would be wise to cut the tips off the cat's claws regularly. Then, even if it performs its rituals in all the wrong places, the stropping will cause less damage.

Once a month, sit down with the cat on its back, held firmly between your knees. With a pair of strong scissors or guillotine clippers, snip the tip off each claw just outside the pink nerve-containing quick. Clipping any closer to the bone will cause pain and considerable bleeding, an unpleasant experience a cat will remember. It is better to err on the side of caution, taking off less claw but clipping more often, and getting little resistance from the cat.

There is a positive side to these little exercises. They help develop good relations between owner and animal, especially important with cats which are always looking for ways to get more attention. Once again, a cat that is accustomed to pedicures at a young age will accept them more readily as years go by.

Nails should be inspected regularly to monitor their condition, the condition of the nail sheaths, and to catch problems at the earliest possible stages. This way infections and deformed or overgrown nails can be spotted early.

Equipment and accessories

Litter tray

Ideally the litter tray should be about 10 cm (4 inches) deep and, depending on the size of the cat, about 50 cm (20 inches) by 40 cm (16 inches); a large cat will of course need a larger box. Essentially the box should be durable, it must be steady on the ground or wherever it is located, and it must be washable.

Some cats are more thorough about burying their excrement than others, and may scratch away vigorously with their hind paws. Cats with this habit should have a litter box with a high rim, or even one with an inward curving edge. Otherwise, you will have constant heaps of litter all over your floor.

For the more fussy cat, a fully enclosed litter box will give the animal the impression that it is safe from prying eyes. Enclosed litter trays may also be more acceptable in appearance; many have deodorant filters in their lids to minimise the escape of unpleasant odours.

A litter scoop is also an essential part of the litter equipment. Buy a strong one, and it is useful to keep a spare. Faeces must be scooped out of the litter at least once a day, and preferably as soon as possible after the cat has used the litter.

Stores now sell litter tray liners, usually made of plastic, which are easily and quickly removed. A reminder: Don't locate the litter box near the cat's feeding area or the cat may refuse to eat or use its box.

Even if your cat goes outside as an adult and no longer uses it, do not discard the litter tray. Your cat will need to be kept indoors after an operation or if it is unwell. Old cats also need litter trays; they often have less control so, without a tray, may have 'accidents' overnight.

Cat carriers

The worst way to carry a cat is in a soft, open bag. Bags can collapse on the cat, are poorly ventilated and difficult to clean. They cannot be closed tightly, and an enterprising cat can easily escape from such carriers.

Rigid cat carriers are far more practical. The best models come apart in the middle, and the bottom half can be used as a litter box. They are easy to clean, and the most practical ones open at the top like traditional wicker baskets. These baskets are practical, but they tend to be draughty, fragile and difficult to clean.

To put a cat in a perspex box is real torture, because a cat enjoys crouching out of view to watch what's going on; it likes to lie in ambush rather than go out and look for prey. So when it is in a see-through enclosure, it feels exposed and knows it cannot hide. Opaque boxes with breathing holes for the cat are preferable. This way the cat can look through the holes at its surroundings.

Wire baskets are easy to clean and can be covered if the cat feels exposed. If the basket does not have a plastic base, provide a waterproof lining.

This cat loves its classic wicker basket, but escape from it is fairly easy. The rigid plastic carrier (facing page) is much more reliable.

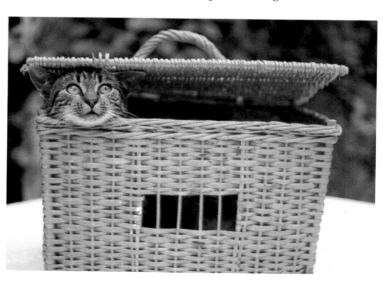

When you buy a carrier consider the ease of getting the cat in and out. It is easier to place an injured cat in a large top-opening carrier than to slide it in through a door in the side. An injured or frightened cat may be impossible to remove through a door without risk to the handler, and it may be necessary to dismantle the carrier around the cat.

It's a good idea at first to leave the carrier where the cat can see it so it will seem less mysterious and not so frightening. Otherwise, every time the owner brings it out, the cat will fear the worst and make every effort to avoid being captured.

Bedding

As a rule, a cat will choose where it wants to sleep. It may even change places from time to time and won't really appreciate an elaborate bed. Nevertheless, some owners are tempted to give cats their own beds. If you decide to buy a cat bed, they can be found or made in a wide variety of designs from the fancy wicker basket to an ordinary cardboard box lined with paper or an old blanket. The bed must not contain any wool if the cat is a wool-eater. Use cotton-covered foam cushions instead. Cats generally like these.

Feeding bowls

A cat should have its own dishes for eating. These should be shallow enough for the cat to eat without getting the food all over its nose – something it dislikes. The bowls should be well cleaned before each feeding, but use soap or dish detergent sparingly. Then rinse well; many detergents have ingredients harmful to cats.

Toys

Cats love to play, even when they are supposed to be staid and middle-aged. Just about anything will distract a cat, from the most sophisticated mechanical toys to a ball of paper on a string. Be very careful with sharp objects you may be using, like a sewing needle dangling from a piece of thread. A cat will play with the thread and may swallow it together with the needle, piercing its tongue or getting it stuck in its throat (see page 164).

Scratching post

It's a good idea to have a scratching post available for the cat and, with luck, the animal will rake its claws on it and not on pieces of furniture or curtains to which it has taken a fancy. Over a period of weeks, the post can be moved gradually to an out-of-the-way location if it is bothering anyone. You will need some sort of vertical pillar, since the cat usually stands on its hind legs when scratching. It may be free-standing as long as it is on a stable base, or it may be a panel attached to the wall. Either way, a log or piece of unplaned coarse-grained wood may do the trick, or you may want to fit it with some burlap or carpeting, which appeals to some cats.

Collar and lead

If your cat wears a collar, it should be tagged with your address and telephone number. However, collars may be dangerous. All collars must have an elastic section so that the cat can free itself if the collar catches on anything. A cat may also get its paw through a collar and, unless released quickly, the collar may cut right through the skin. Some cats can be trained to walk on a collar or harness and lead.

Human-cat diseases

Fortunately, diseases that can be transmitted from cats to humans are rare and, in most cases, easy to control with good hygiene. Keeping the cat's litter tray out of the kitchen, regular vacuuming, and preventing young children from touching the cat's litter will prevent most problems. Sandpits in public playgrounds are potentially hazardous. These are frequented by stray cats that are quite likely to be parasite carriers. (See *Zoonoses – how to prevent them*, page 186 for a fuller discussion.)

Children can also be infested by tapeworms transmitted by fleas from the cat. To be infested, the child must actually swallow a flea that is carrying worms from the animal; the flea could, for instance, bury itself in the jam on a slice of bread. The symptoms are never more serious than a simple intestinal parasitic infection.

Toxoplasmosis is an infection caused by a single-cell microorganism which multiplies in the cat's intestines. The infected cat may then excrete egg-infected faeces and the cycle of human and animal contamination continues.

Those most at risk are pregnant women who can transmit a fatal infection to their unborn children, and anyone with an immunodeficiency disorder.

Signs of distress

General appearance and behaviour

Though cats proverbially have nine lives, in reality they can get sick and die. They are just as prone to diseases as other animals and, all cats from time to time, face fights, falls and risky adventures. There is not much an owner can do to curb a cat's natural curiosity, which often leads it onto distant windowsills and roofs or to the top of high trees in search of birds and squirrels.

Generally an owner can tell when something is troubling the cat – it may sleep all day or be aggressive or unusually listless. In those circumstances, a trip to the vet is in order to make sure nothing is seriously wrong with the cat.

A sick cat will change its behaviour even to the point of misbehaving. In cases where the animal is suffering great pain, has a high fever, or is near death, it will disappear from sight. Cats hide when they are about to die.

If a cat usually goes outdoors, its range of movement must be restricted at the first sign that something is amiss. Any days that it spends away represent precious

Unkempt fur and a timorous crouching position are signs of a sick cat.

time lost to the vet and can lessen its chances of recovery.

If the cat is in pain, perhaps suffering from a broken bone or a dislocation, it may well become aggressive. It may even try to intimidate its owner to avoid being handled and so having to suffer more. Because of this, it takes special skills to pick up or otherwise handle a cat that is suffering in any way. It is best to approach slowly, speaking calmly all the while in order to win its trust. Pick it up by the scruff of the neck, supporting its body weight with an arm under its rear legs. Carry the cat at arm's length, though, to avoid its sharp front claws.

Digestive and urinary disorders

If a cat has digestive problems, it will show its discomfort by becoming slovenly. It will go to the toilet outside its litter, often just beside the box, with frequent bouts of diarrhoea. It may suffer from cystitis, and in that case will also urinate outside the litter. Scolding will not help – the animal is already unhappy enough.

If it is constipated or has a urethral obstruction, it will spend its time in the litter tray trying to defecate or urinate, but not succeeding. If it visits the box frequently and behaves in this way, do not waste precious time plying it with laxatives but take it to the vet immediately. A urethral obstruction can lead to life-threatening uremic poisoning.

Vomiting is not necessarily a cause for alarm, since cats easily bring up a meal at the slightest gastric problem. Frequent vomiting should be investigated, though. If the cat vomits every day, or worse, several times a day, a visit to the vet should be arranged without delay.

If the vomiting is merely a digestive problem, it is easily treated; vomiting due to infections, urinary or endocrine disorders, or tumours can be serious, and may require veterinary intervention.

The cat's fur coat

A cat in good health spends much of its time grooming its coat. So dishevelled or matted hair, dandruff or a coat that feels greasy not only look unpleasant, but are cause for alarm.

A poorly groomed coat reflects chronic suffering or heralds the approach of a serious disease, while an acute disorder will produce an abrupt, spectacular change of behaviour.

Often the coat's condition provides precise clues to what is wrong with the cat. Diffuse or localised thinning of the fur suggests a rash. This calls for a trip to the vet, especially if there are scabs, any sign of parasites, fleas or ticks, or if you suspect that the cat suffers from a hormonal imbalance.

Deterioration of the coat is sometimes due to vitamin deficiencies arising from inadequate nutrition or certain disorders. Sometimes the coat is matted and dry because the cat has failed to groom itself – possibly because it is exhausted, or

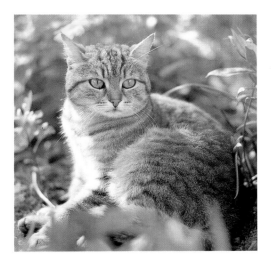

No special intelligence is needed to tell a sick cat (above) from a cat in good health (right). At the first signs of alarm, the owner should consult a vet. If diagnosed in time, most diseases can be treated.

because stiff joints prevent it from moving its head and turning its body in order to reach, and clean, all parts of its coat.

When this is the case, the owner must lend a hand. With arthritic animals, you must be as gentle as possible and respect the cat's sense of pride.

Be especially careful when brushing any ill cat. The task will naturally be easier if the animal has been accustomed to regular brushing and combing. But even when you know the source of the illness or injury, you cannot always be sure what parts of the cat are hurting. Play it safe, and use extremely gentle motions if you must brush its fur at this time.

Making sure the coat looks its best is only one aspect of coat care. What is more critical is ensuring that it is properly aerated and smoothed so that it insulates the cat from cold and humidity.

Appetite and thirst

A cat in good health does not necessarily have to drink a lot each day. If an animal seems inordinately thirsty for a single day, that is entirely acceptable; but if the quantity of water consumed increases each day, something must be wrong. It could signal some kind of serious problem, a fever or a metabolic disorder. Similarly, an excessive appetite may indicate the onset of diabetes. Anorexia, or loss of appetite, is more readily noted as a rule.

Generally, abrupt weight changes are serious warning signs.

Sensory organs

Eyes sealed shut with tears flowing, a grubby, runny nose and dirty, foul-smelling ears are, in themselves, sufficiently obvious problems to warrant a visit to the vet.

It is dangerous for owners to try to diagnose their pets themselves. For example, if the ear is especially painful, it is very important not to administer any medications since the wrong remedy may make certain ear disorders worse.

When the cat's eyes appear runny or have a blue or white film, the cat always needs professional attention.

Cats can sneeze just as humans can for many reasons. Sneezing accompanied by runny eyes or nose may mean feline influenza, which requires a vet's care.

A cat's breath, which is naturally strong, should not smell like urine. If it does, the owner should suspect a mouth infection or perhaps a kidney disease resulting in excessive wastes building up in the body.

Breathing

When a healthy cat is resting, you should barely see it breathing. An animal that is breathing heavily but has not been running, may have a heart or lung disorder. If the nostrils are also dilating at each breath, waste no time in getting to the vet. These are serious signs.

Like dogs, cats do not perspire through their skin, which has no pores. A cat may spread its saliva on its coat, perspire through its paw pads, or pant heavily. When an animal pants, its tongue hangs out and large quantities of air are drawn in and out of the throat and lungs and excess water evaporates from the tongue. These are not breathing motions, however. The amplitude is too small, so the air does not reach the sacs in the lungs. The cat may be panting and perspiring because the weather is hot or because it has just been running. More often, though, the cat is feverish or suffering from anxiety. If panting persists, the cat should be seen by a vet.

Bodily changes

Just as a cat's behaviour is a good barometer of the cat's health, so, too, is its physical appearance.

An enlarged abdomen, for example, is often perceived as weight gain. Since cats frequently have a layer of fat under the stomach, an inattentive owner may not notice the difference between a few extra layers of fat and a bloated tummy. Often the abdomen is distended because of an accumulation of fluid, frequently a symptom of feline infectious peritonitis or liver disorder. Since increased fluid may be a secondary effect of heart disease, prompt treatment is essential.

Deformations or any signs of limb pain, limping for instance, should always be investigated. A young cat may have a growth disorder; an older cat may be suffering from arthrosis (stiffening of the joints). A thorn may have pierced the cat's paw or it may have sustained a wound that has abscessed.

WATCHPOINTS

Good health

Temperature : normally between 38.6°C and 39.2°C (101°F and 102.5°F). A cat's temperature can be taken rectally (see page 210). If it rises near 39.5°C (103°F), it is time to consult a vet.

Colour : the best place to look is the conjunctival mucosa, the tissue around the eyes. It should be a light pink colour. If it is red, the cat is congested, and is likely also to have a fever. If it is dirty or yellowish, an organ such as the liver may be diseased.

Nose : should glisten if the lachrymal canal is functioning normally, because tears keep the nostrils moist. To a lesser degree, the tongue fulfils this function as well. The cat regularly licks its nose, keeping it moist and cool.

Eyes : should not be blinking or red. Redness may be a sign of conjunctivitis or may be caused by glaucoma, be a symptom of a serious general disease, or signal the presence of a wound or foreign body.

Hair : shiny hair indicates a good general state of health. There should be no dandruff or 'pepper' – flea faeces. Long hair can easily conceal a skin disease. If not properly groomed, it does not protect the cat against the cold.

Stools : even if the cat is fasting, it will produce stools, which consist mainly of cellular debris from the digestive tract. Occasional "looseness" or diarrhoea may be due to a change in diet. Consult your vet about persistent diarrhoea.

Appetite : excessive appetite is not necessarily a sign of good health. It may indicate diabetes. Similarly, a poor appetite is not always a sign that something is physiologically wrong.

Worrying signs

Temperature : if it is below 38.6°C (100.5°F), check to see that the thermometer was put in far enough; grease it again and reinsert it gently a little farther. If the temperature is still low, consult a vet without delay, since this could be a symptom of very serious problems.

Colour : the cat may be pale if it has just been suffering from stress. A light colour is normal.

Nose : cracking may indicate a local nose or eye problem or general dehydration, a very serious situation. A nose that is dry, dull and warm may be a sign of a temperature. Check to be sure.

Eyes : if they are gummy, this may be due to simple conjunctivitis, or, worse, a dry keratoconjunctivitis, which requires immediate medical attention.

Hair : the coat reflects general health, but it is a delayed indicator. At the onset of disease, the hair may still be deceptively shiny. Regardless of the cat's state of health, hair fallout may be due to climatic or hormonal factors, or to stress.

Stools : colour depends on food. Since parasite eggs are microscopic, any eggs visible on the surface of the stools are probably fly eggs.

Drinking : if a cat stares at its water dish but will not drink, there could be a serious problem. It may mean the cat is thirsty, but feels too sick to drink. If your cat drinks excessively, it may point to a kidney problem or diabetes.

Straining : if your cat is straining in the litter tray, but does not defecate, it could have a blockage. If your cat is unable to urinate, seek veterinary help immediately.

Wheezing : if your cat wheezes and sneezes, it may have a respiratory infection. Discharges from the eyes and nose could mean the same thing and will need veterinary attention. Even if the cat does not have a fever it may have bronchitis, asthma or a foreign body in the respiratory tract.

Changes in behaviour : despondency, irritability, trembling are serious signs of illness.

Care at home

There are several tell-tale signs that a cat might be ill (see *Watchpoints*, page 208). Some are symptomatic of a particular disease. Others involve unusual behaviour by the cat because of the way the disease is affecting its body. And some signs point to malfunctioning organs or organic systems. Learn to distinguish between general, local and functional symptoms.

General symptoms

Any change in the cat's general behaviour signals something is amiss. The cat may be despondent and sad, may not eat, and may try to hide from you.

Unexplained weight loss may be the first indication of a chronic, progressive disorder. Even if this prospect does not alarm you at first, such an illness is potentially more serious than an acute disorder. It reflects advanced deterioration of various organs and functions.

On its own, a warm nose may only mean the cat has not licked itself for a while. But a dry, cracked nose may be the result of either a general disorder or an eye disorder, since the tears that flow down the lachrymal canal are largely responsible for moistening and keeping the nose cool.

A cat in pain will not express this by crying. Instead it crouches to find a comfortable position, seeks an isolated corner, and may become aggressive.

Local symptoms

These appear at the site of an injury or infection, and thus can help locate the problem. Swelling may accompany a hernia, haematoma, abscess or tumour, while a deformation will indicate a fracture or dislocation. Pus from a wound usually indicates there is an abscess, or an abnormal passage, known as a fistula, between body parts. Nasal discharges suggest a case of rhinitis, and stuck eyelids or discharges from the eyes mean conjunctivitis; vaginal discharges accompany inflammation of the uterus or vagina. Hair loss or scabs indicate dermatitis. A change of colour of the mucous membranes is a local symptom of a general disorder: anaemia if they are pale, liver problems if they are yellow, heart and lung problems if they are dark or purple.

Functional symptoms

Generally these signs point to the cat's whole system being affected by disease.

Vomiting, for example, may originate in the oesophagus, stomach, pylorus (the lower outlet from the stomach), or the intestines. But it is just as likely to indicate overeating as a more serious condition.

Similarly, diarrhoea may indicate a digestive problem, a viral, parasitic or degenerative disease of the pancreas, or even cancer.

If general, local, or functional symptoms persist, get your cat to a vet quickly. The sooner an animal is seen professionally, the sooner a diagnosis can be made. Any instance of prolonged loss of appetite severely reduces a cat's chances of survival. Wise cat owners do not give their cats medicines without veterinary advice. What works for humans can kill a cat. So too can a cat medication administered for the wrong disease.

Before administering care, immobilise the cat

Cats do not take well to being restrained. Perhaps the most important rule in caring for a cat is to act fast and firmly, without being brutal. Exert enough pressure to dissuade the cat from putting up any resistance, but be flexible enough that you do not provoke defensive reactions.

The ideal way to hold a cat is to grab a handful of skin at the scruff of its neck. The cat will be disarmed by this, instinctively reacting passively like a kitten being carried by its mother and adopting a foetal position with paws folded under the body.

As well as being held by the scruff of the neck, the more recalcitrant animals should be pressed down on a table, with the front paws over the edge. The cat, which will then only be concerned with pulling forward to get to the floor, may not think of turning to use its claws.

When a cat is picked up by the scruff of the neck, it adopts a foetal position. It shows no anger and is passive and easy to handle.

Quick checks

If you suspect your cat is ill, listen to its breathing, take its temperature, and check its pulse. A healthy cat will take some 20 to 30 breaths per minute.

To check your cat's temperature, coat the end of the thermometer with vaseline or vegetable oil. Put your cat on a level surface and hold it steady between your body and arms. Lift the tail with one hand and gently but firmly push the thermometer into the cat's rectum for about 4 cm (1½ inches). A reading of between 38.6°C (101.5°F) and 39.2°C (102.5°F) is considered normal. Severe infections can drive the cat's temperature as high as 41°C (106°F). If the temperature gets anywhere near that high, call your vet immediately.

If the temperature is registering below the normal 38.6°C (101.5°F), you may not

Holding a cat by the scruff of its neck at the edge of a table should keep even the most stubborn feline still.

be inserting the thermometer far enough into the rectum; very gently push it in further. If the reading is still below normal, the cat may be suffering from hypothermia, a drop in body temperature that, in extreme cases, can lead to unconsciousness and possibly even death. Treatment depends on the cause. Is the cat receiving any medication? Some drugs may induce the condition. Or has it been exposed to extreme cold or been immersed for a time in cold water?

Check your cat's pulse on the femoral artery, a major blood vessel on the inside of the hind leg close to the hip joint. Put your fingers over the artery where it comes close to the skin and you should be able

Keep those sharp claws under wraps in a towel.

to feel the pulse. Using your watch, count the number of beats for 15 seconds, then multiply that number by 4 and this will give you the pulse rate in beats per minute.

The normal pulse rate is between 100 and 180 beats; a higher rate may mean the cat is nervous or that your cat is ill. Check with your vet.

Pulling a cat's head back causes it to open its mouth and swallow.

Administering pills

Pills are one form of medication a cat can take without too much trouble. Still, many people find liquid medications easier to deal with. Since a cat's claws are a far greater danger than its teeth, it may be a good idea to wrap a cat in a thick towel before giving it pills or indeed any treatment. This effectively neutralises the claws and works as long as being swaddled in this way does not upset the cat too much (see below, left).

Of course you can also administer a pill by placing the animal on a table, sitting on its haunches. Grip the head from behind with the left hand and pull it back (see above). The jaw should be vertical. The lower lip will automatically fall open. You can use the nail of the index finger of the right hand to pull the lower incisors and open the mouth wider, while you slide the thumb and middle finger of the left hand between its lips. If the cat tries to close its jaws, it will bite its cheeks and give up trying.

The pill, which you should hold between the thumb and middle finger of the right hand, can then be dropped between the palate and the back of the tongue. Then push firmly forward with the index finger of the same hand, forcing the cat to close its mouth. The head, with the muzzle still in the air, should not be released until the cat licks its nose – a sign that it has swallowed the pill. If this takes too long, you can rub its nose to trigger the licking reflex or stroke its throat gently.

Administering liquids and pastes

Some veterinary medications are available as liquids and may be given to the cat easily and safely with an eyedropper.

You might also try mixing some of the liquid with one of the vitamin pastes available for cats. Pastes may be the pharmaceutical innovation of the future, at least as far as cats are concerned. They have all the advantages of powders mixed with

Liquids or pastes can be given with a syringe from which the needle has been removed.

fresh cream, and can be prepared in a syringe before being injected between the animal's teeth.

Hold the head as if you were giving the animal a pill. But instead of pointing it upwards, the muzzle is kept horizontal to prevent gulping. The cat can bite down on the end of the syringe as the owner slowly depresses the plunger and the paste is being swallowed.

Some flavoured pastes can be mixed with food without requiring special handling, and it is a good bet that the cat will not reject them.

Administering suppositories

It takes two people to do this. One of them holds the animal down on the table by the scruff of the neck so that it cannot move. Using the left hand, the other takes the tail by the base and pulls it forward over the animal's back, exposing the anus. With the right hand, the suppository is inserted slowly and gently, and then the tail is lowered. Then the cat should be kept still for a few minutes.

Administering eyedrops

Hold the cat with its muzzle in the air, immobilised by the left hand's thumb and index finger, pulling the lower eyelid down with the middle finger. The right hand, which is holding the drop-

per between the thumb, index and middle finger, is supported on the cat's forehead. Pull the upper eyelid upwards with the ring finger, and make sure the eyedrop falls on the cornea or into the corner of the eye. Ophthalmic ointments may be applied in the same way.

Administering ear drops

One person holds the cat in the position used for administering liquids and pastes (see left). The other pulls the pinna upwards and towards him, introducing the nozzle of the dropper into the open

To take a cat's temperature without fuss, lift the tail up over the back. The thermometer is then inserted gradually to the proper depth.

ear orifice, towards the outside and the nose. He should then massage the auditory canal for a long time, holding the pinna in the same position.

The home nurse

Nursing a sick cat requires a lot of patience and concern for a patient who cannot tell you how it is feeling. One of the essential things to bear in mind is that the cat will not behave as it usually does. It may lie there with dull eyes and exhibit absolutely no reactions. On the other hand, it may strike out with its claws and/or teeth.

The key to nursing a cat is to keep it clean, warm, and comfortable and, if possible, in a quiet environment. Have enough food and drink available and, if necessary, help it to eat and drink. Make sure its eating and drinking bowls are kept clean and away from other household equipment.

Always wash your hands both before and after handling a sick cat so that you do not transmit any disease or infection to or from the cat.

And if you really want to be a home nurse, talk to your cat in a reassuring way – it will appreciate that, even if it doesn't understand everything you say.

THE FELINE FIRST AID KIT

What to have

Cotton wool to clean wounds, and especially to make large compression bandages in case of haemorrhage or fracture.

A 10-cm- (4-inch-) wide bandage to wrap around the body, and other bandages for the limbs.

Sterile compresses to disinfect and protect a wound.

Wooden tongue depressors to devise a makeshift splint in the event of fracture or dislocation.

A 5-cm- (2-inch-) wide aerated adhesive tape to hold the crepe bandage covering the cotton, which is isolated from the wound by sterile compresses.

A pair of scissors, preferably blunt-ended, curved ones, to cut dressings.

Hydrogen peroxide (3% or less) to clean wounds.

A saline lotion to clean wounds. Use diluted to clean an irritated or injured eye.

Nail clippers in case the cat gets its claws caught in something.

Metal fine-toothed comb in case the cat gets tangled in the undergrowth or needs grooming.

An eyedropper in case you need to give the cat drops to keep an infected eye clean.

A disposable plastic syringe without the needle, in case you need to give the cat medication.

Mineral oil or hair-ball medication to prevent hair-balls from forming. This should only be given to the cat occasionally.

Flea spray made particularly for cats.

Blunt tweezers to probe safely in the cat's mouth or elsewhere where a sharp pair of scissors might cause injury.

Rectal thermometer to take the cat's temperature.

Not needed

Alcohol, which is a very poor disinfectant, damages tissues, and causes unnecessary suffering to the cat, which will be distrustful of further treatments.

A tourniquet, which is rarely used. Tourniquets must be loosened often at regular intervals. In case of haemorrhaging, a cotton compression bandage poses no danger to the animal's limb, even if it is not quite as effective at stopping the bleeding.

If your cat travels, pack these

The telephone number of your family vet. Even if he or she is not available, a replacement will often provide good advice, and will have immediate access to the cat's medical records.

The cat's vaccination certificate, which will be helpful for a local vet, though he will eventually contact the animal's usual vet.

Water, which may be best carried in a bottle and put into a cat's bowl if needed.

A blanket to catch and immobilise the cat. In case of accident or pain, a cat will often refuse to be touched, even by those who know and love it.

Do not pack these

Medications that are not normally prescribed for the cat. If you are travelling with your cat, ask your vet what medications you should take with you in case the cat falls ill. Your vet will also advise whether a sedative to make your cat sleepy on the journey is appropriate. Never give your cat human medications.

UNDERSTANDING CATS

The territorial boundaries

Range and boundaries

Cats have received mixed reviews from the human race over the years. Many people think of them as antisocial creatures, solitary beings that refuse to share their territory with any other animal. But as most cat owners will testify, their feline friends form attachments to people, and even other pets. Under certain circumstances, cats can live with other cats in large groups. There are colonies of stray or feral cats in our cities living a communal life in parks, gardens, cemeteries, and even in the basement parking garages of high-rise buildings.

Every cat has a territory however small, and many cats lay claim to three. Two of these will be private domains, the third a communal ground, where some cats may gather regularly, others occasionally.

First among the territories is the private or central area, the cat's den, or lair. This is where it sleeps and where sometimes the female has her kittens. The cat will fight tooth and nail to defend that space against any intruder. Within its lair, a cat will sometimes even reject its owner's attentions.

The second territory might be called the cat's 'living space'. In a flat, this will probably include every room. In a house, it usually includes both house and garden, and sometimes the gardens of neighbouring catless homes. A cat will share its living space with other animals in its household, but its resentment of any visiting cats and dogs will be unmistakable.

In urban areas, many cats share the same territory fairly peacefully.

The third territorial area, commonly held hunting and meeting grounds, relates mostly to feral cats, animals that have been domestic and returned to the wild through circumstances – such as abandonment – beyond their control. But cats with a tendency to stray from home and cats with a penchant for nightlife also lay claim to such territories, which they share with other animals they meet there. Open confrontations are rare in such an area. In fact, these feral cats manage not to confront one another, arranging their lives to avoid any unpleasant encounters.

The few fights that do occur in communal areas have to do with seniority, when a younger resident tries to oust an older one from its 'top cat' position. The confrontation is often limited to mutual glaring and intimidating growls, followed by the withdrawal of both parties.

Sexuality plays an important part in territorial rights. Within the private territories, which may be within the communal area or adjoining it, a neutered tom will make do with a much smaller living space than one that has not been neutered, and a queen with kittens will defend a broader living territory than one without offspring. But the more extensive communal territory is more a setting for social than sexual interaction. The several cats occupying a communal territory see it as an area that can be shared; consequently it is not defended as tenaciously as the den or living space. Such communal territories may cover some 20 ha (50 acres).

Cases where feral cats long reverted to the wild live alone in relatively uninhabited regions where food is scarce are rare. In such circumstances, a cat may prowl some 40 ha (100 acres), defending its boundaries against any other cat that crosses them. But obviously no one cat can defend such extensive boundaries 24 hours a day: it must pick and choose which transgressors to challenge.

All territories vary greatly in size. Of the several factors influencing this, food would seem to be the most important. Frequently, in urban areas where food is plentiful, many stray cats are found in a small area. Each has its tiny space or den, often not much bigger than itself, within a living area shared amicably with innumerable other cats.

Territorial marking

Territorial marking is of primary importance in the lives of many animals. This is especially true of cats, which are noted for leaving three different kinds of signals – two involving smell and one visual – to inform other cats of their presence.

A cat's sebaceous glands produce particular smells when rubbed against any object. The glands are found above the eyes on both sides of the forehead, around the lips, and along the tail under the fur. When a cat rubs these parts of its body against a fence, a tree, or even its owner's legs, it is leaving its scent there. This is called marking.

Marking by smell constitutes a sort of 'visiting card' as well as a claim of territorial ownership. Other animals instantly

Cats leave smelly 'visiting cards' around their territory.

recognise the smell as belonging to a cat. Indeed, the smell provides very precise information on the sex of the cat that left the marking, on whether or not it was neutered, and possibly even on its state of health and temper. The sniffer can also deduce from the pungency how recently the mark was left.

Urine is also used for marking. All cats, whether male or female, neutered or not, mark their territory by leaving a few drops of urine in strategic places. This is distinctly at odds with the way they behave in the normal course of urination – when they spray on the ground, then cover it.

When marking with urine, the cat aims its spray not at the ground but higher up – roughly its own height. Thus the smell will readily reach the nose of any other cat passing by. This difference in the positioning of urine can provide useful information. If a cat has begun to mark in the house, its urine will be found on walls, curtains, and around the legs of chairs; but if the animal is simply incontinent because of a urinary infection, the urine will be found on the floor.

Cats also communicate with other animals by visual marking: they mark the places they use – tree trunks, upright posts, or furniture legs, for example – by scratching them with their claws. The cat finds it particularly soothing to produce visual markings because all the time it is scratching, it is also stretching and relaxing the whole body. Scratching hard surfaces is also useful in keeping the claws sharpened for hunting. Scratching is a very strong instinct that persists even in the most domesticated of domestic cats.

Since there is no fighting instinct involved in this kind of marking, it is best to try to limit the damage by sacrificing an old carpet or piece of furniture, or by buying or installing a scratching post (see page 205). Handling the problem of where the cat scratches can be very frustrating and difficult and may require the use of punishment (see page 231).

SEASONED TRAVELLER

When 15-year-old Kirsten Hicks of Adelaide, Australia, was going overseas with her family in 1977, she left her Persian cat, Howie, with her grandparents. So Howie settled in the Outback, some 1,610 km (1,000 miles) from his former home. Then one day he disappeared.

A year later, back home in Adelaide, Kirsten was still mourning the lost Howie when a bleeding, bedraggled cat arrived on her doorstep. Neither she nor other family members recognised the cat at first. But when Kirsten picked it up, the animal snuggled into her arms, purring happily. No one had to wait until the cat was bathed to be convinced that Howie had come home. His incredible journey had spanned wide rivers, hot deserts and the vast wilderness of the Australian Outback.

Obviously there will be times and places where you cannot permit the cat to mark as it sees fit. But it is important to realise that some marking behaviour is vital in a cat's life, enabling it to avoid confrontations and so live at peace in feline society.

Thanks to the 'visiting cards' it distributes around its territory, other animals recognise the resident cat's markings and, depending on the freshness of the marks, can tell if the cat is in the vicinity. In this way, cats organise their comings and goings as peacefully as they can, avoiding potentially unfriendly encounters.

This behaviour illustrates a primary characteristic of feline social life, which is to avoid fighting and other domestic problems within a common living space.

Defending the territory

Although feline social life seems geared to avoiding fights whenever possible, cats can be quite resolute when it comes to defending their living space, especially their most private territory – their lairs or dens.

This defensive behaviour is most intense when a queen needs to protect her kittens. Motherhood gives her great courage, and to protect her offspring she is capable of attacking bigger cats, and even dogs.

Territorial defence is more important for cats that remain unneutered than for neutered ones, and for wild or feral cats than for domestic cats. The arrival of an intruder does not necessarily lead to a fight.

On first meeting, cats take up threatening and intimidating postures. The protagonists begin staring at one another while padding slowly towards each other. They sniff each other's scent, and then the larger of the two attempts to control the other's movements, making various sorts of angry noises calculated to intimidate or at least 'test' its adversary. Its ears stand up and are turned slightly backwards, its whiskers bristle and point forward, its pupils contract and its forehead becomes wrinkled. Pursuing the advantage, the larger cat advances, staring the other cat in the eyes. The smaller cat cowers more, with pupils dilated and ears flattened. At this point, if it sees an avenue of escape, it will retreat slowly and resume a normal position a few cat-lengths away from its adversary.

Sometimes neither party retreats; then a fight begins, ending with the loser on its back and the victor on top, biting and scratching. The loser soon gives up and frees itself to run away.

Cats often defend their territory by threats alone. One animal usually backs down.

Fights, or even mere confrontations, are the basis of a fragile hierarchy; after a series of such encounters, the stronger cats attempt to extend their territory. But they do not necessarily gain supremacy, especially when they are far from home.

Often after several confrontations, two adversaries will come to a tacit agreement to respect one another's rights. This is most likely to happen if they are more or less equal in strength. However, size or status can change, and then hostilities resume until new borders are established.

Cats that share the same household relate to one another in a very similar way, but their confrontations are less violent and more ritualistic. Usually a hiss or a swift slash with a paw will settle matters.

Of course territorial defence extends beyond sibling cats to other house pets and even to people. This may explain why some domestic cats react aggressively when their owners entertain or have house guests. The cat regards the visitors as 'invaders', but its attitude will become less chilly in the long run. It will warm all the sooner if the 'interlopers' do not back down or give the cat any reason to feel he has won any round in the 'Who's in charge?' wars.

You can count on about a month's adjustment whenever there is an addition to the household, whether this is a new baby, another cat or kitten, or some other pet. While a new balance of power is being established, the cat may do some posturing aimed at maintaining or even improving its status in the established pecking order. More often than not, peace returns.

Communal cats and their hierarchy

Feral cats and runaways often live on common territory in variously sized colonies. They prefer quiet fenced-off or otherwise secure areas with a good food supply, ideally an abundance of small wild prey and human food, especially thrown-away leftovers. Cemeteries, the grounds of public buildings, the basements of high-rise buildings, and alleyways behind nursing homes and hospitals are typical of places where such colonies spring up.

Cats in these colonies develop a very complex social structure, based in part on dominant and submissive roles. The concept of dominated and dominant cats is unfamiliar to most people, since by and large our knowledge of feline behaviour is limited to observation of one household pet. But people with two or more cats will have observed feline power struggles. And even in one-cat households, the pets try to dominate their owners. This is often the explanation for a cat's aggressiveness.

The dominant position in cat colonies is neither all encompassing nor permanent. A cat may exert power in some circumstances and be submissive in others. Generally a cat feels more confident the closer it is to home, and it will temper its behaviour accordingly. A healthy young cat will easily wrest power from an older

---

A SIX-YEAR SQUAT

Some cats, like some people, just want to be alone. Such seems to have been the case with Mincha, a black female that climbed a 12-m (40-foot) tree in Buenos Aires in the late 1940s and stayed there for more than six years. Local Argentinians used poles to provide her with daily rations. It also seems that a tom cat or two were granted visiting rights: Mincha had three litters in her tree-top home.

or weaker one. Unneutered cats will oust neutered ones, and cats neutered after reaching adulthood usually dominate those neutered before puberty.

A queen and her kittens form a dominant cohesive unit, resisting all intrusion by other cats. But within a single litter, some kittens will be more active and energetic than others simply because they are physically superior.

In groups of cats living free, the permanence of the hierarchy depends on the size of the territory, how extensively the ruling cat's authority is challenged, and how often he must fight to remain 'top cat'. (Feral cats are generally headed by the most powerful tom cat in the territory.) Hierarchical disputes are common, however, and fights occur often between the established occupants and young cats just reaching maturity that want to take over. Whenever the status quo is challenged, a number of confrontations, sometimes ending in fights, take place over several days until one cat is indisputably at the top of the tree.

Every now and then a ruling animal decides not to assert its prerogatives for a time, making way temporarily for a more submissive cat. When the former ruler wants to be reinstated, it will not openly attack its successor, although it will subject it to constant threats. Usually that is all it takes to get the more submissive cat to step down of its own accord.

With females, hierarchy is a function of reproduction. The older a queen and the

A group's stability is based on a hierarchy, but the pecking order often changes.

more litters she has had, the more power she exerts. There are clearly defined relationships between queen and daughter, or queen and granddaughter where they live together. The oldest female bosses her daughter, who in turn runs roughshod over the females of the next litter, and so on.

During courtship, a queen in heat calls the shots for the toms that pursue her,

becomes momentarily submissive in the act of mating, but within seconds resumes her snarling authoritarian manner. Paradoxically, the dominant male of a group does not necessarily have the right to mate with a queen in heat. She often prefers a less powerful, more submissive tom.

Cats that lord it over other cats not only have access to more territory than their 'subjects', but also feed before the other cats and take first place in all the group's activities. Although age and sexual status are of great hierarchical importance, cats never yield to younger, more active, stronger cats until obliged to by age – at around 8 to 10 years of age – or when tired.

Not all feline relationships are determined by dominance or submissiveness, however. Within the group, cats also develop social, nonsexual preferences. They have grooming companions, playmates, and even 'friends' they prefer to sleep near.

The hunting instinct

Cats are predators, living off the prey they hunt down and kill. Since earliest times, their ability to reduce rodent populations has been recognised and it was largely for this reason that they were so venerated in ancient Egypt. By devouring huge quantities of rats and mice, they protected the stores of grain that formed the major source of wealth for the peoples living along the banks of the Nile River delta. Cats kept European granaries rodent-free in the 1500s (see Chartreux, page 88) and, by devouring silk-worm-gobbling rodents, saved Japan's silk industry from annihilation (see Japanese Bobtail, page 101).

Nowadays wild and feral cats are still seen in European forests, living by hunting alone. They feed mainly on rodents, but also kill baby rabbits and young birds taken from the nest, activities that do not endear them to rabbit and bird lovers.

Hunting behaviour is innate in kittens and is reinforced by teaching from the parent. Kittens at play are serving an apprenticeship. Observation brings instinctual patterns to the fore, prompting them to bat with their paws at anything that moves and bite anything resembling a mouse. These skills improve with practice, but initially are incorporated into play. A kitten is capable of hunting as soon as its neuromuscular development is complete, at the age of 5 to 6 months. The kitten follows a parent and learns the basic tactics: lying in wait upwind, pouncing suddenly, immobilising the prey with a bite to the neck.

Domestic cats no longer hunt out of necessity, since they are usually adequately fed. They hunt for pleasure, and are prone to proudly depositing their booty at the feet of their owners.

Long experience has taught us that a hunting carnivore's instinct to kill dimin-

Through the ages, cats have chased mice. Even in today's cats, the instinct survives.

ishes as its appetite is sated. A hungry cat, seeing a mouse, will chase, kill and eat it. A well-fed cat will still chase the mouse, but will take longer to catch it and will not eat it. The apparent cruelty with which a cat will toy with a captured rodent is actually due to lack of appetite. The cat's instinct has impelled it to catch the prey, but since it is not hungry, it plays with its victim without feeling the need to kill it.

The hunting instinct is still very strong, even in domestic cats. Toms especially carry out a sort of ritualised hunting behaviour involving their owners, attacking their legs, for example, as if they were legitimate prey. Such behaviour is often seen in tom cats living with elderly people. Perhaps the sound of shuffling feet, especially in slippers, resembles that of a prey fleeing through grass. This stimulus may

WILDCATS AND FERAL CATS

The world still supports a few rare specimens of wildcats of the species *Felis silvestris*. These are related to domestic cats descended from the Lybian wildcat.

The wildcat is stockier and stronger, with a striped tail like an alley cat and long thick hair of dark yellow. Unlike its domestic cousin, it has only one litter a year, which explains its rarity. A nocturnal predator, it owes its survival to its small size and night prowling habits, but it is becoming ever rarer and needs to be protected.

The domestic cat, although usually quite happy to live with human beings, sometimes feels a need to revert to the wild state. A cat that does this is called a feral cat. Queens who live out of doors sometimes have their litters there, and kittens born under such circumstances may later become domesticated by hanging around houses until they are adopted by the inhabitants. Other cats will refuse to return to civilisation, preferring the wild life. They survive by preying on birds and various kinds of small animals.

These unneutered cats lead active sex lives and reproduce rapidly. The size of the territory they occupy depends on the amount of food available.

In the wild, feral cats become bigger and stronger than if they had remained domestic. The life they lead means that only those that are more

Feral cats survive by hunting.

resistant to disease, especially to bacterial and viral infections, are likely to survive. Not having been neutered, they continue to develop physically up to the age of 3 or 4. On the other hand, they are at risk from road traffic and dogs. They are often obliged to fight, and continual fighting weakens them. Their life expectancy rarely exceeds 8 to 10 years, almost half that of a house cat.

Populations of feral cats vary in size depending on living conditions and environment. Although they breed fast, many kittens succumb to disease or are killed by other animals. Within a given territory, the number of feral cats varies very little from year to year. Only those protected by humans in special areas increase in population.

This is the case with feral cats living in big-city cemeteries. They are safe from aggression, and people provide them with more food than they need. Animal welfare societies in some countries carry out sterilisation campaigns.

Felis silvestris, the European wildcat.

unleash predatory behaviour in the cat, which may pounce on passing legs with teeth and claws at the ready.

Although this is not truly aggression, owners should nevertheless refuse to tolerate such behaviour. It creates a special hazard for elderly people, who may trip and fall over a cat jousting at their ankles. The best solution is to distract the cat with previously established games.

The cat as 'landowner'

Within the cat's territory, be it a farm or a room, each cat in a sense owns a patch of 'land'. When there are several cats in one household, they often merge their territorial boundaries and join to 'defend' it. Outdoors, the scene is played out on a tougher scale: the city cat may defend an urban area only as large as a back garden, while a country cat may have to cover a huge area that also supports other wild animals. Within the territory the cat will stake out its favourite spots for keeping watch for marauders, and where it can sleep or relax in peace.

In the public territories, that is those not within households, gardens, or other private places where humans exert some control, the cats have a different and communal setup. One area may be designated for hunting, another for cats to meet, and yet another area left free for other animals, particularly dogs, to roam.

The indoor cat has no such gathering to attend and in some cases – especially if it was once an outdoor cat – it will become frustrated. Adding a second cat to the household is often the best solution.

Cats that wander over large areas of countryside not only defend their territory against all outsiders, but may also try to increase its size. However, they do this with noisy threats and aggressive behaviour rather than actual fighting. Sometimes they may try to encroach on a section of farmland that the resident cat has trouble defending. Some male farm cats may try to protect as much as 60 ha (150 acres), but female farm cats tend to be content with one-tenth that space. Urban cats have the least space, and pets may be limited to their own and neighbouring gardens. But such cats have no need to hunt for their food, so their limited territory is sufficient.

The ability of feral and domestic cats to thrive in such vastly different environments highlights their amazing adaptability. Rats in captivity will fight to the death to gain space, even when there is enough for each. Cats, however, survive well even in the most crowded conditions.

Social behaviour

Vocal communication

Since vocal communication is vital for human beings, we tend to be curious about the sounds made by other species. Do other animals understand these sounds? And what do they mean? Students of animal communication say that since cats emit sounds that have a specific meaning, these sounds constitute a kind of language. Cats, say the experts, use this language to communicate not only with their own kind, but also with people and even with dogs.

Experts divide cat noises into categories. One study by New York researcher Dr Mildred Moelk separates cat sounds into three main groups: murmurings, vowels (calls) and high-intensity noises (cries).

Murmuring noises are low-intensity sounds made in peaceful situations with the mouth closed. The sounds are short and are usually made when the cat is enjoying something; perhaps when it is being stroked or groomed. They include a variety of purrs expressing moods ranging from anticipation and pleasure to dissatisfaction and distress.

The vowels, all variations of 'miaow', are clear, easily differentiated noises made with the mouth opening and closing rapidly. Each vowel is used in a different situation – when the cat is asking for food or waiting for it, for example, or when it spies a pigeon out of reach on a nearby roof. A kitten's distress call when separated from its mother is one of the vowel sounds. Almost from birth, each kitten has its own

Each kitten has its own characteristic voice. A distress call alerts the mother, who will hurry to the rescue.

characteristic call, and in this way the mother can recognise which of her off-spring is missing. Low growls are also included in the vowels category of sounds.

High-intensity sounds describe full growls, snarls, hisses and various loud cries made in different situations. They are less specific and recognisable than the murmuring and vowel sounds, and are associated with normal events in everyday cat life. The cries made by tom cats in rut do not serve to attract females – their odour does – but seem spontaneously emitted. By the same token, the scream of a cat who has just received an injection is simply an instinctive expression of rage and fear.

Vocal communication is important in the relationships between people and cats. Neither cat nor owner will know exactly what is being communicated, but the mutual goodwill will be unmistakable. When trying to 'speak' to us, cats are attempting to get closer to us, who can never really know the feline world of smells, vibrations and sounds. Domestication has enlarged their vocabulary of noises, and any owner can encourage a cat to 'talk' more. The more you do this, the better the response.

Body language and facial expressions

Like many other species, cats also communicate by means of body language and facial expressions. An animal's appearance, therefore, clearly expresses its feelings. The facial expressions that a cat uses to communicate with its own kind or with its human companions change with the slightest shift in emotion. Not only do these varying expressions mirror the cat's mood, but they clearly communicate them to the world at large. And unlike people, cats cannot fake emotions. They only show what they really feel.

A happy, relaxed cat has a round face, upright ears, wide-open, normally dilated pupils and relaxed whiskers. An upset cat scowls, flattens its ears, narrows its eyes, and contracts its pupils.

The tail held straight up is a sign of welcome, but when the tail bushes up and flicks from side to side, it betrays agitation well on its way to becoming irritation. A cat with its tail between its legs is frightened and beaten, paralysed with fear. It probably will crouch on its belly next.

A happy cat arches its back when being stroked, and stretches to prolong the contact. However, an arched back and fluffed-up coat also occur in confrontations between cats. By standing its hair on end, the cat is hoping it will appear larger and more intimidating to its antagonists.

The forepaws can express a great deal. A light pat with the claws retracted is enough to quell a naughty kitten who is teasing its mother. A harder blow – with the claws out – is administered to an adversary or an owner who has scared it, or hurt it however unintentionally. Patting the owner's hand gently with the claws half extended is an invitation to play. It resembles the gesture of a cat playing with a toy.

All the signals used by domestic cats to communicate with their owners are the same signs they use for exchanging information with other cats. To understand them fully then, we must learn cat language, an effort they seem willing to make in reverse. They certainly observe us carefully and adapt their reactions to our behaviour.

Just how – and how much – cats 'talk' both to us and to other cats will probably never be known. What we do know is that cats have enough vocabulary – or perhaps it is the way they use it – to express many demands and emotions, from the obvious and persistent request to be petted or fed to the curious chatter made when a bird is spotted through the window.

Highly tuned senses

A cat has at least as many senses as human beings, and it certainly uses them for more purposes than simple survival. Apart from those pets that are never allowed outdoors, cats could not survive without their superb senses of smell, touch, hearing and sight.

Vision

The cat's eyes, rounder than ours, are set in deep sockets and, like ours, protected by eyelids. But cats have a highly developed and mobile haw or third eyelid, called the nictitating membrane. In some illnesses, or when a cat is near exhaustion, this membrane may almost cover the eyeball.

A cat's vision is ideally adapted for hunting, an activity for which sharp eyesight is essential. Its eyes are wide enough apart to give it a total visual field of about 285 degrees, of which 130 degrees are three-dimensional vision. By comparison, the human visual field is 210 degrees, of which 120 degrees are binocular or three-dimensional vision: the cat's rounder eyeball gives it the wider angle of view.

Most cats see shapes almost as well as we do, and can judge distances with great accuracy. Siamese, however, tend to have less binocular ability – the capacity to focus both eyes on an object – than other breeds.

The many rods of a cat's retina are photosensitive in low light and provide excellent night time vision, although in rather soft focus. Under the microscope, various kinds of cells – primarily rods and cones – can be studied. The cones that are sensitive to blue and green are far fewer than in humans, and the cat has no cones that react to red. Because of this it was once thought that cats are almost colour-blind, seeing the world in predominantly pale blue. It is now believed, however, that cats can discriminate between large objects that are identical except for colour.

A cat's ability to see improves sixteen-fold between 2 and 10 weeks of age and cats retain good eyesight even in old age. Unlike dogs, they rarely develop cataracts or retinal degeneration. Only a progressive fading of colour in the iris betrays their age, and this does not imply any loss of function. The fading gives the iris a marbled look. Iris freckles are quite common in cats and are not cause for concern unless there is some change in their shape or size.

The sense of smell

All carnivores live primarily in a world of smells and, except for some hunting breeds, the sense of smell is as highly developed in cats as it is in dogs. It is clear from watching a cat approach an unfamiliar object that smell is of vital importance in identifying anything new.

Since kittens are born deaf and blind, their ears and eyes sealed, their sense of smell is paramount. It is the only tool they have for exploring their new world until they are almost 10 days old.

The mucous membrane lining the cat's nostrils is proportionately much more extensive and more highly developed than the same membrane in humans. This membrane in cats contains some 19 million smell-related nerve endings compared to only about 5 million in humans.

The cat's smell organs include one that we do not have (although several other animals do): the vomeronasal organ, commonly called the Jacobson's organ after its discoverer. This small receptor-lined pouch on the roof of the mouth is also a prime example of the close links between the cat's senses of smell and taste. For the Jacobson's organ connects the cat's oral and nasal cavities and transmits messages to the hypothalamus, the section of the brain concerned with appetite and sexual behaviour.

It is pure myth that what we see as colour, cats see as pale blue: cats are not colour-blind.

When a cat presses its tongue against the roof of its mouth, the Jacobson's organ senses any solid particles the cat may have taken from the air. Should there be any pheromones (odour chemicals from urine and glandular secretions), the cat may react by *flehming*, appearing to grimace but actually savouring the smell. This often happens when a tom gets a whiff of a queen in heat. But the characteristic lip curling is also stimulated by other scents the cat enjoys, such as catnip (see box below).

The sense of smell helps cats find mates and identify friends and foes, tells them what cats and other animals are nearby, leads them to their favourite food. Their noses are particularly sensitive to nitrogen-rich substances.

Hearing

Hearing is the third most important sense for a cat. Since cats often hunt very small animals that can easily hide from them, a cat needs more than good eyesight. The sounds of a small rodent attract a cat's attention, then its sharp sense of hearing enables the cat to find its prey unerringly.

CATNIP

Catmint or catnip *(Nepeta cataria)*, a sturdy perennial plant once used in cooking and for medicinal purposes, inspires odd behaviour in cats. This is caused by an oil the plant secretes to ward off insects that would otherwise eat its leaves. Cats may sniff at the plant or eat some leaves, but are most likely to indulge in ecstatic rubbing and rolling against the plant. In their excitement, some cats adopt the positions of an animal in heat. A few take up peculiar postures, remaining absolutely motionless for minutes at a time, and others indulge in imaginary hunts. Some observers have likened the effect of catnip on cats to that of psychedelic drugs on humans.

Most domestic cats enjoy sampling other herbs besides catnip.

Cats' ears are small but very mobile. Some 10 different muscles enable the ears to turn 180 degrees to locate the origin of a sound. By analysing the delay between the reception of a sound in one ear and then in the other, the cat can determine within a paw's length where it originates.

The cat's hearing is similar to ours in the lower frequencies (around 20 cycles), but a cat can pick up much higher fre-

Especially outdoors, cats rely on their senses of sight, smell, hearing and taste.

quencies than we can. They can receive sounds up into the 50,000-cycle range and are very sensitive to high piercing noises. Mice, however, can hear sounds up to 95,000 cycles, which is good enough to detect an approaching cat.

The ears also play an important part in communication between cats themselves. Flattened against the head they express fear; standing straight up they indicate good health and an even temper.

The cat's inner ears, like our own, are part of the balancing system that keeps the body upright and prevents falls and bumps any time the body moves or changes position.

The sense of taste

The sense of taste varies greatly from cat to cat and it may depend largely on where and how the animal lives. Like all good predators, cats seem able to eat just about everything they catch. However, domestic life may make them fussy, picky eaters.

All the cat's taste buds are found at the end of the tongue and along its sides. There are none on its surface, which carries only large, rough papillae used for licking and grooming. A few groups of taste buds at the back of the mouth complete the animal's tasting system.

The cat's innate tastes do not seem to vary much. Kittens have a natural appetite for their mother's milk, and are fond of other kinds of milk; most adult cats cannot digest milk at all, though some are very fond of it. Kittens especially seem to respond more to bitter, salt and sour tastes than to sweet ones.

Cats also seem to be attracted by a number of foods that are bad for them. Most cats, for instance, adore lung meat (lights), which is of no nutritional value, and liver, which can be toxic in large doses. Regular daily consumption can bring on a very serious bone disease: rheumatoid spondylitis, a condition that may paralyse the animal and lead to an early death.

All cats prefer their protein in the form of meat or fish, are fond of foods with a high proportion of fats, and do not normally like vegetables or fibre. However, they should be fed a balanced diet (see page 198) since an all-meat or fish-only diet can cause severe health problems.

A cat's taste is formed early. A kitten that is always given the same kind of food will later have great difficulty adapting to others. On the other hand, if it is exposed to a number of different foods when young, its adult tastes will be more eclectic.

Cats may sometimes take a sudden aversion to previously relished food, rejecting it completely. It may be that the food made the cat sick, or it may associate it with some other unpleasant event. Either way the cat may continue making the cause-and-effect connection for six months or longer.

The sense of touch

Cats are sensual creatures that derive a great deal of pleasure from touch. When caressed, their whole bodies express delight and satisfaction. They love rubbing their bodies against their owner's legs and they devote a great deal of time to grooming themselves.

A cat's body is entirely covered with pressure and pain receptors that react to the lightest touch. Pressure on any hair is transmitted to sensory cells in the follicle and thence to the brain. Some hairs, stiffer and tougher than others – the guard hairs and especially the vibrissae – are particularly sensitive. These are mostly found as whiskers, but vibrissae also form the eye-

Tastes vary greatly from one cat to another.

brows, and grow in the elbows and the back of the paws above the pads in the forelegs. These bristles sense the movement of air, enabling the cat to 'feel' without touching and to make its way through the darkness without bumping into things.

The hairless areas of the cat's body – the nose and the foot pads – are the most sensitive. The nose reacts to the slightest sensations of heat or cold, particularly in food.

The skin of the foot pads registers the quality of the ground and any objects in the cat's path: it investigates by tapping lightly with its paws. The pads are also sensitive to sound waves or vibrations to the point that cats are generally believed to pick up tremors from impending earthquakes 10 to 15 minutes before people sense them.

Cats can tolerate more heat than we can and show no signs of distress up to a temperature of about 50°C (120°F). Temperatures 5 degrees lower would cause people to feel burnt. This high tolerance for heat may explain why cats sometimes actually singe their fur by venturing too close to a fire in their search for warmth. They are also much less sensitive to cold than we are, since they are protected by fur and have the ability to curl up to help retain heat. To get warm, they start to burn calories at a much lower body temperature than we do, at about 10°C (50°F).

The cat's sense of touch is vital to its survival. By providing information about danger, it reduces the risk of injuries. Touch is also very important in the relationships between people and cats, since a cat's evident enjoyment of its owner's caresses is one of its most endearing characteristics.

Purring

Kittens purr almost from birth in response to their mother's licking and grooming. Adult cats also purr to express pleasure, but a queen will sometimes purr during labour, and some cats purr when confronting a potential aggressor, when very ill or badly injured, and even when dying.

What causes purring? We still are not certain, but there are two main theories. The first and most likely maintains that the sound is caused by the vibration of two membranes, called false vocal cords, found in cats in the larynx behind the true vocal cords. Put your hand gently on the throat of a purring cat and you will be able to 'feel' the sound coming from near the voice box. However, this theory fails to explain why the purring seems to come from the animal's entire body.

According to the second theory, purring is the sound of the blood's turbulence when

The cat's hairless nose leather is one of the areas most sensitive to touch and temperature.

the superior vena cava (the large vein extending from the top of the chest to the heart) is compressed by the cat when it arches its back.

Whatever the true explanation, purring is one of a cat's most unusual and endearing characteristics. Many people are charmed when a cat purrs at their proffered friendship, considering it proof that the animal is happy to live alongside them.

But although purring often seems a pleasurable response to the owner's attentions, its primary function may be communication among cats, especially between a mother cat and her kittens. The sound helps the kittens find their mother in the first weeks before their eyes open. And although newborn kittens will not purr when stroked by people, they do purr when they are suckling. This way the queen knows that all her kittens are feeding well.

Purring also seems to have a calming effect in feline confrontations. Some people feel it actually has a tranquillising effect on the producer of the purr, which would explain the purring of a cat that is injured or in pain or why a queen in labour purrs between contractions.

The sound, then, remains something of a mystery.

Few other animal species purr, although bear cubs have purrs as loud as motorcycle motors when they are nursing.

Cats can communicate

Purring, of course, is just one form of cat communication. Fear or dissatisfaction, for example, may be succinctly expressed by growls, snarls, spits and hisses. Cat owners also believe that cats have a wide vocabulary of miaows that mean different things depending on the way they are produced – long or short, soft or loud, relaxed or intense.

Studies of feline vocalisation suggest a cat's vocabulary contains up to 100 different sounds, some of which are vowel sounds, others consonants. Queens use a particular chirruping sound to recall kittens to the nest, and other distinctive sounds to let her offspring know whether the prey they are hunting is a mouse or a larger rodent.

Nevertheless, some cats rarely 'talk' at all, except for a peremptory miaow when they want something. Other cats become agitated when trying to communicate, and keep on miaowing with intensity until someone responds to their needs. Often, a cat's miaowing, like a baby's cries, is simply its way of saying it is hungry.

Cats under stress – during a visit to the vet, for example – tend to emit a continuous series of long moans quite unlike any sound they produce at other times. And different breeds tend not only to have different cat 'dialects,' but distinctive communication styles. The Persian, for instance, issues short sharp bursts of sound that might be interpreted as: 'Come on, dear owner, I need....' Siamese on the other hand tend to be chatterers, using a combination of sound and body language to grab the owner's attention.

Then there is the peculiar shuddering sound a cat makes when it is indoors watching a wholesome-looking bird outside in territory the cat regards as its own. It occurs when the cat's jaws begin to shudder in a mechanical and strange-sounding way. This may be the cat's inherent killer instinct taking over. As it watches the out-of-reach prey, it automatically goes through the lethal motions required to devour a juicy dinner, although in all probability it will have to content itself with eating its regular cat food in the family kitchen.

But while the cat's vocalisation is not always easy to interpret, its body language is generally unmistakable. Above all tail and tummy are instant giveaways. A swishing tail is a sign of an unhappy cat, whereas a cat with tail aloft and curving slightly is confident and content. A cat at peace with the world will relax on its back and offer its tummy for stroking. A cat with fur bristling is on the defensive, and the whole world can tell that one with lashing tail, smooth fur and pricked ears is poised for the attack.

Purring is one of the cat's most distinctive characteristics, endearing the animal to its human companions.

CAT NAPS

Cats are great sleepers. An adult cat, in good physical condition and fully active, spends 60 per cent of its time sleeping. However, a cat's sleep pattern differs from that of humans. The cat does not sleep for a period of 6 to 8 hours. Instead it sleeps for short stretches which alternate with periods of wakefulness scattered throughout the 24 hours of the day.

The cat's sleep is divided into two quite distinct periods. Phases of light sleep last from 10 to 30 minutes. Electroencephalograph recordings taken during a cat's light sleep show a slow, irregular, wavelike pattern. Although the cat is lying down during light sleep, its muscles are not completely relaxed, and it is quickly awakened by even the slightest sound.

Periods of deep sleep are shorter, each lasting a maximum of 10 minutes. Electroencephalograph recordings taken during deep sleep resemble those from periods of wakefulness, showing periodic bursts of low-amplitude, high-frequency waves of electrical activity. The cat's body, which is extremely relaxed, may be observed twitching briefly and occasionally, and its legs may move. Deep sleep is also characterised by rapid eye movements, and is called REM sleep.

Human beings dream, an activity essential to our mental well-being. Humans prevented from dreaming can suffer hallucinations and other aberrations.

As for cats, their brain activity during their phases of deep sleep is similar to that of dreaming humans.

There is no way, however, of establishing the content of their dreams. It is tempting, of course, to imagine that as a sleeping cat growls and moves its paws it is in swift pursuit of some idealised dream-mouse. But we have no way of knowing what goes on in a cat's mind.

Owners have their own interpretations of the sounds and movements their cats make during periods of deep sleep. But these interpretations are usually projections of the owner's own dreams.

One thing is certain: cats do dream. This is reflected in brain activity that has been observed during laboratory tests. This activity has been found to be similar to that of humans in the same state.

The sleeping pattern of the domestic cat sometimes varies slightly according to the situation it is living in at the time.

An animal left alone during the day in an apartment, for example, sleeps a good part of that day. It becomes more active in the evening and at night when its owner is home to pay it some attention. Cat owners, however fond they may be of their pets, do not always appreciate this increased activity.

Older cats sleep more and more, often lying around for long periods as they did when they were kittens, when they spent up to 80 per cent of their time sleeping.

Social life

Sexuality

Puberty

Female cats, or queens, become sexually mature between 4 and 12 months of age. Males, or toms, reach puberty at about 6 months. Purebred cats or cats kept indoors may reach puberty earlier or later. Health and nutritional status are other factors that influence the onset of puberty.

The female cat experiences the feline heat cycle – oestrus – when she is ready and willing to mate. The cycle lasts 3 to 20 days and occurs at 1- to 4-week intervals. It is repeated during a specific season of the year. For example, in northern temperate regions, the season extends from January to October, with peaks in March or April, June, and September. Generally, the cycles cease between October and December. The cessation may be due to the reduced light levels at that time. Daylight and weather conditions are known to stimulate the hormones that control feline sexual function.

Just before heat begins, a queen is extremely affectionate, rubbing and rolling on the floor with enthusiasm. When heat begins, she becomes restless, howls and calls stridently, and tries to get out of the house to search for a mate. If the queen in heat is stroked, she may take up the mating position: front end pressed to the ground and rear end raised in the air with the tail stiffly bent to one side. If mating does not occur, the queen eventually relaxes until the next cycle begins. If mating does occur, she may produce a litter 9 weeks later.

After males reach puberty, they can reproduce for the rest of their lives without interruption. (However, sexual activity may diminish in the autumn.) This is the time when the male begins wandering and fighting with other toms for the attention of females. The tom also marks his territory with a pungent spray, which is a mixture of urine and anal-gland secretion. It is a sexual attractant. Meantime the female produces odorous secretions, known as pheromones, which serve to attract male cats.

Mating and fertilisation

In female cats, an egg (ovum) is released from the ovaries only in response to the sexual act. The feline reproductive system differs from the human system, where ovulation occurs regardless of sexual intercourse. (Cats are known as reflex ovulators; humans, spontaneous ovulators.)

A queen in heat stimulates the male's interest by her scent and her inviting calls. Initially, she repels his overtures by clawing and snarling. The tom accepts the rejection, but renews his advances. After several advances and retreats, the queen relents and begins purring and rolling

The mating relationship between cats involves courtship rituals and sexual aggression.

provocatively. Eventually, the queen assumes the mating position. The tom mounts the queen from behind and grasps the scruff of her neck between his teeth. The neck bite, together with the stimulation of the male's bony, spiny penis, triggers the process of ovulation. Almost as soon as the penis is introduced, ejaculation occurs. It may be accompanied by a short, sharp howl from the queen.

The sexual act lasts no more than a few seconds. When it is ended, the queen wrenches away from her partner, often sending him on his way with a swipe of her claws. The tom moves off a little way, where he sits or lies watching the queen and grooming himself. At the same time, the queen goes through a display of rolling, rubbing, and stretching. Five or 10 minutes later, the cats resume mating.

Cats may mate up to eight or 10 times an hour. Sometimes the female may mate with several partners, one after the other, until all are exhausted. If fertilisation occurs as a result of the mating, the heat stops soon. The queen's litter appears about 9 weeks later.

In female cats, the prime years for fertility last from 2 to 7; in males, from 2

to 8. Experts advise using most queens for breeding only after they are 1 year old. A queen can produce on average two litters of two to six kittens a year. The litter sizes diminish as the queen grows older. Cat owners who wish to prevent pregnancies are advised to have a female neutered (spayed) at 4 months. If cat owners wish to keep a male cat, particularly for indoor living, it is best to have him neutered (castrated) at 5-6 months. Castration reduces urine spraying.

Development

Birth and maternal behaviour

The gestation period for queens lasts on average 65 days. The most common sign of pregnancy is a change in the colour of the queen's nipples from light to rosy pink, which occurs about the third week of pregnancy. At this stage, vets can diagnose the pregnancy by careful abdominal palpation and by ultrasound examination. They may also use X-rays in the sixth week of pregnancy.

During the first month, the pregnant queen seems physically unchanged. However, she grows quieter and eats more than usual. During the second month, her abdomen is noticeably larger. Physical changes may restrict the queen's activi-

The minute they are born, kittens are protected and cared for efficiently by their mother.

ty in the final stages of pregnancy, but daily light exercise will help to maintain good muscle tone, essential for easy birth.

Preparing for birth

A pregnant queen needs a well-balanced diet. The feeding instructions on commercial cat food products should be followed carefully. The vet may recommend vitamins, minerals or other supplements. Medication, vaccination and worming should be avoided during pregnancy.

A large kittening box in a warm, comfortable and secluded area should be prepared about 10 days before birth. However, the queen may reject it for a quiet spot of her own choice. Some queens give birth in a discreet corner of the house; others prefer places, such as their owner's bedroom, where they can be near people.

During the last weeks of pregnancy, the queen's mammary glands swell. Milk secretions can be seen just before birth. The mammary glands of queens pregnant for the first time may only swell noticeably just before the kittens are born and no milk can be expressed until then.

Stages of labour

The first stage of labour lasts up to 6 hours. It begins when the cervix opens and a plug of foetal tissue passes into it from the uterus. At this point, a clear vaginal fluid may appear. When this happens, involuntary contractions of the uterine muscles begin. The queen heads for the kittening nest, where she breathes rapidly, purring and panting, but in no distress.

The second stage lasts from 10 to 60 minutes. The queen intensifies the involuntary uterine contractions with voluntary contractions or straining ('bearing down'). Eventually, the birth sac – the fluid-filled membrane enveloping a kitten – appears at the opening of the vulva. With a few more contractions, the queen pushes out the kitten. The placenta or afterbirth, which has nourished the embryo, is quickly expelled thereafter.

The kitten usually appears head first, but the tail and hindlegs first is also normal. As soon as the kitten is born, the mother bursts the birth sac and begins to lick the kitten's head so that it can breathe. She bites off the umbilical cord about 2.5-5 cm (1 to 2 inches) from the navel. In the meantime, the kitten makes its way to its mother's nipple and settles down to suckle in peace.

The birth of successive kittens in the litter follows the same pattern. At the end of each birth, the queen eats the placenta. This instinctive habit was originally developed to ward off predators, but it still provides nourishment for the mother until she leaves the litter.

The time between the births varies considerably. It may be as brief as 5 minutes or as long as 2 hours. In some cases, a queen delivers half a litter and stops for 12 to 24 hours before completing the delivery of the remaining kittens.

Labour problems

Cats rarely have trouble giving birth. Generally, cat owners should tactfully oversee but not interfere with a delivery. Too much human meddling may distract a young queen. If labour problems occur, contact the vet immediately. This is essential if a queen fails to deliver kittens after bearing down for more than 2 hours, or if she stops bearing down altogether. In an extreme emergency, put the queen in a warm padded box and take her by car to the vet.

The kitten's development

At birth, the kitten weighs about 100g (3½ ounces) – 70g (2½ ounces) at least, 150g (5⅓ ounces) at most. It is born deaf and blind, possessing only the senses of taste and touch. The kitten has just enough sense of smell to find its mother's teat. Hearing develops at about the fourth day, although the auditory canals are not open completely until the end of the second week. The eyes open in 7 to 10 days. Sight and hearing are fully developed only by the third month.

Immediately after birth, a kitten finds its own particular teat on the mother's breast that it uses until weaned. The teat has a characteristic scent. Avoid bathing the mother in the period following the birth because it washes away the scent. If this happens, the kittens become confused and start to fight.

During the first fortnight of life, the kitten lacks strength, co-ordination, and mobility. The kitten remains in the bed-

The socialisation of the kitten starts with play and games in the first weeks of life.

ding area, cuddled against its mother, sleeping for nine-tenths of the day.

At first, a kitten is extremely sensitive to cold, because it cannot regulate its temperature. The mechanisms for regulating temperature – muscular shivering and the bristling of the fur (piloerection) – start to develop about the third week. By the sixth week, they are completely effective.

The kitten is able to walk and get back to its den after the third week. It regularly leaves the den to explore its surroundings during the fifth week when it also begins to climb. The kitten is completely mobile by roughly the eighth week.

Nourishment for kittens

During the first month, kittens rely on their mother's milk for nourishment. By pushing their forepaws against the mother's breast, the kittens trigger the reflex that provides the milk. Some mothers cannot always provide enough milk for their offspring. In these cases, the fretful kittens cry a lot. Sometimes milk production can be improved with a hormone injection.

If a queen dies or shows no interest in her offspring, ask a vet for milk replacements. Cow's milk is unsatisfactory because the nutritional balance is not right for kittens. There are commercial formulas that match the queen's milk.

At 3 weeks, the kitten can start eating solid food. A commercially prepared kitten food can be used. If the queen's supply of milk is inadequate, mix solid food with a milk replacement. This will speed up the weaning process. By 2 months weaning should be complete.

The kitten learns cleanliness from its mother. In the first days of life, the mother licks the kittens vigorously, which stimulates defecation and urination. She keeps the sleeping den clean by swallowing all waste. Once the kittens are mobile, they start to relieve themselves somewhere away from the den. Towards the end of the third week of life, they begin burying their own waste, covering it over with litter or earth.

The socialisation of the kitten

The behaviour of the adult cat depends on the kind of attention that it received as a kitten. When proper stimulus is lacking, there is a risk of excessive aggression, anxiety, and other behavioural problems in adulthood.

At 2 months of age, kittens are fearless and full of curiosity about the world. Fears born out of experience have yet to take root. Now is the time to undertake the kitten's social education. In a calm atmosphere, introduce the kitten to any other animals living in the same house. If a kitten is meeting a dog for the first time, make sure each is under control.

Put orphan kittens in contact with other mature cats as soon as possible. Orphans deprived of early contact with their own kind frequently show fear and aggression towards other felines. Early introductions help orphans to learn the behaviour pattern of their own species.

Similarly, introduce other humans to establish a sound pattern for good future relations. It is best if several different people gently stroke or hold the kitten every day, provided there is no risk of infection.

Kittens' games teach basic feline skills.

Lessons learned from mother

During the first weeks, the mother cat instils in her kittens the principles of feline life. By washing her kittens, she implants the lesson of keeping their living area clean. Reflex control of urination and defecation develops quickly. By the third week, a kitten learns bowel and bladder control and relieves itself well away from the sleeping area.

The mother's licking keeps the kittens' fur in good condition. The sheer pleasure of the experience encourages kittens to groom themselves. The habit of grooming, started in the first week of life, becomes, at a later stage, an experience shared with the rest of the litter. By grooming each other, kittens reinforce group ties.

The mother also provides lessons in hunting and food-finding techniques. By a process of imitation, observation, and play, kittens acquire all the skills to survive as adult cats.

Learning through play

A kitten born in a litter is rarely alone. With its brothers and sisters, the kitten experiences a wide range of play activities, such as chases, fights, and even surprise attacks on the mother. Kittens learn by playing with simple household objects: empty cotton reels, corks or ping-pong balls. There is a wide range of special cat toys available. For example, a toy bird may satisfy the kitten's awakening hunting instinct.

Play is the essence of the feline learning process. Boisterous games sharpen physical and mental abilities. Fighting between kittens rarely results in injuries or loss of blood. Play also furthers muscular development. It heightens the animal's awareness of the dangers in its surroundings. This, in turn, awakens prudence and circumspection. Finally, play increases the social skills and sociability of the kitten. A kitten's development is rapid during its first 6 months, which is roughly equivalent to the first 10 years of human life (see page 235). What a kitten learns through play in its formative months cannot be taught later. Orphans, or kittens without brothers or sisters, that are denied contact with other cats, usually grow up fearful, nervous and antisocial.

Grooming behaviour

Cats spend much of their time grooming. The habit is the basis of their reputation for extreme cleanliness. Some people believe they can predict the weather by watching a grooming cat. A common sight is a cat passing a licked paw behind its ears. According to folklore, if a cat spends a long time washing behind its ears, the weather will be fine. (Other people believe the same activity foretells a storm.)

Grooming keeps the cat's fur in good condition and calms its nerves. The cat combs its fur by licking. A few drops of saliva dampen the fur and keep it shiny and in good condition. It is the cat's saliva, not its fur, that sets off allergic reactions in human beings.

Licking removes dust, small bits of vegetation and parasites, and smooths out tangled fur. Old cats unable to reach certain body areas due to arthritis or obesity may have tangled fur. Knotted fur becomes extremely dense and damages the underlying layer of skin. Owners can ease the problem by careful grooming of the old cat. In the long-haired breeds, such as Persians, the fine fur tangles easily. Daily grooming with a soft brush keeps the fur in top condition.

The grooming habit is passed from the mother cat to her kittens in the earliest days of life. At birth, she licks away the birth fluids. Later, she cleans their bottoms to encourage regular bowel movements and urination. Once the kittens are mobile, they start to lick each other. The activity strengthens bonds between litter members and reinforces group relationships. By the age of 5 or 6 weeks, they have become completely responsible for their own toilet.

Grooming always has a soothing effect.

Grooming also has a calming effect. When the cat licks itself, it becomes peaceful and relaxed, impervious to outside disturbance. After a prolonged washing, the soothed cat falls asleep.

Grooming problems

A smooth and shiny coat and a normal grooming behaviour are signs of good health and psychological well-being. However, owners should watch grooming behaviour carefully; poor grooming may be the first indication of something amiss with a cat.

Cats with behavioural problems often groom excessively, spending virtually all their waking hours washing. Such activity causes skin irritation which stimulates the desire to lick more. It may cause serious skin lesions and result in self-mutilation. If a cat develops these symptoms, consult a vet immediately.

Toilet training

From an early age, cats are naturally clean. As soon as they can, kittens leave the sleeping den to excrete. This instinctive behaviour is reinforced by the fastidious care the mother devotes to her offspring during the early weeks of life. Thanks to her, their sleeping den is never dirty. The kittens learn to follow her example.

Cat owners appreciate their pet's clean habits. Few owners would be prepared to run round their house or flat cleaning up after a cat. Kittens aged between 2 and 3 months learn quickly, in a few days at most, to use a litter tray.

If the kitten has already been well trained by its mother, all the owner has to do is show it where the tray is. You can also put the kitten in the tray and move its paws in a digging motion. In the case of an untrained kitten, just pick the animal up gently and place it in the tray.

For successful toilet training, put the litter tray in a quiet spot where the kitten feels comfortable and private. Never chastise a cat if it has an 'accident' during toilet training. It is important to instil positive attitudes about the litter tray. A kitten may reject the tray if it is confused or upset by punishment.

Cats prefer different kinds of litter. Owners can choose the best kind for a particular cat from a wide range of commercial litters (see pages 199-200).

When using litter boxes, follow these rules: Keep the box away from the place where cats or humans eat. Avoid any busy areas in your house where people pass by frequently.

Kittens are easily toilet-trained

Provide suitable litter. After cats relieve themselves, they cover their waste by scratching around the immediate area. Modern mineral litters enable cats to gratify this instinctive behaviour.

Never fill the tray with excess litter, or leave the litter unchanged for a long period. Clean out solid waste every day. This prevents an unpleasant smell from permeating the house.

Change the litter and clean out the tray regularly, depending on the amount of soiling. If a dirty litter tray is left unchanged, a cat may eventually refuse to use it and start to relieve itself elsewhere in the house.

If a cat suddenly starts soiling, it may be ill or experiencing some other kind of distress. When the problem arises, consult a vet as soon as possible.

Keeping a house clean is easy if there is only one cat about. Problems may arise if the number of cats increases beyond three or four. To ensure the house stays clean and odour-free, install several litter boxes. If some of the cats are unneutered males, the smell of their spray may spread throughout the house. It is best to have the males neutered to curb spraying and to reduce combative behaviour. Neutered female cats rarely spray indoors, except under stress.

Training a cat

It is often said that humans cannot train cats. The animals are said to be too independent to accept even the slightest constraint. This is simply not true. With gentleness and patience, cats can be taught to live as pleasant companions in houses and apartments. However, it is unrealistic to expect that the animals can be trained as police cats or watchcats. Unlike dogs, cats are not inclined to obey a leader. Only kindness and gentle persuasion will win their co-operation.

Getting to know a mature cat

Before any training begins, it is best to get to know your cat. A newly arrived, adopted or stray animal sometimes has problems adjusting to its changed circumstances. A mature cat with well-established habits and traits is likely to be upset when it enters new territory and meets unknown people. By contrast, a kitten, whose only training has come from its mother, is usually fearless and ready to learn whatever its human companions wish to teach it.

If a mature cat is defensive in its new home, it is unwise to create further stress by imposing a training programme at the outset. There is usually a period of adjustment, which lasts roughly 2 or 3 weeks.

During this period, owners should ensure the animal is properly fed and its litter box kept clean. It is best to set aside time to observe the cat and to consider which habits should be encouraged or curbed.

The older cat will also assess its new family and learn which reactions elicit approval and disapproval. The future domestic relationship between cat and owners depends on the outcome of this period of assessment.

The mature cat sometimes reacts badly to change. For example, if owners switch furniture around, the animal may be disoriented. When guests arrive, it may take a dislike to them. Bad behaviour may continue until the visitors leave. Careful training may eventually modify some of these minor, but unnerving behavioural excesses.

Getting to know a kitten

Training a cat requires time and patience. But the process is usually easier with a kitten. Unlike dogs, cats are not inclined to accept or obey a leader. However, a kitten may see its new owner as a mother substitute, who must receive the same obedient response as the mother cat.

At the age of 2 or 3 months, a kitten is rarely afraid of anything. It usually arrives in the new household with the basic skills imparted by its mother. These skills can sometimes startle its new owner. If a kitten is the offspring of farm cats, it knows how to catch mice. During its first weeks, it watched its mother stalk, attack and kill mice and other prey. A kitten reared in this way may carry on the hunting tradition and seek its owner's approbation by depositing prey at his or her feet.

Hazards and heights

If a kitten is settling into a new home, leave it to explore its new territory in peace. Close the door and windows to prevent the kitten from straying outside.

In a calm and relaxed atmosphere, introduce other people or animals in the

However far a cat falls, it gracefully arches its back and always lands on its feet.

In high-rise blocks, today's kittens face an unexpected danger. Nothing in their short experience can prepare them for the phenomenon of great height. 'Parachute cats' are often reported falling from high balconies and open windows. Some survive, but not all. Owners who live in high-rise flats must be careful that their pets avoid this fate.

Success with reinforcement

The success of any cat-training progamme depends on discouraging unsuitable behaviour and teaching the animal to do whatever you want it to do. This is best done by reinforcing – or rewarding – acceptable behaviour. Reinforcement with occasional titbits is effective, particularly if a cat is hungry. But it loses much of its impact if the animal is spoilt, overfed, or obese. Social reinforcement – caresses, games, and tender words – demonstrates love and appreciation, and strengthens the ties between cat and owner. A stroke, a tickle under the chin, or a light massage of the neck are excellent ways of reinforcing good behaviour.

You must decide what reinforcement works for your cat after observing its conduct. Reinforcement must be effective to maintain a balanced and well-integrated relationship with the cat.

Discouraging bad behaviour

A gentle reproof may be all the punishment that is needed to keep a cat in line. A cat quickly learns the mood and tone of displeasure in your voice. It will respond appropriately if admonished firmly. If, as sometimes happens, you are amused at the same time, a cat may detect this and not take you too seriously.

To ensure good behaviour, follow these rules:

Discourage unwanted behaviour as soon as it occurs. A cat only associates a reproof with an activity that it is doing. Never admonish a cat for some misdeed

house to the kitten. Use play and games to train the cat, and mild reproofs only if its curiosity leads to mischief or danger. Painful experiences will teach the kitten where household hazards are – a stove ring burns its paw, or a door slams shut on its tail.

long past – for example, if you discover the cat scratched the furniture or stole food from a cupboard while you were at work.

Use indirect means to discourage the cat. For example, rattle a rolled newspaper while saying 'No!' firmly. You can use the paper to tap the cat lightly on the nose, or to thump the floor near the cat. (*Never* strike the animal.) A water pistol or water spray is another effective deterrent.

Try to dissociate yourself from the method of reproof. If the cat associates you with a newspaper or water pistol, it may misbehave if you are not around to enforce good conduct.

Avoid any anger that may instil fear in the cat. In some cases, the cat may not understand why it is being admonished. If repeated, your anger may awaken its aggressive instincts.

Finally, apply the chosen reproof systematically until the unacceptable conduct has disappeared.

Controlling natural behaviour

Unacceptable feline behaviour – digging up the soil of potted plants, scratching wood or upholstered furniture, or stealing food – is nevertheless quite normal. It would be absolutely essential to the animal's survival in the wild. It is therefore dangerous to suppress this behaviour entirely, because other more serious problems, perhaps less easily resolved, may surface afterwards.

A cat must be allowed to indulge in its instinctive behaviour, but in a place especially reserved for the purpose where it will not be punished. For example, if the animal starts sharpening its claws on carpets, furniture, curtains, wallcoverings or anything else, provide a scratching post for the purpose (see page 205). A log or an old piece of wood may serve just as well. If possible, take the cat outdoors where it can scratch trees or fences without causing any damage.

Making your cat happy

Some cats always seem calm, relaxed, and satisfied, whereas others are nervous, unapproachable, and aggressive. Owners of difficult cats may be at their wit's end trying to understand and deal with their problem animal. In desperation, they may consult a vet. The outcome may be a realisation that owner and cat are simply not made to live together.

Some people are just not suited to sharing life with a cat. This can be true even when external conditions seem ideal: a quiet home atmosphere, adequate food

TRICKS AND TELEPATHY

If you are going to teach your cat tricks, it is best to begin the training as early as possible. You can build on some instinctive activity that the cat already enjoys, such as hunting, retrieving or jumping. For example, if you want the cat to jump through a hoop, start off with the hoop at floor level. Try to get the cat to walk through the hoop by tempting it with a favourite titbit. Gradually raise the hoop until you can get the cat to jump through at the desired height. Training takes time and patience but, if successful, the cat may delight you and your guests with its stellar jump.

Do not expect miracles of performing skill from cats. You can teach them tricks, but getting them to perform on cue is another matter. Few cats have succeeded as stage or circus entertainers. During the 16th century, the citizens of Brussels devised an 'organ of cats' (see page 40) as part of a royal procession. The infamous musical contrivance amused a public whose only idea of entertainment was taunting and torturing cats. Its popularity faded in the late 18th century. Cat concerts, also known as 'Maiulique' shows, were staged at French fairs during the 1700s. A cat opera was performed near London's Haymarket in 1758. In our modern times, the Moscow State Circus has included feline stars. The Russian trainer Yuri Kouklachev claimed he took 3 years to teach his cats how to jump over hurdles, do handstands and play chess.

You can probably learn as much from cats as they can from you. They delight in playing games – according to their rules – which involve chasing or retrieving. Frequently, cats initiate an activity to catch your attention – for example, sitting on the open pages of the book you are reading.

Some of the ploys cats use in play are essential for their survival. It may be amusing when a cat summons its owners by rattling objects, tapping on doors, or leaping up to push a doorbell. But these skills may help to alert owners to a problem. Cats usually find their way home, no matter how far afield they wander, and some even have the ability to open the front door of the house when they get back. For a cat's convenience, it might however be best to install a cat flap. According to some experts, cat's everyday skills are supplemented by a sixth sense. For example, cats detect vibrations better than humans can. In a quiet house, a cat raises its hackles in alarm as if reacting to vibrations or sounds we cannot hear. Some say cats have telepathic powers. However, it may simply be that their senses are more acute and efficient than ours.

and lots of affection. And yet, the animal is not happy.

Sometimes it seems that it takes more than good living conditions and kind owners to make a cat content. Cats require certain other subtle and often imperceptible qualities from their human companions. A kind of telepathy may exist between cats and humans: it certainly seems that some people communicate better with cats than others. They are more sensitive to the animals and understand them better.

Respect is one key to making a cat happy. We should not force our affections on our pets. Some cats dislike excessive caressing and fondling. If your cat is like this, wait until it approaches you before stroking and petting it.

Another key to the cat's happiness is providing a certain amount of outdoor freedom. Many cats enjoy basking in an enclosed sun porch or patio. Some cat owners have constructed special outdoor houses or gazebos for their feline companions to enjoy the outdoors.

The solitary cat

Since the beginning of the 19th century, the domestic cat has become a much beloved pet in households everywhere. By throwing in its lot with humans, the cat evolved from a wild animal to a companion. However, a companion is sometimes a prisoner in its owners' home.

Some cat fanciers believe the tame cat, unlike its wild relative, was easily domesticated because it never attained full adulthood. Eternally young, the domestic cat has attached itself to humans to ensure its survival. Nevertheless, it needs a social life. It needs to meet and to play with its own species, other animals, and human beings.

The solitary cat develops a close relationship with its owners in the absence of any interchanges with other cats.

However, a cat's life is often solitary. If it starts life as a kitten in a flat, its social contact is strictly limited to its relationship with its owner. Some cat lovers consider the situation unnatural. Yet, cats raised in these circumstances usually adapt

---

GETTING PROFESSIONAL HELP

The best way to guarantee your cat's well-being is to make sure you know where to go if it needs professional help. Check the Yellow Pages, or ask cat-owning friends about veterinary surgeries, boarding facilities and grooming services. Make sure that the professional's office (and office hours) is convenient for you. Compare fees by telephoning around and asking for particular service costs.

Don't wait for a crisis to look for a good vet. If you are going to be visiting a branch surgery, check where you would have to take your cat for surgery or for after-hours emergencies and ensure that this is not too far for you to travel quickly if an emergency should arise. Remember that regular checkups and prompt attention if your cat becomes ill or is injured can save you money and heartache.

If you must board your pet, see if your vet, or the breeder that sold you the cat, can recommend a boarding cattery. Check that the cages are clean and roomy, and that your cat will not come into contact with other animals. Ask about weekly or monthly rates, but expect to pay extra for special services such as grooming. Reserve your boarding spaces early, especially at peak holiday times.

Some pet grooming parlours will bathe your cat, brush and comb its fur, and see to its eyes, nails and teeth. You can do all these tasks yourself, but you could pay a professional to show you how. The cost of tuition, like good-quality grooming equipment, will pay for itself in no time.

---

perfectly and show no signs of disturbed behaviour. This may be because the animal has never known anything else. Without other life experiences, the cat attaches itself to the nearest available person, and appears satisfied with whatever social interaction its companion has to offer. However, a cat quickly reverts to the independent, instinctive ways of its species. If it returns to the wild it will adapt with little difficulty.

Sleep and games

A solitary cat may become bored, particularly if it is entirely dependent on its owner or its own imagination for diversion. It sleeps more than other cats and compensates for its lack of activity by eating too much. Eventually, it becomes fat and out of condition, and devotes most of its waking hours to asking its owner for food.

A solitary cat frequently invents its own games. It tears up cloth scraps, chases dust balls that accumulate under furniture, or just sits in the window watching the birds. It may also make ritual attacks on its owner's ankles. Male cats living alone with an elderly person sometimes do this. Outdoors, this kind of aggressive behaviour is usually directed against real prey.

Owners who are concerned about the well-being of their solitary cat may decide to provide it with a companion. This excellent idea has drawbacks. Problems occur when owners introduce a cat of a different age, or an animal of another spe-

Cats can share cramped quarters but they may be uncomfortable and unhappy.

cies, into a household where a pet is on its own. The pet is unlikely to be pleased when it sees its territory invaded by a stranger. In these cases, there is always a crisis of adaptation. The original animal acts aggressively towards the newcomer, sulks, and goes off to hide somewhere in the house. This difficult period lasts a few weeks. But, in some cases, it continues as long as the two animals share the same household.

The best solution is to adopt a pair of kittens at the same time. They can grow and play together from the start, and are likely to establish a sound relationship for life. It is better to choose two females or a male and a female; two males, even litter brothers, may compete for the territory, even if they are neutered, by spraying urine.

Too many cats?

Some owners opt for several cats – sometimes too many. They love cats and, as long as they can provide food and care, they are happy to live in a household overflowing with cats. Unfortunately, the cats themselves may be unhappy, particularly if space is limited. Nevertheless, they can adapt to crowded quarters. For example, they will organise a hierarchy to avoid repeated fights.

Too many cats in a home can create problems. The household may slip into a dirty, messy and smelly state. Such uncomfortable conditions are undesirable for people and cats.

WHEN CATS WORK

Cats were workers before they became companions. In ancient Egypt and mediaeval Europe, farmers employed 'the harmless, necessary cat', as Shakespeare called it, to protect the grain supply from the depredations of rats and mice. In the Far East, cats kept rodents from chewing sacred scrolls and books in libraries.

Today cats are on rodent patrol in offices, factories, storehouses, museums and other public buildings. The champion of the lot is Towser, who was born in a Scottish distillery in 1963, where he continued working until he died in 1986. According to the *Guinness Book of Records*, Towser caught some 28,889 mice – an average of three a day – during his lifetime. (See also *Awesome exterminators*, page 219.)

The elderly cat

Until the age of 8 or 10, a cat normally enjoys excellent health. From that time onwards, the cat begins to experience the first problems related to advancing age. It may suffer arthritic pains and kidney disorders, and its muscles will begin to atrophy. All these physical problems can obviously affect a cat's behaviour.

As a cat ages, it becomes more placid, and it also begins to sleep more. The cat spends about three-quarters of its time sleeping as it nears the end of its life. It moves about slowly and embarks on new adventures reluctantly. Usually, it prefers to stay safe in its favourite spot, on top of a cupboard or on a windowsill. With age comes a concern for physical comfort. The cat often chooses to sit in a sunny spot or near a radiator or heat vent, where it can warm its old bones and muscles.

Changes in mood and appetite

An elderly cat may become finicky about food. With a diminishing appetite, the cat may sort through its meals, picking out only the choicest bits. In other cases, aging cats become bulimic. That is, they eat incessantly and demand food continually.

Grooming habits change with age. An elderly cat no longer maintains its coat with the same care. Its fur may become dry, damaged and tangled. The cat's mood, too, may deteriorate. It becomes more bad-tempered and irritable, and less tolerant of strangers. When the cat meets unfamiliar animals, it may become aggressive. Or, as is often the case, it may become conscious of its physical deficiencies and slink away to an isolated corner to sleep.

From time to time, unneutered males go prowling in an attempt to recapture something of the sexual excitement of their youth. However, they are likely to be losers in confrontations with younger, stronger toms. They often return home scratched and bitten. To end these exhausting battles, it is best to have the old males neutered (castrated). (If owners want a male cat for indoor living, it is preferable to have him neutered at about 5 to 6 months of age. The operation reduces urine spraying, which begins with the onset of puberty.)

Female cats continue to experience oestrus – the feline heat cycle – until they die. However, the cycles occur further apart with advancing age. An old female cat can give birth to kittens, but her litters grow smaller and smaller, sometimes consisting of only a single kitten. The litters in later life put a great deal of stress on the female cat's whole body. It is therefore advisable to have her spayed. This operation enables the female cat to finish her days in peace and under good conditions.

In old age, a cat needs care from all members of the household, a continual assessment of its state of health, and a suitable diet to make the final years a time of serenity and comfort.

Cats and children

It is easy to understand a child's fascination with a kitten – a little ball of fur that miaows and jumps around, and is so soft to stroke. A child likes the animal's independence and curiosity. Nothing amuses a child more than watching a kitten struggling with its first piece of meat or playing with a ball of paper or a piece of string. Moreover, a child quickly learns to respect a kitten after receiving a quick swipe from its claws.

The cat is frequently a solitary creature. It provides the kind of companionship particularly appreciated by children. The cat also serves an educational purpose. Unlike an inanimate doll or a teddy bear, it not only receives attention and affection, it also returns it. Its demands are few: some caresses and a kind word or two.

Learning from cats

The presence of a cat introduces the child to the animal world. Moreover, it helps the child to develop a sense of responsibility for another living creature. In return, the cat offers its warmth, softness, loyalty and playfulness.

A cat can also bring children together. It acts as a kind of social go-between when a child entertains: visiting young friends may wish to play with the creature, or simply touch or admire it. The cat's beau-

A cat is an ideal companion and playmate for a young child.

ty and elegant movements also provide an early lesson in aesthetics.

If a female cat in the family household is used for breeding, the arrival of a litter is always an exciting event for children. It is the perfect opportunity to observe the miracle of birth. Even very young children want to lend their support when a litter arrives. Later, nursing and raising of kittens put such children in close contact with other facts of life and growth.

AS CATS AND PEOPLE AGE

Compared to people, cats have short lives. A cat of 20 is very old. This table shows an approximate comparison of cat and human ages:

Cat's age	1	2	4	7	10	15	20
Your age	15	25	40	50	60	75	105

And a cat has only one life – not nine!

Some parental concerns

Nevertheless, some parents worry about keeping cats, fearing that cats and children together may simply create havoc in the house. They may also be afraid of cats because they believe some of the myths once used to perpetuate an anti-cat prejudice. According to one myth, a female cat will jump into the cradle of a newborn and try to suffocate it. Although there is no evidence that this has happened, the myth persists. However, it is highly unlikely that a cat would sit for long on a squealing, squirming infant.

Another parental fear is that cats may transmit illnesses. It is true that cats and humans suffer from some of the same diseases. But the diseases are treatable – ringworm, for example – or they can be prevented by vaccination and other medical treatments (see *Zoonoses*, page 186). One health problem is an allergic reaction triggered by the cat's saliva. If this is the only cause of an allergy, you should find another home for the cat. If there are unrelated allergy triggers, it may be more difficult to decide whether the cat should stay or go. A major consideration will be how upset the child might feel if separated from its well-loved companion.

Dogs and cats

'Getting on like cats and dogs' is a popular expression in many countries and cultures. It can denote the close relationship between children or the antagonism between two adults. It can also be used to describe the nature of the ambiguous relationship that exists between our two favourite domestic animals. Generally, cats and dogs get on reasonably well together.

Some breeds – terriers and hunting dogs – remain resolutely hostile towards cats. Fierce hatreds sometimes occur between adult specimens that live outdoors and share the same territory.

First encounters

In urban or domestic settings, cats and dogs meeting for the first time may engage in a game of chase and intimidation. The cat may delight in taunting and teasing the dog. This stimulates a dog's ancestral hunting instinct. The dog pursues the feline intruder. The wily cat may run away or scamper up a tree. Sometimes it threatens its adversary with claws and screams. But, at an opportune moment, the cat dashes away, leaving the dog barking in fury and frustration. Such encounters are usually not serious and rarely

Cats and dogs living in close proximity can often become the best of friends.

end in a real fight. Because the two creatures do not know one another and do not live together, they revert temporarily to the instinctive reactions of their wild ancestors.

Cats and dogs that share the same household often become the best of friends. Many play together free from the fear of attack or retaliation. Female dogs have been known to nurse orphaned kittens. Orphaned cats that were nursed by canine mothers are usually friendly towards all dogs. This attitude may lead to some nasty surprises if the cat encounters dogs unused to its friendly ways.

Introducing new arrivals

Owners need to take special care if they decide to introduce one species into a household where the other already lives. A dog may be willing to accept a defenceless kitten. But a solitary adult cat may be very unhappy if a dog is introduced into its household. It may threaten the newcomer and go off to sulk on its own. The situation is likely to be complicated if the newcomer is an inexperienced puppy that fails to understand the cat's warning signals.

After two or three weeks, the two creatures may come to terms with each other and accept the fact that they are going to be sharing the same household. Unfortunately, their relationship may never achieve the closeness of a dog and cat raised together from an early age.

The cat as companion

The cat became part of the human household about 3,500 years ago. Since then, it has learned to please its human owners and to gain their appreciation. The capacity to adapt to different living situations makes the cat an ideal companion. Many flat dwellers opt for cats as pets because the animals can happily live indoors. Families choose cats because they are less demanding than dogs. For the housebound, the cat can be a comforting and unswervingly devoted presence.

Some cat owners are surprised by their pet's concern if they are ill or depressed. A cat's display of affection is reassuring when things go badly. Just stroking the animal has a relaxing and calming effect that relieves tensions. The cat is wholly dependent on its owners and looks to them for the fulfilment of its needs. Providing for a cat can bolster a sense of responsibility and self-esteem.

The cat is a superb pet for the elderly, particularly the housebound. The two can

Spanish cellist Pablo Casals (1876-1973) with small feline friend.

share common activities, which occur at regular times according to an unchanging schedule. An elderly person and a cat often share mealtimes.

In difficult circumstances, the cat is a model of calm and tranquillity, and a comfort to someone in need. In some instances, the cat provides support for people with physical and mental problems. This may be its finest role and its most significant contribution to the human race.

The cat as healer

During the 1970s therapists first realised that cats have a beneficial effect on the physically or mentally ill. In some cases, children lying in coma recovered after a cat was introduced into their lives.

In 1974, Canada was host to the world's first conference on pets and therapy. One speaker, Dr Michael Fox, an American vet and animal behaviourist, whose books include *Understanding Cats* (1974) and *Love Is a Happy Cat* (1982), said learning to care for a pet made people more sympathetic to human suffering.

In Texas, a study of 100 men and women who had suffered heart attacks indicated that patients with pets had a better chance of recovery. Cats are used in some hospitals and homes to help people overcome or cope with disorders ranging from heart disease and brain damage to drug addiction and alcoholism. Some psychiatrists believe the animals provide an outlet for feelings that might otherwise remain locked in the subconscious of the emotionally disturbed.

Behavioural disturbances

The domestic cat lives in circumstances far different from those of its wild ancestors. So it is not entirely surprising that it still has problems adjusting to our society. Life with humans has compelled it to develop a special form of communication. Some of us, unfortunately, do not understand what cats wish to communicate. The cat's failure to adjust and our lack of understanding can trigger serious behavioural problems.

Generally, cats are well balanced. Vets who are specialists in animal behavioural problems report only one case in 10 concerns cats. The most common feline faults are aggression, fear and dirty or destructive habits. Depression and stress create less obvious behavioural problems. Because a depressed cat is naturally quiet and retiring, and poses no obvious difficulty, the owner may decide to leave the animal on its own even when he or she suspects something is amiss. However, depression and stress require specialist attention.

Aggression

A certain amount of aggression is entirely normal in the life of all animals. It establishes social hierarchies and it also strengthens and protects groups and individuals. It is considered abnormal only when it becomes excessive.

Aggression is a feature of feline sexuality. For example, a female cat threatens and even fights with the male before she permits him to approach her. Males also clash violently when competing for the same female in heat.

In female cats, aggression ensures the survival and well-being of the species. A mother cat retaliates fiercely to protect her kittens and to defend her territory from outside danger.

However, feline aggression may cause problems if it is directed against its owners and other people, or against other pets.

Aggression may take the following forms:

• Territorial aggression is a violent reaction by the cat to an outsider entering its territory or its living space.

• Predatory aggression is rooted in the cat's natural hunting instinct. The cat may play games in which it pursues and ambushes its owner or other individuals. Unfortunately, its overexcitement sometimes transforms a harmless attack into an episode of violence.

• Reactive aggression is displayed when the animal becomes violent due to physical pain, caused by internal diseases, such as cancer, joint disorders, ear diseases, or external injuries, such as blows or bites.

• Deliberate aggression occurs when the cat wants something. It deliberately provokes its owner in order to obtain some desired end. For example, it might threaten or scratch, hoping to get a gentle stroke or a snack.

The antisocial aggression is closely linked to fear. It is common among cats whose early life was spent outdoors and without human company. Because the cats are unused to people, they remain hostile to them in adulthood. Some of these creatures may learn to accept a particular individual, but their conduct towards other humans is likely to be violent and distrustful.

An aggressive cat poses problems for its owners, especially if its violent behaviour becomes established and ritualised. It may even get steadily worse. Any treatment of these problems must be based on

Excessive aggression is a distortion of the cat's natural behaviour.

an analysis of all factors contributing to the outbursts.

Once the cause of the aggression is known, the owners can decide on how best to calm the cat. The owners themselves may occasionally modify their own behaviour. Sometimes the cat may be neutered to reduce any sex-related aggres-

---

STRESS AND DEPRESSION

Cats are sensitive and react as we do to disturbances in their surroundings. This state of tension is marked by symptoms of fear that can lead to aggression, excessive grooming, which can end in self-mutilation, and anorexia or bulimia. A cat may also suddenly become dirty in its habits and may even, in serious cases, abandon its territory to go and live elsewhere.

Depression affects animals that no longer have any defence against the stress to which they are exposed. It may occur, for example, in a cat whose territory has been invaded by another animal and who imagines it has lost the affection of its owners. Or a cat may become depressed if it has been used to living outdoors, and is suddenly confined to a flat. An elderly cat may receive less attention from its owners because it is less lively and more bad-tempered than it once was, and may be pushed into a depressive state.

The main symptoms of depression in cats are prostration, isolation, aggressive behaviour and anorexia or bulimia. To be effective, treatment must be started early. Behavioural therapy conducted by the owners and appropriate medication if necessary can, however, produce excellent results if the problems are caught in the early stages.

---

sion. The use of tranquillisers, sedatives or other behaviour-modifying drugs is highly debatable. The results are difficult to control and only temporarily effective.

There is no doubt that an aggressive animal can be a real problem. However, with our increased understanding of feline behaviour, it is possible to improve some aspects of a cat's demeanour and modify adverse reactions. Getting rid of a cat or putting it to death are extreme solutions, which should be considered only as a last resort.

Fear

Initially, the wildcat feared humans. It was a nocturnal animal that lived in deserts or forests, where it could elude people. The process of domestication erased mistrust. The cat has gradually become accustomed to the presence of people. Nevertheless, it retains some of its ancestral fear. If the animal is highly socialised, it hardly shows. The fear is least evident where the relationship between cat and owner is extremely close.

An animal that lives alone with its owners and spends much of its time sitting on their laps loses virtually all inbred suspicion. It feels free to behave towards its human companions exactly as it might towards other cats. It feels at liberty to impose its will, to become head of a household, and to develop the aggressive behaviour typical of a dominant cat. When a cat knows no fear, it may be difficult to live with.

A moderate degree of fear has its advantages. It ensures that the owner has some control. The cat may enjoy helping itself to food from the family table, but it may be wary of doing this if it is afraid of punishment or verbal rebuke. Fear makes the cat less resistant when it takes medicine or gets a brushing. It enables the vet to examine a sick cat without undue difficulty.

Some cats are fearful of particular situations. In alarm, they adopt a prostrate position: chin tucked in and ears flattened sideways. They are ready to fight or take flight.

The worst kind of fear can lead to panic. The cat becomes uncontrollable, ready to do battle with all its teeth and claws. The terror puts the cat in a really dangerous state. Although its fury usually lasts only a few minutes, it leaves everyone present aghast and at a loss as to what to do.

This panic, entirely unpredictable and uncontrollable, usually has its roots in a fearful event or encounter in early life. The panic may sometimes resurface when the cat is exposed to the original cause of its terror. If its owner cannot protect the cat from the source of its fear, the condition worsens. The animal becomes abnormally aggressive and, ultimately, impossible to be around.

The only solution is to remove the cause of the fear, if possible, and to adopt a calm and understanding attitude. If this can be done, some improvement is possible. But treating a fearful cat is a difficult and lengthy process, one that requires patience and fortitude on the part of the owners.

A detailed analysis of the cat's present situation and its past history often throws light on the source of the problem. It is best to set up a programme that enables the cat to grow accustomed to what it fears and to teach the animal how to live with it or avoid it.

Generally, the cat gradually forgets its fears and can resume a normal life, at

The face of feline fear – dilated pupils, bristling hair and flattened ears.

least as long as it is protected from future confrontations with the original source of its panic.

Behavioural disturbances related to food

The feeding habits of cats living in the wild and of those that live without much contact with humans are often better than those that live with people. For example, neutered animals raised in a pen, and provided with appetising food that is renewed every two hours, react in the same way: every 24 hours, they eat 20 or so small meals spread throughout the day and the night. Their overall intake stabilises rapidly after a few days, they remain in good physical condition, and they do not get fat.

Yet in their daily practice vets are constantly encountering household cats that are obese and, conversely, others that refuse to eat. Obviously, the animals' owners and the conditions of their home life play an important role in the development of feeding problems.

Bulimia is the exaggerated consumption of food. Some conditions such as diabetes, and certain drugs such as cortisone and some hormone medications, can cause a cat to develop an abnormally big appetite. As a result, it becomes significantly overweight.

Such digestive disturbances can only be diagnosed and treated after a full biological examination. But if there is no physical disorder, then the disturbance is clearly behavioural.

Bulimia affects two categories of cats: those that are pushed to eat more by their owners, and those that are depressed or suffering from stress.

Feeding one's cat should be a great pleasure. The animal purrs and rubs itself affectionately against its owner's legs. However, some owners offer their cat too much food, and even stroke it while it is eating. For some owners, this ritual is a genuine pleasure, probably a response to their own anxiety. Gradually, the cat reaches the point where it is consuming two or three times its required food intake. It is the victim of a bulimia created directly, but unintentionally, by its unsuspecting owner.

But other cats seem to develop an excessive appetite without the help of human stimulation. They are constantly begging for extra food or attempting to snatch it while the owner is not looking. These animals are emotionally disturbed and are attempting to deal with their stress by overeating, as others do by overgrooming. Cats that display this behaviour frequently live under difficult conditions that aggravate their anxiety and, finding no other outlet for their unhappiness, turn towards food. But an obese animal opens itself to an increased risk of a number of illnesses.

To treat bulimia, vets prescribe diets that are often as ill-received by the owner as by the cat. The animal frequently becomes aggressive during the treatment, which must be implemented gradually over several months and must consist of special food. Sometimes the animal simply refuses the prescribed diet and never gets down to its normal weight. With this disorder, as with any other, prevention is better than the cure; the problem should be treated the minute the first symptoms appear.

Anorexia, the opposite of bulimia, is the refusal to eat. It may be the result of some illness, or be an acquired behaviour. In some cases the cat refuses to eat anything whatsoever. In others, it is selective – the cat appears not to eat, but actually consents to accept certain foods.

A cat may suffer from bulimia, or excessive overeating, due to stress or poor feeding habits created by its owner.

Complete anorexia is usually a side effect of all the more serious illnesses a cat can contract. The affected animal simply stops eating, and will not regain its normal appetite until the underlying condition is treated or cured. Complete anorexia is rare, however, in cases where the cat is not physically ill. A cat may eat significantly less than it does normally if it is nervous, or during a period of sexual activity, but it is unlikely to stop eating altogether.

Partial, or selective, anorexia, on the other hand, is common. Cats are often quite finicky about their food and have well-defined likes and dislikes. Sometimes, a cat may refuse its food for several days, or as long as a week, simply because what is offered is not to its taste or evokes an unpleasant memory. In these cases, anorexia is temporary and disappears as soon as the animal is given different food. However, when an owner reacts by offering an alternative food, this tends to encourage pickiness about the kind or quality of the food. If anorexia recurs, consult a vet and then make every effort not to give in to the cat's every whim. But this is easier said than done.

Dirty and destructive habits

Normal behaviour associated with territorial marking as well as a certain amount of scratching is to be expected from cats living in flats or in homes where they do not have access to the outside world. Neutering adults and training kittens can help prevent these problems.

Sometimes, however, more specific measures are necessary. Abnormal urination can be a behavioural problem or the result of an illness. The possibility of an illness can be confirmed or rejected following a veterinary examination and analysis of urine. In the absence of any physical disorders, unruly urination and defecation, or urinating or defecating in inappropriate places, are most likely deliberate soilings. There are a number of possible reasons for such behavioural problems. The first is an absence of proper training. A kitten may never have been long enough in surroundings where it could learn clean habits. For example, it may have been kept for too long in a pet shop cage.

Some animals become dirty because the litter they are provided with is different from the kind they have used before. Cats raised in the country, for instance, are used to grass and soil and may not take well to a tray or box filled with mineral litter. The cat may also develop an aversion to its usual litter tray. This is often the result of putting the tray in a place where the cat feels uncomfortable using it. It may be because it is too close to the eating area, for example. Or, it may be because something disturbing or traumatic happened to the cat when it was last in its tray.

Finally, stress and emotional upsets can cause soiling. (These negative influences are extremely wide-ranging and are often difficult to identify. It is only by establishing the cause, however, that a cat with dirty habits can be cured.) Get advice from a vet or from an animal behaviour consultant, since professional help in identifying the cause is likely to be necessary before any remedy can be found.

All too frequently, an owner's first reaction is to punish the cat. To avoid such a mistake, keep in mind that there is always an underlying problem directing your cat's behaviour. Rather, you should try indirect punishment like rattling a newspaper in its direction and saying, 'No!' or 'Bad cat!'

Generally, punishment will not work, and the cat will continue its dirty habits until the source of its stress has been removed and it has been calmly taught to behave differently.

Marking territory by scratching furniture is done mostly by young kittens. If your indirect punishment methods are well conducted, this bad habit should disappear. At the same time, train your cat to use a scratching post (see page 205). Wave a toy in front of the post and whisk it out of the way as the cat lunges for it, so that the cat's claws sink into the post. After a few games the cat will get used to the feel of the post. Jiggle the toy in the air to encourage the cat to climb up the post. Play this game two or three times a day.

Some adult cats that live in flats may become destructive as a result of being lonely and forced to suppress their natural urge to mark their territory. Give them toys, such as objects that roll or that squeak when pressed, and stimulate them to be active by playing hunting games with them whenever you can. If your cat is young, consider getting another cat for it to play with. As a last resort, pet owners occasionally have their cats permanently declawed.

Some cats destroy certain houseplants because they like their smell or taste. Spray these plants with a cat-repellent aerosol. If you have no garden, provide your cat with a box planted with herbs, such as catnip (see page 222), thyme, sage and parsley, and grass.

The future

The social status of cats

Feral cats or tame cats that have gone back to the wild have no legal status and are more often than not regarded simply as nuisances. Are they wild animals that deserve protection, or domestic animals that have strayed away from their homes and which may be subject to some urban or rural bylaws?

Some people believe they should be rounded up by the local authority and sent to a local pound where, if they continue to be unclaimed or adopted, they will be put to sleep. Animal lovers, on the other hand, fight to protect the rights of stray cats. Cat lovers often bring food to the places where feral cats congregate.

For a number of years now, pets, including cats, have been perceived as animals with rights rather than mere chattels. Like all living things, they have the right to live in reasonable conditions, to be treated well, and not to suffer needlessly. However, the law assumes that owners have less control over cats than they do over dogs and there is far less legislation regarding cats.

Unfortunately, many unidentified cats end up in laboratories or are released into the wild and left to fend for themselves, once their owners have decided the cats have lost their initial appeal.

Animal protection associations

There are numerous animal protection associations throughout the world but they vary widely in size and authority. Basically they are formed by groups of volunteers, animal lovers who dedicate themselves to taking in, caring for, and eventually finding homes for the animals they protect.

Most animal protection groups depend on donations raised in various ways. The animal shelters run by charities such as the Royal Society for the Prevention of Cruelty to Animals (RSPCA) and the Cats Protection League (CPL) take care of many of these stray and unwanted cats.

There are also thousands of people who make homes – sometimes good, but often unsanitary – for large numbers of unwanted cats until local authorities step in. In the past, many cases like this have ended with the cats being impounded and rehomed or, in less fortunate cases, destroyed.

Inevitably, the various animal protection groups are forced to destroy a great many animals, under carefully controlled, strict-

ly legal conditions. It is hardly surprising that many members of these groups find it a difficult job. If they have too many stray cats in their pound they may have no alternative but to put them to sleep, even though their mandate is to keep all cats alive.

Some charities fund clinics, where people of limited means can take their pets for checkups and treatment. Often local vets volunteer their time at such clinics.

Nearly all animals adopted from RSPCA and CPL shelters are already castrated or spayed. The only exception might be kittens too young for this procedure – less than 16 weeks in the case of females, 36 for males. Some shelters refund the adoption fee when an owner later produces proof that the animal has been neutered.

Controlling the cat population

The problem of too many cats has been a matter of concern to animal welfare workers for decades. The cat population is increasing all over the world and, in 1993, pet cats in the United Kingdom numbered 7.05 million, of which only about 7 per cent were pedigree cats. Over 4.5 million households owned at least one cat. Dogs, for so long the most popular pet, took second place with a population of 6.9 million.

Cat food sales have increased tremendously, too, with sales of moist cat foods, including the ever popular tinned foods, topping £500 million in the United

Many cat owners have their pets implanted with a tiny electronic tag, that contains information about the cat's identity.

Feline overpopulation is a phenomenon of contemporary life.

Kingdom in 1993. A further £60 million was spent on other cat foods such as complete dry diets, which, despite their nutritional value and convenience, are still far less popular.

The overpopulation of cats is a problem mainly in large cities, where cats can find shelter, food and care relatively easily.

A British organisation, the Universities Federation for Animal Welfare (UFAW), has studied the problem in depth and found that a colony tends to remain stable in size if left alone: sick cats and kittens die and some healthy adults will be driven out or leave the colony if it becomes too big. If, however, an entire feral colony is destroyed, unless the habitat is also destroyed (by building over an open site, for instance) new cats will move into the area and establish a new colony.

Provided that the land owner, the feeders of the cats and local vets can cooperate, UFAW recommends that all cats in the colony should be trapped and examined by a vet. The old, sick or injured are destroyed, healthy young kittens are reared and found homes, and the remainder, including pregnant cats, are neutered, treated for parasites and released back to the colony. Before release the tip of the left ear is surgically removed so that neutered cats can be identified from a distance. The colony will then remain fairly stable but

is monitored by the feeders and should any new cat arrive it, too, is trapped and neutered. Many colonies, both in the United Kingdom and worldwide, have been controlled effectively by this method.

Contraceptives were also tried as a method of feral cat control when 'the pill' became available for cats. Although this had some success initially, it proved very difficult to ensure that each feral female had her pill on a regular basis. It is sometimes used for pet cats as an alternative to spaying but, again, relies on each cat having its contraceptive pill regularly for life.

A male cat can have a vasectomy and the female have her fallopian tubes tied; neither procedure interferes with the cat's sexual activity and, in effect, prevents it from breeding without desexing. However, the sexual caterwauling and other activities associated with reproduction continue, the male will continue to fight and the female, who will continue to be mated, is likely to develop a uterine infection. Most vets and welfare societies therefore recommend strongly that male cats are castrated and that female cats have complete ovariohysterectomies.

The cat populations of the world's major cities can only be effectively controlled either by the recommendations of such groups as the UFAW, or through the use of some form of birth control. Proposals to capture and eliminate abandoned cats are loudly criticised whenever these measures are discussed. Some animal lovers suspect that the fate of animals treated this way would not bear close scrutiny.

The cat protection associations have been effective in some countries, however. In France, for example, the École du Chat has succeeded in giving the stray urban cat a status of its own. This association identifies animals by tattooing them. It also has them vaccinated and sterilised and maintains them within clearly defined areas – the cemeteries of Paris, for example. This approach gives these strays genuine legal status, and has been a successful experiment in population control.

PROTECTION FOR CATS

The movement to protect domestic animals from overwork and cruelty began in early 19th-century Britain. The wealthy landowner and parliamentarian Richard Martin – who was dubbed 'Humanity Martin' by George IV – led the movement. In 1822, the British Parliament passed the first 'preventive act against the cruel and unjust treatment of animals'. Two years later, the world's first humane society was organised by Martin, William Wilberforce (the anti-slavery campaigner), and others. In 1840, at Queen Victoria's command, its name became

the Royal Society for the Prevention of Cruelty to Animals (RSPCA). Similar organisations were set up in France (1845), the United States (1866), Canada (1869), and elsewhere.

Today, domestic cats receive the same widespread and effective safeguards as other animals. Humane societies, as well as organisations concerned specifically with cats, provide shelters and homes for strays and unwanted cats, veterinary care, legal protection and funds for research into cat diseases, behaviour and genetics.

International cat shows

Cat shows are usually sponsored either by individual cat clubs or by the more formal umbrella associations under which the individual clubs fall.

The shows themselves usually last only one day, but some North American and continental shows last two days. Many shows are held in winter, when the cats' fur, particularly that of long-haired breeds, is thicker. At one extreme these shows may be run on rigidly formal lines; at the other end of the scale, they may be more like social occasions. For many years, and in many countries, informal cat shows have been part of local country fairs.

The one thing the formal shows always have in common is that they strive to exhibit the best cats of various breeds, even non-purebred cats. Their goal is to choose the best of each category as a standard for future specimens of each breed.

New breeds and new colourings are also shown, and advice is exchanged between breeders and competitors.

The first shows

The first cat show predates all the modern organizations and is believed to have been held in 1598 at the St Giles Fair in Winchester. By today's standards it was quite a different affair, with cats shown in cages and judged according to their looks as hunters. Records of that 400-year-old show have been lost, but the top award may well have gone to the champion mouser. Later shows saw owners parading around the show ring with their cats, but these often ended in a free-for-all.

The first formal cat show was held in London's Crystal Palace exhibition hall in 1871. It was organised by the English artist Harrison Weir, who wrote many of the rules that govern cat shows to this day. In those days, the more common short-haired cats were shown; later, the long-haired Persians bred for show dominated the competitions. Nowadays there are all-breed shows and specialist shows for individual breeds or groups of breeds.

The National Cat Club's centenary show in 1987 had over 1,800 pedigree and nearly 350 non-pedigree cats but entries have declined since, and in 1992 the world's biggest show was the GCCF (Governing Council of the Cat Fancy) Supreme Show with over 1,400 pedigree and 150 non-pedigree entries.

An early US show, held in 1881 at Bunnell's Museum on Broadway, was not a complete success. A reporter from the *New York Times* observed Mr Bunnell standing in the middle of his museum, fingers bandaged and a deep scratch on his nose. He was surrounded by cats 'half of them yelling, spitting and scratching, as mad as cats can be in uncomfortable quarters and in a strange place.'

Despite Mr Bunnell's unfortunate experience, the idea of formal cat shows along the British line spread fairly rapidly in the United States and then to Australia, Canada, New Zealand, South Africa, most of Europe, and Japan.

The first major formal US show was held in New York in 1895 at Madison Square Gardens. At that show, a male Maine Coon won top honours out of more than 170 cats on show.

Harrison Weir, who organised that first cat show in 1871, standardised the 'points of excellence' for show cats in 1889. The Persian was required to have a silky, fine coat on both body and tail. The Angora was to be woollier, the tail more like a fox's brush. The Russian was to have a woollier coat still;

In British cat shows, the judges' remarks and scores are kept secret until the end of the competition.

The North American style of judging is a lively, entertaining affair with comments made public as the cats are being judged.

its tail was to be shorter and fuller than the Angora's, but with a blunt, tassel-like end.

The colours accepted in the show ring for longhairs were black, white, blue, grey, red and any other self-colour. Tabby cats could be brown, blue, light grey with white or silver. Weir's idea was to standardise the characteristics around the world, but that has not happened. Instead most of the registration bodies have set their own standards, which vary from group to group.

Cat shows today

Cat shows are essentially beauty contests, in which both males and females are allowed to enter. They are not solely for purebred cats either. They may be organised to exhibit only pedigreed cats, or to exhibit only one breed of cat, or they may be wide open to all breeds, pure and otherwise, including the mongrels of the cat world – Household Pets. However, the pedigrees usually reign supreme.

Pedigree cats are judged according to a scale of points for their breed. The scale goes up to 100 points. Cats will lose points if some of their characteristics do not come up to the standards set for their breed by the particular club or association holding the show. (See *Catalogue of Breeds*, pages 68 to 125, for the standards set by the Governing Council of the Cat Fancy – GCCF.)

Unlike most dog shows, cat shows allow cats that have been neutered to compete in their own special class. Most shows present cats in four categories: Adults – unneutered cats of 9 months and older; Neuters – neutered cats of 9 months and older; Kittens – unneutered cats of 14 weeks to 9 months; Household Pets – cats with one or both parents unknown or unregistered. All Household Pets over 9 months old must be neutered.

Before a cat can compete in a show, it must have a vet's certificate showing it has been vaccinated against major feline infectious diseases.

Provided that the cat has been registered with the association running the show, and is of a breed eligible to compete, it is eligible to be entered for the show. It will be judged on its general appearance, its condition, colouring, fur, and whether it has the breed's standard type of characteristics – head, body, tail, eyes and ears.

British shows are very cautiously run and participants must always have a veterinary inspection before being allowed into the show hall. Check-ups are made to ensure that the cats' vaccinations are up to date and that no cats are admitted with parasites, fleas, any skin problems or bald patches, or any signs of illness. A sick cat is instantly disqualified, even if it does not display symptoms until later in the day.

In North America, however, show organisers feel that incipient illness may not be detected in these pre-show check-ups. Also, the cats become upset waiting in the line to see the vet. These shows are self-policing; everyone is responsible for bringing healthy cats to the show and for pointing out any cats that seem ill. If a cat exhibits any signs of being unwell, it may have to leave the show area immediately. This does not happen very often at the major European shows, which are usually vetted shows.

If your cat seems to be sick after a show, take it to your vet immediately. If it has a serious disease, it may have contracted the illness at the show.

The cat show format, the rules of entry and the judging vary from country to country. In most British shows each cat is judged in several different classes, the results are made public when the result slip appears on the award board. In North America the judging is generally done openly with a running commentary by the judges.

In Britain each cat is penned individually alongside others of its breed. The cats must remain anonymous because the judges come to the pens to examine the cats instead of the cats being brought to them. At the GCCF Supreme Show, as in North America and on the continent, the

DISQUALIFYING FAULTS

Cats entering shows have to be in good health. The following conditions will lead to disqualification from GCCF shows:

- General bad condition or undersize
- Any signs of illness
- Any signs of pregnancy or lactation
- Any signs of fleas, scabs or bald patches
- Any declawed cats
- Extra toes, except in Household Pets
- Monorchidism (only one testicle descended) in adults
- Cryptorchidism (neither testicle descended) in adults
- Blindness
- Any signs of sedation.

In addition, disqualification will result in the following circumstances:

- Any powder left in the coat
- Any colouring matter on the coat
- Any trimmed fur (except where clipped for blood tests, etc.)
- Biting an official or refusing to be handled

A pedigree cat must conform to its Standard of Points but the following characteristics will prevent the award of a certificate in any breed category:

- Protruding or misaligned jaws
- Misaligned skull bones
- Reduced nostril size
- Squint (constant cross eyes)
- A fixed deviation of the spine or tail
- Deformed ribcage or sternum

---

cats spend the day in decorated pens and are taken to show rings in order to be judged. Dotted around the hall are booths with the latest cat care products for sale. Often there are places to buy food so that owners do not have to leave the premises during the show.

The judges are cat club members and must have experience in breeding and showing cats. They also must undergo a training programme in order to qualify. The judges may face emotional reactions from upset losers and will often be asked to explain their placings. A good judge must be authoritative, fair, quick and definite in his or her decisions.

During the show cat owners, breeders and spectators mingle to discuss the results, to look over the competition and to talk about the many aspects of their favourite subjects – cats.

Entering a show

Before entering a show, buy a copy of the rules and standards from the organisers running the show, and study them carefully. The rules contain important facts about entry eligibility, entry procedures and the responsibility of exhibitors. For example, to avoid overtiring your cat, you must wait at least 2 weeks before exhibiting it again. The standards for pedigree cats will set out the sponsoring association's guidelines for the ideal cat in each breed, listing colour definitions, and whatever the association considers to be disqualifying features.

Complete lists of shows, with the locations and the names and addresses of show managers, are available from the GCCF. Shows are also listed and advertised in various cat magazines.

To select the show you want to attend think about how far you will have to travel for it. See if there is a local show or specialist show for your breed: a long journey to a large show may be too much for your cat's first outing. Make sure your cat is registered with the correct organisation. If you are interested in showing your Household Pet, contact the show manager to see if there will be Household Pet classes. Send a stamped addressed envelope for a show schedule and entry form. Most clubs offer a reduced entry fee for their members. All shows have a specified closing date for their entries, usually 4 to 8 weeks before the show.

Once you have decided which show you want to attend, send in your entry form and entry fee before the closing date. It is best to do this as soon as possible as some shows can only take a limited number of entries. Enclose a stamped, addressed envelope for confirmation that your entry has been received. The cat must have its registration papers, a certificate of current vaccinations and its confirmation of entry in order to take part.

What you will need

Once your cat is entered for showing, you have to consider how both of you will get to the show. First, you need something to

Many cat-care items make their debut at cat shows. Manufacturers count on the avid interest of breeders to launch new products.

transport your cat. Choose a top-opening carrier of suitable size for your cat to be comfortable but not too heavy for you to carry. Make sure it is sturdy and easy to clean and has adequate ventilation without being draughty. Carriers are available in various sizes in pet shops or by mail order; most cat magazines advertise them. Cardboard carriers are available, but are not suitable for travelling to shows. Cats have been known to escape from them.

At the show your cat will be in a wire pen, with solid partitions between the pens to prevent cats from seeing or touching each other. So that there are no distinguishing features, at all GCCF shows except the Supreme Show the equipment inside the pen must be white; you will need a white litter tray but you can use your normal litter. You will also need plain white blankets of suitable size and number: for instance a longhair adult may only need one thin blanket in the summer but a Siamese kitten in winter would be happier with two or three thick blankets folded to make a cosy bed. It is a good idea to take a spare blanket in case of accidents. There must be a white dish of water in the pen at all times, and when you feed your cat, the food bowl must also be white. If your local pet shop does not have this white equipment, it is available by mail order or from stalls at the show itself.

A well-organised show takes a lot of preparation and planning so that judges, cats, and their owners are comfortable.

At most other shows the cats are confined in decorated pens, usually double size, and are taken from these to the judge. You will need to make curtains to line the pen, together with a floor covering, cushion or bed; the colour scheme should be selected for the cat so that it sets off its coat colour to best advantage. At the GCCF Supreme Show the cats are also in decorated pens but here there is actually a competition for the best pen decoration and some of the designs are quite magnificent, from pure black satin drapery with black accessories to set off a Red Persian, to miniature street scenes with functioning lighting, but always leaving room for

the cat to display itself and to be comfortable during the show.

A comb and brush are essential for grooming. Combs are generally best for long-haired pets, brushes or chamois for shorthairs. A comb is also handy for removing litter or dirt from the cat's breeches. Claw clippers are a good item to have with you, but claws should always be clipped before leaving for the show. Be sure to clip the back claws too, since they are sometimes even more likely to hurt you or the judge.

Some other items you might consider taking along to the show include paper or plastic bags to dispose of litter or garbage, cloth and disinfectant, and a first aid kit. You will need an inexpensive suitcase, too, to carry everything.

At the show

You can ease the tension slightly by arriving well ahead of time. When you arrive, you will receive paperwork, including

---

GROOMING

A show cat must look its best. This means its coat must be carefully cleaned with shampoo, brush and comb. Long-haired cats' coats need the most attention, and the fur should be full and fluffed up.

Be careful how you groom your longhair. Do not use grooming powder just before the show, because any traces will penalise the cat during judging.

The Persian has by far the longest hair. To groom a Persian's fur to perfection will require at least four hours on the evening before a show. But long before the show, its coat must be brushed and untangled daily. Every so often, it should have a bath.

A badly combed Persian is not only ugly, but will suffer from matted hair, which may sometimes leave it unable to move comfortably.

With medium longhairs, grooming is a bit simpler, because the fur, which is flatter and lies nearer the body, gets less tangled, and the undercoat is less abundant.

Shorthairs are much easier to groom, and a good rubdown with a chamois just before the show will give their coat a fine gloss.

Claws must be clipped on both the front and hind legs – but be careful not to cut into the quick of the claw or it will bleed and possibly damage the cat. In some shows, a cat with long claws will be disqualified. In European and some North American shows a declawed cat will be disqualified.

An essential characteristic for show cats is that they must be amenable to handling by strangers, such as the show vet and the judges. If your cat balks at being handled by strangers, then it will not enjoy the show and may be disqualified. You will have to realise that it is just not ready for show business.

Before a British show starts, vets examine the cats and their papers to make sure the animals do not display any signs of illness.

the number of your pen, unless this has been sent out before the show. The pen number identifies your cat for the entire day. Find your pen, set it up, and get your cat used to it. Check the judging schedule. Once judging has started you will be able to buy a catalogue giving details of all the cats in the show and of entries in all the various classes.

At GCCF shows, the judges go around to the cat pens to look at each cat, which means that not too many spectators can see or hear what is going on. The cat's cage must have no personal identifying marks, because the judges are not supposed to know who owns the cat.

Each cat is first judged in its open class according to the standards of its breed. If two or more cats are presented in the same class, they are compared and classed successively from first to last. The certificate will go to the first in the class, but only if the cat merits it. Judges may withhold certificates if they feel no cat is worthy.

The cat is then judged in miscellaneous classes, where it often competes against other breeds; these classes vary but usually include classes for cats bred by the owner, for cats that have never won a first prize or for cats of different age categories. Household Pet miscellaneous classes often include best prepared, friendliest, or longest whiskers. The judge writes comments on each cat on sheets of paper. As each class is completed the judge marks the class placings against the cat numbers on the sheet and on tear-off slips, one of which will be placed on a results board. Exhibitors mark their catalogues from these slips so that they have a record of how their cats, and those of their friends or rivals, have performed.

At the end of many shows, including most specialist breed shows, the open class winners are judged against each other to find the Best in Show Adult, Kitten and Neuter; these may be judged against each other to select the Best Exhibit. If they are included in the show, a Best Household Pet will also be selected. At GCCF shows these Best awards are an honour but do not count towards any title, except at the Supreme Show, the feline equivalent of Crufts, where they are accompanied by certificates and where the Best in Show winners are awarded Supreme titles.

North American-style judging is different and more entertaining for both the public and the presenters. When the cat's judging time is announced, the owner takes the cat to one of the show rings and hands it to a steward in its cage with its number attached. The steward passes it along to the judge and the owner leaves the ring. The cat is judged in the show ring in full public view with a running commentary on the animal's merits or faults.

In North America, each cat is judged individually in its colour and breed class and the top cats in each class are awarded ribbons. After the class judging is complete, these cats may qualify for the top 10 cats in the show awards. When judging is completed the judge announces his or her choice of the 10 best adult cats, 10 best neutered cats, and 10 best kittens.

Cat fancy associations

Each country has at least one controlling authority for all its cat clubs and societies. These associations draw up rules and standards for the various breeds of cat. However, each organisation has a different way of classifying cats during competitions. To make matters even more confusing, some organisations within the same country recognise different breeds as eligible for competition.

Most cat associations are supported by cat magazines, newsletters and periodicals that herald forthcoming shows, giving dates and times, and specifying which breeds will be competing. Many of the associations also provide registration for pedigree cats. In the UK the National Cat Club was formed in 1887 and the Scottish Cat Club in 1894, and both, together with the Cat Club and the Incorporated Cat Fanciers Association of Great Britain, issued separate registrations. In 1910 the Governing Council of the Cat Fancy (GCCF) was set up as the overall controlling authority for cats in the UK, with responsibility for all registrations and titles.

The GCCF, which has no individual members, is made up of delegates from all of its affiliated cat clubs and societies. These may be breed clubs, which cater for specific breeds or groups of breeds, or area clubs, which cater for all breeds but whose main membership is within a specific

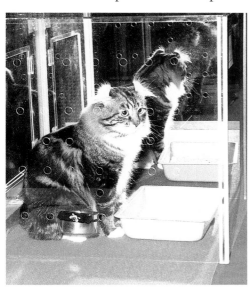

Every device conceivable is used to show the animals off to best advantage. Some cages have mirrors, others fancy curtains.

locality. Affiliated cat clubs in Great Britain have increased in numbers over the years, from 14 breed clubs and 22 area clubs in 1964, to 58 breed and 61 area clubs in 1994, with more clubs seeking affiliation every year.

The clubs run their own shows, licensed by the GCCF, at which cats who are awarded certificates aim to attain the official GCCF titles of Champion, Premier, Grand Champion or Grand Premier. The GCCF also runs its own show, the Supreme Show, at which the higher titles of UK

Grand Champion, UK Grand Premier and 'Supreme' are competed for.

GCCF registered cats may only be shown at shows licensed by the GCCF; apart from small local shows, often run as part of agricultural shows, all British cat shows for many years, and the majority of shows today, are GCCF shows. In 1983 the Cat Association (CA) of Britain was formed and ran its own independent shows until, in 1990, it became a member of the Fédération Internationale Féline (FIFe) and now runs shows under their international rules. The US-based Cat Fanciers Association (CFA) has also held some shows in the UK and there are a few other smaller associations that register cats and run shows, but these are mainly for non-pedigree pet cats.

The Governing Council of the Cat Fancy of Ireland (GCCFI), which registers cats and licenses shows in Eire, liaises closely with the GCCF. Cats may be registered with both organisations and, because there are few shows in the south, many are shown in both countries, so that they can become both GCCF and Irish Champions.

On the continent there are many registering authorities, some of which belong to FIFe, which was founded by the Cat Club de Paris in 1949, while others are independent. In some countries cats registered with one organisation may not be shown with another, while elsewhere the different associations have reciprocal arrangements and cats may be shown at a variety of shows.

The two main registering associations in the USA are CFA, founded in 1906, and The International Cat Association (TICA) which was inaugurated in 1979. In addition to their US clubs, both associations have member clubs and hold shows in Europe and around the world. Other North American associations are the American Cat Association (ACA), the American Cat Fanciers' Association (ACFA), the Cat Fanciers' Federation (CFF) and, in Canada, the Canadian Cat Association (CCA).

Organising a show

Organising a formal cat show is an exhausting job. If it is to be done well, it takes an experienced show manager who must handle not only the details of the competition itself, but also all the pre-show paperwork. The show manager draws up a schedule of classes and invites the appropriate judges according to the type of show, the number of cats and the breeds to be presented. A GCCF all-breed show may require over 60 judges for pedigree cats alone, all of whom must receive a written invitation. The show hall and

Announcing results of the Best in Show competition and presenting the trophies are the high point of a cat show, but perhaps more important than prizes is the shared passion for cats.

penning must be booked and hotel reservations made for the judges. The show manager must also make arrangements for veterinarians to attend to inspect the cats before the show and ensure that one can stay all day as duty vet.

The schedule contains a complete list of classes and judges, together with the rules and regulations for the show. It also includes an entry form for the exhibitor to complete with the names of the cat and its parents, the date of birth, breed number, registration number and the name of its breeder as well as the name, address and signature of the owner and the class numbers into which the cat is to be entered. Many clubs automatically send schedules to their members and many non-members send in stamped, addressed envelopes to receive them.

When entries have closed, the catalogue is drawn up. The cats are numbered in the order of their open class entries and this will be the order in which they are penned in the show hall. Full details of each cat are given under its open class entry but the miscellaneous classes show only a list of cats and their numbers. There is always a list of the exhibitors and their addresses plus a list of the judges and the club committee members. There are also usually breeders' advertisements. The catalogue is sold to exhibitors and visitors, who can use it as a reference guide and to mark up the results.

How the hall is organized depends on its shape and size, the number of cats and stands and the size of the stage. The pens are usually set up in rows and, in an all-breed show, start with the Longhairs, followed by Semi-longhairs, British, Foreign,

Burmese, Orientals, Siamese and finally the non-pedigree Household Pets. There may also be exhibition pens for cats that are on display and not competing. All these must be fitted in to leave space for judges, exhibitors and visitors to circulate and see the cats. Elsewhere in the hall will be stalls selling a wide variety of cat-care products and accessories.

At European and US shows the cats are not necessarily penned in catalogue order and some shows permit cats belonging to the same exhibitor to share a pen, even if they are of different breeds. At these shows the hall also has to be organised to leave sufficient space for the stage or for the judging rings.

After the catalogue and the hall plan have been dealt with, the show manager must prepare the judges' notebooks with a sheet, or sometimes more, for each class; the pen number of every cat in the class must be included, together with the breed number, age and sex of the cat. At some shows each judge may be responsible for a dozen or more classes, with a separate sheet for each.

The show manager must not forget to order the rosettes, prize cards and certificates otherwise there will be some very unhappy exhibitors on the day. Many shows also offer cups and trophies; these must be collected in from the previous year's winners and polished for display on the big day.

After the show is over the job of the show manager is not finished: catalogues must be marked with results for dispatch to the other clubs that may have supported the show, and to the GCCF so that the certificate winners can be recorded.

Organisations for cat fanciers

Enthusiasm for their pets has led cat fanciers to form clubs that set breeding standards, register kittens and regulate competitions that determine the best examples of the various breeds. The following organisations are all concerned with breeding, raising and showing cats.

AUSTRALIA

AUSTRALIAN CAT FEDERATION INC.
P.O. Box 40752
Casuarina, NT 0811

CO-ORDINATING CAT COUNCIL OF AUSTRALIA
P.O. Box 404
Dickson, ACT 2602

Australian Capital Territory

ROYAL NATIONAL CAPITAL AGRICULTURAL
SOCIETY CAT CONTROL
P.O. Box 404
Dickson, ACT 2602

New South Wales

ROYAL AGRICULTURAL SOCIETY CAT CONTROL OF
NEW SOUTH WALES
G.P.O. Box 4317
Sydney, NSW 2001

Northern Territory

CAT ASSOCIATION OF THE NORTHERN TERRITORY
G.P.O. Box 3870
Darwin, NT 0801

Queensland

COUNCIL OF FEDERATED CAT CLUBS OF QUEENSLAND
19 Clifford Street
Towoomba, Qld. 4350

FELINE CONTROL COUNCIL OF QUEENSLAND
40 Union Street
Clayfield, Qld. 4011

QUEENSLAND FELINE ADMINISTRATION
45 Lennons Road
Greenbank, Qld. 4124

QUEENSLAND INDEPENDENT CAT COUNCIL
P.O. Box 41
Esk, Qld. 4312

South Australia

FELINE ASSOCIATION OF SOUTH AUSTRALIA
11 Pembury Grove
Felixtow, SA 5070

GOVERNING COUNCIL OF THE CAT FANCY
OF SOUTH AUSTRALIA
55 Eliza Place
Panorama, SA 5041

Tasmania

CAT CONTROL COUNCIL OF TASMANIA
P.O. Box 116
Glenorchy, Tas. 7010

Victoria

DEMOCRATIC CAT COUNCIL OF VICTORIA
23 Cain Street
West Rosebud, Vic. 3940

FELINE CONTROL COUNCIL OF VICTORIA INC.
Royal Showground
Epsom Road
Ascot Vale, Vic. 3032

THE GOVERNING COUNCIL OF THE
CAT FANCY IN VICTORIA
P.O. Box 318
Belgrave, Vic. 3160

MURRAY VALLEY CAT AUTHORITY
P.O. Box 406
Mildura, Vic. 3500

Western Australia

CAT OWNERS ASSOCIATION OF WESTERN AUSTRALIA
P.O. Box 711
Applecross, WA 6153

FELINE CONTROL OF WESTERN AUSTRALIA
G.P.O. Box 232
Gosnells, WA 6110

CANADA

CANADIAN CAT ASSOCIATION
83 Kennedy Road South, Unit 1805
Brampton, Ont.
L6W 3P3

EUROPE

FÉDÉRATION INTERNATIONALE FÉLINE (FIFe)
Boerhaavelaan 23
NL - 5644 BB
Eindhoven, The Netherlands

NEW ZEALAND

NEW ZEALAND CAT FANCY INC.
20 Warren Kelly Street
Richmond, Nelson

SOUTH AFRICA

GOVERNING COUNCIL OF ASSOCIATED
CAT CLUBS OF SOUTH AFRICA (GCACC)
P.O. Box 532
Florida
Transvaal 1710

SOUTH AFRICAN CAT REGISTER
P.O. Box 4382
Randburg
Transvaal 2125

**Member clubs of the GCACC
of South Africa:**

ALL BREEDS CAT CLUB
P.O. Box 1078
Cape Town 8000

CAPITAL CAT CLUB
P.O. Box 100311
Morreletta Park
Transvaal 0044

CAT FANCIERS CLUB
P.O. Box 5509
Weltevreden Park
Transvaal 1715

EASTERN PROVINCE CAT CLUB
P.O. Box 5166
Walmer, Port Elizabeth 6065

FREE STATE CAT CLUB
P.O. Box 165
Kroonstad, Orange Free State 9500

NATAL CAT CLUB
36 Marion Road
Westriding, Hillcrest
Natal 3610

RAND CAT CLUB
P.O. Box 5836
Bracken Gardens
Transvaal 1452

TRANSVAAL CAT SOCIETY
P.O. Box 3449
Randburg 2125

WESTERN PROVINCE CAT CLUB
P.O. Box 3600
Cape Town 8000

UNITED KINGDOM

THE CAT ASSOCIATION OF BRITAIN
Mill House
Letcombe Regis
Oxfordshire, OX12 9JD

THE GOVERNING COUNCIL OF THE CAT FANCY
4-6 Penel Orlieu
Bridgwater
Somerset TA6 3PG

UNITED STATES

AMERICAN CAT ASSOCIATION
8101 Katherine Avenue
Panorama City, CA 91402

AMERICAN CAT FANCIERS' ASSOCIATION
P.O. Box 203
Point Lookout, MO 65726

CAT FANCIERS' ASSOCIATION
P.O. Box 1005
Manasquan, NJ 08738-1005

CAT FANCIERS' FEDERATION
9509 Montgomery Road
Cincinnati, OH 45242

THE INTERNATIONAL CAT ASSOCIATION
P.O. Box 2684
Harlingen, TX 78551

Care and protection agencies

These organisations are leaders in animal welfare. Their national headquarters (see addresses below) can refer you to local agencies concerned with cat welfare.

AUSTRALIA

ROYAL SOCIETY FOR THE PREVENTION OF CRUELTY TO ANIMALS INC.
4 Hotham Crescent
Deakin, ACT 2600

AUSTRALIAN AND NEW ZEALAND FEDERATION OF ANIMAL SOCIETIES
P.O. Box 1023
Collingwood, Vic.

CANADA

CANADIAN FEDERATION OF HUMANE SOCIETIES
30 Concourse Gate, Suite 102
Nepean, Ontario
K2E 7V7

NEW ZEALAND

SOCIETY FOR THE PREVENTION OF CRUELTY TO ANIMALS, ROYAL NEW ZEALAND
NATIONAL OFFICE
3 Totara Avenue
New Lynn, Auckland

SOUTH AFRICA

ANIMAL ANTI-CRUELTY LEAGUE
P.O. Box 7
66 Marjorie Street
Rosettenville 2130

FRIENDS OF THE CAT
P.O. Box 52429
Saxonwold 2132

SOCIETY FOR THE PREVENTION OF CRUELTY TO ANIMALS, NATIONAL COUNCIL OF SOUTH AFRICA
P.O. Box 82831
Southdale 2135

UNITED KINGDOM

CATS PROTECTION LEAGUE
17 Kings Road
Horsham, West Sussex
RH13 5PP

ROYAL SOCIETY FOR THE PREVENTION OF CRUELTY TO ANIMALS
The Causeway
Horsham, West Sussex
RH12 1HG

SCOTTISH SOCIETY FOR THE PREVENTION OF CRUELTY TO ANIMALS
19 Melville Street
Edinburgh
EH3 7PL

UNIVERSITIES FEDERATION FOR ANIMAL WELFARE
8 Hamilton Close
South Mimms
Potters Bar
Herts. EN6 3QD

WOOD GREEN ANIMAL SHELTERS
Highway Cottage
Chishill Road,
Heydon, Royston
Herts SG8 8PN

UNITED STATES

AMERICAN HUMANE ASSOCIATION
63 Inverness Drive East
Englewood, CO 80112

AMERICAN SOCIETY FOR THE PREVENTION OF CRUELTY TO ANIMALS
424 East 92nd Street
New York, NY 10128-6899

THE HUMANE SOCIETY OF THE UNITED STATES
2100 L Street Northwest
Washington D.C. 20037

INDEX

Credits and Acknowledgements

To identify a photograph or illustration on its page, the following referencing has been used: *r*, right-hand column; *l*, left-hand column; *t*, top of the page; *b*, bottom of the page; *c*, centre.

PHOTOS

Cover: PICTOR/UNIPHOTO
8t: MUSEUM NATIONAL D'HISTOIRE NATURELLE/D. Serrette. **8c:** JACANA/Danegger. **8b:** PREMAPHOTO/K.G. Preston Mafham. **9:** Ed. La Farandole, 1978. D.R. **10t:** MINDEN picture. **10b:** Excerpt from *Les Mammifères* de Carl VOGT, 1884, MASSON S.A, Paris. **11t:** Excerpt from *Précis de paléontologie des vertébrés* de J . P. VETEAU, 1978, MASSON S.A., Paris. **11b:** MUSEUM NATIO-NAL D'HISTOIRE NATURELLE/D. Serrette. **14t:** SUNSET/G. Lacz. **14c:** COGIS/R. Seitre. **15t:** SUNSET/G. Lacz. **15b:** BIOPHOTOS/Heather Angel. **16t:** G. DAGLI ORTI. **17b:** SUNSET/Photo S.T.F. **17t:** COGIS/R. Seitre. **18b:** PHOTOTHÈQUE DU MUSÉE DE L'HOMME. **19t:** JACANA/Ziesler. **19c:** JACANA/McHugh. **19b, 20, 21t:** SUNSET/Animals Animals. **21b:** JACANA/Devez, CNRS. **22t:** GIRAUDON. **22c:** JACANA/McHugh. **22b:** JACANA/J.M.Labat. **23t:** JACANA/Frédéric. **24c:** COGIS/R. Seitre. **25b:** COGIS/Lanceau. **26t:** drawing by W. Kuhnert, excerpt by A. Ménégaux: *La vie des animaux illustrée*, 1903. **26b:** BIOPHOTOS/G. Kinns. **27r:** Excerpt from *A Cat Is Watching* by Roger A. Caras, reprinted by permission of Simon & Shuster. **28t:** G. DAGLI ORTI. **28b:** ÉDIMÉDIA. **29t:** M. HOLFORD. **29b:** R.M.N./Chuzeville. **30:** R.M.N. **31, 32c:** GIRAUDON. **32b:** ÉDIMÉDIA. **33b:** ARTÉPHOT/Nimataliah. **34b:** BRITISH MUSEUM. **34tr, 35b:** G. DAGLI ORTI. **36l:** BIBLIOTHÈQUE NATIONALE, Paris. **36r:** ÉDIMÉDIA. **37:** EXPLORER archives/J.L. Charmet. **38t:** BULLOZ. **39t:** GIRAUDON. **39b:** LAUROS-GIRAUDON. **40t:** GIRAUDON. **40b:** ÉDIMÉDIA. **41:** H. JOSSE. **42:** EXPLORER archives/J.L. Charmet. **44t:** LAUROS-GIRAUDON. **44b:** EXPLORER archives/J.M. Labat. **45t:** COGIS/Lanceau. **46, 47t:** ÉDIMÉDIA. **47b:** H. JOSSE. **48:** ÉDIMÉDIA. **49t:** H. JOSSE/ADAGP/SPADEM, Paris, 1992. **49cl:** Coll. VIOLLET. **49cr:** RAPHO/H. Gloaguen. **49b:** TAPABOR/Kharbine. **50t:** GIRAUDON. **52b:** COGIS/Fr. Varin. **52:** SUNSET/G. Lacz. **52l:** Courtesy of Spillers Foods. **156tl:** COGIS/Fr. Varin. **156bl:** COGIS/Hutin. **156r:** COGIS/Gauthier. **158:** JACANA/J .M. Labat. **159:** COGIS/Amblin. **162l** : COGIS/Fr. Varin. **160r:** COGIS/Remy. **161:** JACANA/M. Viard. **163:** A. GANIVET. **165:** JANSSEN. **167t:** A. GANIVET. **167b:** Cliché Imagerie Médicale ENV of Lyon. **169:** FOTOGRAM/E. Berne. **170, 171, 172:** ENV d'Alfort, Service de parasitologie. **174:** ENV of Lyon, Service de médecine. **179t:** COGIS/Amblin. **179b:** COGIS/Dillschnieder. **180, 181, 182:** A. GANIVET. **183:** COGIS/Lanceau. **184:** A. RULLIER. **185:** ENV of Nantes/Service de médecine. **187:** Sally Anne Thompson/Animal Photography. **190:** DISNEY, with special permission from The Walt Disney Company, France; photo coll. CHRISTOPHE L. **191:** Sally Anne Thompson/Animal Photography. **193:** COGIS/Lanceau. **195:** JACANA/Méro. **196:** FOTOGRAM/E. Berne. **199:** COGIS/Lanceau/Labat. **200:** A. RULLIER. **201t:** A. GANIVET. **201b:** ST. REMY PRESS. **202, 203:** A. GANIVET. **204:** JACANA/G. Thouvenin. **206:** SUNSET/G. Lacz. **207l:** COGIS/Amblin. **207r:** SLIDE/Mauritius/Reinhard. **209, 210tl, 210bl:** A. GANIVET. **210r:** COGIS/Lanceau. **211l:** A. GANIVET. **211r:** SUNSET/G. Lacz. **214:** J.M. LABAT. **215:** COGIS/J.M. Labat. **216:** JACANA/Méro. **217:** FOVÉA/Ch. Lepetit. **218t:** RAPHO/ Le Guillou. **218b:** SUNSET/G. Lacz. **219:** JACANA/Danegger. **220:** COGIS/Fr. Varin. **222t:** COGIS/J.M. Labat. **222b:** COGIS/Excalibur. **223:** COGIS/Gissey. **224t:** COGIS/Fr. Varin. **224b:** SUNSET/S.T.F. **226l:** JACANA/J.P. Thomas. **226r:** COGIS/Fr. Varin. **227:** SUNSET/G. Lacz. **228:** COGIS/Amblin. **229:** FOVÉA/Bacchela. **230:** COGIS/Lepage. **231:** SUNSET/G. Lacz. **232:** JACANA/Axel. **233:** EXPLORER/D. Clément. **234:** COGIS/Fr. Varin. **235t:** COGIS/Remy. **235b:** COGIS/Vidal. **236:** JACANA/B. Rebouleau. **237:** Arch. S.R.D./R. Hauert. **238:** SUNSET/G. Lacz. **240t:** COGIS/Fr. Varin. **242:** Animal Care Ltd. **243:** COGIS/J.M. Labat. **242 to 249:** É. BROCHARD. **250:** Sally Anne Thompson/Animal Photography.

ILLUSTRATIONS

Excerpt from *Steinlen, chats et autres bêtes,* édition Eugène Rey, 1933: 9, 11, 16, 23, 25, 32, 33, 34, 35, 36, 38, 39,43, 44, 50, 51, 52.

Sibylle de Fischer: 7, 53, 63, 189, 213.

Wiiliam Fraschini: 54, 55, 56, 57, 58, 59, 60, 61, 62, 71, 76, 82, 83, 89, 94, 98, 114b,160t, 181t, 186, 203, 205, 212, 242.

Olena Kassian: 146, 148t, 149br, 150c & b, .

Sharon Smith: 65, 66, 67, 68, 70, 72, 73, 74, 75, 77, 79, 81, 82, 84, 86, 88, 90, 92, 93, 95, 96, 97, 99, 100, 101, 102, 104, 105, 106, 107, 108, 110, 112, 113, 114t, 115, 117, 118, 120, 122, 124, 127, 128, 129, 130, 131, 132, 134, 135, 137, 138, 139, 142, 143, 144, 145, 148c & b, 149l & tr, 150t, 151.

Reader's Digest acknowledges with thanks the assistance of the following: Dr. Stuart Halperin, D.V.M., Small Animal Clinic, Veterinary Teaching Hospital, University of Guelph, Guelph, Ont.; Dr. Susan Cochran, University of Guelph, Guelph, Ont.; Dr. Maurice Barrette, Hôpital vétérinaire du Nord, Montreal, Que.; The Canadian Veterinary Medical Association; Canadian Federation of Humane Societies.